Muraille

First edition: March 2019
Printed and bound in Canada by Imprimerie Gauvin, Gatineau
Jacket and book design by Leah Renihan. Jacket photo provided courtesy of Robin McKim.

Playwrights Canada Press
202-269 Richmond St. W., Toronto, ON M5V 1X1
416.703.0013 :: info@playwrightscanada.com :: www.playwrightscanada.com

LIBRARY AND ARCHIVES CANADA CATALOGUING IN PUBLICATION
Theatre Passe Muraille : a collective history / edited by Martin Julien and Samantha Serles with Rae Johnson. -- First edition.

ISBN 978-1-77091-892-4 (softcover)

1. Theatre Passe Muraille--History. 2. Theatrical companies--Ontario--Toronto--History. I. Julien, Martin, editor II. Serles, Samantha, 1987-, editor III. Johnson, Rae, 1953-, editor

PN2306.T62T45 2018b 792.09713'541 C2018-905034-9

Playwrights Canada Press acknowledges that we operate on land, which, for thousands of years, has been the traditional territories of the Mississaugas of the Credit, Huron-Wendat, Anishinaabe, Métis, and Haudenosaunee peoples. Today, this meeting place is home to many Indigenous people from across Turtle Island and we are grateful to have the opportunity to work and play here.

We acknowledge the financial support of the Canada Council for the Arts—which last year invested $153 million to bring the arts to Canadians throughout the country—the Ontario Arts Council (OAC), Ontario Creates, and the Government of Canada for our publishing activities.

Canada Council for the Arts | Conseil des arts du Canada

ONTARIO ARTS COUNCIL
CONSEIL DES ARTS DE L'ONTARIO
an Ontario government agency
un organisme du gouvernement de l'Ontario

Canada

ONTARIO CREATES | ONTARIO CRÉATIF

Theatre Passe Muraille

A COLLECTIVE HISTORY

EDITED BY
MARTIN JULIEN AND SAMANTHA SERLES
WITH RAE JOHNSON

PLAYWRIGHTS CANADA PRESS TORONTO

TO ANDY, LAYNE, AND PAUL, ESPECIALLY

BUT ALSO TO THE THOUSANDS OF ACTORS, PLAYWRIGHTS, DIRECTORS, DESIGNERS, TECHNICIANS, DRAMATURGES, MUSICIANS, GENERAL MANAGERS, STAGE HANDS, STAGE MANAGERS, PRODUCTION MANAGERS, COMPANY MANAGERS, TECHNICAL DIRECTORS, ADMINISTRATORS, FUNDRAISERS, FRONT-OF-HOUSE AND BOX-OFFICE WORKERS, CLEANERS, BOARD MEMBERS, INTERNS, CO-PRODUCERS, VOLUNTEERS, AND—MOST IMPORTANTLY—AUDIENCE MEMBERS WHO HAVE KEPT THEATRE PASSE MURAILLE THRIVING INTO ITS SECOND HALF-CENTURY.

CONTENTS

CHALLENGE AND OPPORTUNITY

CONNECTIONS

DEFINING MOMENTS

16 RYERSON IN THE LATE '70S

INTRODUCTION

BY MARTIN JULIEN

It is no overstatement to say, even for those who have never stepped beyond its walls, that the chronicle and presence of Toronto's Theatre Passe Muraille looms large in the imaginations of Canadian theatre makers and scholars. Infamously founded in the sub-basement of the radical free university and student co-op residence Rochdale College in 1968, the now fifty-year legacy of this experimental theatre is as rich and strange as the multitude of artists, dreamers, blowhards, ragers, and saints that have swept through its histories. Their early style of devised and collective creation, most notably exemplified by 1972's *The Farm Show*, is arguably the single most influential and relevant theatrical development to grow out of English Canada since World War II, and has often been cited as such by numerous scholars, journalists, and practitioners.

Such details and suppositions can be found in many places: academic books, articles, wikis, videos, and classrooms. But what kind of history might this "theatre beyond walls" want to write for itself (if such an ontological sleight of hand might be presumed)? This provocation seemed at the top of his mind when current Passe Muraille artistic director Andy McKim cold-called me in the spring of 2015 to propose my editorship of a publication to commemorate the theatre's fiftieth anniversary. A plan he had hatched in collaboration with former artistic directors Paul Thompson and Layne Coleman, as well as Playwrights Canada Press publisher Annie Gibson and managing editor Blake Sproule, *Theatre Passe Muraille: A Collective History* was to be a groundbreaking book. Dozens of germinal "alternative" theatres had sprung up across Canada in the late 1960s and '70s, but this publication would be the first to honour a half-century of continual existence and production. Our desire and challenge—one to which I immediately hitched my cart—was to create a document that would reflect all the messiness, aspiration, conflict, transcendence, innovation, success, and failure that were absolutely constituent to Passe Muraille's entire social and artistic history. Not a definitive journal of record, sequential history, or consolidated theorization of meaning, but—like the theatre itself—a spun-out and bracing compendium of trial and error.

In essence, the book should look like the theatre.

WE GOT WHAT WE BARGAINED FOR. THERE WAS A TON OF GOODWILL BUT ZERO MONEY.

The thing to do, it seemed to us, was to reach out to and find all the people we could identify and remember—over a five-decade period—and ask for a contribution of some kind. A poem, a recollection, a gripe, an epiphany, a history; a photo, a drawing, a poster, a memo; an aspiration, a wound, an argument, a genuflection. We would organize it all later: instinctively, creatively, generously, but warts and all.

We got what we bargained for. There was a ton of goodwill but zero money. There was inspirational thinking but organizational overload. A working list of contributors was filled with potential, but who to ask? How to find them? And what of those whose experiences with theatre may not have ended on a positive note? We wanted to include all perspectives without censure; but how to convince the recalcitrant to contribute? The better parts of 2015 and 2016 were spent tracking dozens of individuals down and soliciting their submissions. All the past ADs, for sure, but also designers, administrators, actors, playwrights, directors, politicians, journalists, academics, hangers-on, and put-uppers of every stripe over every decade. And we found many. Those who relish hide and seek and those who love dodgeball. Those who need help and those who are waiting to help. Those who are angry and those who are pleased. Those who are still here . . . and those who are now absent. In the end some declined, but most said yes.

Five of the nine artistic directors who have helmed the barnacled vessel TPM are directly represented here. Unfortunately, playwright John Palmer, who helped run the theatre with Martin Kinch and Paul Thompson from 1969 to 1971, has been too unwell to contribute to this publication. Kinch, who decamped to Canada's West over two decades ago, was initially contacted, then "fell off our map," and then reappeared over a year later! Clarke Rogers, who steered the ship from 1982 to 1987, died in 1996; he is well-represented here, though, by visual editor Rae Johnson and many others. Tracking down Susan Serran, a very important figure in Passe Muraille's history who worked as Artistic Producer from 1992 to 1997 and who has a history with the theatre dating back to the late seventies, was a particular challenge for me. Now long absent from Toronto's theatre community and working as a political administrator, Serran declined to directly participate as a contributor but agreed to collaborate with one of her associate directors from the era, Baņuta Rubess, whose excellent compendium is required reading for those interested in a comprehensive account of the theatre's history.

By late 2016, we were lucky enough to get Samantha Serles on board as my co-editor. Various circumstances had precipitated my pulling back on such an active role as sole editor, and without Sam there to enthusiastically dive in mid-process for the rescue, this publication may have stalled entirely. Rae Johnson (who I'd initially tracked down at an exhibition celebrating the archive of ChromaZone, a visual arts collective that was a fellow traveller with Passe Muraille in the early '80s) also committed to a fuller role as visual editor. And the good people at the LW Conolly Theatre Archives at the University of Guelph continued to be a strong, if somewhat geographically distant, resource. (With nearly a hundred boxes of documents on Passe Muraille, to confront that catalogue was to doubt one's own powers of recovery.)

This is not an academic book (though I trust it's of use to scholars) and its intended reader might just be you. It has been an exercise in bold adventure, and, by design, none of the contributions have been vetted with scholarly rigour or forensic investigation. Stories and details certainly diverge and contradict. The editors hope that a singular history—impossible as that is to ascertain—flashes, through co-existence, in these pages. We have strenuously advocated against statements that are hurtful and libellous, but, as editors, we have been resolute explorers in soliciting opinions and perspectives that shake the foundations of an organization that has challenged the very idea of organization. We have tried to be inclusive and worked to solicit and encourage the voices of those often forgotten or left out. Committed to the vital messiness of Passe Muraille's community-based methodology and philosophy, we have tried—even more than usual—to be invisible as editors, and let the subjects speak for themselves, in their own vernacular, with their own voices. The material is arranged by theme and provocation, rather than chronologically, or even systematically.

A scrapbook more than a history. An accretion more than a monolith. An assemblage more than a list.

In the next few years, such venerable homegrown English Canadian theatres such as the Centaur, Factory, Great Canadian Theatre Company, Magnus, Mermaid, Persephone, Tarragon, Theatre Network, Touchstone, 25th Street Theatre, and VideoCabaret will all be turning fifty. I hope that this present volume is a harbinger of the celebration and reckoning that a half-century of creative survival asks of us.

Lastly, a deep bow to Andy McKim for being the dedicated originator, cheerleader, and caretaker of this entire project: it's a "collective history," but it would never have materialized without Andy's passion.

—

THEATRE PASSE MURAILLE IS NOT JUST A BUILDING OR A COMPANY, BUT A HOME.

EDITOR'S NOTE

BY SAMANTHA SERLES

Theatre Passe Muraille gave me my first job in theatre. I was the company's dramaturge from 2010 to 2014, a position that grew out of an internship while I was still completing my studies at York University. Like so many people who have worked at TPM over the years, I found myself within its walls at a time when I was just figuring out where I belonged. For me, Theatre Passe Muraille will always be a place of possibility. So I was thrilled when current artistic director Andy McKim asked me to be involved with this book, even though I did not know exactly what I was getting myself into at the time.

About a month after I came on board as editor, I attended a gathering of artists from Theatre Passe Muraille's first decade. Fifteen people met in the Playwrights Canada Press office, a rather small space to hold so many big personalities and fascinating stories. They talked about the political and social climate that birthed TPM at Rochdale College in the 1960s, the difficulty of selling Canadian Theatre to Canadians in the 1970s, and the struggles and triumphs of creating in new ways.

To me, these artists were legends—many of whom I had studied in university. But as I listened to them talk over each other, laughing and reflecting on their lives as young creators, I was reminded of my peers who are making theatre today.

The spirit of that afternoon greatly informed my approach to the structural editing of this book. From the beginning I knew our objective was not to create a complete linear history of the theatre, but rather to express something about its character—flaws and all. I wanted this book to be a tapestry of overlapping voices who argue, agree, lament, and praise. As I sifted through the contributions that had been gathered and developed by Martin Julien, I was inspired by how many people working generations apart at TPM shared similar experiences. In organizing this text, I looked for pieces that I felt spoke to each other in some way, knowing that different themes and narrative threads will emerge for each reader.

There is no doubt that Theatre Passe Muraille holds an important place in Canadian theatre history. Several articles in this book celebrate the company's influence on our country's cultural identity. But there are also deeply personal stories within these pages. It is clear that for many artists, technicians, and administrators, Theatre Passe Muraille is not just a building or a company, but a home.

I hope it will continue to be a place of belonging for generations to come.

Theatre Passe Muraille ARTISTIC LEADERS

—
THE FARM SHOW
ANNE ANGLIN, MILES POTTER, PAUL THOMPSON, AND FINA MACDONELL.

WHERE HAVE ALL THE SIXTIES GONE?

BY JIM GARRARD

In 1963, a couple of months before US president John F. Kennedy was shot, I was crossing a downtown street in Kingston, Ontario, with an elegant, intelligent, literate, witty young woman named Poppy Gemmell, a fellow undergraduate I'd just met soon after arriving at Queen's University to begin my studies in theatre.

We'd gone to a matinee at the Capitol Theatre on Princess Street. We'd bought wine—"Bloody Red," she called it—and drank it out of the bottle during the movie (I think Debbie Reynolds was in it). At one point one of us knocked the nearly empty bottle over and it rolled noisily down the concrete floor for quite a long time. Everybody in the house—about fifteen people—laughed out loud, Poppy loudest of all. Her laugh was distinctive and beautiful.

Later on, as we crossed the street on our way to supper, she said "fuck!" in a sentence—casually, as though it were nothing. It was the first time I'd ever heard a woman say such a thing. It was kind of a thrill. Even later, she played me a record she'd got from her brother for Christmas—a bunch of young guys with funny haircuts and a funny name—the Beatles, she thought.

It was around that time women started taking the pill—in five milligram doses. That was a game-changer.

A lot of things changed in the sixties.

Theatre, for example, which was becoming my field. Theatre tastes and practices were changing fast. Christopher Fry was going out of style and a new wave of "angry, young" British writers, who'd begun writing about working-class heroes in the late fifties, started washing up on our shore. Brecht too. And Dürrenmatt. Drawing-room drama died a sudden death. Gritty proletarian British realism and cool European abstraction combined to make theatre sexy again.

Our new models were Old World, but America had begun to send great gifts north of the border—its best and brightest—Vietnam War resistors, dodgers, and deserters. These principled young people brought American "know-how" with them, astonishing ideas, improvisational temperaments, political engagement: "rage against the machine."

Rochdale College, where Theatre Passe Muraille (named after a character in a French novel who had the ability to pass through walls, but who unfortunately lost that power one day, right in the middle of a wall and got stuck there) was born and

ROCHDALE COLLEGE, 1960S
VIEW LOOKING WEST, IN BACK ALLEY, FROM THE ST. GEORGE STREET END.

nurtured, was physically located on the corner of Bloor and Huron Streets in the heart of downtown Toronto. Rochdale provided a beacon and haven for like-minded young people and a few elders who fancied themselves part of the "revolution." It was a wonderful, wonderful, free and imperfect environment. To many of us, more than a building, Rochdale became a state of mind.

Rochdale was also an eighteen-storey cheaply built concrete block of apartments, and not far from the university it was striving to escape. No trees. No lawns. Minimal grounds—smaller than the building's footprint. No formal classrooms. No faculty.

I remember meeting the Campus Co-op people from the University of Toronto—mostly recent graduate students with dreams of creating a liberal arts college. Rochdale was their idea. They wanted more freedom, a break with the past, but hadn't counted on the disorder, chaos, licence, anarchy, or any of the other lovely things their idea would attract.

What happened was actually quite great. Rochdale, long in the planning, opened its doors in 1968, not long after the invention of hippies and the beginning of widespread use of LSD. The world was filled with young travellers that year, and many of them made their way to Rochdale to burst the building's seams. Upwards of 1,400 people slept, partied, and learned from one another in a building designed to sleep nine hundred. Lots of other people made the trip in from Scarborough to buy drugs from pop-up entrepreneurs and hang out. Famously, a determined young visionary named Paul Evitts took it upon himself to smash beyond repair the lock on the front door. He wanted Rochdale to be open to all and any fellow travellers. For several wild and woolly years, it was. A great place to break the moulds and try to make a new kind of theatre.

Passe Muraille's first production was based on the play *Tom Paine*, by an American writer, Paul Foster. It was staged in twelve parking bays in Rochdale's sub-basement, painted black and covered with egg cartons to dampen the sound. The original off-Broadway production, directed by Tom O'Horgan, had featured an ensemble of twelve young, mostly American, actor-musicians in leotards playing about sixty roles. The Passe Muraille version was thrown open to anyone who wanted to be in it. About thirty performers of varied backgrounds, talents, and training showed up.

Tom Paine was an epic and satiric American play about freedom—a serious comedy in a fluid form. (It set the urban, international tone of Passe Muraille's first years, but that's another story.) This first Toronto production was closed down by New York lawyers due to some confusion over who had the right to sell us the performance rights we'd paid for in advance and in full. I remember tracking down the playwright on the phone to ask, "What the fuck?" Despite his seemingly genuine preoccupations with freedom and liberty, all he could say to me was, "We're Americans. We're all tainted."

TOM PAINE
MICHAEL J. REYNOLDS CHATTING WITH MEMBERS OF THE AUDIENCE AT 11 TRINITY SQUARE. PHOTO BY BOB NASMITH.

I miss the antic behaviour of that time. Don't get me wrong. Social justice is a great pursuit. Earnest sixties idealism was a powerful force for good; Rochdale had lots of it (and by extension so did Passe Muraille). But I also admired the easy recklessness, the moral abandon of the time and place. Fifty years later our world is filled with senseless prohibitions, needless sanctions. Worse, we're afraid of our own shadows. We can barely choose our own words. The society I live in today feels oppressive and mean.

I don't want to shock anybody and probably won't, but it's important to understand how free-wheeling and irreverent things got to be in the sixties, to imagine the background against which young artists of the day were able to conceive and present their work.

For example, one day in 1969, a young actor—from St. Catharines actually, and a veteran of the Vietnam War—who proudly serves today on the board of Theatre Passe Muraille, knocked on the door of my eighteenth-floor apartment in Rochdale College not long after I'd moved in. He wanted to take me on a tour of the building, to meet some of the people who had jobs there. I didn't know him very well, but he knew his way around "the Rock" better than I did. So off we went. He was stark naked—not even shoes. Down to the second floor we go and drop into the rental office for a chat, visit the registrar, have coffee in the cafeteria, crack jokes with the slow-moving maintenance crew, and so forth. After about an hour of this, he invites me up to his thirteenth-floor apartment, which he shared with a portrait photographer who was legally blind. When we get there, the door was locked. No problem. He reached around and pulled his key out of his asshole. During the entire tour, that's where he'd been storing it. Rochdale was a very good place for theatre.

In early 1970, about a year after Rochdale started paying the rent for a lovely, dusty old former-CBC sound studio in Trinity Square (later torn down to make way for the Eaton Centre), I directed

BOB NASMITH AND JIM GARRARD
PHOTO BY ALEX MACDONALD.

It's important to understand how free-wheeling and irreverent things got to be in the sixties.

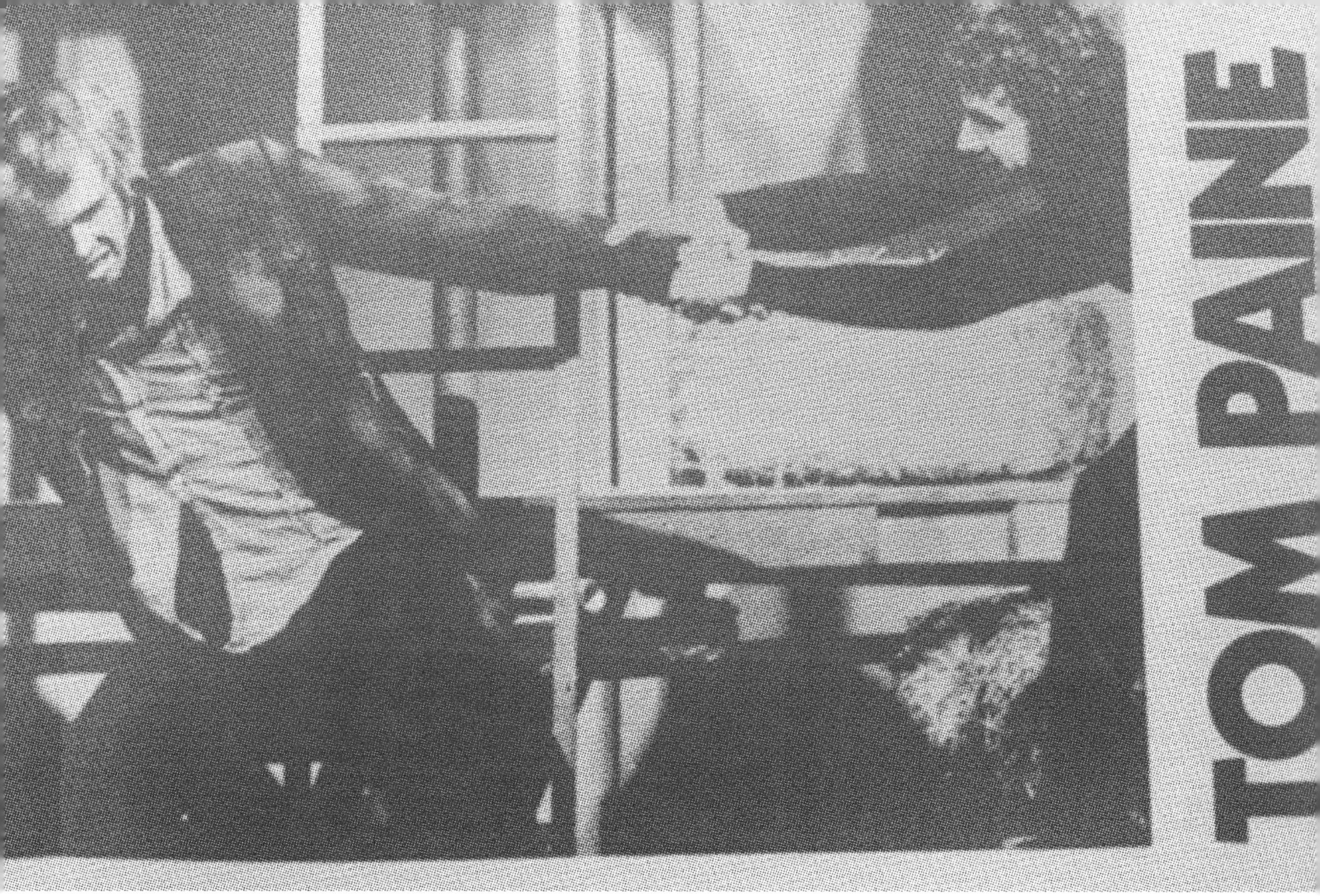

***TOM PAINE* HOUSE PROGRAM**
MICHAEL J. REYNOLDS AND LEN SEDUN.
PHOTO BY LIONEL DOUGLAS.

a play by the great French novelist and playwright Jean Genet called *The Maids*. It was a fine and popular production, an early celebration of gay lifestyles, featuring a very young Kate Nelligan and the legendary Don Steinhouse, with music by Phil Schreibman, costumes and publicity by General Idea, and sets by Lisa Sweeting and Ilana Frank.

Not long after the show closed, I got a call from a now-famous Toronto lawyer asking me if I'd like to meet Genet, who happened to be passing through town. "Sure," I said. Genet was a hero of mine.

I was instructed to show up at the lawyer's office at four p.m. the next day and to bring my car. I did. The office seemed deserted. I sat down in the waiting room. From down the hall I heard voices in an argument. The argument grew fierce, then stopped. Three tall, very beautiful, expensively dressed Black people—one was a woman—came out of a room and passed by me on their way outside. They were all three steamed about something. The lawyer then emerged from the room and came out to me and asked if he could have the keys to my car. He said I should take cabs wherever I was going and give him the receipts next time I saw him. "Sure," I said. Then he took me into the room the others had vacated. Genet was there by himself, the room dark except for small shafts of light coming through the blinds. He didn't look happy. The lawyer introduced us, went away, left us alone. I said a few stupid things in broken French. Genet was polite but monosyllabic. I sat in virtual silence with the great man for about half an hour. Then the lawyer came back and took Genet outside to where my car was parked behind another car. Genet and the beautiful Black people and a couple of others piled into the two cars and drove away. Three days later, on May 2, I got my car back. It was covered in dirt, had been driven hard. I was told it was used as a "decoy car," part of some elaborate plot to smuggle Genet into the States. He'd been barred, I was told, for things he'd written in 1968 about the Chicago riots surrounding the Democratic National Convention. The plot succeeded. Genet slipped across the border at Detroit. He was keynote speaker at the May 1, 1970, Black Panther rally on New Haven Green.

—

WHY WERE THE AUTHORITIES SO PASSIONATE? WHAT WERE THEY AFRAID OF? A MAN FUCKING A PIG? METAPHOR?

Following the abrupt closure of *Tom Paine*, Passe Muraille presented another American play, *Futz*, by Rochelle Owens, at the Central Library Theatre. It was about a gentle farmer who was in love with his pig and, as a consequence, was killed, along with Amanda the pig, by his neighbours.

We had a scene in the play where a young man, wearing a blindfold, pleaded with his mother for her attention. Being the sixties, the young woman playing his mother pulled open her shirt and bared her breasts to him.

The review headline in the *Toronto Star* read: "Futz Brings Nudity and Obscenity to the Toronto Stage." That night the morality squad came to watch the show. The next day I was suspended without pay from my part-time teaching job by the Toronto Board of Education. The cops came back to the theatre that night and every night for thirty days thereafter and charged every member of the company right down to the hat-check boy—who later became AA Bronson of General Idea fame—with obscenity under the Criminal Code.

Four of us, including two lawyers, were convicted. The appeal lasted a year before the new judge agreed to move the court to the Royal Alex Theatre, where *Hair* was playing. The court watched the production, which featured lots of full-frontal nudity. The judge determined that if *Hair* was acceptable to the community—which mainstream popularity demonstrated it was—then so should *Futz*.

Why were the authorities so passionate? What were they afraid of? A man fucking a pig? Metaphor? Why did the police raids on Rochdale require forty cruisers and a hundred cops with sledgehammers? What were people afraid of? Their children?

People took big, needless risks in the sixties. A boy—from Scarborough, we later learned—sat for most of one Friday on the window ledge of Rochdale's laundry room—on the eighteenth floor—with his legs dangling out. It overlooked the second-floor patio, which was for some reason chained shut in winter. I'd been playing cards all night in the second-floor cafeteria, and around four a.m. came out into the lobby next to the patio on my way to take a piss, I guess. I stopped to talk to a couple of people and, as we spoke, we heard an odd plopping sound behind us. The boy had fallen, or jumped—sixteen stories. He lay on his back outside the glass door, a few feet from us. There was a light snow falling and blood began to radiate out from the back of his head, halo-like in the pure white snow.

There was a commotion and quite quickly a black-shirted Rochdale security guard named Pablo appeared with a fireman's axe. Somehow he broke the chain with it. The doors opened and we stepped outside to the boy, who was beyond hope.

Now, a lot of things went on behind closed doors inside the tolerant society of Rochdale College, at all hours of the day and night, not all savoury.

A strange, beautiful thing began to happen. A stream of very young women—it seemed like dozens—came down the stairwell from the apartments above that overlooked the scene. I didn't recognize any of them. They were carrying their coats. They came outside and laid those coats one on top of the other over the body of the dead—or barely living—boy. In silence. I guess they'd looked down from above, saw him lying in the snow, and didn't want him to be cold.

Where have all the sixties gone? Where did they lead?

Where are the Roaring Twenties? The Dirty Thirties? Where is Camelot?

The Disco Years? The nineties? What about the zeroes? Where have all the zeroes gone?

What have we learned?

JIM GARRARD was born in Northern Ontario in 1939. He was the founding artistic director of Theatre Passe Muraille and president of Rochdale College. He has taught theatre at Simon Fraser University and the University of Toronto and has written extensively for film and television.

SOME THINGS I REMEMBER: MY TIME AT THEATRE PASSE MURAILLE

BY MARTIN KINCH

In December of 1969 I became, for a short time, the artistic director of Theatre Passe Muraille.

The previous summer, my friend John Palmer and I had founded the Canadian Place Theatre in the former Puddicombe's Grocery Store, kitty-corner from the Avon Theatre, Stratford, to produce four new Canadian plays, among them John's epic *Memories for my Brother, Part One: Before the Guns*, directed by me and designed by Miro Kinch. Ironically, that year one of the Stratford Festival's rare productions of a Canadian play, Tom Hendry's adaptation of *The Satyricon*, was playing at the Avon. It was a crazy time, a crisis a day as the infant company created some truly original theatre. We worked together, ate together at the Black Swan Coffee House, and slept together round the town, and, like many such experiments, it ended in an apocalyptic final party after which John and I did not speak to each other for many months.

John returned to Toronto to direct a second production of *Memories* at Theatre Passe Muraille on an extraordinary scaffolding set, again designed by Miro Kinch. And, of course, the production was great! That didn't make me all that happy, but it convinced me that Theatre Passe Muraille was the place to be. Some weeks later I approached Jim Garrard about joining the company and was taken on as assistant director of his production of Paul Foster's *Tom Paine*. There wasn't a salary attached. Two months later I inherited the company. I was the artistic director of what was looking like the most interesting company in the country. I was twenty-six.

RICHARD III

My choice of a first production could not have been more ambitious—Shakespeare's *Richard III*. I don't remember its genesis but my notes from that November suggest it was heavily influenced by Jim Garrard's transformational approach to *Tom Paine*, a large dollop of Peter Brook's production of Seneca's *Oedipus*—everybody was influenced by Peter Brook in those days—and a company that was learning how to fill Trinity Square's cavernous space.

From my journal, November 1969:

—

If I did one thing of cultural significance in the time I was at Passe Muraille, it was to invite Paul in and hand the leadership of the company to him.

Clarence Scene
Asheleigh Moorhouse—Clarence
All other actors play ghosts.
They start off as prison bars
(maybe they carry poles).
Then become ghosts swaying bars
that tighten on him as he speaks.
The circle grows smaller until it is
physically crushing him.
He is clawing at the bars.
The actors become the murderers;
the HUMP is the first among them.
They withdraw slowly.
A MURDER DANCE

Lurching Richard is the aesthetic villain. Others perish because they are not aesthetic enough. They are caught on the wrong foot.

This is where it began. It ended a few weeks later with the realization that we simply didn't have the money to sustain a large company and we had to reduce its size. But before that, there was one tantalizing moment when we first viewed the production's opening. The doors from the lobby were flung open and Richard (Don Steinhouse) lurched slowly down the central aisle to join the court, chattering at the stage end of the theatre. A massive hump grew like a hill above his right shoulder. (I see this now as silhouette, but I've probably added the lighting over the years.)

Slowly sensing his presence, the court hushes and turns to face him with a mixture of suppressed humour, contempt, and fear. Richard slowly approaches, his limp and the weight of his deformity slowing his progress. Then he stops, the space between him and the others just wide enough to be palpable, uncomfortable, anxious, and raises his head, smiling. An audible breath. Then suddenly his hump leaps from his back and skitters into the crowd; a dangerous and deranged toy pulling their clothes and nipping at their ankles. Small, agile, quick, and a dancer—Bernice Gai Hune was perfect.

SWEET EROS AND *IN HIS OWN WRITE*

With a significantly reduced company, an evening of *Sweet Eros* by Terrence McNally and *In His Own Write* by John Lennon, adapted by Victor Spinetti and Adrienne Kennedy, became my first and only production as artistic director. This up-to-the-minute combination of Passe Muraille's New York connection—*Sweet Eros* had its off-Broadway premiere the year before—and the extraordinary presence of John and Yoko in Canada—the production sat neatly between their Montreal Bed-in for Peace and the Live Peace in Toronto concert—needed to be a hit. And it was.

Sweet Eros was a sexual shocker, a forty-five-minute monologue hurled at a naked woman tied to a chair, performed with immense commitment by the actors, Maggie Keith and Gordon May. In its critique of "masculinity" and celebration of resistance it was important work, bravely done. In contrast, *In His Own Write* was silly, funny, and remarkably gentle. Certainly it had its flashes of Lennon's pointed satire (plus textual additions by the cast) but, on the whole, it became a sweet tale of a lonely child imaginatively transforming an often grotesque world. The company, dressed by Phillip Hopcraft in matching white jumpsuits combined with their own, less elegant touches, leapt from character to character while Asheleigh Moorhouse presented the young "John" with a sly mixture of innocence and experience. The production even sported a "tiny little tiny pig" puppet that flew above the action singing "with all its might."

And the tickets sold. A surprising amount of money was collected among the Passe Muraille pews during a comic church scene. I was never so personally grateful for the success of a play. The theatre was still alive and I was able to afford the laundromat.

Unfortunately our euphoria was short-lived. Despite the efforts of our producer, the astute Ron Terrill, we still didn't have the necessary budget to support the company. Many of our members were looking for other work and our tenancy at Trinity Square was increasingly in danger.

PAUL THOMPSON

It was around this time that I invited Paul Thompson to join us as a stage manager and director. Paul and I had roomed together on more than one occasion at the University of Western Ontario and had been involved in a number of theatrical projects there. He was a couple of years older and I looked up to him. Paul got things done. He could be more than a little judgmental, but he was optimistic, energetic, and immensely enthusiastic. If I did one thing of cultural significance in the time I was at Passe Muraille, it was to invite Paul in and hand the leadership of the company to him.

A BOND HONOURED

I'm not sure how we chose this play to follow *In His Own Write*—an adaptation of a Lope de Vega play by British playwright John Osborne—but it did reflect an interest in theatricality and high-toned rhetoric that I shared with the director, Asheleigh Moorhouse.

A Bond Honoured was not a success. We were forced to cancel a number of performances, but despite the response Asheleigh had developed some extraordinary theatrical ideas. He ritualized the play's violence by placing buckets of blood around the perimeter, allowing the actors to paint the result of imagined conflicts on their opponents and victims without actually engaging in the expected fight scenes.

I had agreed to perform in the play, but I was simply no actor. I hated the experience. I was still at the stage of imitating performances, which to me had style and a degree of what I thought of as sexy arrogance. God knows how far I got with that—the photographs don't look so bad—but I only need to return to my notes to see how disappointed I was with my ineptitude.

A story went around that Nathan Cohen, the acerbic critic from the *Toronto Star* and a quiet supporter of Passe Muraille, was seen following the performance standing in the snow, beating the door of the theatre with his cane.

I don't remember the conversations as the spring approached. I'm sure there were some. Paul and I must have laid plans, discussed an upcoming season and a new approach to running the theatre. In the end we agreed that he would take over as artistic director. After a summer at the Stratford Festival, I would return (along with John Palmer) as an associate.

SPRING AWAKENING

In Stratford I quickly discovered what I already knew—it was not the theatre for me. And after the experience at Passe Muraille, being an assistant director could be extremely boring. Still, I spent two months working with Peter Gill, Christopher Hampton, and Deirdre Clancy on *Hedda Gabler*. And between rehearsals I created my first original theatre piece, *Separate Cell*, for that summer's Festival of Underground Theatre in Toronto.

Rehearsals for *Spring Awakening* began in September. It was a joy to be back, relieved of responsibility, and wrestling with Wedekind's vision of coming-of-age, lost children, love, and sex. I suspect, however, that my work reflected more than a little of my Stratford experience. At one point Saul Rubinek approached me in a break to tell me that I had to stop directing actors "as if they were Sir Laurence Olivier." At the time I took this as an ungenerous, if slightly funny, comment on the cast and some of the challenges we were facing. But later, after a few more searching conversations, I realized that he was trying to pull me away from the knowing way in which English theatre was often rehearsed and which I had unknowingly internalized. It didn't change me then but it set me on a path to a more curious approach that has been the core of my practice since.

VAMPYR

Two months later, we were at work on *Vampyr*. This devised work created with Shain Jaffe, Phil Schreibman, and a brave company of actors was an all-out attempt to put a Hammer horror film experience on stage. We floated a variety of ideas as to what it meant—I wrote a grant that referred to American imperialism—but the truth is I think we were going for something completely visceral: the terrifying experience, sex, and death.

Taking advantage of the auditorium's size, designer Paul Williams created a rough fantasy of a convent surrounding a central cage that fit perfectly into the Victorian gothic feeling of Trinity Square. Phil Schreibman, an extraordinary composer, writer, and performer, developed

SPRING AWAKENING
ANNE ANGLIN AND GINA LAIGHT.

EXCERPT FROM *VAMPYR* DIARY BY SHAIN JAFFE

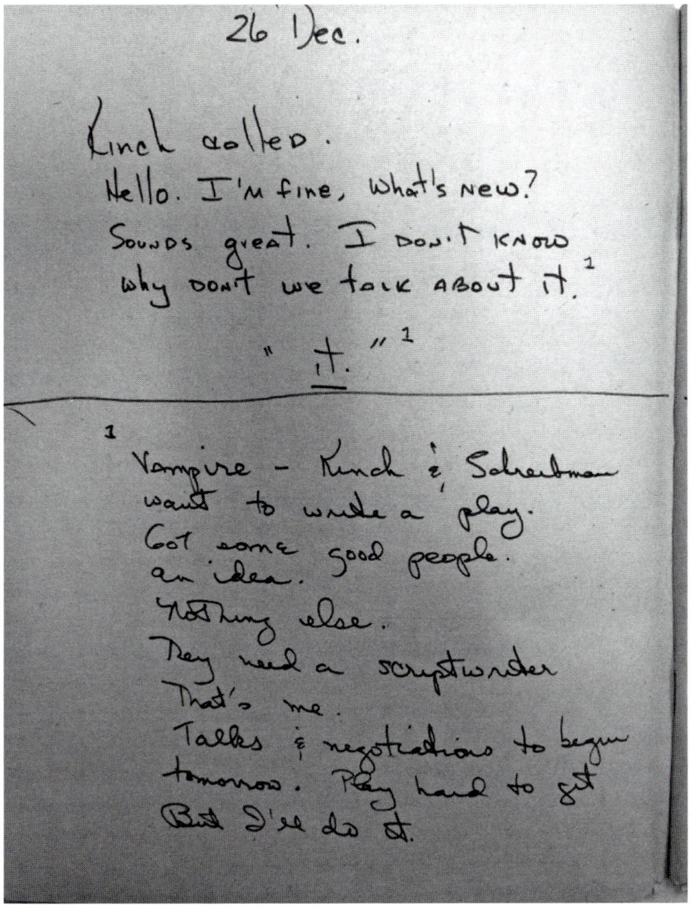

26 Dec.

Kinch called.
Hello. I'm fine, what's new?
Sounds great. I don't know
why don't we talk about it.[1]

"it."[1]

1
Vampire – Kinch & Schreibman
want to write a play.
Got some good people.
an idea.
Nothing else.
They need a scriptwriter
That's me.
Talks & negotiations to begin
tomorrow. Play hard to get
But I'll do it.

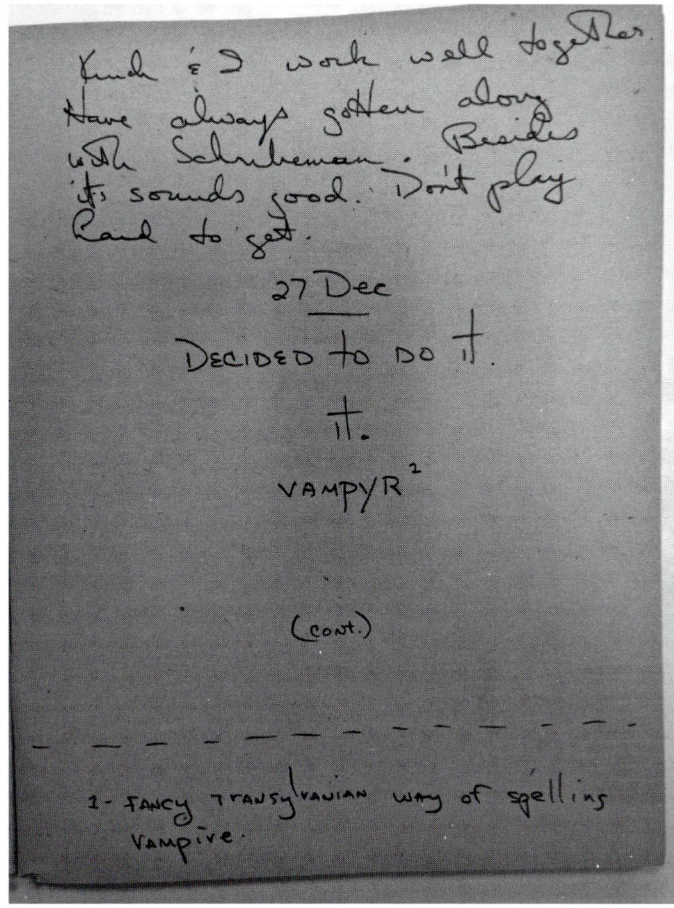

Kinch & I work well together.
Have always gotten along
with Schreibman. Besides
it's sounds good. Don't play
hard to get.

27 Dec

Decided to do it.

it.

VAMPYR[2]

(cont.)

1- Fancy Transylvanian way of spelling
vampire.

a full score for the play. This was melodrama heavily influenced by movies, and it demanded music—what Phil brought to it was a range of dark colours and rhythms intensifying the fear, the desire, and the longing. From the "pit" under the set flowed strains of anxiety and tension that magnified and intensified the experience.

At the heart of *Vampyr*'s creative process was the thirty-six-hour rehearsal, an attempt to get below the pop-culture surface of the material through sleep deprivation. Although I suspect there was some cheating going on—drugs and naps—the experiment yielded amazing results. At the eighteen-hour mark it felt like a silly idea. After thirty-six hours we'd created a show and run it from one end to the other. It was rough. There was lots of work ahead of us. Among other things, we had to create a credible death scene for our lead. Booth Savage was determined—and had a variety of persuasive arguments to the effect—that no one in the play had the power to dispatch a vampire and that we needed to address that in the evening's resolution. I'm not sure we ever completely convinced him, but he played the part with a brooding ferocity and sense of innate power that was truly impressive, and obviously convinced the vampire groupies who ultimately made his life a misery.

Vampyr also gave me my first opportunity to work with Brenda Donahue. A deeply intuitive and truly exciting actor, she was a joy to work with. She died much too young.

Vampyr was my last Passe Muraille production. Nathan Cohen had awarded the production "bouquets of roses," and it was a good time for an exit. The theatre had provided me with a home where I could dream *Richard* and start my Toronto work. It finished any desire I had to be an actor and it encouraged me to explore my passions in *Spring Awakening* and *Vampyr*. For a short time I was artistic director. In that winter of 1969/70, a few of us were able to uphold our belief in exploration and experiment, not always successfully, but with commitment. We kept the theatre alive, and in a time of no money, a great deal of frustration, and frequent discouragement we hung on and ensured that Theatre Passe Muraille would survive to continue its incredible journey.

MARTIN KINCH was born in London, England, and immigrated to Canada in 1948. After graduating from the University of Western Ontario he went on to found Canadian Place Theatre in Stratford, Ontario, with John Palmer and Toronto Free Theatre with Palmer and Tom Hendry. He was the artistic director of Theatre Passe Muraille, Toronto Free Theatre, and Theatre Calgary.

THE THOMPSON YEARS

BY PAUL THOMPSON

ACT 1: ATHLETES OF GOD

My initial impression of Theatre Passe Muraille in the fall of 1969 left me gobsmacked. Jim Garrard's boisterous and overreaching production of *Tom Paine* shook the very walls of 11 Trinity Square and trumpeted a new Toronto. This was not the frumpy and mostly surpriseless city where I'd lived briefly in 1965. Something new was happening and I could play a part. I had work in Montreal, but this felt bigger and newer and the building we had to work in was a glorious treasure chest of possibilities. Of course there were rumours that it would soon be sacrificed to progress and there were financial troubles on the horizon, but Passe Muraille actors were the "athletes of God" according to a director who worked out of La MaMa in New York. No problem.

Of course there were problems. A twelve-member company paid with real money, no administrative infrastructure, great funding schemes with no potential of follow-through. It wasn't a disaster in waiting; it was a disaster happening. I had barely got off the train and my friend Martin Kinch, who had charmed me into coming, called an emergency meeting. He announced he was the new artistic director, that Jim Garrard would devote himself completely to fundraising, that all payment would be box-office driven, and that only actors who could rehearse unpaid would qualify for a last-ditch production to save this amazing enterprise. Six glorious actors signed on. They needed one, so I became stage manager and, oh yes, de facto general manager as I grabbed the keys and the (bouncing) chequebook. The show, a double-billed *In His Own Write* and *Sweet Eros*, was a triumph. The acting was great. Kinch's design was phenomenal. The shows sold out and a quite lucrative tour sprung up. Passe Muraille had been saved . . . for the first time.

OVERREACHING

I didn't have the requisite turtleneck, so missed the picture, but here we were in the spring of 1970 boldly announcing the Festival of Underground Theatre that would change theatregoing in the city of Toronto. The wonder of it was that we succeeded—a non-stop perpetual feast of talent and events

No classics to hide behind, no reassuring knowledge that the theme had worked elsewhere, and no pre-existing script. We would each start from ground zero and, in less than a month of rehearsal, create a fully realized play.

THE FARM SHOW
PAUL THOMPSON, DAVID FOX, ANNE ANGLIN, SEVERN THOMPSON, FINA MACDONELL, MILES POTTER, ALAN JONES, CHRISTOPHER ROYAL, AND JANET AMOS.

that scrambled audiences to surprise venues across the city. All done on a shoestring and headlining a mix of the international and the local. All of us pushing the envelope of discovery: Paris's Grand Cirque with a Tarzan spoof; Bread and Puppet forcing the audience to sit on stage at the St. Lawrence Centre; an original piece by John Palmer, who re-invented *Hedda Gabler* with Saul Rubinek and Luba Goy; a brilliant *Aurore, the Child Martyr* from Quebec; and a stunning fringe program in the inner back streets of downtown at the Global Village (Maury Chaykin and three other two hundred-pounders being "swamp fox" in ridiculous underwear and visual artist Marion Lewis delivering an unnerving and hilarious lecture on the art of the blow job). My own contribution a visually over-the-top and dramatically undercooked adaptation of *Ubu Roi* that ran with the tenor of the times. Of course there were financial troubles, but a brilliant theatre officer at the Ontario Arts Council convinced her organization to declare the Festival of Underground Theatre the success that it so obviously was. Nobody could deny that there was a passion and an audience for the new in this reinvented city of Toronto.

GAME-CHANGER

By the fall of 1970 I was running TPM with a skeleton support staff and an overabundance of emerging theatre talent. There was no money, but the wonder of our theatre space and its potential drove us onward in self-exploitation. Somewhere, maybe around the corner at the Saxony, maybe at Martin's (he always had a nice place), John Palmer and I sat down and agreed to the impossible. All three of us would create major productions (by this point there were already Seed Shows) for Passe Muraille from scratch. No classics to hide behind, no reassuring knowledge that the theme had worked elsewhere, and no pre-existing script. We would each start from ground zero and, in less than a month of rehearsal, create a fully realized play. In the vernacular of the time, mind-blowing.

John Palmer led off with an all-star cast of Anne Anglin, Louis Del Grande, and Saul Rubinek (teenage Bembo Davies is new). They created a nimble and imaginative contemporary farce entitled *Out to Breakfast* that John directed like a Feydeau masterpiece. I have a vivid memory of him creating entire scenes while he watched avidly through an improvised stand-in for a telescope or film camera. John was by far the most talented of our group of directors, and this was vintage.

Martin Kinch followed up with a stunner called *Vampyr*. Nudity, a brilliant set by draft-dodger Paul Williams, thirty-six-hour non-stop rehearsals, a mesmerizing surround score by Phil Schreibman, star performances by the likes of Booth Savage, Brenda Donahue, and Clare Coulter. Martin had found the way of going to the heart of what the new theatre could do well. Classy and new.

My effort had no hope of treading this territory. *Doukhobors*, inspired by our immigrant history in the Canadian West, had to be raw and rough-hewn. Our research information was spotty, the nudity so daunting (the Doukhobors gained notoriety by burning their own homes and protesting in naked marches), that I went through at least three cast configurations before opening. However, the commitment of the actors through this process and the vividness of the story were undeniable. We began to uncover our own history. With these three exceptional achievements it was clear there was no turning back. We had to become a theatre of creation in all senses of the word.

TRIUMPH, HEARTBREAK, AND A NEW APPROACH

"Two thousand years ago I came to save mankind from sin," wails an earnest Sandy Crawley, lodged with his band on a silver platform over the audience entrance doors, "and then it was no enemy, but a friend who turned me in."

Charles Manson a.k.a. Jesus Christ, a new Canadian rock musical brilliantly designed by Paul Williams and stunningly directed by John Palmer, had taken over Passe Muraille and the city. Nudity, dangerous roller skates (toe brakes hadn't been invented yet), headline terrors, and the excoriations of a terrifying Peter Jobin as Manson, the play had it all. The audience perched on two or maybe three levels of scaffolding surrounding the action had to hang on for dear life. And so did our valiant but undermanned support staff. *Vampyr* and *Doukhobors* had been terrific at the box office, but this was madness. The phones went crazy and, like the audience, we hung on for dear life. Over-ambitious and too unwieldy to tour, as we had with *Doukhobors* and *Sweet Eros*, this phenomenon ran its course—and just like that a new crisis arrived. Palmer and Kinch had been invited to take advantage of some new government money in a program called Opportunities for Youth and create a totally new company: Toronto Free Theatre. I argued that we had a brilliant dynamic working at TPM and this model could lead to a reinvention of Canadian theatre. They countered that we were all working for little or no money and their new system guaranteed salaries. I was devastated, for there was really no answer to that.

I didn't know it at the time, but slowly a change of understanding in our approach began to unfold. We had always tried to encourage the new and the experimental. Why not put that goal at the centre of all TPM activities? We would reach out to untested and untried talents not only in our Seed Show projects but for the main stage as well. And this approach would yield extraordinary fruit over the next several years: Louis Del Grande; Hrant Alianak, with his completely original style; guest productions of Théâtre du Nouvel-Ontario, fresh from Earlton and Kapuskasing; Ken Campbell and the creation of Henry Pilk; the birth of Newfoundland's CODCO; and so on . . . This commitment to the unexplored wasn't just shaping our choices of plays, it was having a more pervasive effect on our way of understanding the theatre experience itself. In modern parlance, we started thinking outside the box. Literally.

BEYOND WALLS

Why was I feeling so restless? There was lots of activity at TPM; still more talent than we could possibly use, and the shows were uncovering important parts of our national and personal psyches. We'd done a collective like *Free Ride* (a lively cross-Canada journey about the hippie migration of the early '70s, performed just before *Manson*) and a hybrid like *Buffalo Jump* (just after *Manson*), improvised from a script by Carol Bolt and vividly immersed in John Boyle paintings that rendered whole the On-to-Ottawa Trek and its tragic consequences in the 1930s. We were doing Canadian plays on important themes and were discovering exceptional new actors. Why wasn't that enough? There were long bar discussions, many arguments, and, of course, no solutions. One thing I could try to fix: actors continued to audition with the weakest repertoire of Canadian accents you could imagine. Why didn't we know ourselves better? The budget was long gone and the theatre was closed for the summer, but I had some spare money from a teaching gig I moonlighted at Brock University. We had six actors and six weeks. The plan was to immerse ourselves in some unknown rural area and really learn who those people were, what they thought, and, equally important, how they talked. A crazy idea, with no sense that it might have the makings of a play. Of course, to keep things honest, at the end of our time we would invite these farmers and show them what we'd learned over the time of our stay. My friend Ted Johns had relatives farming near Clinton. Some of them had a sense of humour and a little bit of curiosity. We settled into Ray Bird's abandoned farmhouse and unused barn.

Now there has been a lot said and written about this period of working and exploration, some of it contradictory and almost all of it true. One thing for sure, it was hard to do on all levels: the primitive living conditions, the researching, the actual farm labour, the attempts to find theatre forms for all of the above. None of us had done anything like this before, and apart from rumours of what was happening in the Chinese Cultural Revolution, I had no model for inspiration. There was just us and our work.

Perhaps this is the moment to talk about collectives and the chemistry of companies. None of the triumphs of what was to become *The Farm Show* could have happened if David Fox hadn't decided to take a year's sabbatical from his teaching profession to try acting; if Miles Potter hadn't fled politics in the USA and owed me a favour because I'd welcomed his children's theatre company to TPM; if Alan Jones hadn't insisted on including his girlfriend Fina MacDonell, whom I had only seen fleetingly in a Winnipeg children's play while researching *Free Ride*; if Janet Amos hadn't recently had a baby and was looking for a way to get back into theatre—as long as there was babysitting; if Anne Anglin hadn't decided to marry me, put her classical career on hold, and do original Canadian theatre. That is a lot of "ifs," but it is even more pure talent. They were gorgeous to watch, fearless in their approach, and determined beyond comprehension. The process was every word for painful you can find. There was blood on the floor of the barn when, in the last week of our preparations, Alan Jones balked at the suggestion of further "working" research. He just wanted to be an actor. The Sunday afternoon presentation with the real farmers as our audience was transcendent. None of us would be the same again.

ACT 2: TAKING ON THE COUNTRY ONE PLAY AT A TIME

RIDING A WILD HORSE

Nothing could have prepared us for what followed. The response to the show was otherworldly and both actors and audience seemed to be transformed and more than a bit dazed. What next? Two weeks later in the same barn we tried a second performance, this time without Alan Jones, who was unshaken in his resolve and left the play. The reactions to our work were as vigorous and supportive as the first time round. People from Toronto picked up word of the event, drove out the 130 miles, and wormed their way into Ray's overstuffed barn. They were unanimous: Toronto must see *The Farm Show*. And they were right. Not a peak of nudity in sight and the play brought in crowds as big as *Manson*, *Vampyr*, or *Doukhobors*. None of this could have been imagined, let alone planned. We rode the wave in disbelief, appearing on Peter Gzowski's national radio program several times with excerpts.

I was invited to write a piece on the emerging new theatre (Factory and Tarragon also had strong plays at the time) to be featured on the front page of the *Globe and Mail* Saturday arts section. The theme was "keep the new stuff coming." And we led by example. Rick Salutin approached me with ideas for a play about the rebellion in Upper Canada to be called *1837*. Janet, Miles, and David signed on and we are joined by newcomers Clare Coulter; Suzette Couture; and Neil Vipond, classically trained and a recent convert from having loved *The Farm Show*. With Rick we reached new levels of research and political analysis, but the process of making scenes and

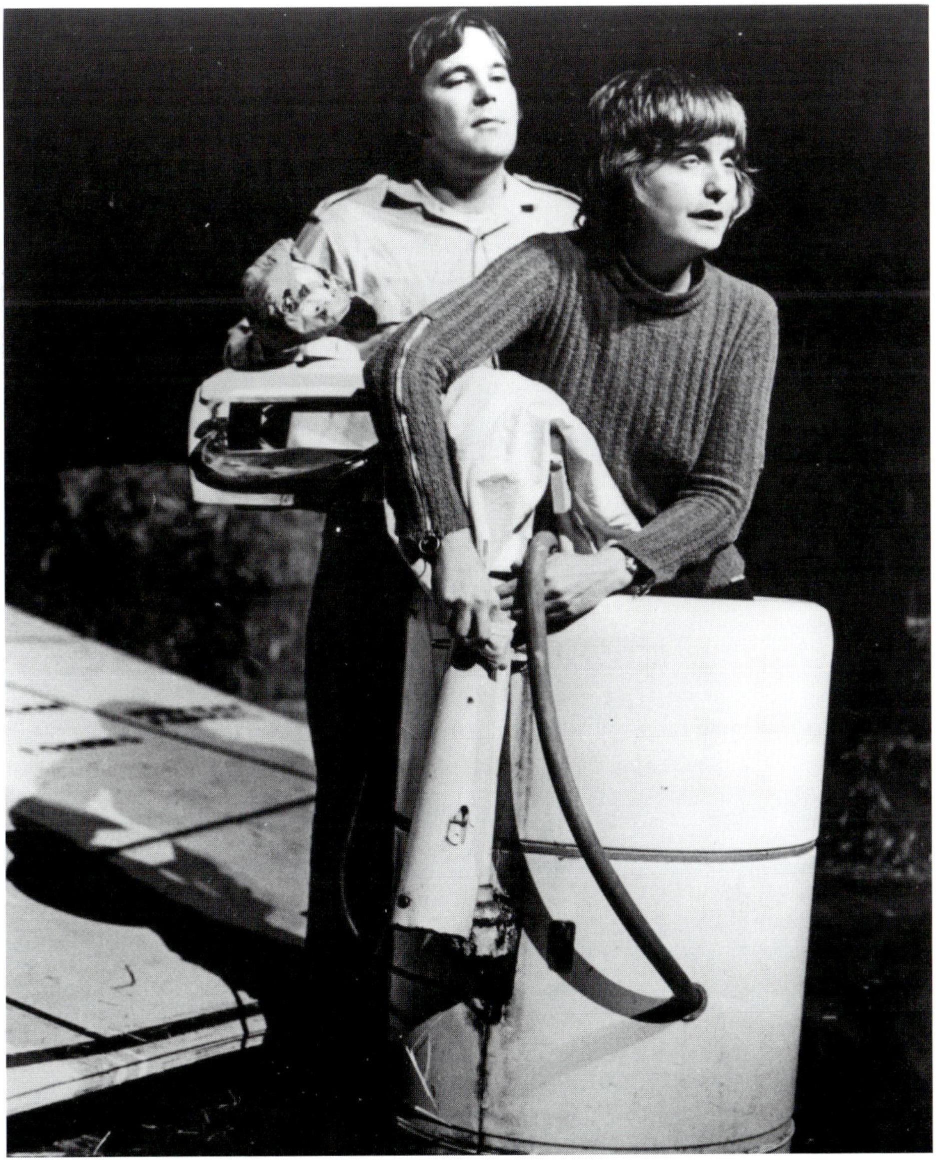

THE FARM SHOW
MILES POTTER AND JANET AMOS.

We had six actors and six weeks. The plan was to immerse ourselves in some unknown rural area and really learn who those people were, what they thought, and, equally important, how they talked. A crazy idea, with no sense that it might have the makings of a play.

making the work remained as elusive as ever. Neil found it particularly painful, but our passion for the theme held us on course, and, guided by a stunning transformation of our stage into an endless forest by the nonpareil Paul Williams, we found our way through to a wondrous and compelling presentation. History had been brought to life and we had our second hit in a row.

It may be time to pause and remember that, folded around this heady romance of success, TPM remained busy developing other emerging work, including a huge, sprawling Lope de Vega directed by Louis Del Grande with Andy Jones, Neil Munro, and ten others; several plays by Miles's children's theatre company; another original from Hrant Alianak; England's Ken Campbell inventing Canadian author Henry Pilk, which shone in Trinity Square before heading off with Andy Jones, Bob Dermer, and Phil Schreibman to the prestigious Royal Court; a new piece from Vancouver with a transgender star and theme; and Homemade Theatre's first creation.

Meanwhile, on the collective front, we continued our surge of discovery—a new collaboration with Carol Bolt, *Pauline*. It focused on the life and art of First Nation poet Pauline Johnson and was created with veterans Anne Anglin, Janet Amos, and a newcomer borrowed from Factory, Peter Kunder. Despite a brilliant set, excellent acting, and inventive dramatic approaches, the show did not win over our recent audiences and performed to what Stendhal called "the happy few." Important to note for all—there was no automatic audience for the new in Toronto. Fine performances and thrilling ideas do not necessarily fill houses. But there was no time to be daunted. Bigger challenges lay just ahead.

A NEW AUDIENCE

Several weeks into the run of *The Farm Show* in Toronto, a woman running the Rhode Island state arts council fell in love with the play and offered us to tour her whole state. "No thanks," came the surprised reply, "we're planning a tour of our own to Canadian farmers." It actually wasn't true, but the more the idea was kicked around, the more we were hooked. Nobody in our part of the world had ever tried to see if there was a rural audience, and certainly nobody with a play about them. Between *1837* and *Pauline*, I cobbled together a three-week tour of Southwestern Ontario. It would play a mix of town halls, high-school theatres, and three auction barns. It would also finish off with one grand finale on the Festival Theatre stage in Stratford. All were produced by agriculture societies, little theatres, or community groups, and the tour had huge help from local newspapers. Again the response was overwhelming. There was a whole new eager and responsive audience in places I hadn't heard of, and the Stratford performance gathered some 1,400 people, amazed to hear their own accents and stories on this magical stage. It was obvious we had to include these people in our future plans. Passe Muraille would definitely be spending much of their future efforts "beyond the walls." But, before the next tour, we launched into our next community-researched creation. *Under the Graywacke* would examine Northern mining from our summer base in Cobalt, the centre of the former glory of the silver bonanza.

It was another huge challenge, with a combination of veteran and new improvisers (Greg Malone, from Newfoundland, was a surprise addition) and the same endless passionate debates about how to make a play. In fact, this template would follow the summer after when we would take on Petrolia and the world's discovery of oil. Each was a landmark in its own way, and each was an invigorating injection of theatre into the home community. Neither would have the outreach possibilities of *The Farm Show*, which was just as well, for we were overwhelmed with the new-to-us touring business. Eager to hang on to our new rural connections, we created two successive productions of *Them Donnellys*, a lustily violent country-and-western-inflected version of the local legend. These plays toured widely in the falls of '73 and '74 and included exuberant performances at both Stratford and Shaw. But before that, *The Farm Show* had to be remounted back at Ray Bird's barn (where poet Michael Ondaatje would take advantage of us in the local landscape for his film *The Clinton Special*), for we were to headline a festival at the National Arts Centre in late summer.

At the same time, in Toronto, there was trouble on the horizon. The long-threatened Eaton Centre would go ahead and our building was scheduled to be demolished. There were demonstrations, sit-ins, and huge lobbying at city hall—to no avail. In the meantime we pressed on with our city season and a flurry of new plays by Hrant Alianak and Louis Del Grande—also another extraordinary first.

Greg Malone brought in a bunch of fellow Newfoundlanders to audition for the Donnelly play. They weren't right, but they were so wonderfully talented that I stole a piddling amount of money from another budget and offered them space and tech support in a modest church hall renamed Passe Muraille East. This "grub stake," as Mary Walsh called it, launched *Cod on a Stick* and the beginnings of CODCO. They quickly parlayed their overnight success into a return home and the creation of one of our truly original theatre companies. We battled on, producing our season all over the city, based in a cramped building with a lot of character just off Yonge and Wellesley. It would be our office/production/rehearsal/modest performance quarters for the next two years. The collective carried on its city version with a vigorous *commedia dell'arte*–inspired look at new Canadians that evolved with Rick Salutin, entitled *The Adventures of an Immigrant*. We booked it into Greek, Italian, and Portuguese community halls. Strong work, but we did not find a way into these communities like we had out of town. Our most powerful performance was when the actors created the show on a streetcar as it travelled through the core of the city. Without our home it was hard to get easily noticed. Our experimentation continued but it definitely got increasingly difficult.

THE TORONTO HIT

Buoyed by our out-of-town popularity and propelled by hungry new actors, experimentation and exploration carried on at an increased pace. Janet Amos directed her first play, a stage adaptation of Dennis Lee's *Alligator Pie*; it would go on to have future lives. CODCO returned with another hit. Ted Johns, who had joined *The Farm Show* company, wrote his first play, *Naked on the North Shore*. We found our ideal Mackenzie in

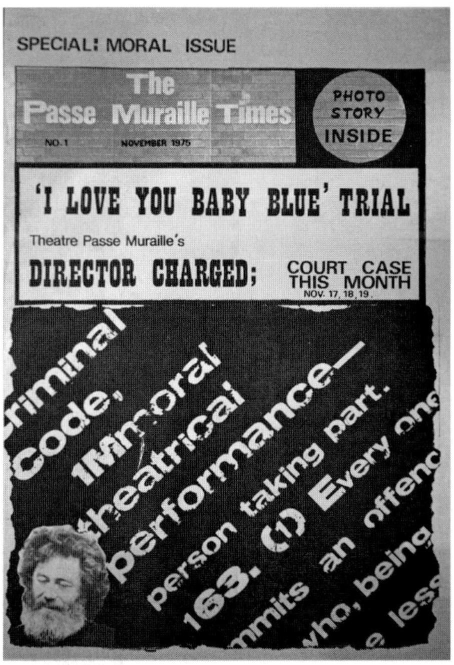

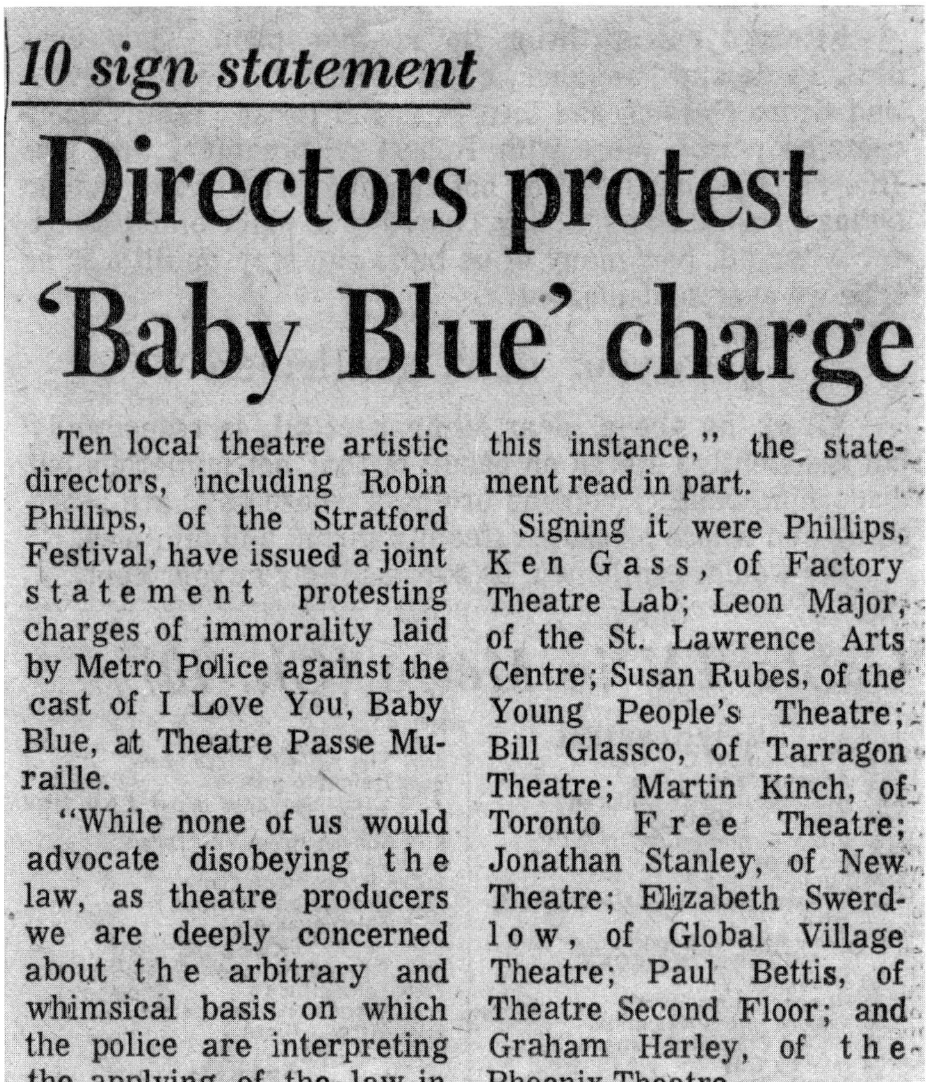

10 sign statement

Directors protest 'Baby Blue' charge

Ten local theatre artistic directors, including Robin Phillips, of the Stratford Festival, have issued a joint statement protesting charges of immorality laid by Metro Police against the cast of I Love You, Baby Blue, at Theatre Passe Muraille.

"While none of us would advocate disobeying the law, as theatre producers we are deeply concerned about the arbitrary and whimsical basis on which the police are interpreting the applying of the law in this instance," the statement read in part.

Signing it were Phillips, Ken Gass, of Factory Theatre Lab; Leon Major, of the St. Lawrence Arts Centre; Susan Rubes, of the Young People's Theatre; Bill Glassco, of Tarragon Theatre; Martin Kinch, of Toronto Free Theatre; Jonathan Stanley, of New Theatre; Elizabeth Swerdlow, of Global Village Theatre; Paul Bettis, of Theatre Second Floor; and Graham Harley, of the Phoenix Theatre.

—
THE THEATRE PASSE MURAILLE TIMES AND NEWSPAPER ARTICLE COVERING *I LOVE YOU, BABY BLUE* TRIAL

Eric Peterson, who would become one of our core collective actors, and with him we fashioned the definitive version of *1837: The Farmers' Revolt*. Like its sister play *The Farm Show*, it had a long touring life, and both were picked up and presented on national television with the CBC. *1837* had the added bonus of original music by John Gray, who had just arrived from Vancouver. Somewhere in there we had time for a four-week tour of rural Saskatchewan with *The Farm Show*. It was also pivotal for the creation by Clarke Rogers of a First Nation's story, *Almighty Voice*, featuring Diane D'Aquila, Hardee Lineham, and Tom Hauff. This too performed in the West. I did a wildly imaginative play/interpretation of ten paintings by artist John Boyle about the Battle of Batoche. Perhaps not too unexpectedly, finding another popular new work in Toronto like *The Farm Show* continued to elude us as we fought for attention in the growing scene. All this would change.

"Passe Muraille Busted for Immoral Sex Play," trumpeted the headlines. It was more than halfway through our season and Toronto the Good had a change of heart. Somewhere in '74 the city discovered sex, and the scene would never be the same. We created *I Love You, Baby Blue*, a full-on collective complete with research and interviews (I'm quoted as describing it as *The Farm Show* for city people). It was as hard to make as any of the others. None of the usual collaborators signed on and we had to start at ground zero with both form and content. Nine brave actors did commit and bared all, both figuratively and literally. We found a desanctified church space off Bloor which held up to six hundred people, and the crowds started coming. We were panned in the press. No matter; both actors and audience claimed differently and this amazing euphoric encounter with the Toronto public surged on unabated for twelve weeks. The cast was exhausted and voted to close, but before that could happen politics entered the scene and we were indeed busted for an immoral play. The theatre community and the city at large were outraged and, with their support, we finished off with two law-breaking encore performances. What a flood of public debate! What a rush! Of course the court case dragged on for years until, represented by a smart young lawyer and fan of TPM,

SOMEWHERE IN '74 THE CITY DISCOVERED SEX, AND THE SCENE WOULD NEVER BE THE SAME.

I LOVE YOU, BABY BLUE
LEFT: DIANA KNIGHT. RIGHT: ABIGAIL WRIGHT, ELIZABETH MURPHY, PAUL KELMAN, DIANA KNIGHT, JOANN MCINTYRE, AND TERRY SCHONBLUM. PHOTOS BY DAVID GROSKIND.

we appeared in Old City Hall and the case was dropped. A victory not only for our committed (and vulnerable) gang of creators, but for TPM as well, for in the midst of the intoxicating run we all agreed to redirect a small percentage of our shares (amounting already to between two to three times the Equity contracted rate) toward the purchase of our own building. An amazing act. And in late spring of '75, with the brilliant negotiations of artist Charles Pachter and $100,000, we gained 16 Ryerson Avenue as our permanent home.

ALL POINTS WEST

We hadn't even completed the sale of our new home in Toronto before the red truck was on the road again. *The West Show* beckoned large. A hugely ambitious project that would embrace more than four thousand research miles and more than five thousand performance miles before we were done. If you look at the photos you might see a change in the faces of our actors. Not so much optimism and youthful energy. We saw them becoming seasoned professionals already sensing how difficult the task of portraying this over-ambitious project would be. We settled into Saskatoon and almost immediately uncovered exceptional local artistic allies such as author Rudy Wiebe, sculptor Joe Fafard, and writer/activist Maria Campbell. Their contributions would be invaluable and allowed us to deepen the work and our understanding of the themes. But the struggle of how to wrap it all up into our travelling show would fuel the debates of rehearsals and post-performance bars for months. The getting of wisdom has its price and we paid it in full. And yes, it was a wise show, full of passion, perception, and the rich performances of veteran collective actors. The effect our efforts had on the local scene was transformative. We connected with a promising young company called 25th Street Theatre, and in return for rehearsal space I offered to pass on our playmaking techniques by creating a parallel local play to be called *If You're So Good Why Are You In Saskatoon?* The company was very talented (Bob Collins, Layne Coleman, and Linda Griffiths connected deeply with Passe Muraille in the future), the theme irresistible, and they uncovered a whole new audience. This changed their approach to theatre and within two years they had their own "west show," a game-changing blockbuster called *Paper Wheat*. Ties between our two companies started solidifying and a decade of exchanges began. So many spinoffs from our Western venture: a Seed Show the same summer in High River and Calgary named *The Alberta Cowboy Show*, created by Paul Kelman; future collaborations with Wiebe, Fafard, and Campbell; Edmonton connections from our performances there; and a very fruitful time with our hosts in Winnipeg, sharing techniques with the aptly named Prairie Theatre Exchange. We were ready to come home.

DIGGING IN

The saga of turning our building into a theatre could be a play itself. What we had bought was an architecturally beautiful derelict that the owner used for storage and dreamed of making into condos. The roof and windows needed major repairs, there was a repository of junk a mile high, and the rats had to be convinced to leave. All this to be somehow squeezed out of our operating budget and done while the acting company was in Saskatchewan. A fantastic group of techies fell in love with the space and worked their asses off for months, scheming how to turn this former bakery into a vital crucible for the development of new work—nothing fancy, but at the core three different spaces that could challenge the imagination and talents of our emerging artists. The techies were our heroes, and partway through the season we actually got to put on shows and begin learning how to play our new instrument. The season was a dazzling flurry of the new and

—

PEOPLE WERE SO EAGER; THEY WOULD SIT ON ANY PERCH, A PIECE OF A STAIR, A WINDOW LEDGE, EVEN THE LADDER TO THE LIGHTING.

the untried. Two women directors, Cheryl Cashman and Janet Amos, took on city-themed plays, Janet's *Operation Finger Pinkie* finishing off with performances in actual offices. A first-timer at TPM, a youthful Des McAnuff fashioned a stunning *Faustus* in our upstairs space, and within the year he would head out to New York. Straight-out-of-school James Roy wrote and directed a play, then headed out of town to the Blyth Festival. The poet David McFadden came in from Hamilton with a magic soufflé of a presentation. Hrant Alianak had several creations, including an over-the-top *Titus Andronicus*, and newcomer Peter Melnick began his unique series. Somewhere in there was a *Brébeuf* with Eldon Garnet and Paul Quarrington and *30 Minutes from Downtown*, an inventively reconfigured downstairs production by Paul Kelman.

There were more, too numerous to list here, because I must finish off with the activities of the core collective company, which included a new piece for our rural touring audience entitled *The Horsburgh Scandal*, starring the legendary actor Don Harron (accepting to work for the TPM exploitive wage) and featuring wonderful music composed and played by John Gray. There was also a challenging tour to Baker Lake, Northwest Territories, where David Fox directed a small team as *they* created and performed *John Hornby*, the second in our Canadian Heroes Series, for the local audience. And finally we finished off with a remount of *The Farm Show* and *1837* in Vancouver, where we were featured in Habitat for Humanity before *The Farm Show* moved on to the Belfry in Victoria. Oh yes, and I would be remiss not to include the return of CODCO, whose *Would You Like to Smell my Pocket Crumbs* became the first box-office triumph of 16 Ryerson Avenue.

TROUBLE IN PARADISE 1976–1979

Be careful what you wish for goes the adage—it may come back to haunt you. Our new beloved building was under fire by the authorities and we continually battled to shape it into various codes of acceptance while keeping the spirit of flexibility and exploration vitally alive. This unsettled period had us alternating productions between our home space and one-off rentals all over town. Also, there was a sea change in Toronto theatre and both nationalism and collectives were starting to be considered yesterday's news. The *Toronto Star*, which had been at the forefront of the new theatre movement with Urjo Kareda's vibrant columns, had done a complete about-face and hired a British critic who was, to say the least, unenamoured of things Canadian. Getting to our audience became harder. To make things worse, my personal life was in tatters; Anne and I had separated for several months before getting back together.

Still, there were positive signs in these messy times. The core collective, with a stellar cast of creators from a wide range of TPM styles (Booth Savage from early Jim Garrard and Martin Kinch; Eric Peterson, David Fox, and Clare Coulter from my own early influence; Layne Coleman from 25th Street Theatre; Joann McIntyre from *I Love You, Baby Blue*; Laine Green from *The Alberta*

Cowboy Show), went to the '76 Montreal Olympics. They were invited to perform in the athletes' village as well as partake in the cultural presentations at Centaur with two new works: the third in our Canadian Heroes Series and *The Athletes' Show*, both written and developed with former Olympian Bruce Kidd. It was a heady experience, although heavy security at the village made it hard to reach our athlete audience. Our best shows happened out of doors in an improvised space just outside the refectory.

Back in Toronto, combined governments ponied up $60,000 to help make our building legal, although this took some time. Meanwhile CODCO returned with another wonderful hit, *Laugh Your Guts Out with Total Strangers*, and we managed somehow to perform that in our new uncertified home. The core company had another coup and we were invited back to the National Arts Centre in Ottawa with a miniseries: *1837*; Ted Johns's *Naked on the North Shore*; David Fox's collective *John Hornby*; and a new creation from Alianak, *The Blues*. John Gray returned to Toronto and wrote his first musical play, *18 Wheels*, and it toured our Southwestern Ontario circuit triumphantly. Alianak created a sequel, *I Love You, Baby Blue 2*, which played at the Bayview Playhouse, and although it couldn't come close to matching the box office of number one, it paid its bills—no mean feat in the new Toronto, where it had become harder to make an impact. But developmental shows in Toronto flourished. There is *The Road to Charlottetown* by poet Milton Acorn and Cedric Smith; a hosted production from Alberta's incipient Theatre Network, *Two Miles Off*; a cutting-edge piece of post-feminist agit/rock/musical called *The Patty Rehearst Story* by the Hummer Sisters; *Cheap Thrills* by Michael Hollingsworth; and others.

Out of town, the collective continued our attempt at dialogue with the whole country by collaborating with Edmonton's Theatre 3 and novelist Rudy Wiebe, making the epic *Far as the Eye Can See*. Along with our regulars, the show would be notable for the performance of Gordon Tootoosis as Crowfoot. After strong houses, it would journey to the Tarragon for the fall season and play as a rare co-production. We were again temporarily out of Ryerson Avenue, and Bill Glassco graciously shared his space, and together we shared with Toronto an important show and author.

But 1977/78 continued the unsettled situation where the city started losing interest in rural connections. First, a wild and exuberant comedy about high and low art entitled *Shakespeare for Fun and Profit*, with excellent performances and a memorable original score by John Gray, played vigorously to our touring audience but found little traction in Toronto. About the same time, a long-planned "CODCO's Great Hits" was cancelled because the group broke up (just like a rock band). We hosted each of the splintered parts, but the usual audience exhilaration was lessened. And when we did get access to 16 Ryerson, we couldn't find the magic liftoff. A rural comedy fashioned together by myself and Ted Johns called *He Won't Come in from the Barn* starring Ted, five actors, and two live cows, was trashed. The *Toronto Star* critic was incensed, proclaiming it "nostalgie de la boue." When the play moved to the Blyth Festival, it broke all box-office records in successive seasons. Obviously, on the main front, something was changing. Our Seed Show program continued to grow in power, most notably the Hummer Sisters's heartbreaking *The Bible as Told to Karen Ann Quinlan*, where their live video treatment took another step forward; and Paul Kelman's highly imaginative adaptation of legendary science fiction writer Judith Merril's *Headspace*. It starred Anne Anglin, who would collaborate later with poet Penn Kemp on *Eros Rising*. Among other Seed Shows, there was an intriguing collaboration with John Gray, Paul Williams, and Eric Peterson. In many ways it would be a game-changer.

AMONG OTHER SEED SHOWS, THERE WAS AN INTRIGUING COLLABORATION WITH JOHN GRAY, PAUL WILLIAMS, AND ERIC PETERSON. IN MANY WAYS IT WOULD BE A GAME-CHANGER.

SWINGING FOR THE FENCES

1978/79 was the liftoff season. The annual report summary claims there were twenty-four productions that took place through TPM. It would be folly to name them all, but I can name some of the most memorable. First, a daring addition to our national conversation when a fearless company headed to Montreal and gutted out an exceptional *Les Maudits Anglais*. We took on the separatist theme in the most nationalist theatre company that we could find, Théâtre d'Aujourd'hui, and performed in our rudimentary horrible Toronto French. They loved us and we were held over. Simultaneously, Claude Jutra and a band of future Québécois stars played their new and glorious *Commedia Dell'Arte* at Ryerson Avenue. We were in heady times again as we followed up with an extensive Ontario tour of *Les Canadiens*, created by Rick Salutin, Eric Peterson, and Ken Dryden, and also notable for the directing debut of Miles Potter. Somewhere in there was a five-week tour of England, Wales, and Ireland with two companies for *The Farm Show* and *1837*, and of course the triumphant return of *Billy Bishop Goes to War* by Eric and John. The Seed Show that had started in Paul Williams's studio had sprouted and grown in Vancouver. It returned as a confident blockbuster with attendance of more than eleven thousand people. "Gleaming with humour, poignancy and believable heroism," quoted one review.

Opportunities galore to share with Seed Shows: VideoCabaret and other Queen street spill-outs; another new work with Janet Amos (*Dream Girls*); Joann McIntyre created a new genre with *Brush-Off* in the Backspace; the home of a Blum brothers' new work as well, *After the Opera*; and among the many other fledgling enterprises, a chance to assist in the founding of Nightwood Theatre. Our scene was bursting with the new. Talent was spilling out all over the place and the arguments about the future forms of theatre in our city and country burned long into the night. I should have been exhausted but truly don't seem to remember whether I was.

THE ANARCHY OF AN AUDIENCE

My favourite moments in Ryerson: creating new stuff in the Backspace and stuffing the Upstairs theatre with an audience on a Sunday pay-what-you-can—especially with a hit show. People were so eager; they would sit on any perch, a piece of a stair, a window ledge, even the ladder to the lighting. They were encouraged to come back during the week for real seats but refused and hung on tenaciously. I got a thrill from the numbers: fifty, seventy-five, one hundred, beyond capacity. The safety Mounties were not yet invented, and we did have the widest escape stairs in the city.

Maggie and Pierre gave me both moments. We took over the Backspace to create the show and, since there were only the two of us, we seemed able to explore, throw away, and reinvent forever. Linda was like an Olympic athlete whose training regime had all been aimed at that moment. I saw what she had gleaned from working on the collectives: the heart of Fox, the spirituality of Anglin, the tenacity and warmth of Amos, the shrewd humour of Peterson's gallery of characters, the theatre inventiveness of Potter, and the sharp mind of Johns. And, of course, her own fearlessness. She was a Ferrari and this was our Grand Prix. She could do anything. We opened in Saskatoon with our buddies at 25th Street Theatre and returned unbeatable. Sundays had me bursting the walls with an audience. Passe Muraille indeed.

Oh, yes, the season had other gems: another brilliant original from Alianak, *Night*, with walls that literally grabbed the character; Ted Johns's *The School Show*; we took over the Horseshoe for the Clichettes and the carnivore half of CODCO and teamed up with Figgy Duff; Clarke Rogers brought real good new writing with *October's Soldiers*; I responded with a writer of my own and *Coming Through Slaughter* by Michael Ondaatje; and out of town another version of the Donnellys broke all box-office records at the Blyth Festival. It was a bursting year on all fronts and no more so than with the Seed Shows: early comic work from Mel Tuck and Sheila Gostick; the launch of the Rhubarb Festival with Sky Gilbert and Cynthia Grant; two separate wonders from Necessary Angel; Tanya Ryga and Sharon Stearns from Alberta's Theatre Network; the *Prostitution Show*; and one of my top forever plays in the Backspace, the chilling *Stallers' Farm*, directed by Peter Froehlich and introducing Kim Renders in a stunning performance. Brilliant timing.

The end of *Maggie and Pierre*'s first Toronto run coincided with my fortieth birthday. I was completely blindsided, being caught up with details of touring to Vancouver, and didn't know about the surprise party. It was a total blowout. Beautiful speeches. I was given the best of presents, a circular staircase that led to nowhere. We got drunk and stoned out of our minds. I had to crash at the theatre, and, at 8:00 the next morning, hungover and sick as dogs, Bob Pearson (who created the staircase) and I took our set-filled truck on the road. We needed to have everything there for Wednesday evening. Three days, three thousand miles of Canadian roads.

MAGGIE AND PIERRE
LINDA GRIFFITHS. PHOTOS BY DAVID GROSKIND.

ANECDOTES

The argument over flexibility and permanent facilities had been a raging battle since we bought the building. I, of course, wanted to offer creators the maximum of choices, accepting personal inconvenience as a trade-off. One actor in particular was not enthralled and refused to share toilet facilities with the audience. A makeshift porta-potty was set up for him and the show proceeded—an excellent play, by the way. Still hugely unhappy, he wrapped his own shit in a newspaper and stormed around: "Where's Thompson's desk?" he growled; "I want to leave him a message." "He doesn't have one," was the reply, "he just borrows one or has his meetings down at the corner."

The hit run of *Vampyr* was in full swing. Booth was playing the title character and managed to parlay that into a free room at Rochdale. Some fans of the show became very intense and one particular young woman was convinced that he truly needed her blood. In her calmer phase we had let her usher the show, but she became noisy and wanted to climb on the stage. I had to physically carry her out of the theatre and into the basement where she immediately made an about-face and sweetly appealed to an offstage Clare Coulter. "Why are you being so mean?" Clare asked me. "She's got a fucking fistful of hair ripped out from my beard. Look at her hand!" She had also talked her way into Booth's room on Bloor Street and handed out all his possessions as artifacts of this man from another world.

The artist Charles Pachter found our building. It needed a lot of work but is beautiful. The owner, Sol Friendly, wanted too much money, somewhere north of $150,000—more than what we could afford—but he was in the hospital with serious medical problems. Charlie visited him, imploring, "Sol? Why not do this? Just once . . . for the arts . . . " There was an unfounded rumour Charlie may have cut off Sol's oxygen temporarily. In any case, Sol agreed to our offer of $100,000. Sol made no mention of his nieces already prominent in the arts, popular agent Pam and powerhouse producer Linda.

Sometime about halfway through the run of *I Love You, Baby Blue*, the *Toronto Star* carried a headline announcing our box office bonanza. The following evening there was an attempted robbery—"Young man," came the stern and authority-filled voice of Lorna-Gail Peterson (Eric's then wife) from behind her station, "we'll have none of that. Why don't you just leave?" He did.

We were high on *The Farm Show* tour audiences, both their numbers and the direct way they responded. What could we give them for an encore? From my days at Western I remembered the sort of nineteenth-century "intellectual frisson" that could be stirred up by our resident eccentrics Orlo Miller and James Reaney when they evoked Donnelly stories—Orlo even had a book. What about a country-and-western, kick-the-shit-out-of-each-other death match on stage with real fire (borrowed from *Doukhobors*)? A cast of thirteen? Even though the numbers were crazy for touring, we had to. This would be our own epic. Booth, who had started with Garrard and flourished with Kinch, was on my case. "I gotta play Will," he growled; "I was born to do it." I was still pissed off at him for bailing out of a couple of my shows, most notably *Doukhobors*. Huge arguments followed. Finally, a solution. He would receive no money for the whole rehearsal period, but if he survived he would get it all. We premiered in Petrolia's reawakened playhouse and Booth got his standing ovation along with four weeks' back pay.

ETERNITY AHEAD

Two years later and we had just ridden a whirlwind. *Maggie and Pierre* played to more than seventy thousand people across the country, including a triumphal week at the Royal Alexandra Theatre. Clarke Rogers introduced the world to a major new talent with Judith Thompson's *The Crackwalker*. Seed Shows were flourishing and helped launch emerging companies such as Buddies in Bad Times, VideoCabaret, and Necessary Angel. *Prodigals in a Promised Land* brought a whole new experience to Ryerson Avenue with West Indian Canadians sharing their stories. There was a change in the wind and my collective/collaborative approach seemed to have lost traction. Plays such as *Torontonians* and *Nathan Cohen: A Review* were unable to surprise or dazzle audiences. Writers like Judith Thompson, Hector Bunyan, and Brad Fraser (with *Rude Noises* in the Backspace) were in the ascendant. Maybe I was a bit tired. Was it time for a change? Clarke Rogers had been working like a dog on this movement for the last couple years. In the usual Passe Muraille tradition he'd been exploited mercilessly. Perhaps it was his time.

My recollection is that the change in artistic direction was made quickly and relatively painlessly. I do remember a rather quirky train of thought that hit me at that time. When we were living at Ray Bird's abandoned farmhouse in the summer of '72, we had a refrigerator donated by the "religious" Lobbs with a sticker on it reading "Eternity Ahead." I had always thought it was pointing a way to the future success of *The Farm Show*. Now it seemed to be clearly referring to my life.

EXIT

Of course there had to be a party. It was a tripleheader farewell, bidding adieu to Bill Glassco, Tom Hendry, and me, held at Toronto Free Theatre. In true TPM tradition, we negotiated the keys to the bar and came close to trashing the place by sunrise. But I was already on another plane of thinking. My farewell gift of service: a glorious ten-speed, put together on a reserve in Manitoba. In the next ten years the bike and I would pedal the equivalent of twice the distance across our country—I would of course travel much farther. And both Theatre Passe Muraille and I would have to reinvent ourselves five full times. Completely.

PAUL THOMPSON is a playwright and director best known for his term as artistic director of Theatre Passe Muraille, where he pioneered techniques for collective creation. He was the general director of the National Theatre School and was appointed as an officer in the Order of Canada in 2008.

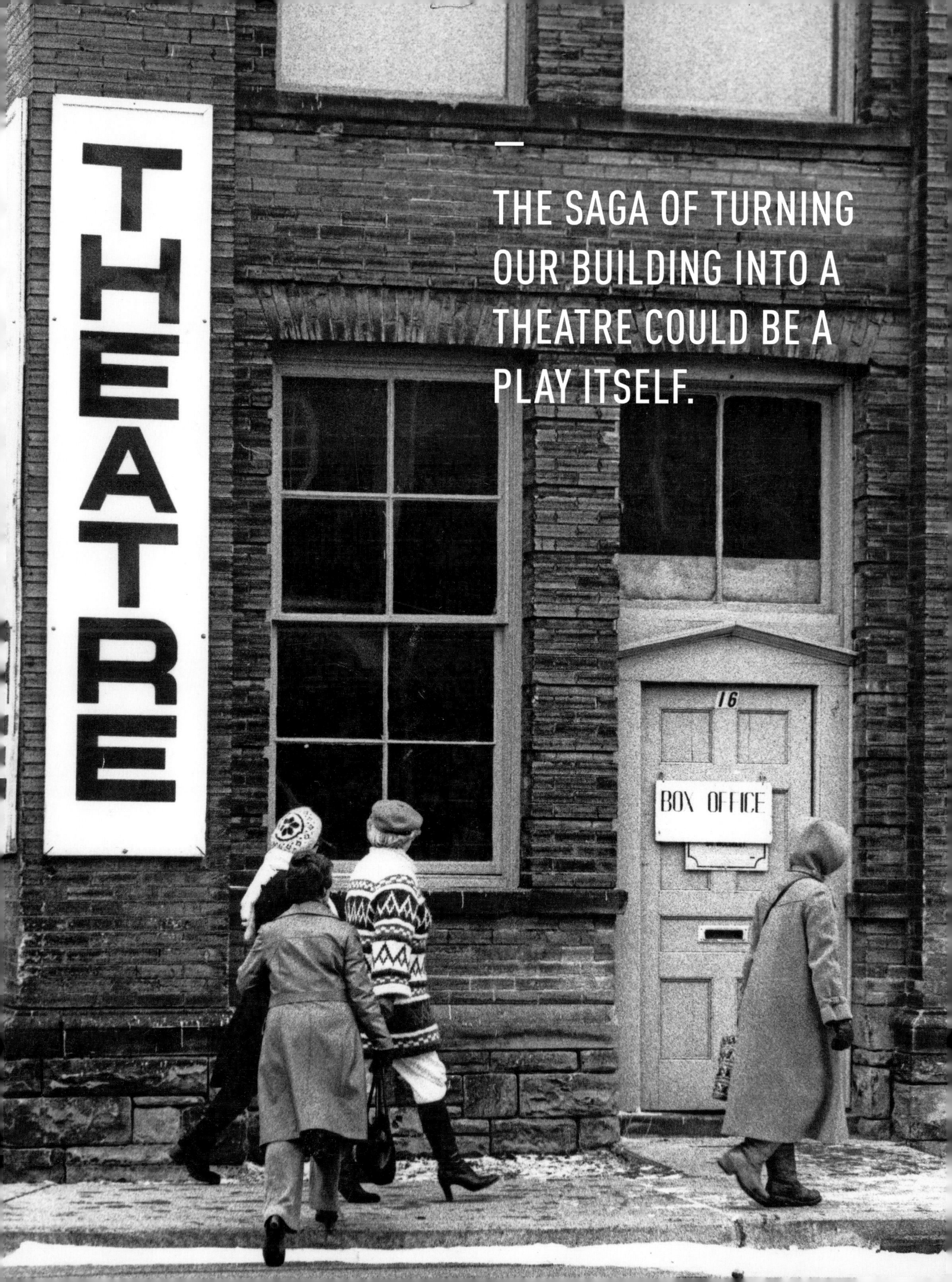

THE SAGA OF TURNING OUR BUILDING INTO A THEATRE COULD BE A PLAY ITSELF.

CLARKE ROGERS
PHOTO BY RAE JOHNSON.

CLARKE ROGERS: A CHAMPION OF CANADIAN THEATRE

BY RAE JOHNSON

Clarke Rogers was the artistic director of Theatre Passe Muraille from 1982 to 1988.

On an August afternoon in 1985 I met Clarke at the Cameron House, a neighbourhood bar and gathering place on Queen Street West, Toronto. He was meeting with VideoCabaret about one of the first productions of Michael Hollingsworth's *The History of the Village of the Small Huts*. Deanne Taylor warned me—"Watch out for him, Rae . . . " After a whirlwind courtship, including a trip to Negril, Jamaica, we were married the following spring on May 24, 1986, surrounded by family and friends from the theatre and visual arts community, in the backyard rose garden of Carole Corbeil and Layne Coleman and their baby daughter Charlotte.

Our first home was my studio on Adelaide Street at John, in a three-storey duplex that has since been demolished, a sublet from my friend, painter Sybil Goldstein. On her return from New York, having few other options at the time, we camped out at Theatre Passe Muraille. Sometimes we slept on the set of *Jessica: A Transformation*, a new play by Linda Griffiths that Clarke was directing. The play was an unruly collaboration between Linda and Maria Campbell, whose autobiography *Halfbreed* formed the basis of the story. The play had a supernatural plot, with animal spirits inhabiting their human counterparts, intervening and guiding Jessica to a spiritual healing from the horrors of racism as a Métis woman from Western Canada. Tantoo Cardinal played Jessica. Susan Hogan played the Unicorn, representing the Celtic part of Jessica's mixed identity. Makka Kleist was wise Coyote. Tom Jackson was the protective Bear spirit and Wolverine, the dark side of addiction. Graham Greene played Crow, the Trickster. I was present for many of the rehearsals and I witnessed an uncanny atmosphere in the theatre. The story and its mythical Indigenous and European references, and the way the events of the protagonist's life were transformed through powerful unconscious forces, still amaze me in their prescience.

JESSICA: A TRANSFORMATION
GRAHAM GREENE AND TANTOO CARDINAL.
PHOTO BY MICHAEL COOPER.

Clarke was a champion of Canadian culture in the broadest sense, often hiring neighbourhood artists to design posters and sets, inviting musicians to perform, bridging the divide between disciplines and arts communities. Clarke was ahead of his time in his interest in Indigenous history. Impassioned and committed to producing new Canadian artists, he supported playwrights like Tomson Highway and Daniel David Moses. He also produced the plays of Hector Bunyan, at a time when other theatres showed little interest in Caribbean and African Canadian playwrights. He supported women and spoke to me often of *The Crackwalker* by Judith Thompson as one of his proudest achievements as director of the 1980 groundbreaking play.

Clarke's early years took him directly from Upper Canada College to working as a stage manager at the Royal Winnipeg Ballet, then in the prop department at Stratford under John Hirsch, and to Theatre Calgary, where he directed Christopher Walken in *Romeo and Juliet*. He brought his love of Shakespeare and new Canadian plays together in the pulse of the 1980s Toronto art scene when he became the artistic director of Theatre Passe Muraille in 1982. Interested in regional theatre, Clarke welcomed CODCO's audacious and sacrilegious brand of Newfoundland humour into Theatre Passe Muraille. When Linda Griffiths and Patrick Brymer's 1983 play *O.D. on Paradise*, about Canadian tourists in Jamaica, was accused of having the actors smoking pot on stage, he took the *Toronto Star* to court. Although the accusations in the review by Gina Mallet had killed the box office, he and lawyer Charles Campbell won a settlement that helped pay for renovations to the building, and set the theatre on solid financial footing.

Clarke had a heroic personality. A dear colleague and friend, artist Tim Jocelyn, was diagnosed with AIDS shortly after completing his *New Dimensions Astrolabe* installation at Expo '86 in Vancouver. It was the early, dark days of AIDS, when revulsion and fear surrounded infected gay men who were being decimated by this new plague. Clarke immediately asked me what we could do. We decided to raise money for Tim and launched a variety show and art auction fundraiser. Clarke opened up the

—
THE HISTORY OF THE VILLAGE OF SMALL HUTS (PART 2)
JOHN BLACKWOOD, PAUL BETTIS, GRAHAM GREENE, MICHAEL COPEMAN, JANET BURKE, PATRICK BRYMER, AND ARTURO FRESOLONE. PHOTO BY MICHAEL COOPER.

***TRAGEDY OF MANNERS* HOUSE POSTER**

theatre to host a very successful benefit for Tim with volunteers from the music and visual arts scenes, engaging the whole community. He had a gift for bringing people together under the cause of art. For Clarke it was always about the "Art."

One of his last productions at Theatre Passe Muraille was a play he commissioned about the Queen Street West art scene. He engaged writer Donna Lypchuk to write *Tragedy of Manners*, a scathing dissection of the art scene that exposed heroin abuse and the new AIDS epidemic. It included a cast of thirty-two mostly non-actors, who were personalities in their own right, inhabiting roles of thinly disguised local art critics, art dealers, artists, and musicians. Although it was not a critical success, it made the cover of *NOW Magazine*. It was truly a community-driven event.

Clarke's dynamic personality and management style simply became too much for his colleagues. After the birth of our first daughter Joslyn, it was time for him to leave the theatre as its artistic director. In 1989, with our babies Joslyn and June and joined by my son Adrian, we moved to a small village in Ontario called Flesherton, two hours north of Toronto. In the rapidly changing economy, it was a time of struggle with little or no work coming Clarke's way. I commuted to my part-time job at the Ontario College of Art.

At first country life suited Clarke, who loved driving the country roads around Grey County and fly-fishing in remote streams, catching trout that he would proudly bring home for us to eat. In 1990 he started an art gallery called Flashtown on the main street and sold paintings by local and Toronto-based artists like Harold Klunder, Robert Markle, Catherine Carmichael, Lorne Wagman, Alan Glicksman, and yours truly. After the press had alerted the public of Clarke's latest venture, art lovers made the pilgrimage to the new gallery in Grey County. The exodus of artists to Flesherton had prompted the *Star*'s Christopher Hume to admonish "the last artist in Toronto to turn off the light." Flashtown Gallery closed in 1992. In its place Clarke created Flashtown Theatre Company, turning the gallery space into a rehearsal hall.

An avid historian, Clarke was excited when he discovered that Agnes Macphail, the legendary parliamentarian, had lived just up the road from us in a tiny village called Ceylon. He dove into research about her life as an early feminist and the founder of the UFO (United Farmers of Ontario), championing the farmers she represented. He began his final writing project, *Agnes Macphail and the Fiddler's Due*. The fiddler was our local violin player and maker, David Prentice, and our daughter Joslyn was often with her father at rehearsals that were part collaboration and improvisation in the spirit of Paul Thompson's *The Farm Show*. Clarke brought the Flesherton community together, artists and non-artists alike. I would tease him, calling him the Mayor of Flesherton, because everywhere he went people would stop him to chat.

In spite of his efforts to create a new theatre community for himself, Clarke became isolated from his former colleagues. It's a tough business. Out of sight, out of mind. And this wounded him profoundly. He taught at the National Theatre School in Montreal under Director Paul Thompson, a seasonal position that was short-lived. It was a struggle to make ends meet. As I commuted to my teaching job at OCA in Toronto, he took on the role of stay-at-home dad, volunteering at our daughters' skating club and at fundraising events like hot dog day at Beavercrest School in Flesherton. He was a hit with the mothers. Yes, he was a ladies' man who could charm his way around anyone.

Still working on *Agnes Macphail and the Fiddler's Due* and his lifelong project, a play he called *Celebration* that had been workshopped at Theatre Passe Muraille, Clarke was also writing an Indigenous version of the libretto for Mozart's *The Magic Flute* for an upcoming production by a local dairy farmer/symphony conductor, in a project called *Symphony in*

THE DAY OF THE FUNERAL HAD A MYTHIC QUALITY, WITH TORNADOES REPORTEDLY SURROUNDING THE AREA, BEFITTING OF THE PASSING OF CLARKE'S DERVISH ENERGY.

the Barn. Nevertheless, I think his fall from grace from Toronto theatre had broken his heart. Even with substantial projects underway, poverty and isolation took a toll. During this time our marriage, and his sense of self, were disintegrating. Only forty-seven, he would say to me that he was an "old man." He had lived an epic life full of drama, fighting for Canadian theatre and culture—experiencing ecstatically creative periods and then the depths of darkness that always followed.

Clarke took his life on April 15, 1996, his forty-eighth birthday. I believe he became lost in his mind, trapped in the maze of his genius imagination, with no way out. His sudden death shocked everyone. He had seemed invincible. Nationwide news coverage reported his death. Clarke's legacy was discussed on *Morningside*, Peter Gzowski's national CBC radio show, with his friend, actor Michael Copeman, and long-time collaborator Linda Griffiths. There was devastation all around. It was palpable. A dark void hung over Flesherton. At his funeral people came up from Toronto and all around, overfilling the modest United Church. His oldest friends Michael and Susan Hogan flew in from Vancouver. David Prentice played his fiddle throughout the service as he would have done in *Agnes* rehearsals. The day of the funeral had a mythic quality, with tornadoes reportedly surrounding the area, befitting of the passing of Clarke's dervish energy.

Twenty years after Clarke's death his legacy lives on in the careers of the many artists he championed at Passe Muraille. He could be exasperatingly difficult and demanding, and in spite of this he recognized talent and had the gift of making those around him believe in the impossible. As a new generation takes their turn, men like Clarke seem rare and exotic in this new professionalized corporate world. I hope that a younger generation will remember the pioneers of Canadian culture like Clarke for their audacity and courage, and take heart to realize their own visionary dreams.

RAE JOHNSON is an artist who began teaching drawing and painting at OCAD in 1988. She has lectured about her work across Canada in universities and art centres. In the early 1980s, Rae formed the collective ChromaZone with fellow artists Oliver Girling, Andy Fabo, Brian Burnett, Sybil Goldstein, Tony Wilson, HP Marti, and, later, Tim Jocelyn.

THEATRE PASSE MURAILLE

Artistic Producer
Susan Serran

General Manager
David Baile

Associate Artist
Banuta Rubess

Associate Artist
Colin Taylor

April 17, 1996

Flesherton, Ontario... Writer and director Clarke Rogers died suddenly Monday, April 15. The Artistic Director of Theatre Passe Muraille from 1982 to 1988, he was renowned for his dramaturgical gifts and for his unerring eye for new talent.

Most notably, Clarke directed first plays by Judith Thompson (The Crackwalker), Sally Clarke ***(Lost Souls and Missing Persons), and Hector Bunyan (Prodigals In a Promised Land)***. He also supported the work of writers as diverse as M.T. Kelly, Anne-Marie McDonald, Brad Fraser and Donna Lypchuck, and worked closely with Linda Griffiths' on her award-winning shows, ***O.D. On Paradise*** and ***Jessica***.

In addition to a legacy of new work, Clarke had a significant impact on some of the country's finest actors, Graham Greene, Layne Coleman, Hardee Lineham, Nicky Guadagni, Susan Hogan, Joe Zeigler, Gary Reineke, Ardon Bess and Tantoo Cardinal.

His tenure at Passe Muraille was marked by courageous risk-taking as well as by a profound understanding that theatre must reflect the times we live in. His work on Hector Bunyan's play ***Prodigals in a Promised Land*** (1981) defined a new era on the Canadian stage. It was the first time a West Indian audience found a home in one of Toronto's alternative theatres.

Clark also wrote three plays, D&C, Celebration and The Agnes MacPhail Story, which was to be presented this summer on tour in southwestern Ontario. In addition to a legacy of new work,

Clarke is survived by his wife Rae Johnson and his two daughters, ~~Jocelyn~~ Joslyn and June. Details of a funeral service in Flesherton and memorial service at Theatre Passe Muraille will be released shortly.

For information please contact: Funeral -

Susan Serran: 504-8988

St John's United Church
Flesherton
Sat. 20 2:00PM.

Trust fund
Girls
Flesh CIBC

16 Ryerson Avenue, Toronto, Ontario M5T 2P3
telephone: (416) 504-8988 box office: (416) 504-7529 fax: (416) 504-8980

Nov 25/81

Paul,

Please accept this letter as notice of my intention to resign from active involvement in Theatre Passe Muraille on December 1st.

As you remember, when I first began working at the theatre it was with the clearly stated intention of stabilizing the production, administrative, and financial areas of the theatre, and developing a forum for the discovery and production of new playwrights. I believed that my ability in the one area ~~and~~ would buy me the opportunity in the other. I think that in both areas I achieved my goals as much as was possible given the circumstances and my talents.

However, after looking at the series of mistakes in judgement, artistic fiascos, failures of planning and general aimlessness of this season, I have come to believe that my presence at and contribution to the theatre is doing more harm than good.

I feel that because I am now lacking the clearly defined goals and ambitions that motivated me through the past 3 years, my own personal direction is unsure, and therefore I am failing to

3

provide the direction and inspiration that is the responsibility of my position.

I take full responsibility for the mistakes of the current season, and for the lack of confidence and direction within the theatre. I offer no excuses or justification for them other than the understanding that they reflect the confusion and aimlessness of myself.

While I know that to leave now is to leave the theatre without a season and to leave you without the support you need and expected, I truly feel that to continue as we have so far this year would do more damage

4

ultimately to the theatre and to myself than my going will cause.

I want to emphasize that I am not resigning out of anger, bitterness, or frustration with either yourself or TPM, but out of a clear recognition that I no longer know what I am doing, why, or even what I ~~am~~ want to do. Having achieved many of the goals I set out to achieve, I have not discovered, within myself, the necessary new goals and challenges to give a purpose to my future or my work.

I would like to continue the NOW WORKS project under TPM's aegis to see if I can rekindle

5

the fire of interest in new writing that I had, but I think that it would be a mistake to place any ~~expl~~ expectations on this work.

With regard to the situation that is created by my going, I believe that Cathy and Susan are capable of producing a season for the theatre, that a portion of the Council grants should be returned on the basis that my departure has seriously affected the plans for the season, and that you should continue to search out your own challenges and goals unaffected by my actions.

I truly did believe that I could provide the impetus and direction

6

for the theatre this year while
at the same time trying to redefine
my own ambitions. I am sorry
I was so short-sighted as ~~to~~
not to see that this was
impossible.

I apologize to you personally
and to everyone in the theatre
for the mess I have made, the
mess I have left behind me, and
the mess my going will create.

I think you know me well
enough to know how much I
regret this decision, but I know
of no other way to remain
honest, sane or useful.

I hope that, when or if I am
able to discover new reasons and

7

new power to accomplish, you will again allow me the opportunity that you have been so generous with in the past.

Clarke

LETTER OF RESIGNATION FROM CLARKE ROGERS TO PAUL THOMPSON, NOVEMBER 21, 1981

"IT WAS THE BEST OF TIMES, IT WAS THE WORST OF TIMES . . ."

BY BRIAN RICHMOND

When I think back on my three years as artistic director of Theatre Passe Muraille, for some reason this over-quoted phrase from Charles Dickens repeatedly comes to mind.

Now, the thought that the most famous writer from nineteenth century imperialist Britain has something to say about the ultra-Canadian nationalist TPM of the late 1980s may seem strange to some. But when one remembers that what characterized Dickens's work was his ability to draw larger-than-life characters that he set afloat on the seas of his dramatic and tumultuous narratives, then the analogy to the people and events I encountered at TPM between 1988 and 1991 might begin to make sense. (Indeed, if I were to go further in this thievery I might even steal one of Dickens's more famous titles to describe these times; although I would be hard pressed to choose between *Great Expectations*, *Bleak House*, and *Hard Times*.)

Nevertheless, I have been asked to write some words about my time with TPM as it celebrates its fiftieth anniversary. And to organize these thoughts around a few of the best and worst of my memories from '88 to '91 seems as good a way as any to do so. As this is a celebration, I had thought of doing only the best, but, upon reflection, this seemed an inappropriate and untruthful way to celebrate the, always beautiful but stubbornly anarchic, soul of this great Canadian theatre.

So here are a few of these fading memories.

The best: The sound of TPM board member Carole Corbeil's voice as I picked up the phone in some nondescript beige motel room in Louisville, Kentucky. The truly fierce and hugely talented Jane Buss and I had concocted a scheme over Christmas cocktails in 1987 to jointly apply for the position of producing artistic director. It was a fun exercise but one that neither Jane nor I thought had much chance of succeeding given that neither of us had been a part of the TPM family up to that point in time. So, in early 1988, I'd decided to jump back into my '87 Nissan Sentra and resume my search for the best methods of new play development being practised in Canada and the US at the time. My next stop involved a series of interviews with those responsible for the Humana Festival at the Actors Theatre of Louisville when Carole (who, in my now distant memory had a voice that contained a warm, velvety intelligence that would steer us through good times and bad) phoned to ask whether Jane and I were still interested in the challenges facing TPM. "You bet!" I said. After calling Jane to confirm this, I jumped into my vehicle and drove the nearly one thousand kilometres in one go. I arrived back in Toronto and started work at TPM on what seemed like the next day.

The worst: The realization that what the board had in mind was for us to do outgoing artistic director Clarke Rogers's

***DRY LIPS OUGHTA MOVE TO KAPUSKASING* HOUSE POSTER**
GRAHAM GREENE, BEN CARDINAL, ERROLL KINISTINO, KENNETCH CHARLETTE, GARY FARMER, RON COOK, AND BILLY MERASTY. PHOTO BY MICHAEL COOPER.

already planned season. Clarke could be an amazing director with a finely honed literary taste (his production of Judith Thompson's *The Crackwalker* remains one of my most vibrant and searing memories in my nearly fifty years of watching theatre in Canada and beyond). The lineup of plays he had chosen for the 1989/90 season were all compelling and worthy of production. The problem was that they were not choices Jane and I had made. And they did not correspond to the business plan we had developed to bring the financial bleeding TPM was suffering under control. Passions rose and were expressed and it was looking like Jane and I would be forced to exit before we had barely begun. But compromises were brokered as we settled into the planning of the season. Little did I know that this opening event would presage the always anarchic administrative and artistic patterns of my three years with the company.

The best: The discovery that we had the opportunity to work with the huge talents of the team of theatre administrators, playwrights, directors, designers, and dramaturges that Clarke and Paul Thompson before him had brought together and which made up the then TPM artistic family. I am referring, of course, to TPM artists such as Linda Griffiths, Carole Corbeil, Layne Coleman, and the brilliant young talents of Jerry Doiron, Peter Hinton, and Stephan Droege. It was not difficult for Jane and I to decide to utilize all of these trailblazers (joined by my long-time collaborators playwright/dramaturge Paul Ledoux and marketing guru Roxanne Moffitt) in key artistic and administrative positions.

The worst: The discovery of rat-infested dressing rooms, putrid toilets, and a deficit the size of a cancerous golf ball that was constricting the voice of this champion of the Canadian experience.

The best: The visit from Shaw Festival's then executive director (the late Paul Reynolds) as he delivered the news that he and Artistic Director Christopher Newton were interested in co-producing our opening production—Paul Ledoux and David S. Young's musical *Fire*. This support, along with rave reviews that generated huge audience enthusiasm, allowed us to enter our first season on a wave of optimism that carried us through the inevitable highs and lows of producing non-profit theatre in Canada.

The worst: The ill-fated production of *West Memphis Mojo* that saw Peter Hinton, Paul Ledoux, and I on phones over several nights trying to solve the merry-go-round of casting mishaps; the fury in the eyes of several board members who accused us of having betrayed the spirit of TPM by inviting to opening night Lieutenant Governor Lincoln Alexander (whose office they saw as a symbol of the imperialism that they so opposed); and the sad tragicomedy of unplanned retribution as, on opening night, Mr. Alexander's wife suffered a mild heart attack (she recovered almost immediately, I am very happy to say) and had to be escorted from the front row of the theatre before the end of the first act. With all this baggage *West Memphis Mojo*, of course, became this season's only critical and audience failure.

The best: The blessing circle led by one of the elders from Tomson Highway's, Graham Greene's, Gary Farmer's, Doris Linklater's, and other cast members' Six Nations communities in advance of the premiere performance of *Dry Lips Oughta Move to Kapuskasing*. The sight of Tomson weeping like a child as the elder told the assembled cast and crew of the huge weight that Tomson had taken on as a storyteller for his people, and his plea for us to do all we could to support him, is a memory that will never fade.

The worst: Jane's decision to leave at the end of the 1989/90 season. Frustrated by her working relationship with the board (and I suspect me), she had guided us to a near break-even season (which was no small feat in that producing environment). Her leaving meant I had personally lost one of the best producing partners I had had the pleasure of working with to that point in time.

The best: The look of unreserved generosity and unmitigated pride in Linda Griffiths's eyes as I and the other artists

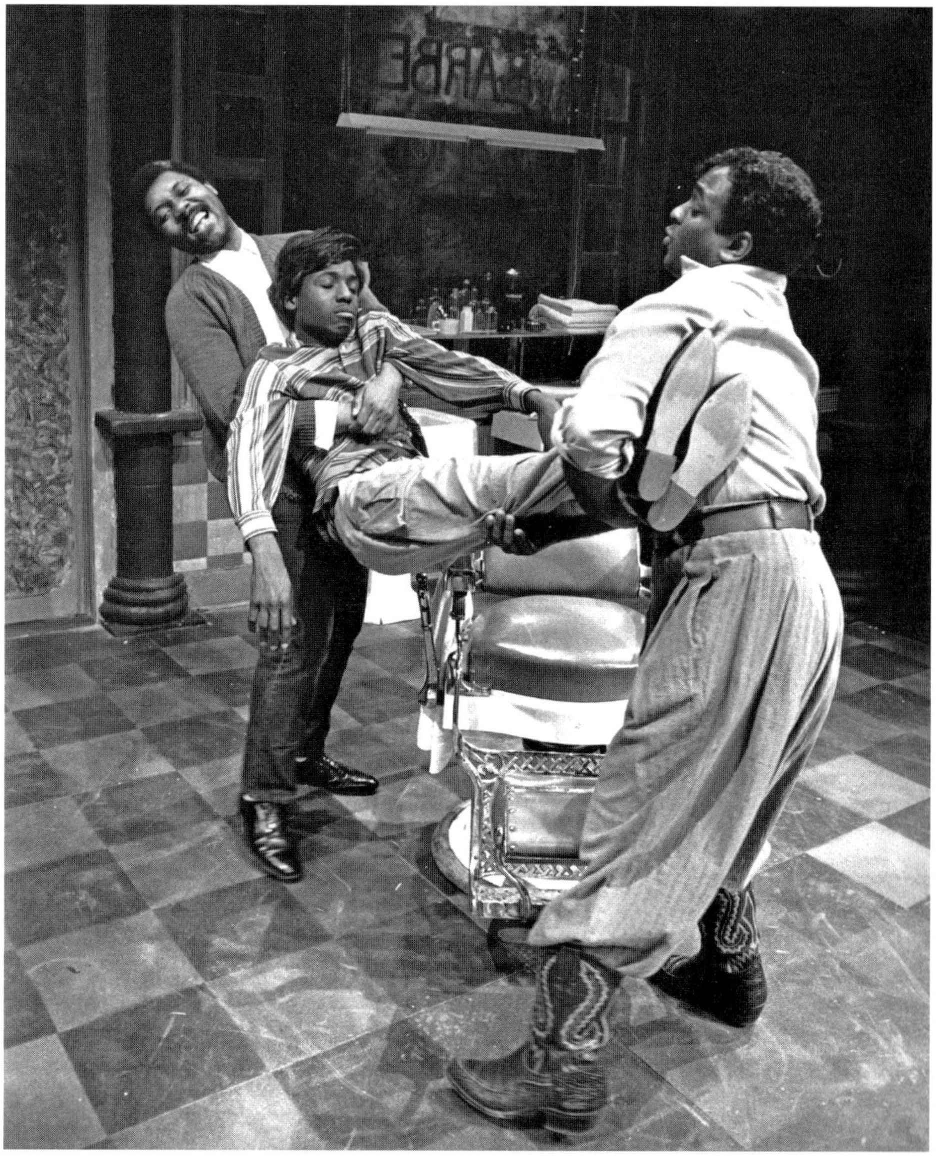

WEST MEMPHIS MOJO
JEFF COOPWOOD, RICHARD YEARWOOD, AND TYRONE BENSKIN.

UNDER THE SKIN
TANJA JACOBS AND MAGGIE HUCULAK.

THE BEST AND THE WORST, THE BLOOD AND THE FLAME, THE MESS AND THE ECSTASY—THESE WERE THE PASSE MURAILLE EXPERIENCE.

walked off the stage of the (I believe?) Winter Garden Theatre carrying what felt like every Dora Award handed out that night for our productions of *Fire*, *Under the Skin*, and *Dry Lips* . . . and, of course, because we are all the children of Dionysus, the all-night revels that followed as we plunged into the pools outside our party site at Roy Thomson Hall and celebrated into the night.

And that's just year one. A quick pass through just some of the next two years' highlights would have to include:

> Worst: A rightfully disgruntled playwright who, in response to my ego-swollen and drunkenly boorish behaviour (at that most iconic TPM watering hole, the Epicure), bleated out in murderous tones that he would "have my head on a stick."
>
> Best: My son Jacob's cartoon left beside my cereal bowl the next morning showing my head on a spear raised over the head of the playwright and his tribe as they danced in their bloodthirsty victory circle; I knew at this moment that Jake had a future as a satirist.
>
> Best: The delight of watching the opening night of Peter Hinton's beautiful and critically acclaimed production of *Abingdon Square* starring Ann-Marie MacDonald, and Robert Lepage's ton of beans falling on the head of a corpulent god in *Echo*.
>
> Worst: The chaos of year two brought on by swelling revenues and even larger expenditures.
>
> Best: The truly magical English-language premiere that my gang of boys delivered with Michel Marc Bouchard's *Lilies*.
>
> Worst: What felt like, at the time, a knife-in-the-back moment following a two-year effort by myself and James W. Nichol to bring Margaret Laurence's monumental novel *The Stone Angel* to the stage.
>
> And finally, the Best-Best came years after I had left TPM. My playwright son Jacob Richmond's new musical *Ride the Cyclone* rocking the roof off this iconic Canadian theatre as the opening night TPM audience watched in rapt attention.

And, in the end, it is the memory of the TPM audience on this night and others that most endures over a quarter century later. They are an audience that is unlike any other in any other theatre community that I have experienced in Canada and beyond. Hugely attentive, endlessly generous, and extraordinarily literate in all things "theatre," they seem to me a key ingredient in what has made TPM such an important feature of our modern Canadian theatre history.

Except, of course, I have not mentioned the other key ingredient. No tribute to TPM would be complete without paying homage to the man who most, in my view, represents the soul of TPM—Paul Thompson. It was Jim Garrard and his successors Martin Kinch and John Palmer who, as TPM's first artistic directors, established the rebellious spirit and the Rochdale-influenced aesthetic that most characterized the theatre as I knew it in the '70s, '80s, and '90s. But it was Paul Thompson with his diminutive Moses-like stature (that always pops up in my memory as bare-chested for no reason that bears any relationship to reality), and his twinkling eyes (which seemed to invite you into some eternal secret that, I am sorry to say, I have yet to discover), who, for me, remains the enduring symbol of this great Canadian theatre. The best and the worst, the blood and the flame, the mess and the ecstasy—these were the Passe Muraille experience. And, for me, these all seem to have grown from the fecund imagination of Paul like the children born from some classic god's mind and body.

To TPM's current artistic director Andy McKim, and to all the TPM artists before and after, I wish us all a happy, happy birthday. It was the best, it was the worst, but it was a time that I would not replace with any other.

BRIAN RICHMOND is the founding artistic director of Persephone Theatre and served as the artistic director for Playwrights' Workshop Montréal, Thunder Bay's Magnus Theatre, and Theatre Passe Muraille. In 2009 he founded Blue Bridge Repertory Theatre in Victoria to facilitate the development of young theatre artists. He is currently a professor at the University of Victoria, and was Chair of the Department of Theatre from 2001 to 2008.

BAŅUTA RUBESS AND KEN MCDOUGALL

MOONWALK: TPM 1992–1997

BY BAŅUTA RUBESS

Nineteen ninety-two through nineteen ninety-seven. Those were heady years. Those were brutal years.

> DAVID BAILE (General Manager, 1993–1996): My very first day at TPM I came in and Bob Nasmith was asleep in the office bathroom floor. The production manager yelled, "Nasmith, why are you sleeping on the bathroom floor?" To which Bob responded, "Where do you want me to sleep, the ceiling?"

> COLIN TAYLOR (Associate Artist, 1994–1997): The theatre when I arrived was in a period of what felt like rapid ascendancy, from near-invisibility and irrelevance to a bold public and artistic profile under Susan Serran and her associates. It was an exciting time to arrive.

The walls of Passe Muraille were seriously shaken when Susan Serran took charge. She burned with energy and vision, and was born to defy convention. She was a woman in power, which is still a convention begging to be defied in the theatre. She was an artistic producer, which was controversial at the time; not a card-carrying artist, but a lover of artists, by nature a nurturer. Her mission was change: though Susan was anointed by the insiders, she was inspired by the outsiders, and opened up the walls to those stuck behind them. In order to do so, she created a triumvirate with Ken McDougall and myself as associate artists. When Ken died, she brought in Colin Taylor, a brilliant thinker and director and a Black man, breaking ground for cultural diversity in the theatre. I have a vivid memory of the very first day Susan, Ken, and I walked into the TPM offices. It was like walking on the moon: a cold, barren, hostile environment. The place looked like someone shouted, "The world is ending in five minutes!" and everyone vamoosed. The place was in shambles.

Susan pulled the theatre back from bankruptcy and opened the stage to an astounding roster of artists, but you'll never read about it, even though I've combed through articles and histories about TPM. There's a cloak of invisibility thrown over women who stick their head over the parapet. It saddens me to see the cultural amnesia. Is it because things ended badly? Because Susan was ousted by the board? Ah, that's a tradition that runs deep in Canadian theatre. TPM has had more than its share of backstage dramas, and I'm not going to parse the details of her departure. Suffice it to say that anyone who poured so much of her life and imagination into our community deserves more gratitude and respect.

A scholarly book called *City Stages* by Michael McKinnie covers our period and claims the theatre survived by celebrating nostalgia. I showed Susan the relevant pages and she snapped the book shut. "Well, *he* got it all wrong."

McKinnie doesn't even record our names. Susan, Ken, Baņuta, Colin.

So I'm going to rebalance the story, place my thumb on the weights.

In order to do so, I talked to Susan, wrote to Colin and David Baile.

Susan and Patti Smith would be best buddies. Both of these women don't hide behind anything. Susan never wore a smidge of makeup in all the time I knew her. She was boldly unfashionable. She wore her hair down to her waist. You could picture her jousting. Her laugh was raucous and her intellect searing. She was a smoker and a drinker, which were important skills to have if you were going to buddy up with the poker-playing patriarchy that founded the theatre. Her piercing eyes could nail you to the chair, and often did. And then she'd share her passion, and show a keen interest in your work, urging you to do more, go further, bite the bullet. She'd ask: Why should we do it? How can we do it better? How is it going to benefit the community? How is it going to change the world?

Paul Thompson brought Susan into Passe Muraille as a publicist in 1978, when she was fresh out of university. A year later she was the general manager and continued in that role for four seasons, launching a slew of successful shows, including *Maggie and Pierre*, which saved the theatre financially by touring the country.

SUSAN SERRAN: I played three different roles at Passe Muraille, in two different time frames. One, when I was very young and extremely passionate, over-the-top excited about getting a job anywhere, let alone at Theatre Passe Muraille, then known as one of the country's greatest alternative theatre companies. *(laughs)* The naïveté really shows through when a year later I would accept the position as general manager. Never seen a Canada Council application from a mile off. Mind you, I became the publicist having never been at the *Toronto Star* or the *Globe and Mail* or anywhere else. It was the days of Paul Thompson and it was not about what was right in terms of time, or anything else, it was about who was right. Who fits into the clan? Do you have the right kind of spirit, the right kind of politics, so to speak—theatre politics versus large politics, which, frankly, I was as interested in the larger politics as I was in the theatre politics. More interested, in fact. Then, finally, coming back [to TPM], in a way, by invitation, in '92, to take over the position.

I don't know if any of those times were right in terms of me and TPM.

If anything, it was the first time that was right, because of my openness, my willingness to push up my sleeves, hop right in, figure it out, learn how to do it, make some kind of a contribution. Nineteen ninety-two was a different story. The place was in deep, deep trouble. The bailiffs had been stopped at the door by a fundraising campaign, but there was no money to be able to actually produce things. It wasn't like you could go in and—*(claps hands like a wizard)*—come up with a fantastic season. It was penny-pinching all around. It was also winning back: winning back artists, winning back arts councils, winning back reviewers, winning back audiences, and, really, winning back even the poor people who were working there, who had gone through hell. Absolute hell, with the ups and the downs, the feuds and the fights, with "maybe the bailiff is coming, maybe the bailiff isn't," and, you know, with the drinking and cavorting and all the other things that went on.

I arrived full of determination; hell-bent on moving it out of the exhaustion and inertia that had taken hold to carve a new exploration of ideas, forms, and communities. I was resolute in my belief that the only way forward was by bringing in a new generation of voices. This was vital: the spirit of innovation and risk-taking; of creating and producing work that would challenge as well as make us reflect on the issues, beauty, histories, and narratives that surrounded us. The theatre was not owned by any past generation of artists; they had been given ample opportunity. This was not to suggest their contributions were not important, but the time had come for a sincere, deep, and meaningful changing of the guard.

One of my first moves, bringing Artistic Associates Baņuta Rubess and the late Ken McDougall on board, was scripted to send a loud, clear message that the doors were opening to a new generation of talent and a new way of doing things. I respected their work; I admired their bold and innovative directorial approaches; and I trusted their curatorial edge, their eyes and ears in our quest to find exciting and essential new voices and content that would connect with audiences and artists in a changing city and country.

* * *

Ken can't tell his version of the story because he died soon after we began. For my part, my theatre life in Canada began in 1982. Passe Muraille was where I saw some of the best theatre, especially in the Backspace. It's where I made my first

WE WERE GOING TO BREAK DOWN THE WALLS. WE WERE GOING TO FILL THE THEATRE WITH WOMEN AND DIVERSITY AND INNOVATIVE THEATRE.

important collective creation, *This is for you, Anna*, a feminist classic-to-come. I saw TPM as my artistic home. In 1992 I even applied to run the theatre. But Susan was offered the job instead, and the first thing she did was invite me and Ken to join her.

Both Ken and I were perceived as outside the mainstream. I liked to push the envelope, making theatre now called site-specific, immersive, or multimedial. I did this as an overtly feminist artist. I'd written or directed or collectively created a significant body of work foregrounding women. By 1992 I was shifting into new territory, exploring film, opera, live music in theatre, delving into my diasporic roots. As a hyphenated Canadian I always felt marginal in the Anglo-heavy theatre scene. The year before I joined the TPM team, I made a show in Riga while Latvia was fighting for independence. Soviet snipers had shot a documentary cameraman in a park, and the slain artist, Andris Slapiņš, handed the camera to his director and said, "Film me," moments before he died. Everyone in my Latvian cast knew Andris. We were working on a play that involved a lot of bloodshed. You couldn't get fake blood in Riga, and I offered to get some from Canada. "Great idea," my Latvian producer said, "you bring the fake blood, we'll supply the real blood."

Experiences like this one coloured my perception of everything. I took politics, particularly the politics of resistance, very seriously. So did Susan. She and I forged an alliance when Susan was still running Theatre Direct. I came to her with the idea of making a play about this new phenomenon called "date rape," and she jumped on it. Beverley Cooper and I wrote *Thin Ice* together and Susan shepherded the play past resistant school boards and toured it across the country. It was a huge hit, and it was the source of a deep understanding between the two of us.

We both admired Ken McDougall enormously. As a queer artist growing up in a homophobic era, Ken knew a lot about bloodshed and resistance. He had an indie theatre company called Platform 9 and tight associations with other innovators like Sky Gilbert and Hillar Liitoja. He was stupendous in drag and assured in direction. Susan and I couldn't wait to welcome him as a comrade. However, our first meeting turned strange. There was a spread of snacks on the table which made Ken turn positively green. A few weeks later he arrived late at another meeting because he had vomited on the street. He had Gothic cheekbones and lamp-sized eyes, and he was so slight of build that he would shop in the children's section. But now he became thinner and thinner. As Susan said, "I remember asking Ken so many times—'Ken, what's the matter? Ken, what can I do? Ken, can I help you?' " Ken insisted that it was some tropical bug he'd picked up in Mexico. Susan and I were sure it was AIDS—which it was—but Ken couldn't bring himself to tell us. Ever.

AIDS was the theme of *The Last Supper*, the most extraordinary show we ever produced. Created by the unsung wild man of Canadian theatre, Hillar Liitoja, *The Last Supper* was a gut-wrenching experience. The Backspace was transformed into a bedroom in which Ken played a man who was dying of AIDS and who was going to commit assisted suicide that night. Sky Gilbert was the doctor with the lethal injection. The audience sat next to the bed and inhaled the slow beauty and sadness of the last hours. But few knew that the main actor was truly dying. Cynthia Roberts and Greg Klymkiw made a film of the piece, and Ken performed his own story, all the way to his last breath, for cameras brought to the hospice. What a champ.

There's a black-and-white picture of me and Ken standing in front of Passe Muraille. It looks like we're in 1930s Berlin, on our way to the cabaret. A cap shades his eyes and I've got a Louise Brooks bob. I look at that photo and think, "Migawd, I'm pregnant." By the time my first child was born, Ken was in Casey House, dying. I'm told he kept a photo of my baby by his bedside. Susan and I wanted to have a candle burning in the theatre in Ken's memory at all times. That candle remains in our imaginations. It's pretty damn bright. And thank goodness his memory is celebrated with the Ken McDougall Award.

After Ken died, Colin Taylor joined us. He was a firecracker of an artist, never lacking for ideas. He'd been an assistant director for Robert Wilson and Paul Thompson. His voice alone could bring you to your knees. He too was committed to expanding the borders of our repertoire and was a dedicated champion of the work of Daniel David Moses. He was also one of the first Black Canadians to hold sway in a professional theatre. He is more than critical of the board's actions in '97; his comments on the debacle throb with disgust and dismay.

We were going to break down the walls. We were going to fill the theatre with women and diversity and innovative theatre. We took the first big steps. But boy was it hard to fill the seats. In 1992 Passe Muraille was the only mid-size theatre without a subscription.

SUSAN: Audience was a huge obstacle . . . In my first time at Passe Muraille, audiences were very inconsistent. You would have a show that would do fabulously well, you would have a show that was dismal in terms of audience . . .

Our team created a Flexpass to suit the unpredictability of people's lives; we designed the Artists' Pass—six shows for $30; we launched a discussion series, the *Passe Muraille Papers*.

SUSAN: We hosted a street festival to reach out to our neighbours and families, trying to get people in the doors of the theatre who had never set foot in it before . . . but the audiences had really, really fallen off . . . and also we didn't have money—very little money to advertise.

There was never any money, and when Premier Mike Harris was elected in 1995, there was even less. Susan would sell as much beer as possible at the bar and skilfully get people to spend their money at auctions of Canadian art. She would risk bidding on work in order to jack up the price; I tried to copy her and got stuck with a (beautiful) work of art I couldn't afford.

Money, shmoney: the art was what mattered most to our triumvirate.

When you make work on the moon, you want it to be stellar. However, it was a balancing act. Susan saw herself as a bridge between generations. Her loyalties to the founders of the theatre ran deep, and every season had to include "the clan." Nineteen ninety-three was the midpoint of Passe Muraille history; we marked the twenty-fifth anniversary in our first season. There's a feature in the *Toronto Star*, with a photo in which Susan stands firmly wedged between Thompson and Garrard. The new guard is still in hiding.

Across all the seasons the work was adventuresome. Ken made a mind-bending show called *Sleeproom* that used both spaces and turned the theatre into a psychiatric institute. Every season featured a play by John Mighton—*Body and Soul, The Little Years, Possible Worlds.*

HEAD IN A BAG
DIANA FAJRAJSL, OLIVER DENNIS, AND DONALD ADAMS. PHOTO BY DINA ALMEIDA.

We showcased a young poet/playwright called Death Waits (now Jacob Wren). Ken directed and Daniel MacIvor performed in his brilliant play about competition, *Never Swim Alone*, the first time MacIvor reached the Mainspace. We brought in a lot of women: our biggest hit show, *The Stone Angel*, was directed by Maureen White, one of the founders of Nightwood, and we programmed a festival for women called the Gathering. Other strong women: Nadia Ross with Diane Cave, Alisa Palmer, Pol Pelletier, Theresa Tova, M.J. Kang, Sally Han, Kim Renders, Naomi Campbell, and more. We fostered the magic and unpredictability of a Czech artist called Jan Komárek.

At the same time, Paul Thompson continued to have a home at the theatre, with the *Urban Donnellys* and a revival of *Maggie and Pierre*, and Hrant Alianak's *Lucky Strike*, a highly imagistic piece was revived. Innovation and/or relevance governed our programming choices, and it's why our team passed on the well-made play *The Drawer Boy*, though later it was a big hit for TPM.

SUSAN: It didn't fit our style, our vision, what we had worked so hard to create at the theatre. [I looked for pieces] that were really responding to the changing times. That for me was a really critical thing and it remains so today: that theatre is relevant. Although Passe Muraille had a history of telling stories that were Canadian stories rooted in Blyth, in *The Farm Show*, and the *Urban Donnellys*—important, important stories—they didn't cast themselves very far outside that particular geographical region, or that kind of thinking. A generation of voices was charting a new theatrical course and we were deeply committed to giving them a home.

* * *

show. The dramedy combined the story of a Soviet spy in Ottawa with vignettes from Romania, Berlin, the rest of Eastern Europe. Nowadays Toronto audiences are game to see plays about Nanjing to Mumbai. But in 1992 my outside-of-Canada story was a box-office disaster, and I was gutted. Every production I'd made until then had either been "successful" or "very successful." It was, as Lemony Snicket would say, a bad beginning.

In 1995 I redeemed myself with Timothy Findley's *The Stillborn Lover*. That show won me a Dora nomination for Best Director, and it did well at the box office. David Fox was perfect as the bisexual Canadian diplomat, and I ache at the memory of the late Marion Gilsenan playing his tragic wife. Findley sent letters from Stone Orchard, saying, "In all our years of theatre, we have hardly ever encountered a company run with such efficiency and professionalism as yours . . . We are, literally, in awe of your entire operation—and at the same time, deeply grateful to have been part of it."

The brochure for the following season, 1995/96, is stylish and confident, with remarkable photos by Cylla von Tiedemann. Susan's portrait has the wind in her hair, and she writes that "every play and every writer in our season is intelligent, provocative, necessary. The artists who work here are among the best in the world. And so is our audience!"

THE STILLBORN LOVER
MARION GILSENAN AND DAVID FOX. PHOTO BY MICHAEL COOPER.

I was at the Berlin Wall when it came down in 1989 and I criss-crossed former Soviet states as the USSR crumbled. I poured my experience into *Head in a Bag*, which I directed in the inaugural season (co-produced with the Great Canadian Theatre Company). That show had me sitting on the back stairs, weeping with frustration. The production manager wouldn't build the set, or would show up drunk and belligerent; the lead actor dropped out a few days before opening, claiming health problems. I had a dedicated cast but a non-existent audience. I got to taste that deadly sinking feeling you get when there are only four people in the house and you cancel the

I'm in that brochure. It would be my last show at TPM, though I didn't know it. The play leaped out at me from the stacks of scripts; it was shockingly poetic and shockingly rude; it was angry; it was funny; it was about living in wartime. A translation from the French by Shelley Tepperman called *Wedding Day at the Cro-Magnons'* from a young Montrealer named Wajdi Mouawad. We co-produced the English premiere with the NAC. Scene One began with a mother screaming "Who bought this fucking cabbage?!" at her son, who had bought the wormy vegetable under sniper fire. Alon Nashman was the hilarious, hapless son, and Arsinée Khanjian made her theatrical debut as an eight-foot-tall bride,

Just before we opened Wajdi said he thought that critics would either really, really hate the play or really, really love it. Well, the critics super-hated it, and the audience stayed away. Wajdi was incredibly idealistic; he felt that every time we performed the piece we were saving a child's life. I wished I could believe him. If Canadians didn't want to see plays about war, I thought, then I wasn't making theatre in the right place. I resigned. I was pregnant again, and I bowed out from theatre-making for a while.

One season later Susan was forced out by the board. Colin left the theatre, too, and soon after I left Canada.

> COLIN: Memories of you and Susan are among my fondest, re: working in the theatre, but I am profoundly disappointed in this organization—as an artist and a human—and would hate to participate in a mere white-washing of its sins and transgressions.
>
> SUSAN: Not only were the numbers of artists starting to grow, but also the number of little companies started to grow. The call-out from these artists was, "When are we gonna get on to the main stages, when are we going to be taken seriously? What's happening here?" And I was going out and seeing that work, and I was meeting those artists, and, to be honest, they were my age. They were my peers. And I thought that the work was relevant. And I thought that those voices were really important, and I shared their frustration that they weren't getting onto the stage, so, when the opportunity came, for me to be able to make decisions of that nature, it was an absolute priority of mine . . .
>
> I had been in the trenches at Passe Muraille, where no matter what happened there was a core group of people who always got their foot—by and large it was always the same people every time—they were always the people first in the door.
>
> But then I got in there, and then I did precisely what they didn't want to see happening. But you know what—I just want to say another thing. Looking back on it, with the maturity I have now, and the self-confidence and everything else, I actually really tried to find a balance. I really attempted to keep them a part of it.
>
> If I were to do it all again? Forget it. Seriously. I would kick their asses out the door.

* * *

Flash forward to 2016, when, twenty years later, Susan and I met again. I've returned to Toronto; Susan has cut her hair. We talk about revisioning, about judging. Susan quotes the preface to Doris Lessing's *The Golden Notebook*. "Remember that the book which bores you when you are twenty or thirty will open doors for you when you are forty or fifty—and vise versa. Don't read a book out of its right time for you."

The lockstep of an official mythology doesn't do the theatre justice. What is the right time? Who has the right stuff? When Susan, Ken, and I walked through the doors of Passe Muraille in 1992, we were in the right place, but at a bad time. We launched and showcased a great group of artists. We left the place in much better shape than we found it. Then we were redacted from the TPM story.

These days, when I go to TPM, no one knows who I am or what I accomplished there. If Susan and Colin came along, they would have the same experience. We are the Invisibles. We know what we did, though. We pushed back the walls. They resisted. We pushed again. We walked on the moon. Many tough steps for us, one giant leap for the theatre.

BAŅUTA RUBESS is a director and writer with a string of innovative productions to her credit in Europe and Canada. Her works laid the foundations for Nightwood Theatre, Theatre Direct, and Tapestry Opera. For four years she was Associate Artist at Theatre Passe Muraille. Her TPM shows include *This is for you, Anna*; *The Last Will and Testament of Lolita*; *Still*; *Head in a Bag*; *The Stillborn Lover*; and *Wedding Day at the Cro-Magnons'*.

KEN MCDOUGALL was an acclaimed actor and theatre director based in Toronto. He served as Associate Artist at TPM from 1992 until his death in March 1994. He is best known as the director of the early works of Daniel MacIvor and Robin Fulford, and for his starring role in Hillar Liitoja's *The Last Supper*, for which he won a Dora Award.

SUSAN SERRAN's career has been a thrilling ride, first at Theatre Passe Muraille, where she served initially as a publicist, then as General Manager and ultimately as the company's first Artistic Producer. She also ran Theatre Direct Canada for a number of years, where she steered the company to national prominence as a groundbreaking theatre for young audiences. After several years with Toronto Artscape, where she programmed the seminal Creative Places & Spaces conference and launched an international, multidisciplinary artist residency, she became Executive Assistant to Councillor Paula Fletcher, one of Toronto's foremost progressive voices at city hall, where she remains today.

COLIN TAYLOR was Associate Artist at Theatre Passe Muraille from 1994 to 1997, where he conceived/co-ordinated *The Passe Muraille Papers*, directed acclaimed productions of Daniel David Moses's *Indian Medicine Shows*, José Rivera's *Marisol*, and Rick Salutin's *1837*. He was formerly a producer/director at CBC Radio Drama and President of Theatre Ontario. He was founding Artistic Producer of (Theatre) WUM and Arts & Science, and has taught and directed across Canada and internationally.

224 Markham St
Toronto, Ont.
M6G 2G6
~~March 30, 1987~~
April Fool's, 1987

To Susan Feldman
Manager
Theatre Passe Muraille
16 Ryerson St.
Toronto, Ont.

Dear Susan,

Please accept my resignation as Associate Artistic Director of Theatre Passe Muraille and as a member of the Board of Directors of Theatre Passe Muraille. I have dared to offer a little philospphy, a hopefully small amount of griping, and quite a bit of history to explain my decision.

In the advent of some theatrical or artistic interchanges, there seems to be a magnetic pull between abuse and love. In my years of work with Theatre Passe Muraile I have continually been showered with, and dealt out, versions of these two things. I no longer know if they are qualities, emotions, or tranjections of artistic temperment, I only know that I recognize the energy created by this polarity, and find myself no longer facinated by it's contradictions.

When Clarke Rogers demanded that I officially become a member of the theatre, I asked him that the word, 'director', not be part of my title, but found later that I was to be called an Artistic Director. It was explained to me that it was time we did something more that just make art, we should take a hand in the institutions that produced art in order to preserve humane places to work and create. It sounded good, but I knew there was a hitch. Maybe it was 'humane'. Maybe it was 'create', certainly it's been a lot of work. Although I have always had a great deal of resistance to this title, in some ways, to my surprise, I actually became an artistic director, which is why I feel I can resign as someone who has actively rendered that service to the theatre. That service has been propelled by a kind of energy I no longer wish to be the fuel of my life. I feel I must rid myself of the position, in order to rid myself of this energy. Which brings me back to abuse and love. The polarities of Theatre Passe Muraille. My resignation has to do with a sincere disappointment in both these words as motivation for human contact or learning. I disown them, as methods of evolution for the human spirit.

It must seem odd, at a time when the theatre seems less propelled by neurosis and hysteria, I should resign the undefined responsibilies of Associate Director, but it is only now that I feel able to let go what has become an impossible position. Notwithstanding this, my associate directorship of Theatre Passe Muraille has been an important part of my life and I am proud of it. I would never deny, in any situation, the love and encouragement I have recieved, but for every moment of that love, there now seems to be an overloaded ballance of gift giving that I am no longer able or willing to give. There is a point when the native concept of 'giveway' becomes masochism, and I believe is no longer pleasing to the spirits.

By virtue of personality or fate, I have lived on the front lines of criticism within the theatre, often being the sole person stupid or brave enough to criticize policies or statements face to face. I have highly critical of many decisions, and paid dearly for my critisms, fighting my way through many horrible and drunken evenings. Drinking plenty myself, I must add. I don't present myself as any kind of saint. In these sessions, I have been capable of egocentricty, of useless radicalism, of unrealistic idealism, but never to the exclusion of my loyalty or dedicaton to the theatre. I have been in the difficult positon of having my ideas solicited, giving extreme opinions, then being confronted for not carying out these opinions. I never presented myself as someone who is interested or capable of complete leadership or administration, believing, and sometimes being told, that my contributions in other areas were valid and important. Sometimes this basic contradiction has been understood and appreciated, but often attacked in unendurable ways. Lately, the attacks have been the rule, as we all struggle to find a place for me when I am not writing a play for the theatre, or acting in one.

I am the only associate director of the theatre never to have asked for, or recieved a salary. I felt it would be easier for me if my directorship was completely without renumeration. Easier to preserve some kind of unique ground, and give myself room for my creative work. It occurs to me that my position has always been unrealistic, that a person with strong views should either be prepared to act on them personally, or keep their mouth shut, but as the Artistic Director was so interested in collaboraton, I thought it possible to live in the half life between action and advise.

As a crisis lieutenant, not a leader, I am no longer needed, or necessary. As a collabortive entity in terms of dealing with the mechanics of the place, I'm at a loss when my suggestions and ideas can't be enfolded into the center of the theatre. I become powerless and useless. Then love disappears and there is only abuse. I feel that on the basis of the work I have offered the theatre, I have justified any degree of difficulty my character has imposed. There is a point when words lose their questionable rough charm and become real insults, that point is often when there is no exchange.

The only time when my relationship to the theatre has been clear and in some kind of harmony has always been when I was working at the theatre as an actor or a writer. These are my true functions, everything else has been a fabrication to avoid lonliness. At these times I have given and demanded enormous comittments from the theatre, not only of the artistic director, but of the working members of the administration, and I have recieved enormous loyalty and generosity. It is at these times, and only then, has there seemed to be any advantage to being an associate Artistic Director. It has meant an insider's understanding of the theatre, and a total output of energy, a commitment to someone who has 'paid.' I would never deny the support I have recieved from the theatre, but I have constantly been reminded of every effort the theatre has made on behalf of my productions , every penny spent, every seat not filled. This is another insider's by product, part of the payment of being that odd thing, an associate director of the artistic.

I freely admit, there have been many crazy and exhilirating crises, ones in which I have fully enjoyed leaping to the fore, but I did so on an individual crisis basis, as a friend of the theatre, always pulling against the official function. I began to feel that I had to pay doubly for working at the theatre. I felt that my creative contributions were never enough, and because of my own tendancies, got caught in a treadmill, feeling no amount of work, loyalty, support or energy was possible to fill the demands of the theatre and the artisic direction. Now that four years of constant and desperate crisis seem to be nearing to an end, can creative work now start to be the medium of exchange?

Lately the amorphous duties of associate director have been very light, yet I find myself in situations where I don't want to be, saying things I don't mean, fighting with lifelong friends, because of my need to rid myself of what has become a negative tie. At the time, I fully accepted the premise, "If you want to have work done here, help to keep the place running. " Now I would say, "I want to work, the place seems to be running fine."

I'm happy to argue in the bar with anyone willing to argue back,but the opposite pulls of dictatorship and democrarcy are too dangerous for me to follow. I am best in the bar, mouthing off to whoever will listen, expecting those ideas to sprout or spoil, depending of the whims of the desision makers. Leave me there.

I will always be a lover, supporter and believer in the essential spirit of Theatre Passe Muraille. Whatever that is. Whoever says they know what it is. I would like to officially thank Jerry, Dara, Vivien, Ken, Susan, and all the various and transitory workers of the theatre. Clarke Rogers has supported me with the full brunt of his contradictions, abilities and inspiration, and there is no question that much of my work has been propelled by his energy, need and love.

I would like to make it clear that I am not resigning over any particular issue.

I will always consider myself,officially or unofficially, to be one of the loose community to whom the theatre is a beacon of hope, art and anarchy. And abuse. And love.

LETTER OF RESIGNATION FROM LINDA GRIFFITHS TO SUSAN FELDMAN, APRIL 1, 1987

HEAVEN ABOVE, HEAVEN BELOW
LAYNE COLEMAN AND LINDA GRIFFITHS. PHOTO BY MICHAEL COOPER.

THE MINISTER OF OPTIMISM

BY LAYNE COLEMAN

I met Paul Thompson and TPM in Saskatoon the year the Vietnam War ended. The price of gasoline had risen seventy percent. I remember the song "Kung Fu Fighting." Paul opened a door for our small and eager company called 25th Street Theatre. His mentorship led to *Paper Wheat* a few years later, which took Canada by storm and became a National Film Board documentary. I was named the artistic director of 25th Street Theatre in 1980 and by then the company was called "Theatre Passe Muraille West." I took it as a compliment.

Clarke Rogers gave me the title of Minister of Optimism. He inherited TPM from Paul Thompson and was going to take the theatre from collective creations into scripted and literary work. Judith Thompson's *The Crackwalker* was the new signpost. Clarke asked me to become his associate artistic director along with designer Jim Plaxton. The idea was to build on what Paul had accomplished in the '70s. That was the year someone laced Tylenol with cyanide and killed seven people. *Time Magazine* made the computer Man of the Year. Carole Corbeil was one of the theatre critics for the *Globe and Mail*. She was not allowed to review any TPM shows. The three of us—Clarke, Carole, and myself—spent most of our nights around Clarke's round table in an apartment where his boxes of books never got unpacked. All his stuff was by the front door and would remain there. Clarke was a raw intellectual and ideologue. He was a finely tuned nerve that needed to talk, and he was worth listening to . . . Carole was more than his equal and she spoke with a low, melodious voice and a vast reference of books and art history. She was worried that men were not awake enough to the art created by women. Clarke was one of those who got smarter the more beer he drank, until he didn't. I was going to be his Hamlet. I loved Clarke and I was falling in love with Carole. Clarke loved TPM like it was his mother. He wanted more than anything to bring it into the promised land.

The actor had been king in Paul Thompson's theatre; the director and writer would be crowned king in Clarke's. The shadow of the early giants of TPM made the *afterlife* of those times formidable. Funding was being clawed back, there were now more mouths to feed, and the '80s was spent mopping up the pain of the '60s and '70s, and there was a lot of residual pain laying around.

I witnessed the changes at TPM after the middle floor of 16 Ryerson Avenue was removed to create one big theatre rather than two smaller ones. The catch was that the big theatre actually held fewer people than could be packed into the two smaller spaces. This was an architectural oddity. It also meant that the design budgets for shows tripled in cost as the larger space with a balcony now meant it was prohibitive to change the room's furniture each performance. As the design budgets went up, box-office potential went down. The Backspace had only fifty-four seats, and that was the jewel in its crown but economically unsound. A way to produce seasons and not be buried by costs related to the space had to be figured out. On top of the theatre space itself, TPM also carried the rent of a shop next door as well as its office space. The model has never truly been sustainable.

One of the things that restrains good art is the housing. The building has been the tail that wagged TPM for a long time. Buying it with the fruits of *I Love You, Baby Blue* was one of those "be careful what you wish for" moments. For a theatre to pass through walls, maybe it is better to have none. But you could not love a building more than 16 Ryerson Avenue was loved. It has to be said that a building can be a rock tied to the ankle of creativity. It is a long prison term through which you have to pay to occupy your own cell. The building defines TPM, and that is not always a good thing. How many marriages and dreams might have survived if it were not for the mortgage?

The DNA of TPM . . . "logical" is not necessarily how things develop and especially not in the arts.

My most vivid image of Clarke during his last days at TPM was him staring into the small eye of a big tin-box computer. One of the early ones that had been donated to TPM by an old Upper Canada College buddy of Clarke's. The Rogers family had money once; his ancestors owned a good deal of land around Niagara-on-the-Lake. You could feel a profound sense of loss around Clarke. It made him awake to Canada in some way. He owned a canoe and it sat like a living thing, a Canadian icon, in the front room of his apartment. I remember him smoking while writing grant applications. He seemed to be happy there, in the saddle dreaming and putting forward writers. Clarke fiercely loved writers and had a way of pushing them, sometimes not in ways they appreciated. But his plays were better for this. When Clarke turned his attention onto you and your work, you felt like you were on a stage that fully had the audience's attention. He was a spirit man, beckoning a writer who might be afraid to join him in the dark part of the forest. He died a few years later after losing the theatre. I don't remember dates. A few years before he died, I married Carole.

TPM has had several major collapses since its beginnings. Every ten years there is usually one. And it has always been saved, but not because the place is so necessary, or even loved in such a way that it can't be allowed to go away. It is perhaps always saved because no one can know what it is they are killing if they put the stake through its vampire heart. The cost of keeping its doors open has been small compared to what would be lost if it had been allowed to disappear. TPM is many things—it is the home theatre of Linda Griffiths and the tribe of Paul Thompson, and as an ark of nationalism it would be tragic to forget its glories. "Canadians, do you love Rebellion?" I never saw the original *1837*, but I was lucky enough to see an anniversary remount. I got what all the fuss had been about.

I was interim artistic director for one year after Brian Richmond moved on. There had been some spectacular

THE PASSE MURAILLE HAMLET
NANCY BEATTY AND LAYNE COLEMAN. PHOTO BY DAVID HLYNSKY.

TPM IS MANY THINGS—IT IS THE HOME THEATRE OF LINDA GRIFFITHS AND THE TRIBE OF PAUL THOMPSON, AND AS AN ARK OF NATIONALISM IT WOULD BE TRAGIC TO FORGET ITS GLORIES.

successes, *Dry Lips Oughta Move to Kapuskasing*, *Lilies*, *Fire*, *Under the Skin*, and others as well. In that year of 1990/91, TPM raised $400,000 with the help of governments and funding bodies, but the company did not have the resources to fund a full season for two spaces. Instead we produced Backspace shows with other partners. Everybody got the same thing: $10,000 and the space. It was a fantastic year despite the challenges and was realized with the help of Sally Han.

I had stopped drinking and smoking by then and one of the standout nights at this time in the Backspace was seeing Daniel MacIvor's *Jump*, directed by and starring Ken McDougall. It was a real Cape Breton play that one. Tracy Wright and Nadia Ross played twin sisters in matching outfits. The two queens of the underground. Ken was the East Coast father. The play had no dialogue, but was one of the more memorable family portraits I have ever seen and am likely to see. At the end of the show I went out with Daniel and Ken, and we met Daniel's boyfriend at the time, the incredible musician John Alcorn, the most handsome man in Toronto for sure. I drank Coca-Cola and had one of the most enlightening evenings of my early '90s life. I saw that the gay community was one I could learn a lot from, and I did.

A search committee wisely chose Susan Serran for the artistic leadership in 1992. Susan was a producer—a very good one with a fine track record. She would be the first woman to head the company. Everyone knew it was more than time for that. She chose two associate artistic directors that were theatre artists and they launched. They brought new energy; they had many successes: *The Stone Angel*, *Sleeproom*, *Head in a Bag*, more Daniel MacIvor shows, and a Daniel David Moses. Then something happened. The Ontario Arts Council drastically reduced its funding and Susan and her associates were forced, mid-season, into a terrifying reality. It is part of the trauma of running an arts organization. There was to be another transition. It was 1997 and I was invited once more to deal with change and instability.

Within twenty minutes of being appointed the new artistic director, I phoned Michael Healey to say that we would be producing *The Drawer Boy*. This exploded the box office and audience projections and defined the theatre again as a David Fox–Miles Potter–Jerry Franken building. This show went on to tour the country and was produced by Mirvish both in Toronto and across Canada. The show seemed to be done everywhere. It was also a play inspired by real TPM history. Michael Healey was a mensch in all of his agreements and dealings with the theatre.

Carole died a short time after this. I found myself in a middle-age crisis about the same time that TPM did. We shared that. The thing about mid-life crises is it doesn't matter if you recognize they're happening. You end up buying the sports car or wearing inappropriate clothing; you generally make a fool of yourself. But fortunately, I had discovered through directing Andrew Moodie's first play, *Riot*, set during the time of the Rodney King riots in Toronto, that there were a number of communities in Toronto that were ready for their close-ups.

I accepted the challenge and tried some new things. One was to hire a company designer, Steve Lucas; he would design all the shows and the company offices and shop. We built a replica Italian opera house inside the Mainspace. We produced two seasons in that configuration. And then Steve opened it out once more and the building got pretty much locked into the configuration that it sits in now. It is a sound one, but when the space is reimagined the theatre produced by it seems to spit more fire.

One of the realities of arts funding in Toronto and Ontario and Canada is that development money used to be granted directly to the theatres. Over time that model was changed. Small companies and individual projects began to be funded, and so money that had once gone to TPM for its development of new work was now missing. What was left was a smaller pool of available resources for administration and production. You had to let the smaller groups and companies do the new play development and then join them in partnership for a slate of shows for a season. This new policy has many positive features—small and new companies get funding to do imaginative things—but the not-so positive is TPM became a kind of grandfather to production. Many of the artistic creation decisions were happening with others. And when the time came to finally produce, the smaller company that TPM would be in production with would often want to market its own name and brand. The host company is seen as already established and not needing the credit. This became more and more of a challenge.

The mothership becomes a husk of its former self. There can be a hollow feeling to running a company where artists come in at a fever pitch and then exit to allow for the next group, and the grandfather has to keep the house in order and never gets to play too much on its own in the creation sandbox. You are always collaborating. A good thing and necessary, but some collaborations are more collaborative than others. And an artistic identity becomes clouded or uncertain, or dimmed. It became almost impossible to produce new scripts from a pile. Everything had to come with a partner or several partners. A playwright could no longer be confident of a production without also having a dowry.

My vision for the company was to produce works of cultural diversity to give voice and presence to those that had not had the microphone or the stage. I felt that the need was so great in Toronto itself and its neighbourhoods that I could not manage to produce work reflecting the rest of Canada, as TPM once did. It had a kind of national theatre identity. This was one of the great strengths of the Thompson years. But the new means and ways of funding made that vision impossible to pursue. Touring grants became harder to get and there was less being offered from other regions. I felt that there was an unintended isolation that was growing. But I could not stop it. And there was a powerful need right in the backyard of TPM. We focused on emerging artists and companies. I hoped that with the growth of representation from all the cultural communities, new audiences from these same communities would be welcomed. And it works, but it happens slowly, with the exception of some brave hits.

I met Weyni Mengesha through the gifted actress Ngozi Paul. Ngozi made me come and see *'da Kink in my hair* at the Fringe. This was a turning point. Trey Anthony had written a play that featured monologues by a number of Black women in different stages of their lives, all meeting at a hair stylist's shop. TPM always had a pay-what-you-can matinee on Sundays. It was at one of these that *'da Kink in my hair* sparked a small riot. People actually began pushing and shoving to get in line for tickets. The lineup was around the block. My daughter saw this show. She was in her teens and she told me that it meant more to her than any show she'd ever seen.

—
THE YOKO ONO PROJECT
LEE PUI MING.

—

It takes a lot of hands and work to do theatre. To plan and produce and market seasons, to acquire funding, to fundraise, to fix the broken furnace, upgrade the air conditioning, heal the plumbing, create a magnificent mission statement. Be a warm and welcoming environment for audiences. Give them a plate of new plays every year. Promoting Canadian content. Always and forever.

She had seen a lot of theatre by this point. When Mirvish became interested in this production, I was asked to give a short talk at the audition. I remember telling the story of the night my daughter saw the play and then looking into David Mirvish's eyes. They were water. I felt like a real artistic director then.

Weyni became the associate artistic director and led a culturally diverse playwrights' group (the most dynamic we ever ran) as well as heading a program for interns and youth. She was key to developing Stage 3 (her name) into a diverse theatre festival. Her time at TPM was a time of learning for me. I knew that I was dealing with a superstar director and theatrical thinker. Her leadership and touch with young people and artists were beautiful to behold. One of her successes was mentoring a young Black woman, about fifteen years old, who created a solo show about her life. As it happened her biological father lived just down the street from the theatre. He had only met his daughter two weeks earlier; he was the youngest-looking father I have met. He came to see her performance and it was memorable. Weyni had a gift for human connections. She could create a unique atmosphere within a show or workshop that somehow warmed everyone's power and confidence, making unusual human contact possible.

We produced *The Yoko Ono Project* with Jean Yoon. Yoko never appeared, but she did send the largest bouquet of pink roses I have ever seen. M.J. Kang; Keira Loughran; Andrew Moodie; Linda Griffiths; d'bi.young anitafrika; Darren O'Donnell; Anita Majumdar; Nicole Stamp; the great Filipino collective, Carlos Bulosan Theatre; Kevin Quain's musical, *Tequila Vampire Matinee*; the Rochdale Project collective; the huge *In the Wings*; Daniel Brooks's new work; Alex Poch-Goldin; One Yellow Rabbit; Daniel MacIvor's company and plays; and on and on. Eight new shows a year. We had a production crew to die for. David Kinsman, Sue Edworthy, Taylor Raths, Jonathan Rooke, Bill Stahl, Mickey Wagg, Mark Ryder, Paula Forst, Jamie Wilson, Christine Estima, Stephanie MacArthur, Laura Bonfigli: a staff made up of loyal and talented administrators. Brenda Kamino made life easier for a season. I was living in theatre heaven.

Joe Pierre wrote a hip hop kind of poetry called *Born Ready*. It was a play developed by Obsidian Theatre and given a showcase production at TPM. It was a show about a gun. A gun found on the stairs of a public housing project in Toronto. It was a celebrated work, but not too many know of Joe Pierre or *Born Ready*. But if it were sent to the lab and analyzed, it would come back positive. This is what TPM can do, and it did not happen anywhere else. I could name many like that.

But all good things must come to an end. And when they end, they end badly. Most often badly. Thank goodness there was a faithful board and a canny and experienced veteran like Andy McKim who stepped up to the plate. It takes a lot of hands and work to do theatre. To plan and produce and market seasons, to acquire funding, to fundraise, to fix the broken furnace, upgrade the air conditioning, heal the plumbing, create a magnificent mission statement. Be a warm and welcoming environment for audiences. Give them a plate of new plays every year. Promoting Canadian content. Always and forever. One of my favourite shows was an all-women's *A Midsummer Night's Dream*, directed by Kate Lynch. Sheer brilliance—what a powerhouse cast. Later, as things got harder to continue, Kate directed several Tom Walmsley plays. Tom is an original and his plays look into dark corners, at bad neighbours (bad neighbours are what Tom calls the thoughts that live in our heads that we'd rather not think).

Well, after three and one-half decades of all-consuming love and work at TPM I have me some bad neighbours and some very fine neighbours. I sat on TPM boards, been an actor on its stages, a writer, a director, a producer, a winner, a loser, a Dora nominee, honoured by my peers, and very tired. But the best of all things is the brotherhood and sisterhood of working with a group of artists, and I call all the arts workers artists. There is a mountain of pleasure and honour in the theatre. Thank you TPM for giving me a lifetime of engagement with Canada and its children. The voices of the young are always rising and coming up. TPM is a place and a home for them. May it always be so.

LAYNE COLEMAN is an actor, director, playwright, and co-founder of 25th Street Theatre where he was the artistic director from 1980 through 1983. He was the artistic director of Theatre Passe Muraille for the 1991/92 season, and then again from 1999 through 2007.

—
***THE DRAWER BOY* HOUSE PROGRAM**

PASSIONATE ABOUT PASSE MURAILLE

BY ANDY MCKIM

PASSE MURAILLE AT A DISTANCE

I was not in Toronto when the so-called "alternative" theatres had just begun to spring up during the first half of the 1970s because I had been studying at Mount Allison University in Sackville, New Brunswick.

Luckily, Playwrights Co-op, as it was then called, started up in 1971, first under the name the Toronto Playwrights Circle, and was publishing quick and dirty 8.5" 11" editions of all new plays. These were immediately available at a variety of locations across Canada and provided me with a lifeline to keep informed about the emerging tide of Canadian plays being produced at these new theatres.

Carol Bolt was instrumental in starting up Playwrights Co-op (along with Tom Hendry and Len Peterson). She was a fierce advocate for playwrights, a powerful female voice at the time. Her play *Buffalo Jump* was produced by TPM the following year. I met her when she visited Halifax five years later. Her political engagement, her self-confidence as a writer, and her sense that an artist is a fully engaged social being in our world inspired me.

While I was able to read plays within months of their production, I also saw some on television. In particular, I was entranced with the CBC TV versions of Passe Muraille's *The Farm Show* and *1837: The Farmers' Revolt*, as well as *The Clinton Special*, Michael Ondaatje's film about the making of *The Farm Show*. Witnessing these groundbreaking events on television began to kindle my passion for Passe Muraille.

My first professional job started at Neptune Theatre in Halifax in 1976. Three years later, Neptune was host to the national tour of *Billy Bishop Goes to War*. Both John Gray and Eric Peterson were in residence at Passe Muraille where they first workshopped *Billy Bishop* in 1978. Later that year the Vancouver East Cultural Centre produced it before it returned to TPM and then headed out on a national tour. It was unique to me. It was also a heady fusion of all of my dreams and aspirations for a more political, contemporary Canadian theatre. I watched it every night of the run. It fuelled my passion even further and I had to go to the source.

MY VISIT TO THE ALTAR

I was finally able to get to Toronto in 1979. I called Paul Thompson out of the blue to ask if I could talk with him. I was astonished when he said yes. After our coffee he asked if I would like to attend that afternoon's rehearsal for *The Farm Show* and *1837*, which were heading out to tour England. I am still moved as I think of his generosity.

Paul took me to the second floor of a Yonge Street office building that had long since been vacated. Broken office furniture littered the dingy space and electrical cords dangled from the ceiling. I sat with Paul amid the litter on the floor and watched as he rehearsed with Canada's acting divinity: Layne Coleman, Linda Griffiths, John Jarvis, Ted Johns, Mary Walsh, Miles Potter, Booth Savage, Mary Ann McDonald, R.H. Thomson, and Terry Tweed. They were rehearsing the liturgy. After that I can't remember anything . . . except floating on a cloud from Toronto back to Halifax.

At that point, "alternative" Canadian drama was less than a decade old and virtually all new plays fit within the "well-made play" form. Except for Passe Muraille. Paul was exploring a collective-creation style, unique in Canada at that time. Others at Passe Muraille—like CODCO, Rick Salutin, Ken Campbell, or John Palmer—were exploring similar collaborative approaches to play creation. Even Carol Bolt was credited as a "scenarist" (not a playwright) for TPM's production of *Pauline* in 1973. Passe Muraille's work was still exploring the social/political dimensions of Canadian history and culture. I was now committed to a life in the theatre because Passe Muraille was showing me how one could combine art and politics in the theatre. Watching from a distance, Passe Muraille rose above the rest of the theatres of the day because it was exploring the cutting edge of that intersection—going well beyond the well-made play.

In 1981 I came back to Toronto for the Toronto Theatre Festival (TTF), a one-off event organized by (the then largely unknown) Garth Drabinsky. TTF was mandated to attract quality theatre from around the world and also to showcase theatre from Toronto. What had the biggest and longest-lasting impact on me was Linda Griffiths's *Maggie and Pierre*. This is undoubtedly one of the top ten theatre experiences in my life. What a remarkably perceptive, resonant, humorous, and magically theatrical play. Linda's performance of all three characters was riveting and she magically captured the charismatic allure of Pierre Elliott Trudeau—our own international star. That day I got to witness Passe Muraille's ascension to the high altar of Canadian theatrical storytelling.

PASSIONATE ABOUT PASSE MURAILLE

When Layne Coleman announced his pending resignation as the artistic director of TPM in the spring of 2006, I felt I was finally ready to apply for the job. I had dreamed about working at Passe Muraille and this was my moment. I already had a twelve-page outline of my vision waiting in the wings.

There were some rumblings about my selection. In particular, I heard the phrase "Tarragon South" used as a criticism of what my selection portended. It made sense to me that people who cared about Passe Muraille would be concerned. In part, it might appear to some that hiring me was evidence that the board wanted to transform Passe Muraille into a "Tarragon South." Granted, Passe Muraille, Tarragon, and Factory were all established within years of each other and are often lumped together as a group. But they are quite different companies, each with their own ethos. There was no rationale for me to change the nature, mandate, or focus of TPM; most importantly, I did not want to.

My contributions at Tarragon came from a personal set of values that were in some ways more in line with those of Passe Muraille. For example, the Tarragon Spring Arts Fair, which I created and ran for years, was inspired by the value of hosting a wide range of independent artists and companies who were developing work outside the bounds of the "well-made play." A case in point was the development, and ultimate production, of *2 Pianos 4 Hands*. It started as a fifteen-minute Seed Show in the Arts Fair. Paul Thompson often remarks that Passe Muraille's biggest hit was a Tarragon-style play—*The Drawer Boy*—and Tarragon's biggest hit was a Passe Muraille–style play—*2 Pianos 4 Hands*.

SELLING THE THEATRE BUILDING

In the fall of 2006 there were whispers around town that TPM was experiencing some financial challenges. By the time of my selection as artistic director in January 2007 the rumours were growing. In the six months before I began in June it became clear that the situation was dire and getting worse.

In response the TPM board, led by Chair Shelley Black, realized something drastic was needed. The two strongest ideas related to selling the building. The first would have us sell it, use the money to pay our debts, and go back to being a company without a venue. The second, and preferred idea, was to sell our theatre building to the city and lease it back. Between Artscape and the board, most of the arrangements to sell the building to the city had been made by the time I arrived. All that was needed was to get it past the city's finance committee in July and a full vote before council in the fall.

Adam Vaughan was our city councillor at the time and a huge advocate of TPM. When the proposal to purchase the building came before the city's finance committee, Adam spoke up to support the idea. It was a stunning performance. From the start, informed passion lifted his words. He has such a profound understanding of the history of the theatre, its relevance within the city, its place within Canadian theatre, and its importance as a Toronto institution. The motion passed unanimously. When it came before

—

PASSE MURAILLE HAS ALWAYS CHAMPIONED THE RIGHT TO FREE EXPRESSION.

council in the fall, our other great city hall advocate, Mayor David Miller, also strongly supported it. When the final vote was counted, there was only one dissenting voice—Rob Ford's.

We got a renewable ten-year lease and received $1.2 million for the sale of the building. The city kept $200,000 of that as insurance against any potential inability on our part to properly maintain the building. We used a large portion of the remaining million dollars to completely erase our debt. It was certainly an odd beginning to my life at TPM, but we were all so grateful that the plan worked and that we could now move forward debt free. But without owning a building we had no collateral. Moving forward we couldn't—and still can't—afford to go into a deficit situation.

TPM'S LEGACY LIES IN THE NEXT GENERATION

One of my greatest joys as artistic director (and perhaps my biggest responsibility) is to program artists who have not yet had a chance to be on the stage of a theatre institution. Talking to Paul Thompson one day, I realized how much he and I agreed on this point. "TPM's legacy lies in the next generation," he said. In my decade or so at Passe Muraille there is no better example of that joy than Anusree Roy.

I was excited to program her first play—*Pyaasa*—for production in my first season. Part of the rationale was a wish to expand our understanding of what constitutes a Canadian play. Even though the play's incidents take place outside Canada's geography, it is a story that fits within the lived experience of many Canadians. At the heart of her story she addresses powerful and uncomfortable realities about the dehumanizing effect of privilege, in any form.

Anusree has since been providing our community with an outstanding body of plays. The craft and economy of her writing is a signature hallmark, especially when her poetic approach to language creates a music in her playwriting. That music is akin to a chamber piece—tight, focused, and detailed—but still very melodic, almost hypnotic.

FREE EXPRESSION

Passe Muraille has always championed the right to free expression. Sometimes the general audience is unaware that the views expressed on our stage are being vociferously challenged by segments of our audience. One example that sticks out for me was when we hosted the National Theatre School's (and Crow's Theatre's) production of *Seven Jewish Children* on a weekend in May 2009. There were some members of the Jewish Diaspora in Toronto who were very upset that this play was taking place at TPM. They complained to the press, to us, and to any public official they could think of, including the mayor.

Notably, the B'nai Brith wrote to Mayor David Miller (as a representative of the city that owns our building) to ask him to close down the production. In Mayor Miller's reply he responded, in part, "I do not believe that censorship of the arts helps further the goals of a society free from anti-Semitism, hatred, bigotry, and other forms of racism. I also feel strongly that public discussion of these important issues provides an effective tool against such beliefs."

To their credit, our board also stood behind the principle of free expression, in spite of the fact that some of them were upset by the play itself. As one board member said, "Given the theatre's mandate, we have to be prepared to take the heat at times, even though we may not personally agree with some of the content." This has been true of our board every time we have come under attack for staging or hosting controversial plays.

For *Seven Jewish Children* we took it upon ourselves to get ahead of the criticism, so we issued a press release about our commitment to the values of free expression. It affirmed that "we have respect for our community and we do not want to cause harm to any, but we do want to take on challenging subjects, in an atmosphere of respect for other opinions. Theatre Passe Muraille is a home for mature, challenging, and sometimes difficult discussions, where all who support that vision will come with an open mind and a willingness to engage in provocative ideas that may not be their own. We invite you to join us in this pursuit."

Most everyone with a critical view restricted themselves to writing letters and emails. But the Jewish Defence League stationed themselves outside the theatre, determined to disrupt the performances. They even erected a huge protest banner outside the theatre and parked a station wagon, with the tailgate open, providing a canteen of coffee and doughnuts to their protesters.

ULTRASOUND
ELIZABETH MORRIS AND CHRIS DODD. PHOTO BY MICHAEL COOPER.

JOHN & WALEED
JOHN MILLARD AND WALEED ABDULHAMID. PHOTO BY MICHAEL COOPER.

LETTERS TO MY GRANDMA HOUSE POSTER
ANUSREE ROY. PHOTO BY LINDSAY ANNE BLACK.

The show was sold out, so the protesters were unable to get any tickets to get inside. However, one of them pretended to be a theatregoer and came inside between shows when the lobby was empty. They shouted at the staff in attendance: "You're anti-Semitic," then, "You're anti-Zionists," and finished off with, "You are nothing but a bunch of homosexuals" before leaving.

Not all demonstrators are as hostile. In 2017 we hosted a rental company's production of a play that drew a lot of public criticism. There were also calls for that show's closure. During the run a very small contingent of respectful protesters wanted to speak to the audience before each show. We made an arrangement for that to happen outside the lobby entrance. This went well but one night the weather was frightful—wind, rain, and cold. Our front-of-house manager decided that the weather was too inclement to be outdoors and he invited the protesters inside to meet with the audience in the lobby. It was a great moment.

BARRIERS

In the spring of 2015 we co-produced *Ultrasound* with Cahoots Theatre. Two years earlier Cahoots's artistic director, Marjorie Chan, had told me about this play by Adam Pottle, a writer from Saskatchewan who was born partially deaf in both ears. *Ultrasound* is about a newly married couple in conflict about her pregnancy, arguing whether or not to abort the baby if it is not going to be born deaf. It was a timely story. Much of the language of the play was in American Sign Language (ASL), and in a co-production we could bring more resources to a project that would need them.

To provide a translation from ASL into English there were English surtitles created by Trevor Schwellnus, our set, lighting, and surtitles designer. We were all really jazzed about this because Trevor designed them to move around the walls of the set so the surtitles would actually follow the actors as they moved. The production featured deaf actors Elizabeth Morris and Chris Dodd playing the deaf characters.

With this play in our 2014/15 season, I decided it was an opportunity to address some of the remaining barriers to theatre in our building. With targeted funding I was able to enact programs geared toward reducing barriers—like offering individual patrons audio technology to assist with hearing, and providing ASL-interpreted performances, audio-described performances, and relaxed performances. It was a big endeavour.

These accessibility programs were an important undertaking for us, and it is fair to say that I threw the staff into the deep end on this one. We wondered whether we could pull it all off in a way that would be respectful of those we intended to include with these overtures. But things went well.

Our first relaxed performance still stands as one of the more impactful days in my life as an artist. It was the first iteration of our new accessibility program and the prospect was both thrilling and anxiety-inducing. We had no idea who would turn out for such an event. It was organized to take place during a performance of *Elle*, Severn Thompson's powerful and poetic adaptation of Douglas Glover's novel of the same name.

Before the performance I was standing at the box office when a family came in with an eleven-year-old son and a six-year-old daughter. I wanted the mother to know that this was a distinctly adult play. She assured me that she understood and that it was fine. I explained again that it was adult material. She said again she was fine. Being an obsessive sort of person I tried for a third time to impress upon her the graphic sexual nature of some of this performance and how it may not be suited to a six-year-old girl. She replied, "Her brother has Tourette's and there is literally nothing she hasn't heard."

That day was full of these kinds of stories, like a fellow I met in the lobby after the performance who said that his partner brought him. He had not been to the theatre at all in his forty plus years and now that he'd been to a relaxed performance he was planning to come again, and again.

I felt that we had done something that day that was more meaningful to me than most anything else I had ever done as a host for the audience. And "everyone" enjoyed the show because they were all "relaxed."

NUDITY ON STAGE—BUT HOW ABOUT OFF?

> *A "clothing-optional" performance in Toronto suggests theatres should reach out to non-traditional audiences—naturists included . . .*
> —Kelly Nestruck, *Guardian*, April 4, 2011

This headline heralded our rather unique attempt to be inclusive. In the spring of 2011 we (Groundwater Productions and TPM) were brainstorming about ways to bring new audience members into the theatre. *Montparnasse*, which was created and performed by Maev Beaty and Erin Shields, featured two characters who spent a good portion of the play in the nude. That led us all to wonder: what if we also allowed the audience to be nude? Heather Ervin, our publicist, called naturist groups and soon we had enough naturists to create a "clothing optional" performance.

You might wonder about the mechanics of this event. When each person arrived the staff was ready with an open garbage bag for each of them. Like a coat check the audience member then deposited all their clothes into their "checked" bag while they went off with their shoes, their wallet, and a towel that they brought to sit on.

> *"You've probably heard this piece of advice dished out to a nervous performer before: to relax, picture the audience naked . . . I would say the advice should probably be rewritten," Beaty joked . . . confessing that, rather than relaxing her, all the naked flesh reflecting the footlights briefly made her self-conscious.*
> —Kelly Nestruck, *Guardian*, April 4, 2011

A SELLOUT

> *The* Toronto Star *has learned that the Harold Green Jewish Theatre has pulled out of its co-production with Theatre Passe Muraille of Julie Tepperman's new play* YICHUD (Seclusion), *which was due to open in early February.*
> —*Toronto Star*, November 30, 2009

Days before this article appeared, the co-artistic directors of the Harold Green Jewish Theatre, David Eisner and Avery Saltzman, had arranged a hasty meeting at TPM to tell us that "they were not in a position to proceed with the co-production." They said, "A major sponsor withdrew their financial support and we [can] not continue with our plans." But by "our plans" they meant TPM's plans, because they presumed that we would follow their lead and also move to cancel the show. With no time to find an alternative co-presenter, we were faced with producing the show on our own, just seven weeks away from the first day of rehearsal. We were left with only two weeks to find the $50,000 we needed to go ahead with the show on our own.

On the plus side, we had never felt more alive and energized than we did then. Everyone jumped on the phones and started to call in favours. People were marvellous, giving us both money and support. In the end, it was with the boundless and effective help of actor/writers Julie Tepperman and Aaron Willis that we were able to successfully fundraise the amount we needed. The theatre community rallied behind us, including

COMING TO TPM WAS A CHANCE TO PRACTISE MY BELIEF THAT NEW WORK SHOULD BE GIVEN A CHANCE TO BE SEEN BY MULTIPLE AUDIENCES, IN SUBSEQUENT PRODUCTION SCENARIOS, IN ORDER TO ACHIEVE ITS LEVEL OF EXCELLENCE.

many members of the Jewish Diaspora, who very much wanted to contribute to our success.

In true TPM tradition, a controversy created a sellout run. But that in no way tells the whole story. *YICHUD (Seclusion)* was one of the more remarkable plays we've produced in the last ten years, and it was vintage Passe Muraille material. It was provocative; it used the talents of the music and dance community, as well as theatre artists; it was set within a contemporary Toronto diaspora/community; and it used every part of our building, indoors and out. Julie's script was really smart and funny and provocative and so very human. Everything about the play was magnificent and the sellout audiences delighted in being treated like intelligent adults.

LINDA GRIFFITHS'S STAIRWELL

Linda Griffiths's untimely death was mourned by all in the theatre community. Linda was an insightful visionary and provocative artist who was involved in more productions at Theatre Passe Muraille than most any other artist. We held a memorial for her and simultaneously set up a live broadcast of the event. At that memorial we chose to honour Linda by naming the stairwell in the Mainspace after her. As you may know, Linda felt a great deal of ownership over TPM.

There were also times when she didn't like to be told how to behave. One of those times had occurred not too long ago. It was late at night in the theatre, after the audience had gone home, and the young bar staff was cleaning up. The staff was always diligent about their responsibility and when they discovered Linda in her favourite stairwell "smoking up" they asked her to please stop. She pointed out to them that she always smoked in the theatre. They timidly countered that it was their responsibility to ask people not to smoke inside the building. This raged back and forth for a bit, with lots of heated debate. Linda became exasperated with the discussion, so she shut down the debate with an unassailable assertion: "Yes, well, this is my staircase."

BUZZ

Collaboration has been an important part of the TPM DNA for me. The theatre was born in a communal political environment at Rochdale, then it developed the collective, or collaborative, play-creation model, then it generated an indie-company residency model while also crafting a variety of co-producing models. So I wanted to create a play-development model for Passe Muraille that could serve our collaborative and creation-based play development needs.

I had read about a Battersea Arts Centre program, created by then Artistic Director Tom Morris, called Scratch. It is a play-development program designed for the needs of creation-based (or collaboratively devised, if you prefer) productions where many elements of the production develop at the same pace. This is unlike a playwright-driven project where the writing comes first and is followed by acting and then design elements. In August 2007 I met with Tom Morris and interrogated him about his Scratch program. What was most persuasive to me is the extent to which audience dramaturgy is at the core of this approach. That conversation confirmed my instinct that an audience-centric kind of process would be an extremely useful component for our development activities at Passe Muraille. I renamed it BUZZ for our purposes and it has become a fundamental part of our play-development philosophy.

At the core, any BUZZ event is usually a low-tech presentation of all, or part of, a new play in the middle stage of its development, while engaging all of the creative team in the presentation. It is important to me to make the event informal. For example, I want to provide the audience with context for the work, so I interview the artist in front of the audience before and/or after the

—
TAMARA MARIE KUCHERAN, JOHN JARVIS, HUGH NEILSON, ERIN FLECK, LIZ JANZEN, HILARY PRUE, ANDY MCKIM, SHAUNA JAPP, RYAN MCDOUGALL, KATE MACKAY, MARTIN IDYAMAT, REBECCA PICHERACK, RANDY HUGHSON, FRANK COX-O'CONNELL, RUTH MADOC-JONES, DIANNE WEINRIB, COLIN ROSE, SANDI BECKER, AND ROBERT ROBINSON.

presentation, in general terms, about their aspirations for the work.

Following the BUZZ presentation, the artists have the opportunity to ask the audience specific questions (in writing) about issues that those artists are grappling with in their play. These questions are generally about issues of clarity rather than issues of choice: "What do you think happened in that scene?" instead of, "Did you like the scene and why?" This specific feedback allows the company to continue developing their piece with information and knowledge received from their most important ally, the audience. We also give the audience the tools for a mediated discussion with the artists over a complimentary beer at the end of the evening!

The BUZZ form of development has been important to me because of its focus on the audience. It is a vital part of what our theatre can offer to collectives, or any collaborative group, at a time in their process when they need to put their work in front of an audience in order to find out what is working. It has been extensively used by a number of the shows we have produced, among them *Kiinalik*, *Elle*, *Acha Bacha*, *Caught*, and *Life, Death and The Blues*.

TOURING *LIFE, DEATH AND THE BLUES*

In Canada our sector too often places prime value on the world premiere of a new play. This can lead us to unduly focus on the "number" of new plays we are producing, and to undervalue the development work done on a play after it has had its first audience, or world premiere. Coming to TPM was a chance to

THE THEATRE BEYOND WALLS PROJECT WAS SO VITALLY IMPORTANT TO ME AS AN ARTIST BECAUSE IT PROVIDED ME WITH A UNIQUE OPPORTUNITY TO FULLY ENGAGE IN WHAT PASSE MURAILLE IS CAPABLE OF.

practise my belief that new work should be given a chance to be seen by multiple audiences, in subsequent production scenarios, in order to achieve its level of excellence. This is particularly true of work that is developed in a collaborative or collective manner where the audience can inform further development of the work.

BUZZ does provide for multiple audiences, but another approach we have taken to play development has been to use touring as another way to give work a chance to develop in front of an audience. Raoul Bhaneja's *Life, Death and The Blues* has been the best example of that.

The show was developed over a decade and a half, with Raoul putting it in front of many workshop audiences. He learned a lot over that time, but it was a hard play to write because it did not have a linear structure. Also, he was striving to find the right story to bring *The Blues* alive on stage while dramatizing the depth of racism that was confronted by blues musicians in North America and remaining responsive to other people's views on the subject.

We had a satisfying run at Passe Muraille, but there were still lots of things we needed to address in the writing and the staging of the production. Our plan was to tour, in part so that we could have more time to rework it and create the play that we all aspired to make. Besides our audiences, we also benefitted from our tour presenters' notes, so we had plenty of feedback to work with.

After touring to five major theatres nationally, the resulting production was about sixty percent different from when we started in Toronto. For example, over time, Raoul shed many of his ironic characterizations, and instead he presented a more authentic representation of himself. This allowed the humour to come more naturally from him while he was also able to plumb the serious elements of the play more successfully.

This experience proved to us that when we are able to play in front of many different audiences, a production is able to reach new levels of excellence.

BEYOND WALLS

In the autumn of 2012 I programmed a dream mini-season. It was huge and unlike anything I had done before or since. Called Theatre Beyond Walls, it was made possible by a large one-time grant from the Metcalf Foundation.

It is no secret that financial challenges and financial instability have been a recurring hallmark of Passe Muraille's history. All to say that the additional resources from this grant were a signature opportunity for me to follow the passion that led me to Passe Muraille in the first place. It was a glorious opportunity to let our imaginations and desires float free.

This one-off opportunity allowed me to feed a core obsession: I made a major investment in developing our community-engagement skills. I programmed sixteen separate and interconnected community-engagement projects that took place in and around the city. I purposefully commissioned a range of emerging, independent, and established artists and companies. Following my desire for an eclectic mix of works, I made sure to include such diverse performance styles as site-specific theatre, collective creation, verbatim theatre, guerrilla-style theatre on Toronto's streets, promenade theatre, and a tech-centric interactive theatre experience set up in Toronto City Hall and Passe Muraille's Mainspace.

At the core of this delightful explosion of activity was a focus on contriving ways to bring the community into our work. I was able to commission five theatre projects by artists/collectives who were mandated to go out into the city to interview people, open themselves to novel experiences, and gather material for their ultimate productions. I will forever cherish the resulting plays, which were grounded in real life and lifted the spirits with their imaginative and humane storytelling: *Fare Game*, which focused on the stories of Toronto's taxi drivers; *The Four Corners*, which featured the stories of a cross-section of people who live and work at Bathurst and Queen; *This Must be the Place: The CN Tower Show*, which had stories from a broad range of Toronto's politicians and citizens; *501: Toronto in Transit*, which featured a bracing range of stories gathered from those who ride Toronto's iconic 501 streetcar; and *The Queen West Project*, which sensitized the audience to issues around mental illness, homelessness, and the stigma of both, with local members of the homeless and mental-illness communities involved in the creation of this quite extraordinary site-specific dance/theatre hybrid.

The Theatre Beyond Walls project was so vitally important to me as an artist because it provided me with a unique opportunity to fully engage in what Passe Muraille is capable of. But only if we have enough resources.

KIINALIK: THESE SHARP TOOLS

As I write this it is November 26, 2017. Three weeks ago we closed our co-production with Buddies in Bad Times of *Kiinalik: These Sharp Tools*. This was a signature event for me. It single-handedly embodied many of my aspirations.

It featured two extraordinary multidisciplinary female artists, Evalyn Parry and Laakkuluk Williamson Bathory, who were supported by an all-female team: director Erin Brubacher, live videographer Elysha Poirier, live musician Cris Derksen, lighting designer Rebecca Picherack, set designer Kaitlin Hickey, stage manager Christina Cicko, and sound designer Aleda Deroche. It featured voices that are usually marginalized, most especially the Inuit voice. It was a devised piece of theatre that was created by writing, talking, travelling, researching, and improvising. It was a collaborative project in which the entire performing, directing, and design team had a voice. Provocative elements in the work tested the audience to confront our own racism, our own latent colonialism, and our discomfort around our sexuality. The enchanting moments balanced the challenging ones. Some of our accepted tenets of Canadian history and pop culture were overturned. It went beyond the boundaries of theatre, employing a wide diversity of performance styles: multidisciplinary elements, traditionally based ritual, popular music, realistic acting moments, moments of performance art, and moments of direct address. There was pure joy and delight to be in the company of such progressive, charismatic performers while they were laying their life and values bare for us to see.

All this and the audience really embraced it . . . with an open enthusiasm I've not often seen in the theatre. At the end of 2017 it was the cathartic and transformative social experience that we all needed in this dark year of hate and rage and stupidity and near hopelessness. It baptized us back into thriving, flourishing human beings.

And in the time since it closed, I have felt the euphoria and elation that comes from striving for an elusive goal and then achieving it. All the hard work we undertake, all the shared obstacles we face, all the defeats we accept as part of the work we aspire to do . . . they melt away in moments like this.

MY JOY

The act of putting on a play, and inviting people to come and see it, is presumptive. By definition it means that we assume a responsibility to that audience. We undertake to show them something that is meaningful, challenging, and relevant while perhaps inspiring them to imagine a different future. It is a very socially engaged activity. It is what drew me into the theatre. I was not attracted just to the *form* of theatre necessarily, or its commercial potential. I was looking for something that fused the emotional potency of art with an intellectual exploration of contemporary political life. Theatre can be that cauldron for me and Theatre Passe Muraille has always exemplified it in practice.

ANDY MCKIM was the associate artistic director at Tarragon Theatre from 1985 to 2006 before becoming the artistic director of Theatre Passe Muraille in 2007. He is the recipient of the George Luscombe Award for his contribution to the development of new Canadian plays, the Silver Ticket Award from TAPA, and was awarded the Bra d'Or by the women's caucus of the Playwrights Guild of Canada.

Theatre Passe Muraille

SEEDS OF CANADIAN THEATRE

—
CIRCUS GOTHIC
JAN KUDELKA. PHOTO BY ROSS SCOTT.

TPM FIFTIETH ANNIVERSARY REUNION

On March 11, 2017, several artists involved in Theatre Passe Muraille's first decade gathered in Toronto to reminisce about the founding of the company and its influence on Canadian theatre. The following is an excerpt from that conversation featuring Hrant Alianak, Janet Amos, Anne Anglin, Layne Coleman, David Fox, Jim Garrard, Shain Jaffe, Maggie Keith, Paul Kelman, Bob Nasmith, Bob Pearson, Alan Rosenthal, Booth Savage, Andrew Scorer, and Paul Thompson. The dialogue has been edited for length and clarity.

GARRARD: I went to LAMDA in 1967/68, and my wife came to visit me there. She was doing a French course, and she had a book called *Le Passe-muraille* by Marcel Aymé. It's about a guy who has the power to go through walls, but he loses his power and gets struck. I thought, that's a really interesting concept; when I get back to Toronto we'll have an English theatre called Theatre Passe Muraille. Which was completely stupid—nobody could pronounce it and they all thought it was a French theatre.

I was enamoured by La MaMa, the leading New York alternative theatre company, and they did a London season where I saw a very interesting production of *Futz* and a wonderful production of *Tom Paine*. So, being a Canadian, I didn't do anything original. I came back and did remounts, re-imaginings, of those two plays.

KEITH: So you came back, and how did you pick Rochdale?

GARRARD: Well there was an officer at the Ontario Arts Council, Charlotte Holmes, and I went to her and I said, "I want to start a theatre company, what should I do?" And she said, "Why don't you go see Dennis Lee," who became a children's poet; he was one of the intelligentsia of Rochdale as it was forming. So I went to see him and he said, "Yeah, that sounds good," and then I ran into Paul Evitts, and he arranged for a coach house for us and we put out the call, anyone can come, and we ran workshops for six or eight months and then we did a production of *Tom Paine*, which got closed down, and that was sort of the first public performance.

SAVAGE: Where did you do that?

GARRARD: In the basement of Rochdale, and if you go down there to this day you will still see the parking bays painted black . . . we put egg cartons up to muffle the sound.

At one point Kinch and Thompson and I and several other people associated with the company were all living at Rochdale.

When I first did *The Farm Show* we made thirty dollars a week and I thought, "I can't make a living doing this; I'll just do it as a goodbye to theatre."

UK TOUR OF *1837: THE FARMERS' REVOLT* & *THE FARM SHOW*
JOHN JARVIS (1), LINDA GRIFFITHS (2), LAYNE COLEMAN (3), BOOTH SAVAGE (4), R. H. THOMSON (5), PAM BRIGHTON (6), TED JOHNS (7), DAVID PAPAZIAN (8), UNKNOWN (9), DON FINLAYSON (10), MAUREEN A. DOOL (11), MARY ANN MCDONALD (12), STEPHEN GEORGE (13), PAUL THOMPSON (14), MARY WALSH (15), TERRY TWEED (16), JIMMY ADAMS (17), AND PAUL KELMAN (18).

Rochdale provided us with some rehearsal space, props, and initially the people who came to answer the call to be in the show. We said anyone can be in a show, all you have to do is show up. And so a lot of really interesting people showed up, and some were stage-worthy and some were not. Eventually we whittled down an ensemble of twelve, similar to La MaMa.

Rochdale took a long time to die; it kind of ran out of resources. And Passe Muraille changed, it became a real theatre and got funding, so there was a friendly separation that took place over time.

NASMITH: Rochdale was still managing the rent for Theatre Passe Muraille at Trinity Square, and we had a big fund-raising initiative called Play On and On. We would take various aspects of Rochdale and go out West or to Montreal and my contribution down to Brock University, where I had gone to school. So the Rochdale connection did remain strong for several years, through '74, '75.

THOMPSON: And the thinking extended beyond that, of course.

SAVAGE: How did you get the Trinity Square space? How did you afford that?

GARRARD: Well we did a production of *Futz* at the central library, which got busted—it was quite notorious. The morality squad came every day and issued summons to everybody, right down to the hat-check boy.

ROSENTHAL: *Futz* broke the ice. I mean a woman bared her breasts, we had fake dicks sewn on our costumes, and a guy was in love with his pet pig and was simulating sex. That was it. I remember getting a call from the stage manager and she said Jim called to let everyone know we were probably going to be raided that night . . . And at the end of the show we just got changed and ran down the fire escape and ran away. And the next night when they came to arrest us the CBC was there with cameras, so all they did was hand out summons. But we sold out every night after that. The morality squad had to buy tickets every night.

SAVAGE: So Jim is, for me, the soul and the heart of Theatre Passe Muraille, and Kinch was the intellect—not that Jim wasn't also. And what would Thompson be?

GARRARD: The seeds! He planted the seeds.

SAVAGE: Yeah, or the sire.

GARRARD: Well I remember you all got fifty dollars a week, there were twelve of you, and we couldn't make payroll. It was very close to Christmas. I had a fancy recording device and I was on my way to the pawn shop to get the cash for payroll.

Thompson was coming in, I didn't know him very well, but he was the production manager at the time, and he said, "Where are you going with that?"

I said, "The pawn shop," and he said, "Give me that," and he took it out of my hands and back into the theatre. Of course he didn't think it was important to pay the actors. So that was sort of the symbolic transition of power.

KELMAN: I think that politics ran through everything we did under Paul. I came in around the summer of '72 and everything was political. I think that was the reason I was drawn to it. Because it wasn't just play-acting, it was about saying something about something that meant something. And the politics were inherent in the way we created plays too. Paul had a certain kind of political attitude; he gave you just enough rope to either succeed or hang yourself. And it was so democratic in a way. When we did *I Love You, Baby Blue*, he said you can go through the rehearsal period with me and the other actors, or you can not go through the rehearsal period and come up in six weeks with ten minutes worth of the show, and if it's good you'll get paid and we'll use it. So it's up to you. And because it was about sexuality in Toronto, he cast the women first and the women cast the men. I can't think of a play that didn't have political implications.

THOMPSON: One of the impulses was that activity had to keep going on to keep the actors interested, and so that the potential audience would know where to go in case something interesting came up. Jim was running Theatre Passe Muraille but he pulled two of the most interesting directors I knew, Martin Kinch and John Palmer, into the dialogue that was going on. And that ended up being the ultimate blueprint for Passe Muraille. There was never one director vision, one director impulse, but a series of activities, influences, and styles. When Hrant [Alianak] came in he brought a whole original style, and that was an exceptional gift for the city.

There was a physical, theatrical vocabulary that was emerging in the environment, if not out of the building itself. We shamelessly stole from each other; if anything was working you would find it in somebody else's show pretty soon afterward.

ALIANAK: All this exciting stuff was going on at Theatre Passe Muraille; for some reason I was drawn to that theatre more than any other theatre. Every time you saw a play there it was adventurous, it was risky. And I met a guy named Louis Del Grande who directed me in a kids' show somewhere else; he was working at Theatre Passe Muraille as well and he was looking for a play. So I had a whole bunch of little short plays, but I said, "I have a play, if you want to look at it." Spent a few days putting them together and pretending it was a full play, gave it to him, and he did it. That was *Tantrums* in 1972. And it was a very big success, but it was only sixty percent of what I wrote and it really bothered me, so I felt that I needed to direct my own stuff. So I went to Paul—I think there was an upstairs storage space—and he offered me the room for free and said, "Do short plays; after our show we can tell them to go upstairs and see yours."

So I did that for a year. I did about four or five short plays up there. Just to learn how to direct. And then I did my first major play, *Noah's Kiosk*, downstairs, and on opening night the set fell on the audience. It was disastrous. And I remember Paul came to me and said, "Now is the true test—are you going to accept failure or are you going to go on?" I took that as a challenge.

SCORER: The summer of '69, that's when a whole bunch of noon-hour lunch plays were done at Trinity Square. We used to go out onto Yonge Street and try to drag people in off the sidewalk to watch the shows. And actually we had two people from General Idea involved, one who is still alive, Michael Tims [AA Bronson]. It was a pretty magical summer, one little show after another.

FOX: I was a high-school teacher but I quit teaching and came to Toronto looking for work as an actor. I had met Paul Thompson at Western. I didn't know Paul was connected with Theatre Passe Muraille at that time, but I worked with Martin Kinch at Western as well. So I tried to phone Martin Kinch because I didn't know anything about what theatres existed in Toronto, but Martin never returned any of my calls. And then finally Paul, who I think was stage manager at that time, took over as managing director. I phoned and phoned and phoned and he actually responded but his answer was, "Well why don't you apply to one of the much smaller theatres in town." I said, "I thought Theatre Passe Muraille was one of the smaller theatres!"

And then several weeks later Paul phoned and said, "I want to do a play about mine workers in Sudbury or farmers where I grew up in Southwestern Ontario, do you want to audition?" I said okay. So to audition I had to sit on the back of a tractor and tell a story about my family, then tell a joke using only colours.

AMOS: When I first did *The Farm Show* we made thirty dollars a week and I thought, "I can't make a living doing this; I'll just do it as a goodbye to theatre." But then things happened and Paul started to use Equity contracts and giving a portion if there was extra money, so suddenly we were able to make a living. And the work was, to me, the most interesting thing around.

When you are performing, it's not just what is given to you. You have to learn how to speak the way that person is speaking and have the mannerisms, but when you get on stage you have to make it bigger, it becomes fuller and bigger because you are bringing a kind of importance and strength to that character. And that was the most exciting thing of all, to see these ordinary people on stage who suddenly became iconic characters. And the material worked everywhere. It worked in England, it worked in Vancouver, it worked in the city. And even when we did a little bit of it a few years ago, most of the audience hadn't seen it before, and people just laughed and carried on. We heard, "Oh that's just like my mother," and "Oh I love that," and it's a power that I had never experienced in the theatre. And that's why I kept working in the theatre. I would have quit otherwise because I was bored.

ANGLIN: We were doing a show out West and trying to find stories everywhere. Joe Fafard, who is a wonderful sculptural artist, lived in Saskatchewan and he said, "I've got a brother who is a lawyer as far as the road will take you up North." A place called La Ronge. He was called the Flying Judge because he flew to Indigenous communities all over the place, trying to keep the peace. So Bob and I drove, and halfway up we ran into this wolf on the side of the road. Dead. Roadkill. I said, "We've got to stop and do something here. Let's put it in the bush."

And Bob said, "Let's take the tail off first." So he brings out his knife and takes off the tail, we put the dead wolf in the bush, and go on to meet the Flying Judge, who says to us, "You should go next door, there is a Métis woman and she'll skin that tail for you." We did—we went next door and the woman was extremely shy at first, but then she took the tail and slit it open and took out the bone—all the while talking about her life.

So that night we were all camped out in tents and I wrote out everything that she said. In fact, I wrote it up like scenes. The next day we were in rehearsal and Paul says, "Okay, who's got something," and I say, "I've got a script." And he goes "What?" So I read it, very emotionally, and when I finished there was total silence. "Well what do we do with that?" Paul said, "It's a script, that's like going backwards." We rehearsed the scene and it actually worked, but it was such another direction for us to go in, because usually we discovered the dialogue after having an audience for a week.

KELMAN: One year, I think it was '74, we did twenty-three productions. Including Seed Shows, which were one-thousand-dollar budget shows. But twenty-three productions, that's the most of any theatre in the history of Canada, ever.

The first time we did the *The Alberta Cowboy Show* was in a barn. Only three people showed up, a chicken, and a cow.

SAVAGE: We opened *The Athletes' Show* in the Olympic village tent, but nobody came. The only people there were guys with machine guns, standing around the edge. So we all said, "Well what's the point of this, let's just go home." Foxy said, "No, no, we've rehearsed the show; we're doing the show." Which is true David Fox. So we did the show for three guys with machine guns, the first performance of *The Athletes' Show*.

AMOS: Paul went from community to community finding venues, auction houses, schools, barns—and finding people in them who would be interested in sponsoring a show they had never heard of about farming. And then he had to find places for the actors to stay because we were all billeted. Because we had no money. I don't know how you did that, Paul, but you reached into a whole world of people who had never heard of theatre.

And then we went to Stratford and nobody bought tickets; we were doing [*The Farm Show*] in the Festival Theatre, this huge, huge space. There were no tickets sold, but at about one thirty people started to arrive at the box office in their pickup trucks. The whole parking lot was filled with pickup trucks. We had to delay the show because so many people came at the last minute. It was people who had never, ever been in that theatre before. We felt like we were creating a whole world for these people. And Paul did that.

KEITH: There was a chant that some of you might remember, and it was, "Passing through walls, passing through walls, we pass through the walls of your mind." And I can remember it was a great warm-up before you went on. You got together like in a football huddle and would chant: "PASSING THROUGH WALLS, PASSING THROUGH WALLS, WE PASS THROUGH THE WALLS OF YOUR MIND," and out you'd go.

* * *

HRANT ALIANAK made his debut as a writer in 1972 at Theatre Passe Muraille with his play *Tantrums*. Other plays he has written and directed include his gangster trilogy, *Night*, *Passion and Sin*, and *Lucky Strike*, as well as *The Blues*, *The Big Hit*, and *The Walls of Africa*.

From 1972 to 1976 JANET AMOS appeared in Theatre Passe Muraille's productions of *The Farm Show*, *1837: The Farmers' Revolt*, and *Them Donnellys*. She also directed, stage-managed, and ran the lights for *Operation Finger Pinkie*.

THE FIRST TIME WE DID *THE ALBERTA COWBOY SHOW* WAS IN A BARN. ONLY THREE PEOPLE SHOWED UP, A CHICKEN, AND A COW.

ANNE ANGLIN is an actor and was a member of the core company at Passe Muraille in the '70s, collaborating on such celebrated collective creations as *The Farm Show* and *The West Show* among others.

LAYNE COLEMAN is an actor, director, playwright, and co-founder of 25th Street Theatre where he was the artistic director from 1980 through 1983. He was the artistic director of Theatre Passe Muraille for the 1991/92 season, and then again from 1999 through 2007.

DAVID FOX played rural characters in the premieres of several historically significant collective creations at Theatre Passe Muraille, including *The Farm Show*, *1837: The Farmers' Revolt*, *Far as the Eye Can See* (with Rudy Wiebe), *Les Maudits Anglais*, and *Them Donnellys*.

JIM GARRARD was born in Northern Ontario in 1939. He was the founding artistic director of Theatre Passe Muraille and president of Rochdale College. He has taught theatre at Simon Fraser University and the University of Toronto and has written extensively for film and television.

SHAIN JAFFE was a co-creator of the TPM production *Vampyr* and was the executive director of the Toronto International Theatre Festival.

MAGGIE KEITH was among Dora Mavor Moore's last students at the New Play Society. For financial reasons, she refused Mrs. Moore's offer of a place at the Webber-Douglas School of Acting in England. After performances at Hart House Theatre, Maggie joined the company at Theatre Passe Muraille. Returning to university, she earned an M.A. in English, but could not keep away from theatre. A series of "me too" experiences rendered Maggie unemployable by the local cabal of directors. Too many lengthy regional contracts ended her marriage. Leaving theatre in despair, Maggie worked in co-op housing and freelanced as a writer and editor for art institutions and the co-op movement. Her children's novel *Patrick and the Actors*, illustrated by Glenn Priestley, was published by Penumbra Press. She is now Communications Officer at the Agency for Co-operative Housing in Ottawa, taking classes at the Acting Company, and trying to write ten-minute plays.

PAUL KELMAN is an actor and playwright and was a member of the core company at Passe Muraille in the '70s, collaborating on *Les Maudits Anglais*; *I Love You, Baby Blue*; and *The Alberta Cowboy Show* among others.

BOB NASMITH is an actor and was a member of the core company at Passe Muraille in the '70s, collaborating on such celebrated collective creations as *The Farm Show* and *The West Show* among others.

BOB PEARSON provided many of the set designs during the early years of TPM and acted as company carpenter, helping to convert the space at 16 Ryerson into a theatre.

ALAN ROSENTHAL is a film, television, and stage actor as well as a narrator and voice actor, and appeared in early TPM productions such as *Futz*.

BOOTH SAVAGE is an actor and playwright and one of the first actors to perform with Theatre Passe Muraille.

ANDREW SCORER is an actor who performed with TPM on many early productions.

PAUL THOMPSON is a playwright and director best known for his term as artistic director of Theatre Passe Muraille, where he pioneered techniques for collective creation.

OUTSIDE THE VICTORIA PLAYHOUSE, PETROLIA
ERIC PETERSON, JANET AMOS, PAUL THOMPSON, ANNE ANGLIN, AND TED JOHNS.

Passe Muraille

TPM AND THE COLLECTIVE PROCESS: MY VIEW

BY RICK SALUTIN

I returned to Canada after ten years of study in the US and elsewhere in late 1970, coterminous with the FLQ kidnapping crisis in Quebec. I had the luck to plunge into the middle of the nationalist theatre renaissance—or just naissance—in Toronto. It focused on Canadian plays for Canadian audiences.

This actually mattered. There had been impressive theatre activity here for many previous decades. Those involved, like Mavor Moore and the Davises (who started the Crest), were skilled, professional, and committed. The one thing they weren't particularly concerned with, as I learned whenever I talked to them and quizzed them, was Canadian scripts. "It never occurred to us," said one of them. They were doing theatre by Canadian actors, directors, designers, in Canada for Canadian audiences. But the script issue was being overlooked.

I don't know how you explain that except that different generations focus on different matters. That's more or less what being part of history means. I think this urgency for Canadian scripts was one of the forces behind Passe Muraille and Paul Thompson's vision. The collective-creation process was part of that era, everywhere in the world that theatre was done. But elsewhere it did not fill the need we had here for our own scripts.

Scripts are hard to develop; or rather, I should say, playwrights take a while to develop. But the urgency was there, the sense of need, and one way to shortcut the process was the collective process. There were other reasons, but that was among them. I had done scripted work prior to working with Paul at Passe Muraille in the collective method, but it was clearly a speeded up way to make a play, and in the bargain I learned a lot about what works on a stage.

Another benefit of the collective approach is that it emphasized the live and especially the oral nature of theatre. Many of us grew up thinking of theatre as a branch of literature, i.e., of the written tradition. Theatres were where you went and they read the scripts to you. Or at you. You could know the play by getting a copy of the script. Plays were in effect holographic versions of movies: three-dimensional and live, but not basically different. The collective method helped reclaim theatre's essential nature as an oral form of culture.

I'd like to add that, to my surprise, I found that little brought out egomania in theatre people like the collective process. I'm not sure why. Some of it was probably due to the competitive nature of the approach: actors, for instance, are not handed a part. They have to create it, and the more they create the more they get to perform and then reap the complex rewards of being on stage.

Let me finish by saying something about the historical nature of the collective process itself. When the Shaw Festival contacted me recently about doing *1837*, one of the Passe Muraille collectives, it became my responsibility to collect and distribute the royalties as we'd long ago agreed. I had a hard time remembering the formula for dividing them. There had been many productions but they were frequently by small companies that paid little or nothing. I got my head in knots trying to remember the percentages. I mentioned it to my son, who was seventeen at the time. "Surely," he said, "it's written down somewhere." Then he shook his head and said, "Or is it one of those crazy seventies things where no one ever wrote anything down." How true. It was like the play itself in that respect, though eventually the script became set and printed.

That's what happens. First you do plays about history from some lofty perch where you view it from above. Then you become one more distant piece of it yourself (yourselves).

Playwright RICK SALUTIN worked with Theatre Passe Muraille throughout the 1970s. His work included the collective creations *1837: The Farmers' Revolt* and *The Adventures of an Immigrant* and the scripted plays *The False Messiah*, *Nathan Cohen: A Review*, and *Les Canadiens*.

1837

Theatre Passe Muraille
11 Trinity Square

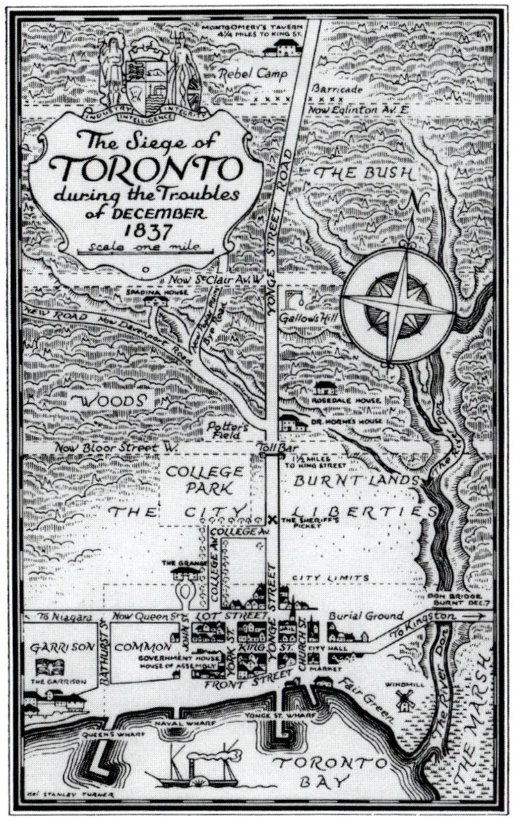

ACT I Summer 1837

ten minute intermission

ACT II Winter 1837

The final scene takes place April 12, 1838.

This play was made by:

JANET AMOS - actor
CLARE COULTER - actor
SUZETTE COUTURE - actor
ED FISHER - stage manager
DAVID FOX - actor
MILES POTTER - actor
RICK SALUTIN - writer
PAUL THOMPSON - director
NEIL VIPOND - actor
PAUL WILLIAMS - designer

production: ED FISHER, LUCIEN PARMENTIER, ELIZABETH FAJTA, PAUL WILLIAMS.

Special thanks to Bill Fleming, the St. Lawrence Centre, Pioneer Village.

poster: Linda Jurcisek.

Theatre Passe Muraille receives assistance from Canada Council, Ontario Arts Council, Metro Toronto, and works in association with Trinity Church and Rochdale College.

1837 HOUSE PROGRAM FROM 1973

GETTING MIXED UP WITH THEATRE PASSE MURAILLE

BY ERIC PETERSON

I got mixed up with Theatre Passe Muraille one night in the early 1970s, after a performance of *Under the Graywacke*, a collectively created play about a mining community in Northern Ontario. The experience stirred a deep sense of familiarity in me that was so direct and intense that I felt, in some inchoate way, proprietorial about the piece—that it belonged to me. This sense of connection was entirely new to me. In my experience most (if not all) plays and movies were stories from somewhere else, anywhere else, rather than here. Every one of them required an imaginative geographical and societal translation for appreciation to occur. I could enjoy their universality "here," but it had been created out of the specifics of "there."

Fatefully, I lingered after the play to congratulate the actors and thank them for my experience, ineffable though it was. Not that I realized it at the time, but I was meeting many of the colleagues and collaborators and friends that are lovingly enshrined in my mind as Theatre Passe Muraille: David Fox, Miles Potter, Janet Amos, Ted Johns, Anne Anglin, Clare Coulter, and as fate would have it, of course, Paul Thompson himself.

I introduced myself, saying that I too was an actor. What happened next, it seems to me—as I remember now—was that I almost instantly found myself north of London, Ontario, outside the small town of Lucan, capering along a rural road called the Roman Line on a stormy night with some of the above named, conjuring the ghosts of a long-past feud and massacre. "Part of the rehearsal process," I was assured, for *Them Donnellys*, the first of many plays over the next ten or fifteen years that I was to do with Passe Muraille.

My memory renders this time as an impressionistic montage of places, faces, stories, and characters. So my portrayal of Grouchy Ryder, with a burning barn beam held aloft, the lighter-fluid flames soaring high along its length, bellowing his vengeance on Jim Donnelly, morphs in my mind to the wail of powwow songs in one ear and fiddle jigs in the other, and me at Batoche on the banks of the South Saskatchewan River, where the Riel Rebellion came to an end. This scene, in turn, melts into a pig barn where I'm wrestling young pigs—the pigs only slightly more panic-stricken than myself—so that farmer Loeb can castrate them. "Part of the rehearsal process," I was again assured, for going into *The Farm Show*. Now dissolve to "the barrens" and Baker Lake, the school gym crowded with every man, woman, and child of the community watching our world

1837: THE FARMERS' REVOLT
ERIC PETERSON.

IN MY EXPERIENCE MOST (IF NOT ALL) PLAYS AND MOVIES WERE STORIES FROM SOMEWHERE ELSE, ANYWHERE ELSE, RATHER THAN HERE.

premiere of *John Hornby* and our rendering of two "bushed" trappers dividing in homicidal rancour their partnership and all its equipment right down to the single kettle, which must be chopped in two to avoid murder. This is portrayed by two of us standing ass to ass, one bending one way—the handle—and one bending the other way—the spout—the axe then falling between, chopping the kettle in two. The entire audience erupted in ribald hilarity, not our intended effect, but understandable when we learned the audience had not seen a kettle but two mating dogs still locked in post-coital engorgement being chopped apart. Cross-fade to Melville, Saskatchewan, the morning after the first night of our two-night stand for *The West Show*, at which we had an audience of all of five people. I'm meeting with the Canadian Legion sponsor in the legion hall, trying to get to the bottom of the dismal turnout of the night before in this city of four and a half thousand people. The Legion guy is sympathetic but unfazed as he declares that, "Shit, we hadn't done too badly." He'd had a Legion funeral recently and he couldn't get six pallbearers. Perspective is everything. We cancelled the second show.

So it went. A whirl of cities and towns all over the country, east to west and back again, south, north, north, south, labouring to articulate theatrical themes and stories of what it was like being a Canadian living in Canada and presenting it for Canadians to watch and verify, wherever that audience was likely to be: church halls, civic auditoriums, under the flag poles of the athletes' village at the Montreal Olympics, theatres, disused railroad stations, sales barns, streetcars, anywhere we could get to and they would come to watch.

One last image has to be of Paul Thompson; visionary of this entity called Passe Muraille and, for me, its heart and soul. Illuminated in the near blizzard conditions by the van's headlights, he's standing on the shoulder of the Trans-Canada Highway, his red wool-blanket habitant coat with the black stripe and peaked hood flapping in the wind; the snow whirling around him; his coat, hair, and beard all blowing in the same direction as he waves us on our way.

I had gone to *Under the Graywacke* a young actor, dreaming of himself on stage in the West End of London or in front of the cameras in Hollywood, my version of that Canadian migratory instinct for finding self-realization elsewhere. Then I got mixed up with Theatre Passe Muraille and there has been no glittering London, New York, or Hollywood; instead there has been the ever-ongoing search for that deep note of identification and ownership in an audience's appreciation—the exact thing that thrilled me so many years ago when I first got mixed up with Theatre Passe Muraille.

ERIC PETERSON is an actor who helped found Tamahnous Theatre before joining Theatre Passe Muraille, where he played principal roles in several collective creations, including *The Farm Show* and *1837: The Farmers' Revolt*. In 1976 he worked with John Gray to create *Billy Bishop Goes to War*.

Passe Muraille

I DREAM

BY BOOTH SAVAGE

I'm alone and cooling on a winter's bench with yellowing so-so reviews in my otherwise empty pockets, my terrible familiar secret dream. Friendless, hopeless, imagination-less, and so, so, fucking cold—chilled to a solid from the inside out. First the heart/soul/mind becomes crystal, then the less vital organs. Folks pass by. Once in a while one of them stops and asks me if I'm the guy from some television show with Gordon Pinsent they saw when they were a kid. They won't leave until I run my resumé by them, and, of course, they don't remember any of the shows I call out. They think they've done me a favour by vaguely recognizing me, and assume, kindly I suppose, that I'm in research for another, more grizzled part.

In a few months, but always before spring, I'm dead. They peel my body from the bench. Bits of old reviews come away as they pry me from the cold aluminum. Back at the morgue they identify me by a shard of cruelty some *Globe and Mail* critic visited on me years ago, the hateful note still impossibly stuck to my rigor mortised fingers. An enterprising young clerk follows the trail of this middling review to discover my true identity. "Old Actor Dies Frozen and Broken" the small heading reads in the obits of the next day's *Sun*. No one claims my body. I enter eternity via an unmarked grave in Potter's field. Dumped without ceremony or an audience. A bit like one of my plays at TPM back in the day.

> CREATION: 1. The act or process of creating. 2. The fact of being created or produced. 3. Something that has been brought into existence or created, esp. a product of human intelligence or imagination.
> —Collins English Dictionary.

THE TPM SHOW
ACT 1
SCENE 1

A young man—terrifically handsome, long hair sweeping over his shoulders, bare chested, muscled, pec deck flexed, canines dripping blood as he descends an elevated platform at the rear of a cage or cell—twists his mouth into an unholy snarl as he steps into the torchlight that is the sole (soul) source of illumination. He moves with deliberate purpose toward a cloaked figure standing near the front of the cell. As the young man nears the figure, the torchlight, as if commanded by the young man himself, reveals an older man (a Catholic priest?) kneeling just beyond the cage with his head bent in what we might assume to be an attitude of prayer.

YOU DON'T NEED AN IDEA; YOU NEED AN OPENING NIGHT. START WITH RESEARCH, THAT'S ALWAYS A GOOD PLACE. SOMETHING CONCRETE.

The younger man reaches the limit of the cage and peers through the iron bars. The "priest" lifts his head—he is studying a few pages of type. The younger man looks deeply into the older man's face.

Dissolve to a few weeks earlier. An abandoned downtown storefront.

OLD ACTOR: Thrillers are good. With sex. Naked girls. Fit young men. Make it a rule play. Rule number one: it opens on the day we say it's gonna open. Rule number two: no one gets to quit. Rule number three: that's enough rules for now.

YOUNG ACTOR: Okay. We're here—let's get started.

OLD: Sounds good.

YOUNG: Whatta we do?

OLD: Build a cage. Hang some lights.

YOUNG: We don't have any lights.

OLD: Okay. Build a cage.

YOUNG: What about the scenes? The play? The story?

OLD: That'll take care of itself.

YOUNG: How?

OLD: I don't know. The magic of theatre, I suppose.

YOUNG: How did you guys do it?

OLD: I forget. There's no formula. You just hope someone takes the reins and starts pulling.

YOUNG: I don't have any ideas.

OLD: You don't need an idea; you need an opening night. Start with research, that's always a good place. Something concrete.

YOUNG: What was it like back then?

OLD: God, who remembers?

YOUNG: You were stoned?

OLD: Probably.

YOUNG: And there was sex?

OLD: Oh yeah.

YOUNG: Who decided which plays you'd do?

OLD: That I don't remember. Someone showed up with an idea and seemed like a decent leader and away everyone went. I'm boring myself to death here. You guys don't really care about any of that. That history's useless and boring, not worth memorializing. You're the future. What is it you guys want to do?

YOUNG: We just want to act.

OLD: Some things never change. But somewhere along the line someone has to step up and lead. That's where we're at. Waiting for a leader—

YOUNG: Like Godot?

OLD: Why not do that play instead?

YOUNG: Been done too many times. The festival's doing it again next summer anyway. Besides—too many characters.

OLD: If I were you—and I'm not—I'd go for amusing or thrilling. You like those long, angry speeches, with plenty of irony, things to move quickly, lots of tension and smart-talking guys, right?

YOUNG: I don't know—

OLD: It's okay you like that. We all like plenty of throat-grabbing action. Grab 'em by the throat and never let 'em go. That was Billy Wilder's advice.

YOUNG: That's what a vampire does.

OLD: Yeah, but we can't just do a vampire story—not that vampire story—I think we've covered the reasons for that.

YOUNG: So?

OLD: It's always about family. Think of a family and go from there.

YOUNG: Tell me about the family.

OLD: Christ, actors love to talk—anything but get down to work. We've got a play to get open in three weeks. We've got to get the damn thing written and rehearsed and publicized and built. It's not gonna write itself, is it?

YOUNG: That's for sure.

OLD: Okay. So here are we. In the second act.

YOUNG: Really? The first act is done?

OLD: Not done, but in pretty good shape. We have to figure out what happens in the second act. I think we should have an exorcism and an orgy—not necessarily in that order. I think once the old fart priest finds out that Paul Destrie has won over all the nuns and they're all cavorting naked in his cell that he has to finally pull the big ace out of his sleeve and go for the climactic exorcism.

YOUNG: That sounds good.

OLD: You'll have to write some great music for that—big—lots of piano and drums and bass chords.

YOUNG: You're a musician now?

OLD: I'm just telling you what you'll need to make it dramatic. We need big drama here. All lit by torchlight.

YOUNG: The fire marshal might have something to say about that.

OLD: We'll keep him in the dark.

YOUNG: An orgy, eh?

OLD: Yeah. The three nuns all come at once to the cage. By now they've all been bitten and completely won over to Destrie's side of things. They're his brides now. Jesus isn't even a memory—in a procession—torches and bare breasts—better if one of them is completely nude.

YOUNG: I don't think you'll talk the girls into that.

OLD: Too shy?

YOUNG: Yeah.

OLD: And Destrie is waiting for them, accepting their offerings, allowing them to serve him.

YOUNG: Sounds like a nice fantasy. How'd you ever get away with that?

OLD: It was a different time.

YOUNG: Maybe we should update that?

OLD: Update? I thought this was a history lesson. You can't go changing things to suit the modern era. It was different. Things were different.

YOUNG: But you're showing that back then artists were way behind the curve. Women were starting to emerge as full partners even then, weren't they?

OLD: It's got nothing to do with that. It's a story that is placed in an indeterminate century or two before any of that. Women were . . . anyway, these women are medieval nuns. How advanced can they be?

YOUNG: But don't you want to give a little hint that you avant-garde theatre folks were at the actual vanguard of this kind of thinking? Maybe a little revision here wouldn't be bad—you know—to help with sympathy?

OLD: For who?

YOUNG: For you. For it.

OLD: We don't need your sympathy.

YOUNG: All right, an orgy with bare-breasted girls. I'm not saying I don't like it. I'm just saying we may run into a few difficulties, that's all.

OLD: They agreed.

YOUNG: Who agreed?

OLD: Brenda and Clare and Chris. Nobody cared. Besides, it's in their contracts.

YOUNG: You had contracts?

OLD: No, we didn't. We had an understanding—that was enough.

YOUNG: I think we have to let the women discover those choices for themselves.

OLD: Oh, do we?

YOUNG: I think we have to build the story to the point where the women make their own decisions about how and what and why they react to the vampire. Then, if they feel like getting naked and having an orgy, it'll be organic.

OLD: Jesus. What a lot of bother. Why can't we just say that that's the way it happened, and that's the way it's gonna be.

YOUNG: It doesn't work that way anymore. I'm not saying it won't happen, but we just have to be a little more sensitive to the times. It needs to be organic.

OLD: What about the exorcism?

YOUNG: That's a little old fashioned too. I think in your day it had more meaning

NO. WE'RE ALREADY COMMITTED. THE POSTER IS DONE. THE ADS ARE OUT THERE. WE'RE DOING THIS ONE.

because of—well, because—but now I don't think anyone's gonna be impressed.

OLD: It's a show about a show that happened forty-five years ago. Can't we find a way to make it appear like . . . I don't know, that audiences were not so jaded?

YOUNG: Maybe we just have to be cleverer.

OLD: You're making this way harder than it has to be.

YOUNG: Just trying to keep you honest.

OLD: All right—that's the second act fucked.

YOUNG: No. Let's just reconsider things from a new point of view.

OLD: If you don't want to do the play we did then let's just pick another play.

YOUNG: No. We're already committed. The poster is done. The ads are out there. We're doing this one.

OLD: We had a lot of rehearsals just like this where nothing got done because we'd sit around and argue and discuss until finally someone said let's just try something, anything, and see where it goes—even movement for movement's sake is better than the eternal wrangling that actors without an audience or a playwright would rather waste their valuable time doing—that's why a lot of those collectives were a collection of monologues—actors getting fed up and coming into rehearsal with an idea or a song or something that didn't require anyone else's co-operation or agreement. Peterson would just show up and dazzle us all with a bit of virtuosity and Fox would go from there. They didn't think about it. They didn't scheme or plot or get bogged down in all that excess, they just jumped in with both feet—and if it worked, great, if it didn't, they'd try something else. We need to have a little more of that genius, a little less apologizing.

YOUNG: Apologizing? For what?

OLD: Not being smart enough or clever enough or witty enough. Just pick something—some event—some tiny bit of the story and jump in. In the end it's gonna be your ass hanging out there. My advice is not to wait too long. Have a bunch of alternatives, then you can choose which ones work and toss out the ones that don't. Fill the space with moody, dark, soulful music—percussive and twangy and eerie and torchlight. You can hide a lot of sins with torchlight. Have a couple of bare-breasted nuns moving about in a creepy old nunnery carrying a torch and visiting the ailing but still sexy vampire in his cage. All that temptation and nuance and impending peril and sex ought to be enough to fire the imagination . . . If that doesn't cut it you can always do what Phil, Géza, and I did when we were stuck.

YOUNG: Yeah?

OLD: Go to the alley out back and toss rocks through a hole in the fence.

BOOTH SAVAGE: I think I'm safe in saying that Jim (Garrard) not only invented TPM, but he invented me as well. When he chose me to be a part of the "company" in the summer of 1969 my life altered course forever. I can't say with certainty what I was before, but ever since I have been a believer in risking it all for the sake of (artistic) freedom. TPM for me has always been the place where I (and everyone else) could (and did) dare anything.

THEM DONNELLYS 1974
GARY REINEKE, DEAN HAWES, TED JOHNS, AND BOB O'REE.* PHOTO BY DAVID GROSKIND.

WHEN THE MODE OF THE MUSIC CHANGES: REFLECTIONS ON THE EARLY DAYS OF PASSE MURAILLE

BY TED JOHNS

What follows are things which I observed, experienced, or heard about during my time at Passe Muraille during the 1970s. Many other things were going on within the city and elsewhere but these I cannot begin to catalogue or even try to track down.

At the time there was a competition between Passe Muraille (largely paperless) and Tarragon (largely literary). For better or for worse, it was won by Tarragon. Better in the sense that things became more predictable, straightforward, and reliable (dull?), but worse in the sense that Tarragon has contributed to the relentless institutionalizing of the arts in our time which—after the golden age, the silver age, and the bronze—leads inevitably to the age of lead.

Tarragon was founded in 1970 by Bill Glassco, a gentleman scholar (as Google has it), a scion of a wealthy family, and a graduate of Princeton and Oxford. His theatre looked and functioned like the department of a well-endowed university. Tasteful photos of the past adorned the walls. Writers commanded a special place of honour (alongside management), and they, like its subscription audience, were much cherished.†

Passe Muraille was founded in 1968 by Jim Garrard. Its origins were in the chaotic and rebellious atmosphere of Rochdale

* Bob was from Fredericton and his brother Willie (recently inducted into the Hockey Hall of Fame) was the first Black player in the NHL. Bob was also an excellent athlete but he failed to catch on with the CFL and, in the days before colour-blind casting, found acting a very tough go. Who wrote plays for Black Canadians?

† Unfortunately, Tarragon has recently removed all photographs from its lobby, leaving bare white walls and a computer screen. Pamphlets and posters from other theatre groups are no longer allowed. Presumably this is so Tarragon can now present itself as a "brand" rather than a troupe of players.

college and its first major show *Futz* was raided by the police.† It's more of a "space" than a theatre. It used to be a factory, and efforts to convert it still seem improvised. Nothing on the walls suggests anyone ever worked there. As one girl said, "When you come in here you think you can do anything. Because there's nothing here."

I don't want to be too hard on Glassco because he was for a brief time one of my lecturers at college. In my opinion he was an honest, caring man. A man who was, as they used to say, "of great integrity." But he was truly the last person on earth I would have expected to start a theatre.

For him, theatre was an acquired taste.‡ He had never acted professionally, never written a play, had certainly never improvised, and would have been terrified to mount the boards without a script. His comic sense was very faint—I can't recall him ever making a joke. He was great at cracking the whip but equally great at taking people aside for long heart-to-heart chats. His wealth was sufficient that he never took a cent in salary. He hung around with Stratford types and even went to theatre school in New York—but in his heart of hearts I think he thought theatre's true function was to illustrate the written word. His highest praise was to say an actor "took direction well," which for Passe Muraille actors§ sounded suspiciously like, "Please check your brains at the door."

Hence Glassco created a theatre where playwrights of sufficient prestige are said to be "in residence."¶ They have offices. They write, they meet, they discuss, and they have "readings." The readings evolve into "workshops," i.e., a script conference with actors. Further drafts appear until at some point someone declares the thing "ready," at which point it starts down the long pipeline into production.

All this is much admired and much imitated. Academics like it because it's so academic. Writers like it because it is so secure. Councils like it because it is so bureaucratic. Audiences like it because, theoretically, there seems to be some kind of quality control. Artistic directors like it because they don't have to think of ideas for new plays—the writers come up with the ideas and the dramaturges grind through the acres of unsolicited manuscripts. And, finally, critics like it because it makes their work easy—familiar writers doing familiar work.

The word "tarragon" suggests it aspires to be a little bit of spice in the mix. However, it is now the theatre whose model dominates all others. For many it is not just a way of doing things, it is the only way.

We're talking about the sixties here. Theatre was not a career, it was a diversion. In 1962 I remember running into Dave Bolt, who said he wanted to be an actor. Doing Canadian Theatre. I thought he was mad. Where on god's earth would he act? What would he act? Years later, in 1968, the great British director Clifford Williams told the then apprentice actor Janet Amos, "You know, you people should be doing your own work." She too was mystified. What would this work look like? Who would want to see it? Who on earth would want to direct it? Anyway, lots of good plays were being written elsewhere. Why bother making your own? Still later, the great John Hirsch told the Canada Council, "When I started, the idea of making a living as an actor in Saskatoon wasn't even a dream."

Toronto was a city with two theatres. The O'Keefe Centre, which was a cavernous roadhouse, and the Crest, which was a small professional repertory about to exhaust the wealth of its founders. The Royal Alex was about to be torn down and businessmen claimed that what we really needed was a freeway right through the centre of town. Somewhere off in a church basement George Luscombe, a.k.a. Toronto Workshop Productions, was doing an improv show called *The Mechanic*. There was no CanStage, no Pantages, no Winter Garden, no Princess of Wales, no North York Civic Centre, and certainly none of the small theatres and small festivals which give them oxygen.

Anyone with literary aspirations was on the first cattle boat to Europe or the first train to New York. Why? Because the little Canadian publishing houses (Anansi, Talon, Coach House, Coteau, etc.) hadn't got going, nor had the little literary magazines and bookstores, nor

* Jim Garrard says that Rochdale paid the rent for Passe Muraille for five years—a measure of how much they valued the theatre in spite of their own financial difficulties; cf. the University of Toronto, which periodically has qualms about whether they should support Hart House.

† The cast of *Futz* was arrested, charged, and convicted. During their appeal, rich Toronto backers brought the big American musical *Hair* into the Royal Alex. After the court viewed it and its much more blatant nudity, they decided in their wisdom? hypocrisy? cowardliness? to overturn the conviction.

‡ Acquired may sound pejorative but it probably applies to more than a few professionals in this country. Acting is pretty hard to fake but directors can fumble along. In time they learn refinements—when to push, when to lay off, how to get a performance from the rehearsal hall to the stage. In terms of basic organization Glassco could learn it, I could learn it, and people pouring out of theatre schools have learned it. The point is that all this is remote from those very rare people who can actually create things in the theatre, the Brechts, the Dario Fos, the Ken Campbells, the

§ The kind of actor who thrived at Passe Muraille was given to taking creative initiative. Paul called them his cowboys. He told Mary Walsh she should be careful around the cowboys because they were growing antlers. "What about me?" she said; "why can't I have antlers?" "You don't need antlers, Mary," he told her; "you've got wings."

¶ Quotes because people don't actually reside there. It's a pretentious way of saying

Can Lit people, nor had the critical mass of people who were interested in this stuff been created because we were still a young country, etc., and we had no tradition, etc., and it would take years and years, etc., all of which was upended when the Trudeau government introduced LIP grants (a Local Initiatives Program) which, to the horror of conservatives, allowed young people to get money for projects however unlikely and to spend it more or less unsupervised. Some day some particularly dedicated Ph.D. candidate will document how many of these teeny handholds eventually blossomed into many of our cultural institutions today. Governments like to hand out truckloads of money to institutions, and trainloads of it for "security," but they are extremely wary of giving even slight amounts to individuals. Questions in Parliament. Unworthy people. Threats to the family. Chances of scandal. It is an experiment unlikely to be repeated.

Keep in mind that our national theatre at the time was essentially the Dominion Drama Festival and it was not until 1960 that a Canadian was deemed fit to judge the regionals, and not till 1965 was a Canadian (Guy Beaulne) deemed capable of judging the finals. Until then British or American professionals (or sometimes even military men!) were brought in and, then as now, they flattered the poor Canadians shamelessly ("This is as good as anything in the West End" or "This should be on Broadway"), thus ensuring a fat stipend and their safe return. Obviously some people got experience here and some people found their métier,* but what I am saying is that if you thought you could start a theatre in 1970 devoted to Canadian works and you thought you could make a living at it, you had to be either barking mad or very wealthy.

Not only that but, as the academics of the day were quick to inform us, Canada had no tradition of original theatre. It was a slow process they told us. You had to start people off gently with something easy, say, *Our Town*. Then you moved up the ladder to, say, *The School for Scandal*. If that proved difficult, you retreated to *A Christmas Carol* or *Hobson's Choice*, and if that went well you might launch a haymaker like *Mourning Becomes Electra*, although that might be a stretch. Then as now a recent hit from London or New York was the best bet, but to show that you were a creative theatre every now and again you might throw them a curve like *Waiting for Godot* or even, with proper precautions and fair warning, a "Canadian" play, say, Robertson Davies's *Eros at Breakfast* or James Reaney's *Colours in the Dark*.

* A generation of theatre people including big stars like William Shatner, Donald Sutherland, Christopher Plummer, William Hutt, Kate Reid, Frances Hyland, Jane Mallett, and Roberta Maxwell got their starts at Hart House (1919), the Crest (1953), the Stratford Festival (1953), the Shaw Festival (1962), the CBC (1936), the Alumnae Theatre (1918), Dora Mavor Moore's New Play Society (1946), and Amelia Hall's Canadian Repertory Theatre (1949) and Montreal Repertory Theatre (1930). But not by doing Canadian plays.

SHAKESPEARE FOR FUN AND PROFIT—A CANADIAN DREAM (OR, IT SURE BEATS FARMING)
LINDA GRIFFITHS, DAVID FOX, CONNIE KALDOR, TED JOHNS, ALAN BRIDLE, AND DONNA BUTT. PHOTO BY DAVID GROSKIND.

It could take years, perhaps generations, but, with proper tutelage, eventually people would catch on. As in a constitutional monarchy, eventually the commons would take over.

This theme was reflected in a Passe Muraille collective called *Shakespeare for Fun and Profit* (1977), which was essentially *A Midsummer Night's Dream* wherein the Canadians were the mechanicals—a situation which an older generation of actors would instantly recognize. As the Canadian actress Beth Amos used to say, "Oh, to be in England now that England's here."

The concept was Paul Thompson's. He had the idea. He raised the money. He hired the actors.† And he turned us loose. David Fox played an academic director who worked out his blocking at home and then brought the maquette into rehearsal and directed the play by moving the figures around with his back to the actors. Every now and again he would look around and be appalled at how little the actors resembled anything he had imagined. Every year his character went to London (England). He'd seen all the great Lears, all the great Hamlets, and like many before and since had been utterly swept away by an art he could love but could not reproduce.

Similarly Alan Bridle played a bartender who reluctantly took on the role of Puck but then became so smitten by it that he couldn't bear to return to his old humdrum life worrying about crinkle-cut french fries and replacing sixty-watt bulbs. Connie Kaldor played the captain of a women's softball team shanghaied by social pressure into playing one of the play's inane lovers.

As a person and an athlete her character was so many light years removed from this essentially courtly love parody

† In those days Thompson didn't offer you a role. He said something to the effect that he was organizing a kind of card game and asked if you would like to "deal yourself in."

IF YOU REALLY WANTED TO IMPRESS PAUL, YOU GOT UP ON THE BANDSTAND AND SANG A COUNTRY SONG.

that the effect was either grotesque or comic depending on your point of view. However, she did sing (she is now a famous singer) and John (*Billy Bishop*) Gray wrote the music. Linda Griffiths played a visiting English star à la Maggie Smith who was booked for so many years in advance she scarcely knew what day it was. Donna Butt played the Queen of Athens and the wife of John Bottom (myself). The Bottoms go to Stratford to learn how to do plays and are astonished and utterly baffled by its gay subculture. It was a striking illustration of what Joan Didion calls "dreampolitik"—a situation where two societies occupy the same space without being aware of each other's existence.

This play toured Southwestern Ontario and played to large audiences in Petrolia and Blyth. It finished with a run at what is now the Bluma Appel Theatre at the St. Lawrence Centre for the Arts. Paul organized a pit where people could get cheap tickets to stand close to the stage and watch as they did in the old Shakespearean theatre. I drove a tractor down Front Street. In spite of these hijinks the critics were not amused and not a smidgen of this play survives. No audiotapes. No videos. No paper.

Still, for all its joking around, *Shakespeare for Fun and Profit* was toying with some very important ideas, in particular the thought that only by winning the approval of the dominant culture (be it US or UK) would you be able (or even allowed) to make your own. It is not surprising that alternative theatres of the day tended to style themselves as "underground" theatres, a term which the very much above ground critics found amusing because nobody in Canada was being put in jail for doing—ha ha—Canadian Theatre.

However, in retrospect, I suspect that more than a few of us were under RCMP surveillance, as were Tommy Douglas (for advocating health care), Michael Ignatieff (for organizing a teach-in), Northrop Frye (for supporting peace organizations), and Nathan Cohen (for editing a labour newspaper). Rick Salutin (union organizer) would have been a prime candidate, as would George Luscombe, Cedric Smith, Ken Gass, Paul Thompson, and even, god help us, Rita MacNeil.* Then and now the Tory brain tends to think that art is a form of recreation and should come under the purview of tourism. Like golf courses, art should be privatized and, whatever else it is, it should not be construed as a form of knowledge much less as a legitimate form of protest. Unions, socialism, talk of social justice—all these are suspect and the wise arts organization stays clear of them. For example, in 2002 the Playwrights Union of Canada went to a great deal of trouble to change its name from the Playwrights Union to the Playwrights Guild of Canada largely, in my opinion, to avoid being associated with left wing tendencies.

More recently (2012), Tarragon encouraged Michael Healey to write *Proud*, (about Prime Minister Harper). For reasons the theatre would not divulge, they suddenly refused to produce it.

Healey resigned (after eleven years as playwright-in-residence) and went public with his story, asserting that Tarragon was intimidated by the prospect of losing federal-government funding.

"They're extremely good at controlling the message," Healey said of the Prime Minister's Office. "I think they're so good at controlling the message, they have the board of Tarragon doing it for them."†

Richard Rose, the artistic director of Tarragon, has publicly denied that he turned down Healey's play for fear of losing funding. The rest of the arts community has been wary, however, since the Toronto SummerWorks Festival saw its federal funding cut in 2011 after it produced *Homegrown*—a play that, the PMO said, "glorified terrorism."‡

The first play I worked on was called *Under the Graywacke* (1973). It was directed by Paul Thompson and produced by Theatre Passe Muraille. To audition for this as-yet-unnamed play "about Northern Ontario" you had to do five Canadian accents. You then had to go to

* In 2008 the Canadian Press revealed that historians Steve Hewitt and Christabelle Sethna had sifted through hundreds of pages of declassified files detailing the RCMP Security Service's interest in women's groups that began flowering in the late 1960s. RCMP spies infiltrated the women's movement in the early 1970s, monitoring marches and rallies to keep an eye on feminists, including Rita MacNeil, who would become a much-admired Maritime songstress. "She's the one who composes and sings women's lib songs," the officers noted and made some attempt to connect her to a "foreign power." Poor Canada.

† See Ian Brown, "Michael Healey and his play Proud," *Globe and Mail*, March 17, 2012.

‡ The Tory's love of supervision continues. When ministers of the crown routinely accuse environmentalists of "hijacking the agenda," "laundering foreign money," and using "... funding from foreign special interest groups to undermine Canada's national economic interest," one may assume that files abound in both official languages. In Eastern Europe citizens of the former Soviet bloc can now view the files kept on them by the secret police. In Canada we do not have that privilege.

UNDER THE GRAYWACKE HOUSE PROGRAM
TED JOHNS, CLARE COULTER, AND MILES POTTER.

a rundown bar in a sleazy part of town and strike up a rapport with the locals without making them feel suspicious or violent. This entailed dancing to country music with some of the resident gals and drinking a large quantity of draught beer with the resident guys. If you really wanted to impress Paul, you got up on the bandstand and sang a country song. This could be tricky because, as we rapidly discovered, people can be very touchy about their music. Mean drunks abound.*

The final cut included myself, Saul Rubinek (now a big movie actor), Miles Potter (now a big director), Géza Kovács (also in the movies for a while but, of late, "blue"), Clare Coulter (later a big Tarragon actor who also did well on British TV), Anne Anglin (ex-Stratford actress and one of the few people with actual training), Jacquie Presly (whom I've lost track of), and Greg Malone, later a founder of CODCO but, at this particular time, was searching for his soul and deeply unhappy. It was a motley crew and I cannot imagine a group of people with less in common or with more contrasting styles. Paul explained this by saying he didn't think of us as actors but as "forces," each of whom might bring some unique quality to "the mix." What that quality was he didn't specify.

Into this concoction you now add a large portion of Northern Ontario, which, then as now, is an uneven mix of dreams and desolation and heartbreaking beauty. It's hard rock mining country, lumbering, sport fishing, and a few small farms. Southern Ontario is coloured by people from the British Isles, Germany, and Holland—reserved, hard-working, reliable. Northern Ontario is much more flamboyant—lots of French,

* This kind of hands-on research had been by now well established not only in *The Farm Show* but in shows like *Free Ride,* which required each actor to hitchhike across Canada.

Finns, Russians, Swedes, Indigenous peoples, and oddballs from almost everywhere. In a bar in Northern Ontario you could meet people from almost any class of society—sometimes people who had made and lost a million maybe two or three times. Unlike the South they didn't care if you were rich or poor, taciturn or loud-mouthed. Life, they knew, could blow you to pieces in a twinkle and yet . . . and yet . . . as in the theatre or the stock market or the racetrack, dreams could come true. In fact, they did come true. It is said that the shortest conversation in the world is between two prospectors meeting in the bush. Nobody wants to betray what could be a fortune through a slip of the tongue or an unwitting clue. How many mines have been discovered because somebody stumbled onto something someone else had overlooked? A lot.

In the poolrooms and restaurants you could follow the stock market and listen to the rumours. Mining is half flim-flam. The trick is to keep the investors interested, make it look like there's big money rolling in (maybe there is). Trucks going in, trucks going out. Big secrecy. Guys flying in. Guys flying out. Wearing suits. Maybe they're from Bay Street. They say one guy had an American accent (or maybe it was German). Somebody said they were looking at drill core. Others said they were drinking champagne. Every Sunday it seemed half the town was off with their dynamite working their claims. Actually, when you think of it, few people looked as if they really belonged in the jobs they were doing. But they were giving it the old Northern try—until things got better. There were other things of course, but mining was by far the biggest campfire in the forest. It cast its weird and flickering light over everything and of course over us, the newly arrived.

We set up shop in an abandoned stone building a few miles outside of Cobalt. We sat around looking out the vacant windows and contemplating the solitude. I don't recall ever seeing a stage manager. At the time I thought this was normal and did not realize that such an oversight was enough to send Equity ballistic. Not to mention the stage managers. Stage managers are no friend of collectives because if there's no script, no lights, no time sheets, no call boards, and no big production machine to organize, what are they there for? Not that this deters them. They would be quite happy to sit in an empty room all day if necessary. In fact, I've seen them do it. They will stare at the wall, watch the clock, announce the break, and take home a salary much higher than any of the actors, even though there's no one there. It's worth stating that they have acquired this power by legitimate means because they are great goers to meetings, takers of notes, proposers of motions, voters on amendments, and creators of rules. As a result they are happy dwellers in the very heart of bureaucratic theatre.

I am quite aware that in a "normal" theatre good stage managers facilitate things, smooth over disagreements, anticipate problems, help create a good working environment, and, indeed, act as the "perfect head waiter" as Miles once put it. However, the bad ones are abrasive, create problems, and make everyone dread coming to rehearsal. As soon as the director leaves the show, it is the stage manager's duty to give acting and blocking notes and make up a semi-secret show report that is shipped off to the director, wherever he or she may be. Some take advantage of this to act as spies and to hang around during warm-ups and note who says what to whom, especially about the absentee director. Finally, having watched many hours of rehearsals and having observed more than one bit of boneheaded direction and appalling misuse of talent, many stage managers aspire to be directors, although when they do, as Paul put it, they usually "direct like stage managers."

Our designer was Paul Williams, who was forever grateful to Paul because, by giving him a job, Paul allowed him to qualify for landed immigrant status, escape the Vietnam War, and eventually become a Canadian citizen. He didn't work in an office but was out every day exploring the countryside. A mine lasts from about thirty to fifty years and then the place is abandoned. Towns sit empty. Huge machines flop about like rusting dinosaurs. Every so often he would bring in something for us to play with. Some oddball contraption he'd found or maybe a strange plant or a crystal. One day we came in and he'd suspended a rope from the ceiling. He left it there for a while until we'd done almost everything imaginable with it and then he took it away and brought in something else. Some days he'd just sit there and take notes and think. Or he'd tell us about some interesting place he had found and take us there. In later life he built a boat and sailed it from Vancouver to Nova Scotia. Being green, I thought this was what designers did.

So what went on in these "rehearsals," these so-called "repetitions" as the French call them? Well, to begin with, we started with "show and tell." Describe, for example, your trip up there. Describe where you're living. Your first impressions. If you started to talk you were almost immediately stopped. The idea was to show, not tell. To perform, not narrate. Gradually you started to realize that everything has an emotion. Travel has an emotion, colour has an emotion, buildings have an emotion, and this can be translated into sound and action and transformations. Someone's account of their trip might be, say, half an hour long and contain, maybe, six words. Eventually we made our way through all the stagecraft first introduced in *The Farm Show*—word painting, freeze stops, voice portraits, illustrated poems, monologues, physical transformations, etc.—all of which is now common in theatre classes but were new then. What we did not do was form trust circles, play theatre games, or draw on personal or confessionary experience.

Then there were the people. We tried to pick up accents, phrases, bits of conversation. For example, two guys are sitting on a park bench. One guy, out of nowhere, suddenly says, "Lonely. Talk about the desert. You should see that Regina." Or, "Look at her. She's not wearing enough clothes to clean a shotgun."

We started to learn the geography: the Tri-Towns, Elk Lake, Larder Lake, Kenogami, Swastika, Matachewan. We started to search out what people did, what they worked at, what they talked about. We created characters. We had one exercise called "scening in," wherein one actor would assume a character and the other actors would zoom in from all directions confronting them with sudden choices, e.g., "I'm your father" or "I'm your grade-six teacher" or "I'm a character from a movie," etc. We had another thing called "mind tracking" where people would wander around thinking about things and then every now and again someone would utter a word or a phrase or sometimes break into a song or a monologue. Some might choose to partake in the monologue and even create a scene. Others might keep going or they might stand and watch until that person finished their piece. Then the wandering would resume until someone else thought they had something they'd like to try. This could go on for hours. Some days, if everybody got into the zone, it could be quite astonishing. I don't think any of this material was ever used, but it got us thinking.

Sometimes Paul would set us exercises—write a song, say, or take a trip in the woods, "Show me three characters you saw in the bar last night." That sort of thing. Linda Griffiths claimed that her career began when she started to describe a movie and Paul interrupted to say, "Why don't you *be* the movie?" The point is we were not making scenes here and we were certainly not even thinking about making a play. We were discovering the ingredients of whatever it was we were going to make the play about later. So week after week we ground away until all the obvious things had been said and done and it became harder and harder to think of new things. The efficiency curve dropped like a stone. However, if I were to make a rule about playwriting, I'd say write until things start to get hard. Then throw everything out and start from there, because that's when things get interesting and that's what your play is probably going to be about. I didn't make that up, by the way. So it's probably someone's intellectual property and it might be wise not to think about it unless you have written permission.

As you can see, this is all a long way from having a reading or conducting a workshop. Not only was there no writer, but Paul got very spooked if he saw anything written down, especially if it resembled a script. He was convinced that scripts (like stage managers) made actors stupid. It deadened their ears, dulled their eyes, made them stop thinking and looking and, most important, it made them lazy about remembering things. He believed that if you concentrated hard enough your body would remember things, even if your brain did not, and if neither remembered it probably wasn't that important anyway.

When I protested the waste of what I thought were some pretty impressive performances, he replied with the story of Virgil throwing his manuscript into the fire until a friend restrained him and convinced him to write it all again. "Which was probably good—because I'll bet his memory of it was way better than it actually was."

Well, yes, maybe, but tell it to the library at Alexandria. Tell it to all the lost Greek plays. Later people brought in tape recorders but it didn't really help. People still couldn't remember. But he was right about one thing—writing, acting, and publicity occupy three completely separate parts of the brain. Paul also embraced and perhaps even encouraged the idea of perpetual chaos in rehearsal because all workers in the theatre have their own way of seeing things. The actors see things one way, musicians another, designers another, marketing people another, production people another, and, as Paul would occasionally concede, even the "word people" (i.e., writers) had a need for satisfaction, although you will note they are ranked a distant fifth.

As an aside, I should say that this kind of paperless theatre had other benefits. The eternal question for an artistic director is, "Where are you going to get ideas?" Out of your own head? By talking to other theatre people? By listening to the marketing people? I mention this because it is sometimes thought that artistic directors sit around their offices and pick through unsolicited manuscripts until they find five or six they like and that's their season (sort of like a publishing house). In practise, this is like trying to run *Maclean's* with whatever happens to get thrown over the transom. You might find one or two good things but, to be creative, an artistic director (like *Maclean's*) has to come up with ideas and commission them, or at least make sure somebody is working on them. If they don't—well, there's always the Tarragon model. Without paper the artistic director, even more than the actors, is reduced to listening to what Walter Bagehot called "the murmurings, the whisperings, the stirrings of the people." Without paper, the artistic director becomes another searching soul almost immune to the herd thinking of the regional theatres.

Graywacke is a sedimentary rock formed from accumulated sand or mud at the bottom of ancient lakes. Minerals are rarely found there because it is non-volcanic. One day Géza (one of the actors) came in with a show and tell. He had gone into a second-hand store to buy an electric teakettle. An ancient mariner emerged. "You wanna buy a teakettle? Sit down!" Some whiskey appeared. "I got some glasses around here somewhere." What followed was a series of free associations, which concluded with the following:

> The geologists told him—and
> the prospectors told him—and
> the miners told him—they
> said—gulp—there's no gold
> under the graywacke—but he

said—gulp—give me five more
feet—and they done it—and
there was nothing—and they said
whaddaya want now?—and he
said—gulp—give me five more
feet—and they done it—gulp—
and there was nothing—and he
said—gulp—give me—gulp—
five more feet—gulp—and
they hit—gulp—and there was
silver—five foot of silver—and—
they were rich—rich beyond all
comprehension rich—gulp—
rich—here—take the goddam
teakettle—I don't need it.

And so our play* acquired a title—a title which to my mind illustrated as well as any the state of Canadian Theatre. We too were looking for theatre in a most unlikely place. We too were pounding on with no end in sight. We too had received much advice to the contrary. Still, four weeks of this was enough to drive you nuts. We were getting to the point where we couldn't remember what we had done or where we were going or why we were even there. Poor Greg and his girlfriend Whitey were practically ill with homesickness. Saul's girlfriend was organizing a strippers' union (or maybe it was prostitutes; I didn't press her on the details). She was not in a good mood. Géza and his girlfriend retreated into a blissful world of love. I remember them dancing naked in the rain. Miles gritted his teeth and soldiered on. But you know things are coming apart when rehearsals close down for long periods so people can talk about what exactly it is they think they're doing when they're acting. Also, keep in mind that I was not really an actor. I had been in a few drama-club productions and I'd carried a spear during *The Farm Show* tour but, believe me, that is not the same thing.

What I was learning was what an amazingly plastic and creative machine an actor can be, especially when we delved into what Thompson called "the primary colours"—sexuality, fear, hatred, etc. "Two heads are better than one," I once told Michael Ondaatje, "and when you get five or six actors working off one another, things can get pretty crazy. Crazier than anything anybody'd ever think of on their own." "Maybe," he said, "but when a writer is sitting alone with his typewriter, things can get pretty crazy there too." Having read some of his novels I don't doubt it.

So . . . maybe what we were doing in these long rehearsal sessions was creating a concoction of craziness similar to the wild and unchecked unconscious of a great writer, what D.H. Lawrence called his "demon" and what we called, for want of a better word, "work." For me it was a combination of confusion, disorientation, and disintegration that I really couldn't understand. I used to think I was learning something and that we were actually getting somewhere and then the next morning it would suddenly seem all useless and incomprehensible. Especially with regard to acting.

Saul took me aside: "Ted, this is a craft. There are tricks to this stuff. You've got to separate things out. First, you turn. Then, you look. Then, you pick up the brick. If you do that, it's funny. If you don't, it's not."

Clare gave contrary advice: "You've got good energy, Ted. But that's all you've got. Stop imitating Saul. You look ridiculous."

Paul: "Ted, you don't seem to understand that these guys are actors. As soon as they get an audience, they're going to jump ten feet. You're going to be left so far behind you won't know what hit you. Sometimes you look like you haven't a clue what's going on."

Keep in mind that my previous experience of drama had been more along the lines of T.S. Eliot's "Tradition and the Individual Talent" or his meditations on the Tudor translations of Seneca in *Selected Essays: 1917–1932*.

Don't laugh.

I used to think I was learning something and that we were actually getting somewhere and then the next morning it would suddenly seem all useless and incomprehensible. Especially with regard to acting.

* *Under the Graywacke* is available in copy-script from the Playwrights Guild of Canada in a version transcribed and edited by myself.

Without Seneca it can be argued we wouldn't have Elizabethan verse. And without Elizabethan verse, well where would we be? "Few things that can happen to a nation are more important than the invention of a new form of verse," Eliot intoned. It's possible that he stole this from the French symbolists, as was his wont, but I was deeply impressed.

Then I discovered that the old rascal had stolen it from Plato. "When the modes of music change, the fundamental laws of the state always change with them," said Plato, or at least someone writing down whatever it was Plato said—which made me think of Shelley and the unacknowledged legislators etc., not to mention Thomas Browne's "what song the sirens sang, and what name Achilles assumed when he hid among the maidens," etc. All wild and heady stuff.

Then I heard The Fugs singing it and it showed up in their album, *It Crawled Into my Hand, Honest*.* So what had begun as an esoteric bit from Eliot? Plato? Shelley? the symbolist poets?—was suddenly as common as mud. Kids were dancing to it at rock concerts. It was bouncing off the walls. The world was coming apart.

Meanwhile, back at the rehearsal shed, Wanhope was rife. Miles and Saul, desperate for material, signed on for a "traverse" with some geologists. This turned into a cruel and soul-destroying march through a cedar swamp and up long hills that left Miles white with exhaustion. Saul, who is not a nature lover, sought refuge from the heat, the blackflies, and the mosquitoes by sitting in a secluded lake until he suddenly realized he was covered with bloodsuckers. His screams could be heard for miles, but the geologists, who have legs like Clydesdales, never turned back.

As an actor Saul loved "the business of the business" and eventually became obsessed with the labyrinthine twists and turns of fortune that each mine seems to entail. Miles, for his part, finally cracked the invisible wall that prevents non-miners from entering mines and returned with weird tales from the underground. Clare settled her formidable will into the character of Ma Bijoux, a woman with a flypaper husband (Géza) who rumbled about in her truck seeking reusable metal. (Years later I tried to revisit her character in my play *Cricket and Claudette*.) Anne transformed herself into beautiful songs of winter and the landscape. Jackie finally got a grip on the handcuffed world of women in the North and Greg latched onto Paul Hermiston, a gem collector, a curator, and a lone and quavering voice defending the North.

I mention all this to emphasize how very much collectives are the creation of the actors and how, in Paul's shows at least, actors were under extreme duress. In a paper-oriented theatre actors are not hired to have opinions.† Their function is to make the writer look good or, better still, the director.‡ This is in stark contrast to Passe Muraille rehearsals, where the main reason you were hired was to have opinions and to have more and more of them until your nerves were shredded and your brains were exhausted.

Early on I thought, "Well, we'll make up a group of skits and presentations and then Paul will pick out the best and we'll string them together and that will be the play." Gradually I started to realize that not only were our skits and presentations pretty low on the Richter scale but, worse (and this is when the bottom really fell out), Paul really hadn't a clue what he was looking for. His great gift was the ability to sit through days, if not weeks, of complete bullshit. Like John Franklin or Henry Hudson, he just thought that "out there" there was probably something. If we didn't find it, that wasn't his fault. It just wouldn't be found, that's all. In a normal play actors go through their own personal journeys, but this was different. This wasn't a journey. It was a collapse. The ship had sunk. The lifeboats were drifting about aimlessly. Not only was there nothing there, but people had given up looking. What kept me going was the thought that this would soon be over—which is why it was particularly difficult when I discovered I had been fired from my job at the university.

The chairman sent me a note saying there'd been a big meeting and the department (not him) had decided that I "lacked a mature attitude to my discipline." Standing as I was in a phone booth in late-night Cobalt surrounded by, let's face it, some pretty unlikely people, I couldn't help but think that maybe they were right. Maybe I did lack a mature attitude. Could I appeal? Should I appeal? Did I really want to appeal?

I consulted Paul. Did he, in his considered opinion, think I had enough talent to survive in professional theatre? "Come on in," he replied. "The water's warm."

The actors were no help. They were baffled by my consternation. I had at least six weeks more work. On an interesting project. With nice people. What more could I possibly want? I muttered something about a "career" but the idea of a career suddenly seemed so remote that I suppressed the thought and indeed it never surfaced again until recently, when I heard some kids talking about it in theatre school. I think the collegial atmosphere of the theatre arises from actors sharing their insecurity and terror and their outrageous turns of fortune. When actors meet they are usually celebrating their own survival. I tend to think of us as a frail flotilla floating on the open ocean clinging to each other by our fingertips.

* The Fugs changed Plato's "When the modes of music change, the fundamental laws of the state always change with them" to the more musical "when the mode of the music changes, the walls of the city shake" which is probably more about Joshua and the walls of Jericho.

† Shakespeare may be an exception. As John Hirsch once said to some poor struggling actor, "Why did you audition for this part if you didn't have some ideas about how to do it?"

‡ I am reminded of Noël Coward's comment, "I will always despise talented directors who choose a stinkingly bad play (*Marat/Sade*) just because it offers directorial opportunities."

Some are born, some are made, and some have it thrust upon them. I was now in the latter category.

Graywacke opened in an old movie house (the now refurbished Classic Theatre in Cobalt). The audience was entertained and appreciative but not smitten. Around Clinton, with *The Farm Show*, many of the actors made lasting friendships with their characters. Forty years later people still wanted to see the play and still talked about it as if it had happened last week. Here it was different.

One night we were invited to an after-show party. I remember trooping along in the darkness looking up at the bottomless abyss of the Northern sky. Some New Yorkers were there—Jewish people up for a good time in the primal wilderness. Inside there were drinks and laughter. It struck me that our host was just a tad overexcited but I thought nothing of it. Then I saw Saul and Greg being hustled off. Strange. I saw our host arranging chairs for a performance. Stranger. Time passed. Then the door opened.

Saul was lying on the ground with his shirt open holding a large knife with the point resting on his chest from which blood in the form of lipstick trails spread in all directions. Greg was dressed up as Goebbels and our host had slicked his hair down and stuck on a moustache so he looked like Hitler. He placed a needle on the gramophone and announced, "Saul shall play the Jew. Greg shall play Goebbels. I myself shall play Hitler." He then pulled himself to attention while Hitler's voice bellowed from the gramophone and the crowd roared, "Ein Volk! Ein Reich! Ein Führer!" As the record trailed off into a roll of drums, our host started in, "Sieg Heil! Sieg Heil!" ("Hail victory!"). After some preliminaries about the glories of existence in general, he started in on the injustices of federalism and the viciousness of the Ontario government.

—
THE SCHOOL SHOW
TED JOHNS. PHOTO BY JOHN MOFFAT.

> You could take Japan! And you could helicopter it into Northern Ontario! And you'd have to send the Mounties out to find it—it's so vast!
>
> And yet Japanese commerce sails on every sea, on every ocean—and we could do that too! The lines of demarcation have been drawn just below North Bay!
>
> Why do we pay a dollar for a loaf of bread when they can ship out ore for pennies a ton!

Saul's Jew squirmed and yelled out some kind of craziness. Greg stepped forward and delivered an impassioned version of whatever script he'd been given. The New Yorkers gripped their chairs in stunned amazement—as did we all. Apparently our host had been rehearsing all this for years and finally he had some actual actors to flesh it out. Talk about underground theatre. Talk about the "Volk." Talk about—dare I say it—dreampolitik.

I wonder if Saul ever recalled this evening when in later years he was doing *Unforgiven* with Clint Eastwood. Or Greg, when he was running for city council in St. John's, or *Das Kapital*, as CODCO put it. But I do believe our host was right. Northern Ontario should be a separate province. Until it is, it will always be Southern Ontario's second or third or possibly fourth thought: a minority culture within a minority culture. It is said that the servant always knows more about the master than the master knows about the servant. If so, I was getting a real eye-opener. I felt like Aeschylus when the eagle dropped a tortoise on his head. Except, of course, it didn't kill me. It just woke me up and made realize how little I knew about where I lived. How my education had largely been about other places.

Graywacke opened to some acclaim in Toronto, mostly because we had the amazing good fortune to have Urjo Kareda as the leading drama critic of the day. Like his predecessor Nathan Cohen and his illustrious contemporary Kenneth Tynan in England, he had a formidable intellect and a powerful prose style. When I add that we also had Jamie Portman at Southam News

Service and Mark Czarnecki and later John Bemrose at *Maclean's*, and that these people covered theatre right across the country—even small theatres—people are incredulous. These days if you're a critic in Toronto and you have to cover perhaps two or three hundred shows a year there is a danger your brain may go at least partially dead. But that's no excuse. The critic has a guaranteed income. The people he reviews do not, and it has been a long time since we have had critics who resembled anything like a reliable guide to what's going on in the city, let alone the country. Mostly they just stumble along in the wake of the hoopla. They are, as one critic told me, in the business of writing publicity, not criticism, and the sooner I got used to it the better.

Urjo was originally Estonian (one of the more moving prayers at his funeral was in Estonian), and I remember his large figure, always in a hurry, pushing up to the very front row of Clifford Leech's lectures on Renaissance drama. He was a ferocious hard worker, intent on getting high marks, and thinking deeply about his subject. He was that rarest of creatures, a critic who had actually prepared himself for his role as opposed to being assigned the job because he was deemed too dim for sports and too erratic to review cars. Like Nathan Cohen before him, he early on seized upon Toronto Workshop Productions and Passe Muraille as lively places and, as he settled into his job, he became a formidable force. I was playing *Naked on the North Shore* to half a dozen people until Urjo's powerful review sent me off on tour for the next decade. CODCO was doing *Cod on a Stick*, a Punch and Judy show with a satire on the CBC stuck on as an afterthought, and they too were playing to almost no one until Paul got Urjo to review their work. Suddenly they had a radio show, a tour of Newfoundland, and were the cradle of a whole series of great new shows like *Would You Like to Smell my Pocket Crumbs*; *Sickness, Death & Beyond the Grave*; *Laugh Your Guts Out with Total Strangers*; *Festering Forefathers and Running Sons*; and *Pleasant Irish Priests in Conversation* (about their sex lives), culminating in *This Hour Has 22 Minutes*. I'm sure there are many other examples, but what's exciting here is the idea that a major critic had, first, an opinion that mattered; second, was deeply engaged in the struggles of the scene; and, third, would actually seek out new work as opposed to waiting for the paper to send them off on a yearly update of the Broadway shows.

I can't recall Urjo's exact words but other audience members claimed *Graywacke* was much more riveting, imaginative, and far-reaching than *The Farm Show*, and some were quite smitten by it. One night, long after everyone had left, two people were still sitting in their chairs apparently much moved. I stopped to speak to them and they turned out to be Eric Peterson and his wife Lorna-Gail. Eric said they were from Saskatchewan and that he had been working in Vancouver and wanted to be an actor. They said it was a show unlike anything they had ever seen before and it had redefined what they thought of as theatre. They were absolutely entranced. Shortly after Eric joined up with Passe Muraille and went on to help make the first and second *Them Donnellys*, *The Adventures of an Immigrant*, *Oil*, *The Horsburgh Scandal*, *John Hornby*, *Far as the Eye Can See*, *Canadian Heroes Series Number 1: Gabriel Dumont*, *The West Show*, and *1837: The Farmers' Revolt*—as well as taking part in remounts of *The Farm Show* and *Alligator Pie* and helping to organize, especially through Lorna-Gail, a Saskatchewan tour of *The Farm Show* and, later, *The West Show*.

I mention all these titles to emphasize just how fast shows were being churned out. I arrived at Passe Muraille in April 1973. By November I had done a tour of *The Farm Show*, culminating in a performance at the Stratford Festival Theatre; a film by Michael Ondaatje (*The Clinton Special*); a run of *The Farm Show* at the National Arts Centre; gone up north for eight weeks to make *Graywacke* followed by a run in Toronto; and rehearsed and made *Them Donnellys* and gone on a tour with it through Southwestern Ontario, again culminating in a performance at the Stratford Festival Theatre.* Along the way, I typed out *The Farm Show* (mainly from memory), edited and published it with Coach House Books, and suddenly realized I was now a professional actor and a member of both Equity and ACTRA—all in the space of little over half a year.

On average I would say it takes a playwright six months to a year to make a play, or, if they are blessed with a dramaturge, many years. With paperless theatre, given the right actors, one could create a new show in six weeks, eight weeks, three weeks, even ten days.† All this was just Paul's work. In addition Hrant Alianak was producing *Noah's Kiosk*, Louis Del Grande was producing *So Who's Goldberg?*, Carol Bolt was creating *Pauline* (about Pauline Johnson) with the collective, and Cheryl Cashman was doing *City: The Toronto Show*. Add *The Alberta Cowboy Show* directed by Paul Kelman, *Breathing Space* directed by Jordan Deitcher, *30 Minutes from Downtown* directed by Howie Cooper, *Operation Finger Pinkie* directed by Janet Amos, *The False Messiah* by Rick Salutin, *Follies of Conviction* by James Roy, *Brutal Paradise* by Peter Melnick, *Remember the Truth Dentist* by Heathcote Williams, *Field of On*

* When I looked up *Donnellys* on Wikipedia, I was startled to see that Tarragon was given extensive coverage along with Peter Colley and some others, but there was not one word about the six different productions that emanated from Passe Muraille: *Them Donnellys* (1973), *Them Donnellys* (1974, a completely different show than the first, with a live band and real fire), *The Death of the Donnellys* (Blyth, 1979), *Urban Donnellys* (1980), *The Outdoor Donnellys* (Blyth, 2001, 2002, and 2004), and *The Last Donnelly Standing* (Blyth, 2016). I tried to remedy this but I am not sure if I was successful.

† Jim Garrard once said half-jokingly that the influence of Paul's collectives set Canadian playwriting back a decade.

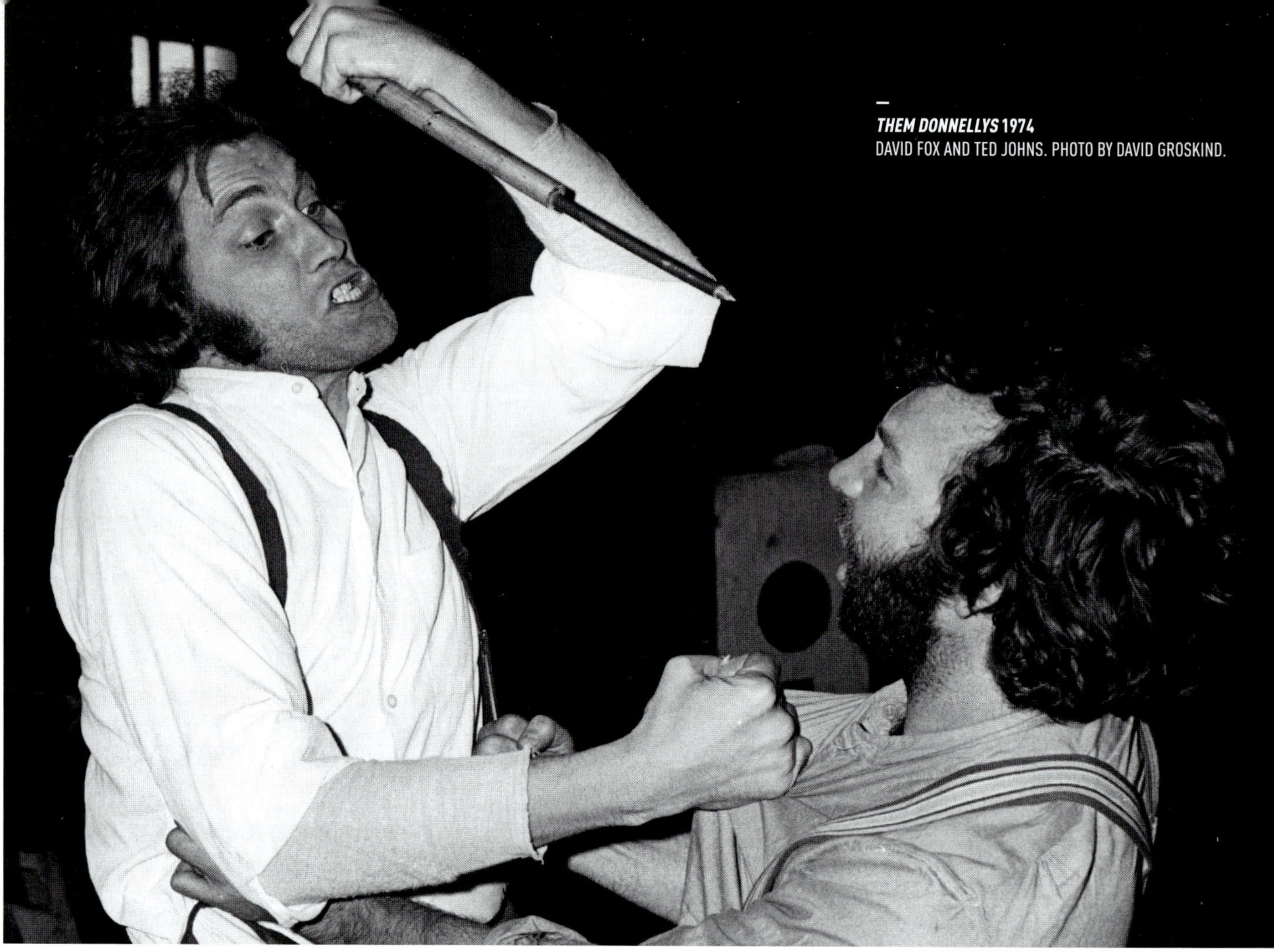

THEM DONNELLYS 1974
DAVID FOX AND TED JOHNS. PHOTO BY DAVID GROSKIND.

and Off by David Type, *Show of Shows* by Homemade Theatre, *Simone* by Megan Terry, *Canadian Heroes Series Number 1* based on paintings by John Boyle, etc., etc.

Even though Passe Muraille was about to lose its building, and most of its papers were carried around in a big bag slung over Paul's shoulder, it was a busy place. When David Fox phoned to ask if he could audition for his first job, Paul was not being entirely outrageous when he suggested he "try one of the smaller theatres." The theatre was producing between ten and twenty shows a year. In addition Factory Theatre, Toronto Workshop Productions, Toronto Free Theatre, Open Circle, Actor's Lab, Global Village, Young People's Theatre, and several others were also pushing out new material that I knew about but which, sadly, I cannot begin to document here.*

What a great pity Nathan Cohen was not there to see it. With his cape and cane, his double black coffees in his giant double-cup mug, his four packs of cigarettes a day, and his massive critical cudgel laying waste right and left, he would have had a wonderful time. As it was we had Urjo, who was gradually putting together a reputation and a philosophy and evolving into an arbitrator of a national culture. All this came to a sudden halt when Robin Phillips hired Urjo as a dramaturge at Stratford. I do not think this was an accident. I doubt very much that Stratford had any special need for advice about Shakespeare, but by giving Urjo a sinecure and of course flattering the boots off him, Phillips effectively defanged him. Poor Urjo. Having a life-threatening car accident didn't help. I remember Paul and I visiting him in the Stratford hospital. He was in great pain. His weight was a burden. Things looked pretty grim.

Then Glassco came along and said his great work at Tarragon was coming to a close and, bypassing the messiness of an actual search, he hired Urjo, whom he claimed was his only worthy replacement. Urjo toiled away with his playwrights and directors and, year by year, he put out plays and met his quota—but he was down among the pigeons now. He was no longer a hawk riding the mighty updrafts and signalling the currents of change. He may have been no Nathan Cohen, and certainly not a Kenneth Tynan, but when he hung up his critical skates, as far as Canadian Theatre goes, a light went out of the world.

* I am not a scholar, but the best book on this period that I have come across is by Denis Johnston, a theatre professor at the University of Victoria. It is called *Up the Mainstream: The Rise of Toronto's Alternative Theatres, 1968–1975* (Toronto: University of Toronto Press, 1991).

TED JOHNS is an actor and playwright who started his career in theatre with Passe Muraille. He was a core member of the collectives for several notable TPM creations, including *Under the Graywacke*, *Them Donnellys*, and *Oil*.

THE ATHLETES' SHOW 1976

BY BRUCE KIDD

I fell in love with Theatre Passe Muraille over *The Farm Show*. I was deeply moved by the boisterous affirmation of rural Ontario life, especially David Fox's (Bruce Pallett's) spirited critique of the political economy that kept farmers down, and the fact that TPM first staged it for audiences of farmers and their families in auction barns and community halls. I wanted to do the same for athletes. It was the summer of 1973 and the Montreal Olympics were quickly approaching. Although everyone expected Canadian athletes to win with pride in Montreal, many of them were broke, going on welfare, and stealing food to stay alive, and rarely listened to. I had just helped create an organization called the Artists-Athletes Coalition for the Cultural Celebration of the 1976 Olympics, because the Montreal organizers were threatening to eliminate the traditional Olympic arts festival as a cost-saver. One of our demands was the commissioning of new Canadian works of art about sport as part of a full festival. It was a heady moment of activism and cultural nationalism. I couldn't imagine a better example of what we wanted than a play about Canadians in the Olympic sports, so I sought out Paul Thompson. He had been an intercollegiate wrestler, loved the Olympics, and embraced the idea immediately.

So in the spring of 1976, with a grant from the Canada Council, we introduced the cast Paul recruited—Layne Coleman, Clare Coulter, David Fox, Janet-Laine Green, Joann McIntyre, Eric Peterson, and Booth Savage—to athletes and coaches, training gyms, track and swim meets, and all the political arguments, and Paul and the actors improvised scenes in Toronto and Lennoxville (where Paul was directing Herschel Hardin's *The Great Wave of Civilization*). John Gray composed the score; John Boyle did watercolours of great Canadian athletes that we turned into plywood cut-outs that the actors played to; Paul Williams, Michel Catudal, and Bob Pearson designed and built a wooden track to serve as the set, and somehow, magically, we brought it into Montreal as a play. It was performed at the Centaur Theatre the week before the games, then after the opening ceremonies moved it into a tent in the Olympic Village (next to the spot where the Canadian army paraded just before

—

***THE ATHLETES' SHOW* HOUSE POSTER**

opening curtain every afternoon) to show the athletes. In the final days of the games, we broke it up into wordless scenes (for those with little English) and staged it in the dining hall.

The play was everything I had dreamed about. It affirmed the importance of the Olympic sports in Canadian nation-building, while it critically examined the myths surrounding some of Canada's and the world's greatest athletes (Tom Longboat, Ethel Catherwood, and Vladimir Kutz). It dramatized the lives and loves of the current crop of Canadian Olympians, and the politics of Mayor Drapeau, the driving force of the games, Olympic selection, and athlete funding. In the final scene, David Fox played me reliving a great race. I still get shivers from the memory. Over and over, Paul and the actors brought new interpretations to familiar stories and debates. For example, Coleman's characterization of Longboat, the Onondaga distance runner who had long been belittled by racist sportswriters as an unthinking "natural," infused him with perceptive and courageous agency and prefigured his subsequent rehabilitation. (*Maclean's* voted him Canada's top athlete of the twentieth century.) McIntyre gave poignant voice to the fear and anger generated by the Olympic sex test that jump-started a Canadian tradition of opposition to the practice. The play was a hit wherever we took it, and to my great relief, the Canadian athletes liked the scenes about their sports and themselves the best.

In subsequent years, Paul did other plays about sports. In 1987/88, we collaborated on *The Games of Winter*, a play about Canadian athletes in the Winter Olympics that was improvised by a collective, then scripted by Miles Potter. Starring Dennis Robinson as Pheidippides, the witty but ethical ghost of the original marathon runner; John Jarvis as Poindexter, a cynical television executive whose antics anticipated the corruption of today's Olympic Movement; and Catherine McNally as the courageous Ottawa figure skater Barbara Ann Scott, it was performed in a string of towns and cities from eastern Ontario to Calgary in step with the Olympic torch relay. Then at the Winter Olympics, it played the Olympic Village before full houses of athletes. Again, it was the athletes who loved it the most. Some of them stayed after the performances to give us tips on how to play themselves.

But I still remember the summer of 1976 most fondly. It was one of the highlights of my life.

BRUCE KIDD is a Canadian academic, author, and athlete. He is an honorary member of the Canadian Olympic Committee and volunteer chair of the Selection Committee for Canada's Sports Hall of Fame, and is the principal of University of Toronto Scarborough.

MY APPRENTICESHIP AT THEATRE PASSE MURAILLE

BY PAULA JARDINE

In the summer of 1973, my high school graduation year, I saw an article about *The Farm Show* in *Star Weekly Magazine*, and I said to my mom, "This! This is the kind of theatre I want to do!" A year before we had been to see Tom Wood and John Neville in a restoration comedy at the old Citadel in Edmonton, where I grew up. They were fab, of course, but I had ranted to my mom all the way home with the pure outrage of a sixteen-year-old about how completely irrelevant the theatre they were producing at the Citadel was, and how I wanted to do theatre that was about my real life, about where we live. Apparently I wasn't alone, and it was the beginning of a very exciting time of Canadian theatre; a time of exploring/searching for/grappling with "what is Canadian identity?" I wrote to Paul Thompson at Theatre Passe Muraille, and said how I felt, and that I would like very much to apprentice with them. He wrote back to say that they did not have an apprenticeship program. Seeing as I had already told everyone I knew that I was going to Toronto to apprentice with TPM, I wrote back to say I would be arriving on such and such a date, 1974 (sometime in January, I think).

I took the train. In those days that was the cheapest option; travelling standby, in coach. It was a four-day trip. I ended up sitting next to Trevor Boddy, now a well-regarded architectural critic, who invited me to his parents' house for Sunday dinner and to watch the TV broadcast of *The Farm Show*. The night before I left Edmonton, for some reason I thought it was a good idea to cut my bangs really, really short. The result was a kind of sticky out fringe that looked like I had cut my hair with nail scissors. So that's what I looked like when I arrived, the unsolicited super enthusiastic and slightly weird looking seventeen-year-old.

They were rehearsing *I Love You, Baby Blue*, a collective creation about sex intended to get them out of their crampy little building on Breadalbane. And I guess it worked because then they bought the Ryerson Avenue building.

But when I arrived they were still on Breadalbane, a small two-storey brick building in a back alley off Yonge. I got put to work answering phones for *I Love You, Baby Blue* (it was a sold-out smash hit) and running the follow spot, which included doing a tight close-up on Paul Kelman's penis, part of a magic trick that saw his member rise to a stiffness capable of holding the magician's top hat. Maybe you had to be there.

The morality squad came and shut us down at one point—we had advance warning, and I was so mad when Paul Thompson told me I had to take the night off because I was underage and it wouldn't be cool for me to get arrested. I pleaded, "But I'm almost eighteen!" as if it would have made any difference to the police. We weren't closed for long, as I remember. I think the police just had to be seen as doing their job or something. Clayton Ruby was our lawyer.

Apprenticing at TPM was about the best and most thorough education and training I could have received. I was put to helping out with office stuff (including how to write grants, which mostly I learned just by watching), hanging lights, sweeping stages. I was assistant to the costume mistress for *The False Messiah* by Rick Salutin; I got to be in it too, as a young girl, and the back of Saul Rubinek's throne, and I did sound effects with John Gray. Anne Anglin, Clare Coulter, David Fox. John Palmer. It was an amazing time—really, the luck of timing. Passe Muraille was where I started to learn a lot more of the true history of this country, and where I grew up in Treaty 6 territory.

Starting with the John Boyle series of paintings, *Batoche, Batoche*, I got to be part of an experimental piece interacting with and responding to his paintings about the Riel Rebellion at Batoche, and Gabriel Dumont's escape to Buffalo Bill's Wild West Show (and his alleged affair with Annie Oakley). I was no good at brilliant improv like the others—Miles Potter, Eric Peterson, Ted Johns, and Janet Amos—but I think I did do one really good death scene, falling in stages from a great height. Despite my lack of improv skills, I was invited to join *The West Show* if I wanted—at first with no pay, my grandpa gave me some money so I could do it, but the cast, led by Janet Amos, complained and made Paul pay me. Connie Kaldor was invited on that one too. We were the Westerners, along with Eric Peterson, who's from Indian Head.

We worked with Rudy Wiebe, whose *The Temptations of Big Bear* I had already read, thanks to my mom, and Joe Fafard designed the set. He also brought some of his ceramic sculptures, Big Bear and Riel, and maybe Gabriel Dumont too, I can't remember. Riel was stolen. We had left him at the 25th Street Theatre Centre over the weekend and when we came back on Monday he was gone, and as far as I know he has never been returned.

Theatre Passe Muraille also funded my first three productions.

The first was a collective creation (what else?) with the after-school program in Kensington Market. The kids wrote the script and had their moms translate it into Portuguese. They designed and built the set—a replica of the market made from cardboard fridge boxes—and performed it simultaneously in English and Portuguese.

My second show was a dark little children's show I adapted from a book of children's poems by Susan Musgrave, *Gullband Thought Measles was a Happy Ending*. My third and last show produced with the help of TPM was another dark story by the late Sharon Riis, *The True Story of Ida Johnson*.

I think I missed the mark on that one—Nightwood Theatre did their own adaptation later that year that was much better. (Even though we really were altogether too casual about the fact that the protagonist murders her babies and burns the family trailer to the ground.) A couple of weeks ago I got to see *John & Waleed* perform in the Mainspace at TPM. I'm pretty sure it's been more than thirty years since I'd been there. I really appreciated that the space was cleared back to its edges, with the stage and set floating in the centre. It made it easier to remember where things were for different shows, Des McAnuff's *Faust* was kind of where the stage is now, and I remember the first night of *Maggie and Pierre* in the Backspace, and behind us is where the pigpen and cow stall were for Ted Johns's *He Won't Come in from the Barn*—those pigs stole the show every night.

I have complicated feelings about Paul Thompson and what kind of director he was/is. But I'm super grateful for the unparalleled experience it was for me. Wouldn't trade it for anything. Around about the same time I was reading *The Theatre and its Double* by Antonin Artaud, in which I read these words, "You must speak to the audience in a language they understand." *The Farm Show*, to me, completely embodied that view. It felt like coming home, or a kind of defiant and elusive sense of being my real self.

PAULA JARDINE's work has focused on reviving and redefining community arts and the artist's role in the community. Her work explores and cultivates cultural forms that celebrate and connect us to each other, the land, and natural cycles. Paula's training background is in dance, theatre, and writing, with an emphasis on Canadian history and folk traditions in ritual and seasonal celebrations.

Apprenticing at TPM was about the best and most thorough education and training I could have received.

CODCO
ROBERT JOY, CATHY JONES, DIANE OLSEN, MARY WALSH, GREG MALONE, ANDY JONES, AND TOMMY SEXTON. PHOTO BY PAM HALL, COURTESY OF ARCHIVES AND SPECIAL COLLECTIONS (COLL-178), MEMORIAL UNIVERSITY OF NEWFOUNDLAND.

BLACK WITH FILTH

ANDY JONES

My first trip from Newfoundland to Toronto was in the spring of 1969. I soon heard about *Futz*, a play that had been performed the year before and in which the protagonist has carnal knowledge of, and is arguably in love with, his pig.

My scruffy elite friends thrilled at the scandal this had caused in Toronto the Good. I was sorry I had missed it, but I went to see that same company's production of Chekhov's *A Marriage Proposal*. I was surprised that the theatre was so dirty that the fronts of the main character's white gloves were black with filth.

I knew at that moment that there was a place for me in the Canadian theatre. It was clear that I would not need a smoking jacket or an English accent. It was a turning point in my life.

In 1972 I returned and auditioned at Passe Muraille, where I got my first job in Upper Canada. I have since performed at Passe Muraille in all my one-man shows and in all the sketch comedies of CODCO. We have always felt that it is our spiritual home in Toronto; we love it like we love our pigs, and it is still filthy. What's with that?

In 1972 ANDY JONES's first two roles in Upper Canada were in Passe Muraille's *Dog in the Manger* by Lope de Vega, directed by Louis Del Grande; and *Pilk's Madhouse*, written and directed by Ken Campbell. In 1973 CODCO was actually started with a $300 investment from Paul Thompson. The main character in that dusty production of *The Marriage Proposal* was played by Asheleigh Moorhouse, who had been one of those given a summons by the Toronto police for his role in *Futz*.

PASSE MURAILLE AND ME, BODY AND SOUL

BY JERRY WASSERMAN

When I came to Vancouver from the United States in 1972, I was a student actor with a Ph.D., hired to teach English at UBC. I knew nothing about Canada, its history or theatre. Within a decade I was a Canadian nationalist, teaching Canadian drama and acting professionally in Canadian plays. Theatre Passe Muraille had an indirect role in all those transformations. I experienced the company's influence and work as a West Coast AmeriCanadian coming to terms with life in my new country, discovering an exciting new theatrical culture at the moment of its ascension.

Sensational productions of David Freeman's *Creeps* at Vancouver's Arts Club and *The Bacchae* from Tamahnous Theatre initially opened my eyes to Canadian plays. My first professional acting gigs were in David Fennario's *On the Job* at the Arts Club and Tom Walmsley's *The Workingman* with Vancouver's New Play Centre. (Decades later I chaired the board of that company, renamed Playwrights Theatre Centre and run by Martin Kinch, who regaled me with stories of Passe Muraille's early days.)

Passe Muraille started worming its way into my consciousness when *Canadian Theatre Review* appeared in 1974/75 with accounts of the goings-on in Toronto's alternate theatres, and college productions of *The Farm Show* and *1837: The Farmers' Revolt* showed up in Vancouver. *The Farm Show* didn't impress me—too rural, too local, too much mime. *1837* was another story: I was struck by the Canadian revolution that never was. Rick Salutin's rehearsal diary in the published script told fascinating stories about the play's creation. And the rumours of Eric Peterson's brilliance in both shows were substantiated by his jaw-dropping performance in the 1978 Vancouver premiere of *Billy Bishop Goes to War*.

Both Peterson and John Gray were UBC alumni and original members of Tamahnous. Gray directed *The Bacchae* that so impressed me. Peterson acted in an earlier version, then left for Toronto and joined Passe Muraille. Gray soon followed, and while touring in *1837* they co-created *Billy Bishop* in classic Passe Muraille style, mythicizing Canadian history in a tour de force of minimalist staging and bravura acting. A few years later, Linda Griffiths brought *Maggie and Pierre* to Vancouver and I was hooked.

All these shows operated on the principle of what I came to call Can-Do Canadianism. Characters disadvantaged by geography, gender, power imbalances, or their own limitations overcome those obstacles through sheer will, cleverness, perseverance, and imagination, the plays' themes reflected in their collective style and theatrical strategies. More than breaking down walls or making theatre as popular as bowling, that was what Theatre Passe Muraille came to signify for me.

Experiencing these shows made me see Canadian theatre, and through its prism Canadian life, in a new light. There were other reasons—Vietnam, Nixon, Reagan, my wonderful Canadian wife—but anyway, I was soon a convert. In 1985 Talonbooks published my first edition of *Modern Canadian Plays*. It included both *1837: The Farmers' Revolt* and *Billy Bishop Goes to War*.

I had my most intense Vancouver experience of a Passe Muraille play performing in the 1977 City Stage production of *Doukhobors*. We eight actors had to repeatedly take off all our clothes and set fire to our miniature onstage houses to indicate the Sons of Freedom Doukhobors' protests against private ownership, materialism, and Canadian law, and it was rumoured that the show might be shut down by the morality squad for our nudity or by the fire marshal for our conflagrations. Director Ray Michal, also City Stage's artistic director, felt the pressure. He left the show a week before opening, Jane Heyman stepping in for him.

Things I recall most vividly about *Doukhobors*: the rehearsal when we stopped miming taking off our clothes and just did it. The actor who seemed to have his scrotum connected to his vocal chords; when he sang naked his balls moved up and down. The nerves I felt going full frontal in that 150-seat theatre when my students came to a performance. Doukhobors from the Fraser Valley who brought us gifts of borscht and lit matches in the audience in solidarity with our fires. The Doukhobor woman on a day-pass from Oakalla Prison who sat in the front row and stripped naked when we did.

Theatre Passe Muraille helped shape my view of Canadian theatre and my world view, too. It gave me a new sense of just how potent theatre could be, body and soul.

JERRY WASSERMAN is a Vancouver actor, critic, UBC Emeritus Professor of English and Theatre, and recent inductee into the BC Entertainment Hall of Fame. Theatre Passe Muraille played a central role in both the Canadian Theatre History course he taught for many years and his *Modern Canadian Plays* anthology (now in its fifth edition). Performing in *Doukhobors* was a highlight of his stage acting career.

DOUKHOBORS (TPM PRODUCTION, 1971)
PHIL SAVATH, ALAN JONES, KAREN SANDERSON, DINI BAKER, BOB AARONS, AND JEANETTE COLLINS. PHOTO BY BOB NASMITH.

Passe Muraille

ADMIT ONE: PASSING THROUGH THE WALLS

BY JUDITH RUDAKOFF

In 1977 I was a Ph.D. student, newly arrived in Toronto, studying at the University of Toronto's Graduate Centre for Study of Drama. I was ostensibly specializing in contemporary Canadian theatre, even though there were few related courses available to me other than independent study arrangements. I soon realized that living in a city that was on the way to becoming the third largest theatre centre in the English-speaking world, where theatres committed to developing and producing Canadian theatre were thriving, provided me with the option of experiential learning. I was keenly aware that there were walls between professional theatre and academe, and I desperately wanted to find a way to live beyond the limitations of those walls, negotiating citizenship in both worlds.

Over the next few years Artistic Director Paul Thompson and then his successor, Clarke Rogers, gave me opportunities to do just that, even though I was a Ph.D. candidate with lofty, naive, and somewhat inflated expectations of what I could offer to Canadian theatre and what it could offer to me. Nevertheless, despite my lack of professional practical experience, TPM opened its doors to me: I read unsolicited manuscripts and wrote dramaturgical reports; I tore tickets as Assistant Front of House/Assistant Box Office Manager (sharing duties with playwright Anne Chislett who read me excerpts from drafts of what would become her first major hit play, *The Tomorrow Box*—which premiered in 1980 at the Kawartha Summer Theatre—as we sat in the lobby during the shows); I did whatever basic administration work needed doing in the mornings (Brenda Darling took over these duties in the afternoons). Ironically, it was my typing skills rather than my commitment to contemporary Canadian theatre that brought me my first substantial dramaturgical task, during the development of the legendary one-person play *Maggie and Pierre* by Linda Griffiths with Paul Thompson.

Those of us working in the office knew that Linda and Paul were working on something new in the Backspace. Just the two of them, every day, would spend hours together, with Linda improvising in the character of Prime Minister Pierre Trudeau, his young wife Margaret Sinclair Trudeau, and a political reporter named Henry. Paul, ever the instigator, worked indefatigably with Linda to create hours and hours of material that was recorded each day. When it came time to transcribe and edit the wealth of recorded material into a script, Paul called upon me (and Kit Dawson) to do what, in the Talonbooks published version of the play, would be called, with great generosity, "initial script preparation."

My involvement with *Maggie and Pierre* went beyond the developmental stages of the play, which previewed in the TPM Backspace in November 1979 and premiered in the Mainspace in February 1980. My husband, Myles Warren, was the stage manager for the production, and had devised the backstage magic that facilitated more than a dozen quick costume changes that the three character portrayals required of Linda. When the play finished its lengthy run at TPM, a cross-country tour ensued. Over two years the production would play to sold-out houses over long runs in theatres in Montreal, Ottawa, Edmonton, Calgary, and Vancouver, with short tours to Saskatoon and New York City (where, curiously, producers insisted on adding a second actor, Eric Peterson, to play the role of Henry).

By then I was finished my doctoral coursework and qualifying examinations at U of T, and in the throes of writing my dissertation. This gave me the freedom to travel with my husband as he stage-managed the touring show. I think it was Paul who gave me the title "Publicity Assistant." My duties and responsibilities were minimal, and rather . . . fluid. Mostly I attended publicity events with Linda where she typically spoke to the assembled members of the local media and answered their questions in character as Pierre, Maggie, or Henry. (For example, in Calgary, I accompanied Linda and carried the white stetson hat she would wear when talking to the press as Pierre.) While this might seem an insignificant role to play, touring with this uniquely Canadian production was, for a student of contemporary Canadian theatre, an extraordinary experience.

Each night, during the performance, I would sit in Linda's empty dressing room, or one adjacent, with the stage speakers on, working on my dissertation. I listened to *Maggie and Pierre* night after night, city after city, and while I don't really remember much about what my dissertation had to say about contemporary Canadian theatre, I can quote long passages from *Maggie and Pierre*, verbatim, to this day.

One of the most fascinating aspects of following the show from city to city across the country was observing the audience and press reactions to the content. In Montreal, where the Anglophone audiences at the Centaur Theatre still harboured vestiges of Trudeaumania, the play was about Pierre as a tragic hero. In Ottawa, in the audience each night there were serious-looking men wearing trench coats, suits, and shiny leather shoes who watched the show stone-faced: secret service, perhaps? No government representatives ever made themselves known to us, and Trudeau did not attend a performance. The most vivid recollection I have of audience reaction came from the Vancouver run of the show, in Sinclair territory, where the play was always about Margaret, the tragic heroine. True to form, attention-loving Maggie saw the show at the Vancouver East Cultural Centre one evening, and the atmosphere was electric as patrons watched both the show and Maggie's reaction to it. Afterward she came out with the cast and crew to party at our favourite post-show pizza restaurant in English Bay. Watching Maggie preen and hold court at one end of the table as Linda, at the other end, kicked back and unwound after a long show while the rest of us sat between them, transfixed, was an event in and of itself.

While I was a witness, not an active participant, the opportunity to experience this piece of Canadian theatre history first-hand was a privilege. As a novice dramaturge and contemporary theatre documentarian, watching a quintessentially Canadian production play out across the country gave me a greater understanding of audience politics than any theoretical lecture in a graduate program at university, or a chapter in a textbook could ever have offered. And for that I'll always be grateful.

Ten years later, in 1991, I edited *Dangerous Traditions*, an anthology of four plays from the Theatre Passe Muraille chronology (Blizzard Publishing). Each play, in its own way, was to my mind "dangerous" and exemplified the spirit of TPM. John Palmer's *Before the Guns* (originally produced as *Memories for my Brother, Part One: Before the Guns*) was produced at TPM in November of 1969, a sprawling, challenging play that broke through the walls of realism and demanded audiences relinquish expectation of linearity and colloquial speech. Palmer's engagement with youth and rebellion, a lifelong compulsion, fuelled this dramatic exploration of confusion and despair. First staged under the direction of Clarke Rogers in May of 1984, Sally Clark's *Lost Souls and Missing Persons*, her initial professional production, broke the rules of what a relatively small-scale theatre could produce in terms of scope of narrative, size of cast, and scale of production, and presented audiences with twenty-three characters and thirty-two scenes. Focused on loss and death, this play presents a quirky narrative, from Clarke's typically ironic perspective, about finding your soul and an affirmation of life. Linda Griffiths and Patrick Brymer's *O.D. on Paradise*, set in Jamaica on Jim Plaxton's realistic beach set complete with sand, lapping water, and the theatre thermostat set at a tropical level, had its Toronto premiere in frosty January 1983, and was embroiled in a scandal when the *Toronto Star* erroneously reported that actors on stage were smoking weed. A lawsuit ensued, was settled out of court, and the cast exonerated—they were smoking strawberry tea leaves—but the damage had been done: a major sponsor balked, and the hit play didn't have the type of production afterlife it could have sustained. Founding artistic director Jim Garrard's *Peggy's Song*, which premiered in February 1988, a tightly wound mystery that delves into the psychological makeup of its small

—

TPM HAS ALWAYS BEEN IMPOSSIBLE TO DEFINE AND THEREFORE CHALLENGING TO DOCUMENT OR CHRONICLE.

cast of characters, examining the boundaries of traditional and unconventional relationships in frank and uncompromising ways, rounded out the volume.

The anthology also contains a chronology of TPM productions from what I termed "The First Era," 1968–1974, ending with the demolition of the performance spaces at 11 Trinity Square after *Toronto Pixie Caper*. This section of the book contains archival photographs from some of the theatre's early productions and events. I worked with two tireless and resourceful assistants, Beverly Taft and Sally Szuster, to track down and verify information, photographs, and obtain permission to publish those images. This led to some adventures. One actor had left Toronto and was living without the benefit of technology on the side of a fjord in Norway. We faxed the "permission to publish" document to a neighbour of his, living on a nearby cliff, who shouted the contents of the document across the water, obtained verbal permission to sign for him, and faxed us back the executed document. Another actor, because of a newly found commitment to ultra-Orthodox Judaism and strict religious observance, would no longer deal directly with a woman with whom he was not acquainted, requiring a conversation through a locked apartment door, and, after much convincing, the sliding of the permission form under his apartment door for approval with a signature.

Details of the play calendar were gathered from a multitude of sources in print that included *Canada on Stage* (CTR Publications, 1975), Denis W. Johnston's *Up the Mainstream: The Rise of Toronto's Alternate Theatres* (University of Toronto Press, 1991), newspaper reviews and articles, archived press releases, original theatre programs, and posters. It quickly became apparent that there were many discrepancies: names spelled three different ways in three different sources, actors who were members of Canadian Actors' Equity Association performing outside of association rules under pseudonyms, dates that didn't coincide. I decided to go back to the source and, with the help of Beverly Taft, track down as many of the original artists as possible to check facts. This method did not prove as fail-safe as anticipated, as some contributors had only vague memories of details. As with documentation of any historical oral tradition, and despite our best attempts at accuracy, there may still be errors and omissions in the published chronology.

What I cherish most from the experience of compiling and editing *Dangerous Traditions* is the contact the project gave me with representatives and work from different eras of TPM, and the resulting first-hand understanding of how contemporary theatre research is inextricably tied to human interaction.

TPM has always been impossible to define and therefore challenging to document or chronicle. TPM is a community, not a set of rules, a mandate, or a building. Perhaps that is one of the reasons for its longevity: beyond walls TPM has been and continues to exist as an uncontainable entity, identified by its resistance to boundaries and to elitist notions of inclusivity/exclusivity.

Today "I am"—as I wrote in the introduction to one of my recent books, *Dramaturging Personal Narratives: Who am I and Where is Here?* (Intellect, 2015)—"hyphenated: I work as an academic-artist, documentarian-practitioner in theatre-dance within this culture–that culture." For demonstrating that a career beyond walls was possible, for all I learned from my involvement with TPM and its artists, and for taking a chance on me, I offer my gratitude and respect.

Developmental dramaturge JUDITH RUDAKOFF has worked with emerging and established playwrights and artists for several decades, nationally and internationally. Her books include *Performing Exile: Foreign Bodies* (Intellect, 2017); *Dramaturging Personal Narratives: Who am I and Where is Here?* (Intellect, 2015); *TRANS(per)FORMING Nina Arsenault* (Intellect, 2012); and *Dangerous Traditions: A Passe Muraille Anthology* (Blizzard, 1991). A professor of theatre at York University, Rudakoff is also a member of Playwrights Guild of Canada, and the Literary Managers and Dramaturgs of the Americas. Among her jobs at TPM were Assistant Box Office/Front of House Manager, Administrative Assistant, Publicity Assistant for the national tour of *Maggie and Pierre*, and, briefly, Dramaturg.

AS A DIRECTOR PAUL THOMPSON IS HALF IMPRESARIO AND HALF COLLAGIST OR MONTAGE MAKER. HE WRESTLES AND PERSUADES STRANGERS TOGETHER.

PAUL THOMPSON

BY MICHAEL ONDAATJE

Years ago, when the sculptor Joe Fafard first came into contact with Paul Thompson, he said, "When Paul Thompson dies he will probably die of enthusiasm."

Paul had hunted down Fafard in Pense, Saskatchewan, simply because he liked his sculptures and his celebration of place and he now, simply, suggested they make a play together. This was and is Paul's great pleasure and essential method of theatre—bringing together diverse talents, bringing together various "enthusiasms." This "stone-soup" technique has led to a strange, wonderful, mongrelized theatre. As a director Paul Thompson is half impresario and half collagist or montage maker. He wrestles and persuades strangers together. Apart from his usual team of actors, he has brought onto his stages a famous goalie, roller skaters, an aging fiddle player he met in a bar, singers, jazz musicians, schoolteachers, ivory-tower poets, and prairie sculptors to make those plays with him. So that in the end when we talk about "Paul" we are talking of a changing collective of artists.

I'd met and worked briefly with Paul in 1968. Paul was in training at Stratford (something like Abbie Hoffman at West Point), and John Hirsch—another great enthusiast—brought us together to work on dramatizing a long poem of mine. Paul's ideal theatre has always welcomed poetry along with roller skating and the step-dancing; he's never been scared of any of the arts, just as he has never been hesitant about any possible theatrical location. He's already done plays in auction barns and Toronto streetcars.

But it was *The Farm Show* that I saw a few years after the Stratford meeting that converted me totally into what Paul was really doing—which was to expand the boundaries of art—to widen and deepen it into our real lives. *The Farm Show* was and is a wonderful and very essential piece in our theatre history. And I, who had just a polite affection for theatre, was stunned by its possibilities. Hearing Janet Amos as a farm widow speak about an accident devastated me with the power of real speech. And the structuring of this play by Paul and his company in some way taught me about how to shape a book, more than any other novel or critic or writing school. How scenes were nestled and juxtaposed against each other. How politics was brought into a play casually and personally and so was made to feel an indelible part of life. How a scene evolved from a real everyday place into a metaphorical one.

The Farm Show also taught me how one could write about one's own place. Paul had taken the company to the farms in Perth County and made them research and compose a sort of biography of a place. It was a landscape he himself had grown up in. I still see that play as Paul's autobiography and self-portrait. It was his childhood map. Because the play was full of true complexities, because it was not just a play about "farmers" for "Toronto," it was also empowering for the community it was about. When the play went on tour to towns such as Listowel and Blyth and was performed in auction barns it always got a standing ovation.

For years I'd had my own past locked up within me and it was only after seeing *The Farm Show* and making a documentary on it that I was able to write about my family and the place I had come from in Sri Lanka. *Running in the Family* is, I suspect, full of uncredited devices gleaned from Paul and his company.

Paul made his dramas occur in landscapes and they concerned themselves with issues that were seldom written about. But he also brought an odd magic to those plays. "Passe Muraille" means "going through walls" and this is what all his works did. He has always climbed through walls into some surprising dimension.

Let me give you an example. In *Shakespeare for Fun and Profit* a theatre group starts up in the small town of Seaforth, Ontario, and they decide to go to Stratford to see how it should be done. At this point we cut to a production of *A Midsummer Night's Dream* at the Stratford Festival and the scene where a Maggie Smith–like Titania (courtesy of Linda Griffiths) falls asleep bewitched. We know that she will fall in love with the first person she sees when she awakens, and so we wait for Bottom to appear. But at this point one of the small town's company who has been lost backstage during a tour, now accidently walks onto the Stratford stage and thereby into the "rules" of the play. Titania/Maggie Smith awakens and falls in love with this mechanic from Seaforth. (I think played by Ted Johns.) We have now gone through a wall. And now Paul follows up the conceit. What happens is that Maggie Smith leaves the Stratford company and returns to Seaforth to live with Ted Johns.

The American theatre and film director Elia Kazan hated being called "Gadge," his nickname as a result of beginning his career as a techie. "Gadget." He was the guy who began by fixing things backstage. Paul slipped into theatre that way too, as a stagehand, then stage manager. Yet both of them are similarly subtle and surprisingly intimate with actors. (This is surprising because Paul is not the most verbal of directors. He will stand in front of you, using tortured body language in order to get you to go further with the scene . . . You find yourself talking and writing out of politeness. Someone has to say something. You'd have to call this technique of directing "creative bullying.")

Paul often speaks of the necessity of creating characters on stage with a certain amount of "thickness." All his characters are three-dimensional, even the villains. We seldom see a cliché of a person. The portraits are always generous. There is always someone real talking on stage. In some of his plays he has opened up historical characters for us—as in *1837*, his great work with Rick Salutin. Or by giving Anne Anglin a chance to dramatize the poem "The Song My Paddle Sings" by Pauline Johnson, which I always thought was an old chestnut. With it he created a truly powerful moment on stage.

Whenever a journalist interviews a writer, no matter how often the writer refers to his peers, the eventual article only speaks of the writer's career and self-obsessions. There seems to be no sense of the artist reading other writers or seeing other art; he or she just seems to emerge suddenly on the half-shell with no help or influence from his or her peers. Paul Thompson is someone who has had an influence. He is one of those who has been remarkably generous with fellow artists. Dennis Lee, Ken Gass, bpNichol, Roy Kiyooka have nurtured and supported those around them. Paul, as a friend and as a director, has had a tremendous influence on us. But more important, professionally, he was never meagre with his support for those on the outside. He has always left the stage or the theatre company open for a takeover, a revolution. And in a way that is why Passe Muraille always has these necessary revolutions. He has always made everyone around him riskier.

Influence is a difficult thing to tack down. James Tate said about working with the poet Donald Justice, "I think I learned more from watching him put on his overcoat than from anything he ever said." Well Paul never taught anyone how to dress. I told him once that if he didn't wear his Hudson Bay blanket-coat he wouldn't be recognized.

I think it's important to remember another Passe Muraille soul when we celebrate Paul. He was a cohort, a co-conspirator against the kind of theatre we were expecting to see when the '60s began. He took over at Passe Murraille from Paul in one of those revolutions that Paul inspired. This was Clarke Rogers. I would hate to imagine the Toronto theatre scene without the influence and work of those two spirits. And I'd like to quote something Clarke wrote in a letter when he was living in Europe in the last years of his life:

> Our apartment is well away from the Arno, a good country klick, near the Piazza Beccaria, one of the old gates to the city. The piazza, however, is named for the man responsible for the abolishment of capital punishment in Italy. The way they can change a name of an ancient piazza to commemorate the passage of living history, in a city that drips with the names of the famous—Michelangelo, Giotto, Dante, Gramsci, Medici, etc.—makes me envious of a culture which is not afraid of its living self. Can you imagine changing a street name in Toronto? Only Quebec—God I get tired of saying that—has the guts to get rid of whoever-the-fuck-Dorchester-was to remember René. The lesson here is not moralistic, simply that what was, no matter how great, is not

necessarily better than what is, or recently has been. Here streets and piazzas change their names to respect the ongoing life of the people who live here. Adelaide, Richmond, Wellesley, Carleton . . . is there really no one who has superseded the importance of these people in our lives and whom we could honour by renaming these streets? Honouring, in the civic sense, is simply an aspect of self-awareness and self-respect.

What Clarke says here, beautifully, is what the real revolution was about among the small theatres and publishing houses many years ago, and why companies like Passe Muraille and Factory and Tarragon and Buddies and Nightwood have come into existence. The alternative was permanent worship to the old gods. The alternative is still *Cats*, *Phantom of the Opera*, *Beauty and the Beast*—those musicals that could be from Mars.

In this time of recurring conservatism, not just in politics but within the media toward the arts, it is worth remembering the dedication of Clarke and Paul and their determination and their selfless love of the art. I hope their names inspire a hundred streets and avenues.

MICHAEL ONDAATJE is the author of several award-winning novels, as well as a memoir, a non-fiction book on film, and several books of poetry. Among other accolades, his novel *The English Patient* won the Booker Prize in 1992 and the Golden Man Booker in 2018; *Anil's Ghost* won the *Irish Times* International Fiction Prize, the Giller prize, and the Prix Médicis. Born in Sri Lanka, he lives in Toronto.

PAUL THOMPSON OUTSIDE THE NATIONAL ARTS CENTRE, OTTAWA

He has always left the stage or the theatre company open for a takeover, a revolution. And in a way that is why Passe Muraille always has these necessary revolutions. He has always made everyone around him riskier.

PLANTING A SEED

BY KIM RENDERS

In 1978 Maureen White and I were cast in Open Circle's production of *The Splendor and Death of Joaquin Murieta*. This was my first paid gig in Toronto. We all got a hundred dollars a week, usually in the form of a crisp hundred-dollar bill. In hindsight I realize what a pot of jam I had landed in. The show was a mélange of burgeoning talents—Allegra Fulton, John Blackwood, Allan Merovitz, and Arturo Fresolone are some of the names I remember. And a group of Chilean musicians that went on to heat up the Danforth as Compañeros.

It was in the midst of this creative energy that Maureen and I got together with Cynthia Grant (who was also working on the show) and Mary Vingoe to create Nightwood Theatre. The four of us had ideas and drive, and we were bursting at the seams with energy. Our first production was an adaptation of Sharon Riis's novelette, *The True Story of Ida Johnson*. We used live musicians, backlighting, projected text, movement and masks, and original poetry to create our theatrical impression of what Riis had written. From page to stage. But with our own unique artistic twist.

Perhaps not surprisingly our production got the attention of Theatre Passe Muraille. I have a memory of seeing Paul Thompson and Clarke Rogers waiting in the lobby after the show, hands in pockets, grinning from ear to ear. I feel like they were jumping. Everything back then, my world, my life, was just so big, so full of movement and colour!

They loved the show. Or did they love us? Thompson helped us negotiate with Factory Theatre to move *Ida* over to the Factory Mainspace (at Adelaide Court Theatre at the time) for a longer run, and then, most unbelievably, he gave us what he called "Seed money" for another show.

What's important to note is we hadn't asked for money. Outside of some help to remount *Ida Johnson*, we had no further expectations. We weren't developing anything at the time;

we didn't have any specific ideas for a new show. Paul just handed us a cheque, gave us access to the Backspace, and told us to go crazy. Make some theatre, he said.

Boom.

How we made *Glazed Tempera*, a theatrical adaptation of the paintings of Alex Colville, is a muddle of memories for me. I do remember that we dove into the process without asking how or why we were going to do this. We invented our own approach to collaboration; we used textbooks and photos to create a script; we rejected narrative; we worked with movement—just because. We created a style of theatrical presentation—non-linear, poetic, layered, multidisciplinary—that came to define our work in those early days.

I felt like I lived at Passe Muraille back then. We seemed to have full run of the building. (Is that possible?) I have a vague recollection of back rooms where we gathered to brainstorm and rehearse. I remember late nights and sneaking into the main office to use the Passe Muraille stamp machine for our mail-outs. And there were so many opening-night receptions, and Thompson's birthday party, and helping to clean up afterward, meeting so many people. And we were there. We had been invited. We were Nightwood Theatre.

Who knows what would have happened if Passe Muraille hadn't supported Nightwood in those early times? I like to imagine that the four of us would have made it without that leg up, and yet . . .

It is a fact that we were supported. We were given confidence, we were given a space, some time to play, and, most importantly, we were given a seed. To grow. With no expectations. Nothing required in return.

"Make some theatre."

And perhaps that made all the difference.

KIM RENDERS was a founding member of Nightwood Theatre. She worked in theatres across Canada, including over a dozen shows at TPM, where she was nominated for a Dora Mavor Moore Award for her performance in TPM's production of *Staller's Farm*. She was the artistic director of Theatre Kingston from 20072011 and ran her own company, Chipped Off Performance Collective, dedicated to working with Kingston artists toward the creation of large-scale community-engaged performances, until her death in July 2018.

1980

GLAZED TEMPERA

by NIGHTWOOD THEATRE

THE PERFORMERS:

Kim Renders
Peter Van Wart
Maureen White

Quotes of Alex Colville on tape are read by Jack Messinger

Cynthia Grant. . . . . Director
Timothy Crack, Flight Productions. . . . . . . .set and lighting Design
Peter Chapman and Steve Mackay, Late Capitalism. . . .. Sound Designers

Tony Ramsey. Technical Director
Boghos Kalemkiarian. . . . . .Scenic Artist
Kim Renders. . . . . Costumes
Caroline Wuschke . . . . Sound Operator
Robert Caspary . . . . Photographer
Sky Gilbert. . . . . Publicity

With the belief that theatre is the potential meeting ground for all art forms, Nightwood Theatre chose the works of painter Alex Colville as the inspiration for Glazed Tempera. The piece was conceived by Kim Renders, Maureen White and Cynthia Grant.

Phases in Glazed Tempera:

descending
geometry
the sea
the picnic
winter
departure
permanence
cat's cradle

We acknowledge the influence of Mabou Mines' Southern Exposure and the films of Marguerite Duras.

This season Nightwood Theatre has produced the following original works: The True Story of Ida Johnson, Soft-Boiled, Gently Down the Stream, and Psycho-Nuclear Breakdown and co-produced Handke's Self-Accusation.

Glazed Tempera was developed with "Seed" money from Theatre Passe Muraille and some assistance from the Ontario Arts Council.

Special Thanks: Cliff Simon's Sign Painting, Family Trust Real Estate, Karl Moritz, A Space, Factory Theatre Lab, Steve Allen, Be Wright, Bob Pearson, Terry Crack, and Pebs Shea

—

GLAZED TEMPERA

PETER VAN WART, KIM RENDERS, AND MAUREEN WHITE. PHOTO BY ROBERT CASPARY.

***GLAZED TEMPERA* HOUSE PROGRAM**

FOR VIDEOCABARET INTERNATIONAL

D. ANNE TAYLOR
MICHAEL HOLLINGSWORTH
ALAN BRIDLE
CHRIS CLIFFORD
SHAIN L. JAFFE

FOR SWORD BROTHERS PRODUCTIONS

VICTORIA STOECKLE
CHRISTOPHER GERRARD-PINKER
ANGELA THOMAS
BRAD CURRY
DAVE RICHARDS
JUDY SHINER

FOR THEATRE PASSE MURAILLE

CLARKE ROGERS
JIM PLAXTON
BRENDA DARLING
BIRGIT WORLIDGE
LINDA LEE
AMANDA MILLS
WHITFIELD SLIPP

FOR THE CAMERON PUBLIC HOUSE

HERB TOOKEY
PAUL SANNELLA
ANNE MARIE SANNELLA

* *

MAY/JUN '84

VIDEOCABARET INTERNATIONAL
SWORD BROTHERS PRODUCTIONS
THEATRE PASSE MURAILLE
THE CAMERON PUBLIC HOUSE PRESENT –

FIGHT

JOANNE HOVEY

BOB NASMITH
JACK MESSINGER
VIDEO–THEATRE
DIRECTED BY–
C.GERRARD-PINKER

—

***FIGHT* HOUSE PROGRAM**

RIGOLETTO
TRACEY MOORE AND DANIEL KASH. PHOTO BY MICHAEL COOPER.

Theatre Passe Muraille

BEYOND WALLS

TPM MEMORIES

BY AVIVA ARMOUR-OSTROFF

I wouldn't call myself a history buff, but I do love the feeling that old architecture inspires . . . a sense of lives lived, days before cars, petticoats grazing cobblestone, and even the faint smell of powdered wigs.

So I suppose I love the feeling of history, not so much the facts of it. Perhaps that's why I spent so many years in the bowels of Passe Muraille . . . that underground where horses were once fed and the flour was stored for the bakery; it vibrated with what came before.

I don't know what the building was built over, but it would not surprise me in the least if a very unique collision of magic rock created the vortex that funnelled the greatest of artists into the smoky cave. Or perhaps it was simply the handmade Ping-Pong table and the two-dollar beer. It was certainly the present-day company that drew me there religiously (I mean, Alan Rickman was once there, for fuck's sake!), but it was also the ghosts of those that came before us.

Layne Coleman was there in body, and so was the ghost of a young Layne, Hamleting around. Nasmith and Thompson, there in the flesh, Griffiths and Garrard, all alive and singing, but just behind them, singing in harmony, their pioneering baby selves, mining the way for their own elders. And there, woven in with the weight of the past and the fleet of the present, was also the buzz of the future.

To be able to straddle history, to sit in it, to recognize your part in the future of it as you shape the past, is a testament to the remarkable place that TPM is. Transcending time . . . stinking into the floorboards with a funk so potent even a hard-core renovation couldn't excavate the imprint of talk, work, sweat, love, tears, sex, drugs, rock 'n' roll, ideas, laughter, and creation that has grown in that place. This is my theatrical heritage, my history, my today, and my tomorrow.

AVIVA ARMOUR-OSTROFF is an actor, playwright, director, and producer and a member of ARC (Actors Repertory Company). Her acting credits include *He Left Quietly*, winner of the SummerWorks Best Production Award, Annie Sullivan in Western Canada Theatre's *The Miracle Worker*, and Layne Coleman's film, *The Shape of Rex*.

PASSE MURAILLE AND THE SPIRIT OF TRINITY SQUARE

BY MILES POTTER

Picture yourself walking on Yonge Street, either south from Dundas or north from Queen. Travelling on the west side of Yonge, pushing through the throngs (remember, all the pedestrian traffic is on the sidewalk), you come to the midway point of the block: the Superior Restaurant is across from you on the east side of the street, and on the west side you can slip out of the crowds and into a small alley—an alley that opens into Trinity Square; Scadding House to your right; the Church of the Holy Trinity ahead, fronting the square; and to your left is a large brick building with a set of double doors up some steps. You go through those doors and enter a vestibule: now to your left is another set of doors; move through those and you now find yourself in a huge, black, seemingly limitless space. Without lights the ceiling is invisible, the walls distant, no pillars to block your view of the huge mysterious space.

What you have entered is a turn-of-the-century Eaton's warehouse, the home of Theatre Passe Muraille in the late '60s and early '70s. It was in this space that many of the theatre's iconic productions were first produced. While shows were done earlier at Rochdale, and of course while many shows will be done later in other spaces, there was some alchemy about this combination of a truly black-box theatre (whose dimensions would put other "black box" pretenders to shame) and a crowd of late hippie/anarchic-but-hopeful theatre folks that appeared to spin the strangest material into gold. Not every show produced there was a barnburner, but there was enough to provide momentum, and combining that with the energy still burning from the sixties and Local Initiatives Program grants and perhaps a lucky combination of artists converging on Toronto made the alternative theatre scene of the '70s a unique event in Canadian theatrical history. At least that's how I remember it.

Some other things I remember from the period: the set for the original *1837*, a series of ramps and soaring "trees" made of rough lumber with the bark still on it; the theatre smelled like a forest, and the bark-sided columns soared up and out of sight into the dark, beyond the lights. I also clearly remember the audience laughing at a serious reference to Yonge Street; it was explained to me, a recent immigrant, that Canadians were unused to hearing local place names in their theatres.

I remember giant red banners descending from the ceiling for a production of *Bethune!*, and for a play about Charles Manson a piano wire was stretched from the attic (you had to be a brave technician to venture into that "ancient" attic) to the floor; at a pivotal point, blood was poured on it and it ran down the wire, illuminated and glistening—as explicit as it needed to be. I suppose my "thesis" is that although the Trinity Square home only lasted a few years before its walls were destroyed to make way for commerce, and it was not even the founding home for the theatre beyond walls, there was an explosion of sorts that occurred in those years and in that particular space; the after-echo of it is still reverberating. Whether it was *The Farm Show* or *Vampyr* or *Doukhobors* or *1837*, in my mind the "spirit" of Passe Muraille may have been seeded in Rochdale, but it bloomed in that vast dark warehouse, and wherever the theatre had to go afterward, touring across the country, another alley off Yonge Street farther north, various churches and halls and barns, and finally (perhaps) Ryerson Street, somehow a little bit of the spirit of that vast, almost-infinite-feeling space came with it; a spirit that said "anything can happen."

On the "anything can happen" front, jump ahead almost thirty years and into another dark space. It was the first preview (of two) of *The Drawer Boy*. We were finishing tech on a "found" stage at one end of the Ryerson space with a table and some props on it. The actors were working something out when a nice woman who (I guess) was in charge of PR (or at least was given a rotten job), slipped into the seat next to me:

"Um . . . I just wanted to let you know that no one is coming."

"Sorry . . . what?"

"Um—no one is coming tonight."

"You mean—the preview?"

"Yes—we have no reservations or . . . we haven't sold any tickets."

"None? No one?"

"As far as I know . . . "

There followed a discussion about various theatre schools in town and phone calls that could be made. The upshot was that the first preview was done for about eight people, and the next night maybe a dozen. The actors soldiered on as actors do, and we came to opening night with a new, unknown play produced on no budget and previewed for a handful of polite strangers. But Passe Muraille being what it is, the opening night was of course packed with all the usual downtown and Queen Street suspects, and no one, including us, knowing what to expect. As the second act moved toward its conclusion, there began to be a strange element in the atmosphere of the room. It is difficult to describe, but I began to sense two things: first, no one was moving, no audience shifting; and second, it began to feel that the audience was breathing with the actors. I had only had one other experience like it, in the first performance of *The Farm Show*, the play that had partly inspired *The Drawer Boy*. We had been so busy and preoccupied with getting this "little" play on, I for one gave very little thought to its place in the history of Theatre Passe Muraille. I sat in the balcony, looking down on the final moments of the performance as the lights very slowly went to black, and it was over. We sat for a moment in the dark, in total and complete silence. We could have been in Trinity Square, and for a brief moment, in the dark, in the silence, we were—and then the place erupted.

I haven't included any of the names of the artists involved in these stories; there are too many, and I hope you know who they are. I wouldn't have liked to inadvertently leave someone out, and if you are curious there are many sources to learn about them. Without these artists there wouldn't be the kind of Canadian theatre you know today.

MILES POTTER began his career with Toronto's Theatre Passe Muraille creating such iconic works as *The Farm Show*, *1837: The Farmers' Revolt*, and *Them Donnellys*.

FACADE OF 11 TRINITY SQUARE
PHOTO BY MALCOLM LENNOX. PART OF MALCOLM LENNOX FONDS, CITY OF TORONTO ARCHIVES, FONDS 351, FILE 2.

"DO YOU WANT TO STEP ON HIS OXYGEN TUBE OR SHOULD I?"

FROM CHARLES PACHTER: CANADA'S ARTIST

BY LEONARD WISE

Having outgrown his house on Shaw Street, Charlie sold it in early 1974 and bought his first building at 24 Ryerson Avenue, near Queen and Bathurst, and named it Artists Alliance.

With a ten thousand dollar loan from Margaret Atwood for the down payment, Charlie was now the proud owner of a twelve-thousand-square-foot building with parking for twenty cars, all for a hundred thousand dollars. He moved to a three-thousand-square-foot loft on the top floor; rented studios to fellow artists, writers, journalists; started a co-op gallery called ARTERY; and became janitor, landlord, consultant, renovator, mediator, and event organizer.

When Charlie noticed an abandoned derelict building next door to 24 Ryerson with its doors sealed, he climbed up the fire escape to try to find a way in and look around. But he was caught by a cop. "What do you think you're doing?" inquired the officer. Charlie had enough presence of mind to mutter, "I'm sorry, officer, but I lost my pussycat." The cop replied, "Okay, but just don't go in there." Of course the moment he left, Charlie sneaked in. What he saw was a derelict old building with high ceilings, dust floating through shafts of sunlight, a few pigeons flying around, garbage strewn everywhere, but it looked haunting like a Piranesi etching. He realized immediately that this place would make a wonderful theatre.

With some sleuthing he found out that the owner, a man named Sol Friendly, was in a sickbed in Toronto General Hospital. Charlie told theatre director Paul Thompson about the building and convinced him that the two of them should visit Sol to see if they could make a deal. As they entered his hospital room, Charlie joked to Paul, "Do you want to step on his oxygen tube or should I?" Charlie schmoozed with the old man. "You're not in great health," he observed, "maybe it's time you let go of the place." A few weeks later Paul got the building for $95,000 and Theatre Passe Muraille had a new home.

LEONARD WISE is a lawyer with a parallel career as a television performer, food critic, and screenwriter. He is the author of seven books, including the bestselling *Toronto Street Names*. He lives in Toronto.

CHARLES PACHTER, one of Canada's foremost artists, is a painter, engraver, sculptor, draftsman, historian, and speaker.

MY HOMETOWN

BY CHARLOTTE CORBEIL-COLEMAN

Theatre Passe Muraille is my hometown. It's the place I see on the inside of my eyelids before sleep and the place I won't return to for the holidays. I grew up with the exquisite myths and the sober realties, the magic and the mould.

This building has seen me, and being seen is always complicated. Passe Muraille may mean "beyond walls," but I know that building has walls because they're always watching me. They caught my very creation, the flirtation between my parents' eyes. They saw me through a betrayal that led to my birth. They winked at me, a baby in a backstage basket. They caught me, as a little girl, playing on sets and staircases when no one else was looking. They let me sleep in their green room. They noticed as I studied actors before and after shows; I learned to love by listening to actors' vulnerabilities, the whispers of fears and egos. I watched plays again and again on their stages, amazed by everything that stayed the same and everything that changed. They held me at my mother's memorial. They allowed me to hold court within them while I was electric with grief.

They saw me become a teenager; I learned to flirt down in the shop and on the roof. They listened as I filled up the Backspace with a play I wrote. They saw me through my early twenties when I left and then returned a few years later to direct a play in the very style their theatre was created in. They witnessed me lose their duchess, Linda Griffiths, too soon. They held me again as I said goodbye to another kind of mother, at another memorial, inside them. I'd like to think I've earned their respect, their ghosts, their love, but the real magic of Theatre Passe Muraille and its walls is that they don't care about any of that. They let us do the storytelling while they stand strong and watch.

CHARLOTTE CORBEIL-COLEMAN is a playwright and screenwriter; her mother Carole Corbeil was a theatre critic and novelist, and her father Layne Coleman was the artistic director of Theatre Passe Muraille for over a decade.

ELLE
SEVERN THOMPSON. PHOTO BY MICHAEL COOPER.

MOLECULES IN MOTION

BY SEVERN THOMPSON

Theatre Passe Muraille was a second home for me when I was growing up. I'd bound up and down the stairs pretty much feeling like I owned the place along with the other theatre kids. My father Paul had told me about his own sci-fi version of the French story *Le Passe-muraille* that he wrote in high school. Instead of a man who could walk easily through walls, my dad's story was about a boy who had detention at school. The boy had learned in his science class that all solid matter was made up of molecules that were constantly in motion. The trick, he figured, was to find the exact moment when the molecules were aligned and a person could cross through a solid structure without resistance. The boy set to work, trying to push through the school wall again and again until it finally happened and he escaped . . . only to fall to his death, realizing too late that he was on the second floor. Not the most optimistic of stories, but I was still inspired to push my hand against solid walls and tables just to see.

All around the theatre I watched artists, technicians, and administrators work to accomplish what must have seemed impossible at times—successful new Canadian plays. These people were and are still my heroes, endlessly fascinating on and off the stage. Off stage there would be dramatic shouting matches and fantastic parties. On stage there were so many brilliant productions and vivid memories for me, such as the incredible transformation of the theatre into a tropical beach for *O.D. on Paradise*, my mother Anne's heartbreaking performance in *The Stone Angel*, Clare Coulter in *Alligator Pie* stuffing her mouth with Weetabix cereal and then slowly spitting it back out to the delight of young audiences, Bob Nasmith in *Young Art* shouting riddles while his head sat on a table inside a glass bowl, Linda Griffiths masterfully playing all three characters in *Maggie and Pierre*, and Nancy Beatty as the tortured poet Elizabeth Smart.

A couple of years ago I was preparing to open the play *Elle* that I'd adapted from a novel and was performing in at Passe Muraille. I was cursing myself a little for coming up with this "brilliant" idea of writing such a demanding role. There was a preview with a small audience, and I was still trying to figure out what kind of play it was that we'd created. After the show a young woman who'd been there told me that she'd seen a ghost-like figure of a woman standing near the west wall in the theatre, behind the seating. She'd sketched a picture of her vision and when her boyfriend (who worked at the bar) took her over to Linda Griffiths's Stairwell, she recognized Linda's photo as the figure she'd seen. Linda had passed away a year and a half before. Was it really Linda that the woman had seen? Or was I somehow manifesting Linda's memory because she felt so present there? Hard to say, but to me it felt as though I'd somehow managed to cross over, to walk through the wall and safely materialize on the other side.

SEVERN THOMPSON is an actor, director, and playwright. Her father is Paul Thompson, who was the artistic director of Passe Muraille for twelve years, and her mother is actress Anne Anglin.

Passe Muraille

WHERE DID THESE PEOPLE COME FROM?

BY JOHN JARVIS

I once knew every part of that building on Ryerson Avenue; every one of its shadowed corners and every bit of its luminous, dusty stages. It seems like only yesterday that we breathed it all in: a smoky, sort of sensual, drink-drenched, coffee-fuelled world of what seemed like never-before-told stories. Paul Thompson, who bought the old building in the first place, insisted on constant exploration, constant interaction with the world outside, forever throwing us into collectives with a driven, toe-twirling abandon. How else could one find oneself, as I did, bare naked in an empty bathtub spouting off the top of one's head in language barely within one's grasp to understand?

Clarke Rogers was the other head of this new nationalist beast. With a flurry of sleepless words he marshalled playwrights and designers to give a new voice to the theatre, to be fearless with their edgy urban tales, and to never give up pushing against everything that seemed conventional, even when the theatre itself, its very bricks and mortar, teetered on the brink of financial collapse. It was a building where great friendships and high humour were born by all accounts, where every stone of the Canadian landscape was turned over and examined and poured into like the creation of a brand-new world. Brilliant, terribly flawed, surprising, and wonderfully intense. It was a golden time; one that was formidable for the careers of so many of Canada's great theatre artists.

I'll only describe my first play in the Mainspace, as it was an important baptism by fire in my life, and one that isn't forgotten too easily. It was 1978 in Paul Thompson's hugely popular collective *Les Maudits Anglais* with David Fox, Linda Griffiths, Diana Belshaw, Paul Kelman, Bob Pearson (building the set), and myself. We had begun work in Montreal that summer in the heart of separatist Quebec with an ambition to discover and perform our "Anglo" story using the very *joual* of their language. With Québécois playwright Claude Roussin creating a surprisingly true vocabulary from our improvisations and the intellectual guidance of Canadian poet Gary Geddes, we took the good people of Montreal by storm.

I began the play on roller skates as the spirit of Quebec, Le Bonimenteur, swooping about spiritedly—if not at times rather clumsily—pointing out our band of Anglo intruders to a constantly full audience of Montrealers who sat dumbfounded before us. I can still see David Fox on opening night rise from his character's deep slumber and speak those immortal words:

LES MAUDITS ANGLAIS

(A Theatre Passe Muraille Québécois creation)

Directed by:
Paul Thompson

Scripted by:
Gary Geddes

Translated by:
Claude Roussin

Set Design by:
Paul Williams

Costumes by:
Michael Joy

Lighting Design by:
Nicholas Ayre

Original Set Constructed by: Bob Pearson

The Cast:
Diana Belshaw
David Fox
Linda Griffiths
John Jarvis
Paul Kelman

For Theatre Passe Muraille:

Paul Thompson, Artistic Director
Donna Lebo, Administrator
Nicholas Ayre, Technical Director
Kitten Lyons, Office Manager
Scot Whitham, Master Carpenter
Stephen Allen, Master Electrician
Susan Serran, Publicity

Theatre Passe Muraille receives assistance from The Canada Council, The Ontario Arts Council, Metro and City of Toronto.

Special Thanks to Jean-Claude Germain and all those who helped at Theatre D'Aujourd'hui, Montreal, and The Touring Office of the Canada Council.

Toronto Theatre Alliance

announces

ALL - MAYORAL CANDIDATES MEETING

at

ADELAIDE COURT, 57 ADELAIDE STREET EAST

MONDAY, NOVEMBER 6 7:00 - 8:00 PM

in association with

Canadian Actor's Equity Association
Canadian Conference of the Arts
Dance in Canada
Professional Association of Canadian Theatres

We seek a dialogue between the mayoral candidates and all those interested in theatre and dance.

We feel all voters should be informed about the candidates' attitude toward the performing arts.

Do we have a vital place in the cultural life of Toronto?

Do we have a responsibility to the community?

Does City Hall have a responsibility to us?

JOIN US NOVEMBER 6 AND SUPPORT THE ARTS

"Whoo! J'ai pense pour un moment que j'étais derriere les lignes d'ennemis . . . Hi! Je suis d'Ontario. Charlie McCrae . . . Ou sont-je? Ou etre je?"

The audience erupted with a bemused delight that night as we had completely surprised them. Where did these people come from and how did they learn to speak like that? When we arrived later in the fall at Ryerson Avenue we were a play performed entirely in French that required English subtitles for our Toronto audience to fully understand. The building was alive that night with pure linguistic combustion. Who are these people and where did they come from? It was a perfect irony, of sorts. The *Globe* critic at the time, Brian Johnson, wrote, "They displayed a kind of courage, a disregard for appearances and 'acceptable' positions which is unique in this country. And the result is a totally unique show."

I remember a very hot August rehearsal for *Les Maudits Anglais*. Linda was restless and, let's just say, wonderfully unhinged. She paced about the stage muttering a jumble of thoughts and frustrations and rising emotions. "What are we doing here? It's the height of arrogance! We're insane to think we can tap into the soul of this place!" Paul leaped into action and convinced her to stop pacing for a spell, sit down, and tell us who she was, and what it was that she wanted to say. It began with a slight curl of the lip and then a sharpening of the eyebrow, then her voice launched in with that trademark nasality right from the very soul of her body, and slowly and quietly she raised her head and her eyes sparkled as if from a vision. She said something like, "You're not the only one around here with balls . . . " We were wrapped in Linda's genius; we were tumultuous in our response. Pierre Trudeau, the character, was officially born and a new language poured out of her like a great reservoir of liquid thoughts, some of them molten and scorching, many of them crackling with humour and a biting, sardonic wit. I can still see her chaotic raven hair flying about, her arms slicing the air for clarity, her thoughts giving a stupendous glow to her beautiful, impassioned face. It was a moment for the ages and still seems as if it were yesterday.

When I think of all the extraordinary artists that floated their ideas within its walls, whose spirits constantly drift about us, I find myself amazed and deeply thankful for a time when the actor, the designer, the director, and the playwright all fought together amidst blasted bricks and untold ambitions to forge a memory and leave a legacy for us all to keep hanging onto throughout our forever interacting lives.

JOHN JARVIS is an actor born and raised in Toronto.

—

***LES MAUDITS ANGLAIS* HOUSE PROGRAM**

LES MAUDITS ANGLAIS
DIANA BELSHAW, JOHN JARVIS, DAVID FOX, AND LINDA GRIFFITHS.

—

The audience erupted with a bemused delight that night as we had completely surprised them. Where did these people come from and how did they learn to speak like that?

KNOWING THE BACKSPACE

BY DAVID DEGROW

Everyone knows a theatre in a different way. When you see a show, you know a theatre for an hour or two. If you're a designer or a director you are in the room for a few days or a week, even though you've been imagining the space for several months before. If you act you spend a couple of weeks in the space, even a month or two. When you're the space technician you spend half your waking life there for a couple of years. What each of these experiences shares are the small histories you develop. Where they differ is how detailed those histories can become. Spend enough time somewhere and, eventually, everything has a story. Let me tell you a few of mine.

It's probably easiest to remember getting the space ready on a show night; running shows was what you did most. You walk up to the red graffitied doors and pull them open using your key as the handle. It never occurred to you to install an actual handle on the door, but you did screw on the angle iron that keeps skaters from bouncing off of it (the dip in the curb and the ramp up to the stage door made it perfect for a wall ride). You feel along the brick wall until you find the rheostat. It's a rheostat instead of a switch because you needed to dim the lights for the opening of *Jesus Chrysler*, when the audience started the show in the stairwell. You open the door on the right that you had to fix when *Madre* needed it to slam off stage, and you realized that turning the knob didn't do anything.

You walk backstage, which consists of an aisle stage left bounded by the wall and the too-skinny steps on stage and by the ever-draughty stage door and the green room at either end. You've kept that aisle clear of set pieces ever since you had to move a bunch of furniture at the command of three fire inspectors. You later learned that they were firefighters who had been pulled off an actual fire to do this, because people protesting *Seven Jewish Children* had reported a fire exit was blocked to stop the performance. You turn the corner into the theatre and walk up the eight levels of cascading red carpet and black leather seating. You climb into the booth, duck under the pipe that runs through the middle of the room (which still hurts like hell if you walk into it, no matter how much padding you wrap around it) and turn on the work lights.

You pull the vacuum out of the furnace room. That room used to be filled with old lights that were too big for the Backspace (or the Mainspace for that matter), so you traded them to Ryerson University for the pipe you used to rebuild the grid. You vacuum up the dirt and salt of last night's audience from the stairs and behind the seat backs. The holes in those leather back pads used to be covered in black gaffer tape until one very hot summer when the adhesive started coming off on people's clothes. So you pulled it all off and patched the holes underneath with automotive leather repair kits from Canadian

Tire. You collect the seating pads left from last night and stack them in the box at the entrance. This box that was built (by a very skilled high-school intern) to hold the extra cushions you bought for documentary screenings after *Highway 63: The Fort Mac Show*, because if someone was going to stay for three hours you wanted them to have two cushions.

You fill the mop bucket in the green room, holding your breath to avoid the smell that you were never able to find the source of, and carry it back on stage to wipe off the footsteps of last night's show. You've put something new on this stage almost every week. You've set up dozens of sets on it, focused hundreds of lights at it. You've climbed under it and over it, filled and sealed the holes in it, replaced the skin. You've painted the floor black twenty or thirty times. You've painted the walls five or six times: once a year, and then every time someone writes on them in chalk. Chalk never really comes off anything. You've put lights in the walls, built two-storey houses, rigged a wall of leaves to reveal a stripper pole, dripped blood from the ceiling, covered the floor with granulated cork, and dropped balloons on the audience. And next week you'll do something else.

You empty the bucket and climb up to the booth, sit at the desk, and look down on the stage. You've seen hundreds of performances from this seat. The first show you called from here was *Pyaasa*, the show that started your best friend's career, and yours. You've watched new writers tell their first stories, and actors with decades of experience lose their lines. One Fringe, when your second technician's child was born, you ran seven shows in a day, and back then you didn't have air conditioning. You watched a man in a zebra-print thong perform extremely acrobatic yoga with a huge swastika painted on his chest. You ran a show where an urn containing the ashes of the actor's father was a prop. And as you wait for the actors, the audience, and the show, you look up at the ledge of the booth window, where you line up all the thank-you cards people gave you at the end of their runs. And it's nice to be reminded that a show isn't everyday for everyone else.

That's how I know the Backspace. Remember one of my stories the next time you're there.

DAVID DEGROW is a designer, technician, manager various, and one of the co-artistic directors of Theatre Jones Roy. David was the coordinator of the Theatre Passe Muraille Backspace for many years.

NORTH EAST CORNER OF THEATRE PASSE MURAILLE, SHOWING THE BACKSPACE, 2014
PHOTO BY PETER MACCALLUM.

IT'S THE SPACE FOR ME

BY ERIN FLECK

It's the space for me.

Don't get me wrong, it *is* the people of Theatre Passe Muraille—the artists, the audiences, the leadership, and the staff—that make TPM the incredible place it is, and make the important work that goes on inside those walls happen every year. And I've felt incredibly lucky to have called Theatre Passe Muraille a home since starting work here in Toronto.

But when I think of my memories of TPM and my time there, the most visceral are of being within its different spaces, and the different people I was in each of them. Early on Andy McKim brought me to the theatre in his first year as artistic director, training as a marketing coordinator under the mentorship of the general manager, Colin Rose. I was just out of university and was already on board helping to found an emerging artist program with the theatre, the Elephants in the Room. At the same time I was sometimes working the balcony bar during shows, sometimes selling tickets as box-office staff, and doing all the jobs you do when you're twenty-three, just out of school, and need to make money to make your art. I'd go from the office on Wolseley, approving poster designs for the rest of the season, to the darkness of the upper balcony watching *The Drawer Boy* for the fourteenth time, while eating Kit Kats ferociously—but quietly—and sometimes confusing audience attendees buying wine at intermission who had happened to be in a marketing meeting with me earlier in the office.

When you're an artist that wears many hats, to find an artistic community that encourages that part of you is integral to your success. I had my first play grow and be produced in the Backspace; I threw my first shadow-puppet show at the wall on the Cabaret stage. *Those Who Can't Do* . . . and Caterwaul Theatre exist because I was given a space to experiment, to take risks, and to find myself as an artist within the building. The people that make TPM run are as adaptable and nurturing as the space they occupy and let the work that happens inside change the space as much as it propels young artists to create, think outside the box, and get things done.

For such a lively building, for all the hectic adventures of producing, performing, and collaborating I was a part of, I do find it funny that most of my nostalgic memories centre on moments of quiet. Trying to read by a sliver of light through the balcony window curtains while perched behind the bar during a performance, because no matter how good the play was, I'd been watching it for three weeks. Being one of the last people in the building after a late-night event in the Cabaret Space, somewhat tipsy on Steam Whistle, looking over onto the empty Mainspace stage while stacking chairs and contemplating the possibility of ghosts on the stairs. Trying to breathe in that tiny Backspace green room before opening a show and wondering if there was still time to flush the toilet before the other show in the Mainspace started because I wouldn't be backstage again for ninety minutes.

They're always memories of balance, of different aspects of myself: producer, administrator, performer, creator, all tied up in one human dreaming, hoping, making plans, always moving. Much like the theatre itself, still there, keeping everything and everyone together inside it, and making art happen in Toronto.

I'm so thankful for it.

ERIN FLECK is a playwright, puppeteer, and performer based in Toronto. She is one of the founding members of the Elephants in the Room and Crapshoot, Theatre Passe Muraille's emerging-artist program and late-night new work cabaret. Erin has toured her Dora-nominated one-woman show *Those Who Can't Do* . . . to Victoria, BC, and New York City since the show's premiere at Theatre Passe Muraille in 2011.

DREAM COME TRUE

BY ATOM EGOYAN

For years I had come to see shows at the beautiful old building. I vividly remember experiences at the space upstairs and hearing the footsteps of those shows when I was at a play downstairs. I was disturbed when there was talk of losing the floor and connecting the two spaces. I thought something would be lost, that an intimacy would disappear.

One of the beauties of any cherished theatrical space is that coming back will always evoke the shows that were seen there before. Would that vanish once the spaces had been reconfigured so violently? Would there be any trace of those important nights of theatre I had witnessed?

I needn't have worried. The Theatre Passe Muraille Mainspace was an architectural wonder, and it remains one of the best places to see live theatre in the city. The acoustics and sightlines work beautifully, and there's even a cozy bar/coffee lounge with stools that directly overlooks the stage.

One of my strongest memories of this new space was seeing my wife, Arsinée Khanjian, perform in the English-language premiere of Wajdi Mouawad's *Wedding Day at the Cro-Magnons'* over twenty years ago. I was watching from upstairs, and it was a huge moment to see someone so close to me inhabit a space that I associated with such magic and transformation. Afterward, it was a thrill to walk into the backstage area and explore the spaces that had been so mysterious and inaccessible before. It was like walking into the arteries of a body you thought you knew.

A year later I would see Arsinée in another play at the Mainspace—the haunting meditation on the Armenian Genocide called *Beast on the Moon*. Again, there is something so powerful about seeing someone so close to you undergo a complete transformation. In this case, she became a young girl.

While theatre is clearly a collective act of transubstantiation, it becomes even more evocative when there is some vestigial image of a roof on top of your head that separated you from the sound of actors playing in something else while you watched a show downstairs. I was shocked when I discovered that the radical renovation of this special theatrical space happened in 1983.

I was only in my very early twenties, yet I had already seen so many shows at this theatre. This was long before I had made my first feature film. All I could think about was the theatre and how much I wanted to be a part of it. I had been selected to be in the inaugural edition of the Playwrights Unit at the Tarragon a couple of years before, and a professional production at *any* space would have been a dream come true.

The dream was now coming true many years later as I saw my loved one become someone else in the place I could only fantasize about.

Before he became a filmmaker, ATOM EGOYAN was a member of the first Playwrights Unit at Tarragon Theatre. He recently directed the North American premiere of Martin Crimp's *Cruel and Tender* for Canadian Stage as well as several critically acclaimed operas. His production of Samuel Beckett's *Eh Joe* for the Gate Theatre (Dublin) won the Irish Theatre Award for Best Director.

INTO THE THEATRE AND THROUGH THE WALL

BY JUDITH THOMPSON

Theatre Passe Muraille is the funky beating heart of Toronto. I am not in the building itself very often, but when I pass by it on my yellow bike—and especially when I am in the audience or on the stage—I know that Passe Muraille is, in a way, my body in this city. And my soul. Unexpected corners, dusty and creaky but clean and fresh, both big and small with unbreakable bones, a splashy red door and just, well, happy. A happy place suffused with its history.

Passe Muraille is not shiny or sleek, and the seats aren't fancy. It's exactly what Canadian theatre is at its best: raw, real, with sloping floors and groaning walls. The shine of Passe Muraille comes from the underneathness, not the surface. People who live in Rosedale and shop at Whole Foods do not go to Passe Muraille—they never did. I am guessing they don't like the smell: Passe Muraille still smells of Toronto in the late seventies–early eighties; the Toronto of Rochdale and Kensington, of strip clubs and sit-ins and beads and bare feet and the air fragrant with pot and patchouli and people actually saying "groovy" and "far out."

I met Passe Muraille when I was twenty-five and my whole life changed. I had just graduated from the National Theatre School of Canada, which was, for me, like being released from captivity. Three years locked in a cold tower with no windows, chained to the floor, but absolutely, stupidly believing it was the best place in the world. A textbook case of Stockholm Syndrome.

Finally, I was out; I was free. It was exhilarating. I was free to breathe, to speak, and to sing full-throated instead of strangled by fear. Toronto seemed to me a kind of urban Garden of Eden; even though I had loved Montreal, as an Anglo I never really felt I belonged there, and anyway, we really didn't have time to experience the city. Toronto was a drug: addictive and galvanizing. I moved into a big house on Albany Avenue with eight other young people, most of them medical students, and one of them—the one who became my husband—an English student. Every moment was thrilling, and every new day full of possibilities. Auditions, meetings with CBC casting agents, readings, my own writing, more auditions, and more writing. I was happy for the first time since my childhood, though at the same time, my

THE CRACKWALKER
GRAHAM GREENE AND HARDEE LINEHAM. PHOTO BY JOEL BENARD.

world was collapsing: my beloved father was very sick, and in Kingston. I went back every weekend with my wild hometown friend who would later star in my play *Lion in the Streets*. She was going back to a scandalous affair while I was going back to a family home that seemed to be sinking into the ground.

I had begun *The Crackwalker* in Montreal on a desperately lonely weekend, and I continued to write it that first summer out, on a desk that was made out of a door. I wrote for about two hours every day, and then I would call my friends and read them what I had written. When it was finished, I sent it to my mentor Michael Mawson—the great Michael Mawson who also grew up in Kingston and had been the one faculty member at NTS who believed in my writing. He was taken by my many mask character monologues and advised me to listen to old recordings of Ruth Draper at the Toronto Reference Library, which I did. Once he read the play it seemed to possess his heart and soul and he became its greatest champion. He tried to convince every theatre in Toronto to do it and almost all of them slammed the door. Theatre Passe Muraille opened the door wide. Michael walked into Theatre Passe Muraille and put the play in Clarke Rogers's hands, and said, "Do not say no, do not say no; you are doing this because it must be done." Clarke read it and declared it deadly depressing, and a play he had to do.

So then began the torturous dance of creation within the walls of Passe Muraille. It was the forming of my identity as a theatre maker; Clarke Rogers was fully dedicated to the play, and for that I will always be thankful. He virtually climbed inside it with me and the cast: Joann McIntyre, Géza Kovács, Jane Foster, Graham Greene, and Hardee Lineham. It's as if we were in a deep dark bat cave and all we had were our headlamps. Clarke came to rehearsal with electric energy that was at best galvanizing and at worst frightening. When there was conflict, the girl part of me wanted to just run away and never come back, but the artist in me stayed and fought for everything I knew to be right. The stress caused me to break out in painful and hideous cystic acne, droopy eyelids, sleepless nights with lots of crying; now the broken-down quality of Passe Muraille truly reflected my interior and exterior being perfectly.

I think Paul Thompson was the artistic director at the time, though I am not certain. Every now and then Clarke would

—

PASSE MURAILLE IS NOT SHINY OR SLEEK, AND THE SEATS AREN'T FANCY. IT'S EXACTLY WHAT CANADIAN THEATRE IS AT ITS BEST: RAW, REAL, WITH SLOPING FLOORS AND GROANING WALLS.

bring me down to the basement offices and hand me a pen and order me to sign, and soon I would have a small but life-saving cheque. I suppose it was one of those OAC artist-in-residence grants that they were handing to anyone who wanted it in those days . . .

So the play opened and the audience reaction was volcanic. They devoured the play and every aspect of the production. It was the most thrilling moment of my life. My father had died the year before and I believe that this was his posthumous gift to me. I remember the standing ovation perfectly, the hoots and hollers, and the great revelry afterward. Someone told me I should be chained to a typewriter. I was flying high. My husband Gregory and I set out on our bicycles the next day in the cold November rain to buy a newspaper, we were so sure it would be a rave. We opened the paper to the arts section and there we saw an evisceration. The reviewer hated the language and referred to the characters as creatures one would "find under a rock." Class hatred ruled the day.

I cycled down Bathurst to attend every performance, and much to the chagrin of some of the actors and our stage manager—who I think might have been the amazing Cynthia Grant—I gave acting notes after every performance. I knew it was against Equity rules and I didn't care. We were aiming for perfection. We had very small audiences for the first week or so, but word of mouth is powerful, so by the second week we were filling the Backspace. The Backspace! It is still one of my favourite theatre spaces in the world. Its odd configuration, awkward little balcony, and tiny stage were just perfect for this play. Years later, in 2010, my play *Such Creatures* would premiere there, with Maria Vacratsis and Michaela Washburn, directed by Brian Quirt. The space was ideal for *The Crackwalker*, absolutely unique, and seeing-the-sweat-on-the-actors'-faces intimate. I still adore that space. Jim Plaxton's design was a giant sewer that filled the stage—a stroke of genius at the time, if a bit on point from today's perspective.

One moment in the production that Clarke devised is still celebrated: he asked Graham Greene, who was playing the Man, to make his entrance from the alley outside the theatre. Suddenly, in the middle of the play, the exit door was pulled open and a big drunken man with long black hair stumbled all over the stage and even threw up on cue. Some of the audience gasped and stood up in their seats. They only sat down when they realized, a few lines later, that Graham was part of the play. Many people tell me that this was the most memorable moment of the production for them. In hindsight, I feel that the shock was a sort of cheap trick that drew on the inherent bigotry of the mostly white and middle-class audience. But it was unforgettable.

In the last few years, as the artistic director of RARE theatre, I have turned to collective creation with communities who are seldom seen on our stages. My work in this form (*Sick*, *Rare*, *Borne*, *Wildfire*) is surely inspired by *The Farm Show*, which was created by Paul Thompson in 1972 with Passe Muraille actors. The company lived among the people of Clinton, Ontario, for a summer, and created characters and movement pieces based on their experiences. When I think of collective creation, of Canadian cultural nationalism as a reaction to the years of the cultural colonization by the US and the UK, I think of Passe Muraille. When I think of fighting tyranny, I think of Passe Muraille. When I think of speaking truth to power, I think of Passe Muraille. When I think of the voices of the marginalized, in those walls, shouting, talking, whispering. When we perform in Passe Muraille, we know that our words, our ideas are flowing through those old walls and being absorbed in the air, the sidewalks, the flowers, and the trees. Passe Muraille was one of the very first, and it shall, I think, be the last standing.

JUDITH THOMPSON is a playwright, director, and actor whose career began with the production of her first play, *The Crackwalker*, in the Backspace of Passe Muraille.

THEATRE AS A VERB

BY ROB KEMPSON

I was lucky enough to call Theatre Passe Muraille my home for four years—as both a staff member and as an artist. Andy McKim granted me my professional debut as a writer with our production of *The Way Back to Thursday* in 2014, and I was the associate artistic producer from 2011 to 2015. However, more than any project or position, he granted me the possibility to fall in love with a place, and with an organization. And for that, I am eternally grateful.

As I was trying to put this notion into words, this idea of falling in love with this place, I kept searching for a metaphor. Passe Muraille is like . . . what? A perpetual phoenix rising from the ashes? A complicated but loving family? A story, but one that is non-narrative and non-linear in form? None of those things felt right. The love I have—and I think the love we all have—for Theatre Passe Muraille is rarely perfect and never pure. It's an affection that is challenged and constructed and forged through hard work and dedication. Through a belief in the cause.

So then I thought about the cause. Theatre alone, though a charity, doesn't feel like a "worthy cause" on its own. But the innovation of theatre, of the form and of the discipline itself, is an exciting prospect. Or perhaps theatre that reflects the causes we encounter in contemporary Canada. Theatre that addresses social injustice. Theatre that activates protest. Theatre that changes the world. Passe Muraille does all that, but it all felt a bit wanky and pretentious when I wrote it down, and that is certainly not the character of this wonderful place.

And so I considered adjectives; how could I describe Passe Muraille? How could I describe my experiences there and the way that they have shaped me as a person and an artist? In truth, all the adjectives I thought about seemed flimsy. Certainly Theatre Passe Muraille is at times inspirational and offensive, joyful and subversive, provocative and pedestrian. Apparently, it is paradoxical. But none of these adjectives were sticking.

And then I realized how to talk about this place; I realized it with such clarity that it seemed dumb not to have found it the moment I sat down. Theatre Passe Muraille cannot be described through metaphor, or with adjectives. It cannot be described as a cause. Because it is *action*. Theatre Passe Muraille is a list of verbs: struggle, move, change, grow, create, adorn, imagine, discover, evolve, explode, break, breakdown, work, work, work. This place made me comfortable in the grey area, where the mess is. Because that's where the work is. That's where the magic is. I feel so privileged to have spent some of my career surrounded by that action and I know that it will pull me back again soon.

ROB KEMPSON is a theatre artist and educator, working as a playwright, composer, performer, and director. He spent four years working as the associate artistic producer at Theatre Passe Muraille under Andy McKim. During that period he performed in the world premiere of his musical *The Way Back to Thursday* in 2014, expanded the After Hours programming with the creation of the Songbook Series and Body Brake, developed new educational programming such as Student Creation Week, and worked with countless resident artists and companies. He has also been featured in four BUZZ Festivals. But Rob's crowning achievement was the year that the TPM staff went to Medieval Times for their Christmas party.

—
THE WAY BACK TO THURSDAY
SCOTT CHRISTIAN, ASTRID VAN WIEREN, AND ROB KEMPSON. PHOTO BY MICHAEL COOPER.

Theatre Passe Muraille

OPEN DOORS

KEYS

BY ANN-MARIE MACDONALD

Paula Schappert and I were descending the grand staircase of the Monument-National theatre in Montreal. We were second-year National Theatre School acting students and feeling all existential. Sitting cross-legged on the first landing, back against the wall, sporting a dirty blond Afro and a buckskin jacket with fringes, sat Paula's erstwhile lover, smoking a cigarette. Paula didn't use terms like "boyfriend." Clarke Rogers reeked of stale cigarettes, coffee, booze, and theatre. He was rangy and mellifluous. It was like meeting Mick Jagger. I had no idea what to say to him. And I never would; even so, Clarke would go on to make space for me to unlock my voice and start writing. He never imposed his taste; he never got in the way. He made the barriers disappear.

And he never hit on me. We worked together for days, one on one, while I improvised a one-person show about gender identity and sexuality that I never wrote, but which has fed me like an underground spring, and has recently surfaced to flow through a book I am working on now.

It was from Paula that I first heard of Theatre Passe Muraille. She had said to me, in 1978, across her rickety kitchen table on Montreal's "Main," through the smoke of her Gitanes, "I wouldn't say this to anyone else, just you. You're a writer, and when you go Toronto, you should go straight to Passe Muraille."

I did go straight there, but I was too shy and self-consciously uncool to approach any of the baby boomer gods and goddesses. Instead I went to see the first show I could: Linda Griffiths's *O.D. on Paradise*. I had just moved into my first very-own apartment, and the landlord, taking me for a nice responsible girl, handed me the key with the solemn proviso, "Don't lose it. It's a Medeco." I went to a Sunday matinee performance. The set consisted of a real sand beach. Afterward, I couldn't resist walking on it. And I dropped the key in the sand.

When I did arrive for real at Theatre Passe Muraille, it was via Nightwood Theatre, which was my first spiritual home. TPM became my second. It was like having a set of godparents whose job it is to help you keep the faith. Nightwood was my godmother, and Passe Muraille was my godfather. I did many shows at TPM, in both spaces, and I saw countless. I grew up there.

When Bev Cooper and I came to Clarke to apply for Seed money to develop our political comic spoof of Nancy Drew, he

—
ABINGDON SQUARE
JOHN GILBERT, GREG SPOTTISWOOD, JOANNE MILLER, ANN-MARIE MACDONALD, AND CAROLYN HETHERINGTON.

had us meet him at the Black Bull for lunch. He ate beer and talked about image banks, the collective unconscious, Marshall McLuhan, postmodernism. I don't know if we said anything. And I don't know if he had read the script we submitted or even our application. Ultimately, the whole lunch was an elaborate "yes." I think it was Clarke's idea that we should do a seat-of-the-pants late-night weekly series, then rewrite it into a three-part show in rep; except he made it sound way more theoretical.

He never imposed his taste. He never got in the way. He said yes.

By the time I had that lunch with Clarke, Paula was already dead. And when my first novel came out, Clarke had been dead for several months. Both died by their own hand. Too young, too sad. Both beautiful. I am grateful to have had them in my life.

I searched for an hour, until the stage manager told me she needed me to clear the set, and I never found my key in the sand. But who needs a key when you can pass through walls?

ANN-MARIE MACDONALD is an author, actor and playwright. She has co-created and performed original theatrical work such as *This is for you, Anna*; *Nancy Drew: Clue in the Fast Lane*. Her first solo-authored play, *Goodnight Desdemona (Good Morning Juliet)*, was honoured with the Chalmers Award, the Governor General's Literary Award, and the Canadian Authors Association Award.

Passe Muraille

MY DOORWAY TO TORONTO THEATRE

BY DEREK BOYES

Passe Muraille was my first Toronto theatre home. I had been plucked from Vancouver's thriving scene by John Hirsch to go to Stratford in 1984 and once I saw the depth and breadth of the talent in Ontario, I knew I had to relocate.

The door to Passe Muraille was opened by Bev Cooper, who I had gone to theatre school with in Vancouver at Studio 58. She made the move to Toronto several years before me and was a very generous conduit to the local Toronto scene. She had joined forces with Ann-Marie MacDonald and they were writing and starring in a weekend late-night version of an ongoing Nancy Drew mystery series. I went to see it and was thrilled by its daring satire and very funny dialogue. I was offered a walk-on for the next week and quickly agreed to join the fracas. I was to be dressed as a thief and get caught by Nancy in a brief preview of upcoming episodes. When spotted, I ad libbed, "*Sacré bleu*, it's Nancy Dreu!" and my door opened a little further.

There were some wonderful collaborations with Bev and Ann-Marie over the next few years. A full-length three-part production of *Nancy Drew: Clue in the Fast Lane* that allowed me to play one of the Hardy Boys and many villains. My first Hardy Boy team had me matched with Henry Czerny, who was seconds away from his Hollywood career but was a delight to play with. His schedule didn't allow him to be part of the holdover run so his parts were passed to Stuart Clow, who became my Passe Muraille partner for several years after the run.

As Bev and Ann-Marie continued to write together, Stu and I reaped the rewards of their creations. He played Bob Hope to my Bing Crosby and we each got to play dozens of wacky characters as *The Road Shows* hit the stage.

Both Stu and I were cast in Layne Coleman's *Blue City Slammers* that had what felt like a cast of thousands. I was thrilled to get to soak up Layne's caring, thoughtful, and slightly off-kilter directing style and his deep love and appreciation for the respect and safety theatre artists were offered under Passe Muraille's roof.

I wouldn't have believed it at the time but what appears to be my strongest legacy at Passe Muraille was the talk show that Kate Lynch, Bev Cooper, Arlene Mazerolle, Stuart Clow, and I produced in the closing years of the 1980s. I modelled it on a talk show that Jon Bryden, Colin Mochrie, and Ken McDonald built in Vancouver before I left and I felt it would work a treat in Toronto. Stu got a band together; I researched interviews; we all wrote sketches and acted in them and we did close to thirty shows over four years on various sets and backdrops that were playing the Mainspace at the time. Highlights include Ken Dryden performing his first live theatre sketch, Elwy Yost failing a movie quiz, Elliott Gould giving us the silent treatment until he realized we were on his side, and Simon Bradbury riding his Harley on stage and reciting an epic poem about biking. Arlene somehow always managed to convince a local pizza joint to send us free pizza so every show would have a snack for the audience. Not bad for a two-dollar cover charge. My favourite food moment was when we had chicken wings delivered and as a stand-up comedian (our one and only) was delivering a hush-provoking unfunny monologue, the sound of one hundred people sucking on chicken wings was deafening.

I feel very fortunate to have had Theatre Passe Muraille in my life as I began my Ontario theatre journey. I treasure the mentorship I received from those who had created and cared for its creative life. I admire their ability to overcome the challenges of their leaking, creaking, barn-smelling building and offer Toronto a daring, caring, and sharing place to dream and perform.

DEREK BOYES continues to be an active part of Canada's theatre scene since graduating from Vancouver's Studio 58 in 1979. He landed in Toronto after his first season at Stratford in 1984 and found an early Ontario home at Theatre Passe Muraille. Credits there include *Nancy Drew: Clue in the Fast Lane*, *The Road Shows*, *Blue City Slammers*, and the live theatre talk show *After Hours* he hosted and co-created. He is now a resident artist with Soulpepper.

NANCY DREW: CLUE IN THE FAST LANE
HENRY CZERNY AND DEREK BOYES. PHOTO BY CHERYL DANIELS.

CAUGHT
JAKOB EHMAN, MEEGWUN FAIRBROTHER, AND SABRYN ROCK. PHOTO BY MICHAEL COOPER.

WHEN I THINK OF THEATRE PASSE MURAILLE

BY JORDI MAND

When I think of Theatre Passe Muraille a number of impactful memories come to mind. I think of being involved in my first production at the theatre. The play we were working on was raw and real and wonderful. It also had a lot of swearing in it. The show was being marketed to high schools, a number of which cancelled their tickets because of the language. Regardless of what that impact might have meant for the company, TPM stood by the piece every step of the way. They did not apologize; they did not appease. They knew it was a story that needed to be told. And it did.

I think of being asked to join a small group of artists who worked with TPM to create their first set of emerging artist programs—programs that actually gave young people the chance to showcase themselves and their work. Shortly after, a number of theatre companies in Toronto launched similar kinds of programs. But TPM was one of the first to lead the way at the time.

I think of being asked to present a new play of mine at TPM's BUZZ Festival (a play intended for three male actors) and being encouraged to act it out entirely on my own simply so I could feel what the story was like on the inside. Those are just a few (there are many, many more), as Theatre Passe Muraille has played a meaningful role in my artistic life over the years—as they have for so many other artists in Toronto.

JORDI MAND is a Toronto-based playwright and TV writer who has worked with some of Canada's most prominent theatre companies. Her plays include *Between the Sheets*, *Caught*, *This Will Be Excellent*, and *Brontë: The World Without*. Jordi was a Resident in the 2017 Bell Media Prime TV Program at the Canadian Film Centre and has been a playwright-in-residence with Theatre Passe Muraille, Carousel Players, and Nightswimming Theatre. She is a past member of Tarragon Theatre's Playwrights Unit and the Stratford Festival's Playwrights Retreat. Mand is a graduate of the National Theatre School of Canada.

—
THE TALE OF THE TOWN
LISA MARIE DILIBERTO, FIXT POINT. PHOTO BY DANIELLE LOMBARDO.

THE TALE OF THE TOWN

BY LISA MARIE DILIBERTO

Was it 2008? I think it was. And I was the definition of emerging artist. Looking for opportunity on every corner, any way to get noticed, to meet people, to strut my stuff. One-minute pitch session with Andy McKim at Theatre Passe Muraille. One minute!? Okay, fine—I'm in.

I took my big *Tale of a Town* storybook, put on my best costume and my funniest voice, and presented my timed-out turn.

This led to a meeting, and another, and then a production in association and, finally, a season opener spot in 2011 for *The Tale of a Town—Queen West*, where I led crowds through the streets and alleys and into a reclaimed six-thousand-square-foot space to hear stories gathered about the living memory of this legendary Toronto strip.

But this was just the starting point. We just knew that there were so many stories and memories like this waiting to be recorded and shared in so many other communities. That's when my husband and co-creator of *The Tale of a Town* said to me, "Why don't we interview people in every province and territory across Canada?"

That's what I've always loved about Charles—he's so ambitious.

So I said, "Yes, let's do this! But first . . . let's have a baby!" because I guess I'm pretty ambitious too. We got ourselves a road map. We bought a Jeep and a storymobile—our recording studio on wheels—and me, Charles, and our baby son Zevon set off to tour the country!

Since then *The Tale of a Town* has toured to every province and territory in Canada recording stories and creating performances in collaboration with hundreds of local artists (and in the meantime we had another baby too).

In 2017 we returned back to where we started, at Theatre Passe Muraille, to tell the tale of our journey across the country in search for the meaning of main streets in Canada and that will feature some of the thousands of voices we have recorded from coast to coast to coast during this epic family adventure.

LISA MARIE DILIBERTO is the artistic director of FIXT POINT and co-creator of *The Tale of a Town*, a site-specific theatre and media project that has now toured to every province and territory in Canada. She is a Dora Mavor Moore Award–nominated director and has a range of experience in the field, most notably as playwright-in-residence at Theatre Passe Muraille, associate artistic director at Jumblies Theatre, and education coordinator at Canadian Stage.

Passe Muraille
TORONTO

BY JONATHAN SEINEN

It was a cold, blustery day in January 2010 and I was in Kensington Market when I got the phone call. Charlotte Corbeil-Coleman said that Theatre Passe Muraille would like to program the Toronto premiere of *Highway 63: The Fort Mac Show*, Architect Theatre's first production, into their next season.

Georgina Beaty and I had formed Architect Theatre in 2008 as we wanted to make a play about life at the heart of what was then the world's largest industrial project and, to our minds, the most important story in Canada: the Athabasca oil sands in Alberta. We, as a country, were being defined by the oil industry and yet what did we actually know about the people who lived and worked there? Fort McMurray was just north of where I grew up, and we wanted to see what it was like on the front lines. So Georgina and I brought together theatre artists from across the country—Layne Coleman, Charlotte Corbeil-Coleman, and Greg Gale—to pile in a borrowed car, drive up Highway 63, and share an unfurnished condo for three weeks in the depths of winter to see what stories this city had to share with us. We interviewed locals, toured the work sites, and experienced life in this twenty-first century boom town. And after we developed the show in Alberta, a fictional narrative mixed with theatrical portraits of residents, we instinctively felt that TPM would be the right Toronto home for the work. In the hopes of which, we presented a one-off of *Highway 63* in the back room of the Cameron House and invited Andy McKim.

And a few months later I got the call.

Passe Muraille became the home of Architect Theatre, where we were in residence from 2011 to 2013. After *Highway 63*, TPM commissioned us to turn our attentions to the uniqueness of Toronto and its recent past. Our team expanded to include Ingrid Hansen and Thomas Olajide, and *This Must Be the Place: The CN Tower Show* compared the city during the tenure of Mayor Rob Ford to the civic transformation of the late 1970s and was also a meditation on finding a home and looking for love in Canada's largest city. We transformed TPM's Mainspace into an alley stage—Lindsay Anne Black's set design was a scramble intersection—where we portrayed many community members we had interviewed and recreated city council's debate over a plastic-bag ban. We performed original songs about making your way in this town. We invited the audience to go speed

And there was something about that night—the humidity of midsummer, the clear sky, the lights on the tower, the being a part of something, downtown, at this festival in this historic theatre—that I thought to myself, *anything is possible.*

dating and to take a dance class with us and asked them what it takes to thrive in this city.

These first two productions established us as a contemporary expression of that great collective-creation tradition that TPM initiated here in Canada, and Architect Theatre's formative relationship with Layne Coleman connected us to that lineage of going out and doing first-hand research, improvising the material, and then crafting a play. For us, TPM was a place where making theatre about people and places that are not the centre by artists outside the centre with a sometimes-off-centre methodology was welcomed. Architect Theatre has continued to evolve our approach to documentary theatre yet grounding that process in the real through works such as *Like There's No Tomorrow*, informed by stories we heard along the route of the proposed Northern Gateway Pipeline in BC; *Unknown Soldier*, inspired by the actions of Chelsea Manning; and *Extremophiles*, which considers, through magic realism, motherhood in an era of climate change. Passe Muraille was a significant anchor for this formative period of our theatre company.

On a more personal note, growing up in Western Canada, my road to Toronto was a long one. But I remember the first moment when I felt, *this must be the place*. Still a student, I was at my first SummerWorks Festival in 2006 acting in *You Like It*, a queer reimagining of Shakespeare's play. And one night, after seeing a show at Passe Muraille, I walked out through the big red doors, and, looking to the southeast, there it was, the CN Tower. And there was something about that night—the humidity of midsummer, the clear sky, the lights on the tower, the being a part of something, downtown, at this festival in this historic theatre—that I thought to myself, *anything is possible*.

Turns out, it is.

JONATHAN SEINEN's involvement with TPM began in 2011 as co-artistic producer of Architect Theatre and an actor in *Highway 63: The Fort Mac Show*. Architect Theatre was in residence at TPM from 2011 to 2013 when Jonathan directed *This Must Be the Place: The CN Tower Show*. Elsewhere he directed Saga Collectif's *Black Boys* (Buddies), acted in *Body Politic* (lemonTree/Buddies), and wrote/directed *Unknown Soldier* (SummerWorks). He was born in Terrace, BC, and raised in Slave Lake and Edmonton, Alberta.

I'M NOT GOING TO EMAIL YOU, ANDY MCKIM!

BY BILAL BAIG

The first time my writing had ever been presented in a theatre in Toronto was at Passe Muraille.

It's April 10, 2014. It's the gala event fundraiser at the Paprika Festival where a twenty-minute excerpt of my play will be read. I'm wearing a really sharp blazer. I've stuffed six of my friends in my mom's van and we drive off from theatre school in Etobicoke to 16 Ryerson Avenue. We've got under an hour and there's a lot of traffic. I'm driving especially poorly because I'm incredibly nervous and somehow I managed to get the boy I like into my mom's van. Win. We arrive to the event four minutes before it starts. Double win.

I'm not listening to my own play. I'm examining the brick walls of the Mainspace. I'm shaking my leg. I'm trying to stop and focus. At times people in the audience laugh. At other times I hear a few gasps. Twenty minutes pass, the excerpt ends, and one of my biggest dreams come true.

I started writing *Acha Bacha* the spring before, and that was my first experience of writing non-white characters in a play. Then, when some of the characters started speaking in Urdu, I convinced myself I'd never hear this play aloud. Impossible. I began to make peace with the idea that hearing my play aloud would only exist in my dreams. I thought: Who can act *and* speak Urdu in this city? This doubt quickly stemmed into a greater doubt: Who would ever want to hear what I have to say as an artist?

So, when the excerpt ended and my leg finally stopped shaking, it hit me: the impossible became possible. A dream turned into reality. People listened.

Dan Daley was the magician who assembled the entirely South Asian cast (who could act . . . and speak Urdu!) for the reading. The Paprika Festival connected me to Djanet Sears, who worked with me as a dramaturge for six months leading up to the gala event. The festival gave me the space to share what I needed to say through the play and Theatre Passe Muraille was the building that held that space.

Another dream came true on that evening of April 10, 2014. I met my theatre hero. Anusree Roy talked to me. We sat on the bar stools closer to the mini-stage upstairs and chatted for maybe five minutes. My life was complete at the end of those five minutes. So, later that night, when Andy McKim gave me his card and asked me to email him the full play, naturally, I died.

Well, no, obviously I didn't actually die. I just couldn't believe it. No way. This isn't real. I'm not going to email you, Andy McKim. This is a trick!

Then, after some time passed, the voice of reason entered my head. This voice belonged to my dear mentor Damien Atkins. I recall Damien telling me that he initially didn't send his play *Good Mother* to Richard Monette at Stratford when asked to because he too didn't believe Richard's interest in his play was a real possibility.

And so I thought about this word a lot: possibility. How do we define what's (im) possible? What if it's possible that the boy in my mom's van liked me too? Or that Anusree had a good time talking to me? Or, what if, people not only listened to the excerpt of my play, but felt things or saw images or representations of themselves for the first time in theatre? And what if that could allow them to dream of other possibilities?

So, I did it. On May 21, 2014, I emailed Andy.

BILAL BAIG is a playwright and actor. His first play, *Acha Bacha*, was produced by Theatre Passe Muraille in association with Buddies in Bad Times in February 2018. His other plays, *Khwaja Sera* and *blue eyes killed him without blinking*, are in development at Buddies and Factory Theatre, respectively.

So, when the excerpt ended and my leg finally stopped shaking, it hit me: the impossible became possible. A dream turned into reality. People listened.

ACHA BACHA
BILAL BAIG. PHOTO BY TANJA-TIZIANA.

Some theatres have mandates about diversity. It's part of their whole costume as a company. Then there are those who actually practise it . . . inclusiveness . . . and their desire and willingness to hold such compassionate and supportive spaces helps take the sting out of those who just have it on letterhead.

SINGING PRAISES

BY MICHAELA WASHBURN

First off, I have always experienced Andy McKim as a warm, welcoming, and gracious human being, and it doesn't surprise me that the same can be said for my experiences with his staff. I believe when we are led well we have the potential to become exceptional leaders ourselves.

I have had the absolute pleasure of working at Passe Muraille on a few occasions, but a stand-out memory for me was during the run of Judith Thompson's *Such Creatures* featuring Maria Vacratsis and myself, directed by Brian Quirt.

This wasn't my first rodeo, but I was still in the process of reclaiming and integrating my spiritual practices as an Indigenous person of mixed blood with my holistic practice as an artist. That in itself has had its ups and downs, and although I have witnessed a shifting landscape of growing understanding and open-mindedness over the years, unfortunately, there are still times when the negative memories can stay with us long after the time has passed.

This, however, is not the case with TPM.

Backspace. 2010. Due to the heavy nature of the play, it was my preference to clear the energy of the space and ask for the story to be a safe place to meet and have an exchange. I would ask for protection for, as well as express gratitude for, all those who helped bring this story to the stage and for the audiences who would come to share in it. To aid me in doing this, I checked with Andy that it would be okay that I burn sage and smudge the space prior to each performance. Not only was Andy receptive to the idea, but the first time I smudged the space he and many members of the company and the creative team joined in as well. Talk about integration. What a gift!

One evening there were some patrons who were quite upset and complaining as they entered the Backspace to take their seats, as they were adamant they could smell marijuana. I could hear the altercation from the dressing room, and once again began to feel uncomfortable having remembered some not-so-pleasant experiences in other theatres in the past. I especially felt for the folks having to field this energy on what I believed was my behalf.

What transpired has forever lived in my mind as one of those moments where an ally rose to a gentle defence of a positive intention.

I could hear David DeGrow, the Backspace coordinator at the time, calmly explain smudging to patrons who were entering the space. I listened as he spoke of the ritual and its intent while acknowledging their concerns. He navigated the situation with such grace and generosity that I felt compelled to speak with him about it afterward. I shared with David that I could hear the altercation from the dressing room and wondered if perhaps I should change what I was doing to avoid future misunderstandings. I really wasn't interested in causing disruption, and certainly didn't want him to have to be in that position over and over.

Instead, David reassured me and encouraged me to continue on with my practice. He acknowledged the value of what I was offering and seemed to take pride in the fact that he could speak to "smudging" as articulately and wonderfully as he did and was willing to do so again. This is powerful medicine.

Some theatres have mandates about diversity. It's part of their whole costume as a company. Then there are those who actually practise it . . . inclusiveness . . . and their desire and willingness to hold such compassionate and supportive spaces helps take the sting out of those who just have it on letterhead.

It is an honour to be associated with TPM in any capacity. I am exceptionally grateful for this opportunity to sing their praises.

Based in Tkaronto, MICHAELA WASHBURN hails from Alberta and is a proud Métis artist of English, Irish, French, and Cree descent. Michaela has had the privilege to play on the deck of Passe Muraille's Backspace a few times, in Judith Thompson's *Such Creatures*, Falen Johnson's *Salt Baby*, and most recently as a guest in Donna-Michelle St. Bernard's powerful piece *Sound of the Beast*. Washburn is also a frequent patron of TPM and considers it one of her theatrical homes.

—

SUCH CREATURES
MICHAELA WASHBURN. PHOTO BY ALEX FELIPE.

A STRONGER ARTISTIC COMMUNITY

BY WEYNI MENGESHA

Theatre Passe Muraille gave me my first professional artistic home. When I was applying for theatre school at eighteen I could not find a Black Canadian female monologue to audition with. By the end of my first year in school I had switched to the directing program because I wanted to work with playwrights to put stories of colour on stage. The next year when Trey Anthony approached me to direct a new play she had written called *'da Kink in my hair*, filled with Black female monologues, I was ecstatic. Trey raised whatever money she could and we toured the play to Fringe festivals and small venues, until we got our shot with a co-production at TPM. I still remember how we screamed when Trey told us that Layne Coleman had come to see a showcase and wanted to program it. We visited the theatre together as a company and were moved. I remember looking out from the stage at the house and thinking, "The characters need to enter through the audience; I want everyone to experience all these Black women beside them as they take the stage."

Layne was so supportive of the show from the beginning. He also supported our desire to get involved in the marketing, and some of the unorthodox ways we wanted to target different communities. On opening night I met Paul Thompson (who I had only read about in theatre school). He came up to me with a wide smile and said, "The house hasn't shaken like this since *Billy Bishop Goes to War*!" Paul has since given me many great words of advice on my journey as an artist, and Layne Coleman became a very important mentor. I was embraced as a new member of the TPM family. I continued to work there for years, first as a dramaturge of the Playwrights Unit, then as associate artistic director. I was lucky to have been able to work on plays that went from the Unit to Mainspace productions. Eventually I started to get more directing offers and spoke to Layne about leaving to pursue my career. He didn't flinch; he told me I needed to get out there, take risks, and be the best artist I could be.

That was my experience of TPM. Supporting individual artists not just for the benefit of TPM but to build a stronger artistic community. I'm so happy that TPM's pitch program and BUZZ continue to give new artists a place to be heard. Thank you, TPM, for giving me my first professional directing job and an artistic home where I was able to grow.

An award-winning director and dramaturge, WEYNI MENGESHA started her career directing *'da Kink in my hair* across North America and in London, helping build it into an international sensation, and composing its Dora-nominated score. Mengesha is also a committed mentor for new talent and a producer of youth arts initiatives.

TPM & I

BY JOSEPH JOMO PIERRE

The incubation that re-energized me.

Theatre Passe Muraille was the misfit theatre to me. It was the store with the toys that were too loud, too bright, or might cause some toddler to lose a limb. Not sure where I fit in, maybe all of the above or, at least under the direction of Layne Coleman, allowed to be all of the above.

In October of 2005 Layne and Weyni Mengesha hurled a bucket of "colour" onto the Toronto stage with the Stage 3: Word. Sound. Power. festival. On any night you could have witnessed the works of Anita Majumdar, Nicole Stamp, d'bi. young anitafrika, and myself. This was the sort of reflection that I believed deserved to be on the Toronto stage. Writing for me was about making sure that this voice was included in the history of Toronto/Canadian theatre. With one blow they introduced artists that continue to do that. It is the sort of thing that companies now aspire to. But at that moment it never felt forced; it wasn't about appeasement of any sort. TPM believed in the value of our voices, and we bought into the vision of Layne and Weyni.

Grateful for the friendships and working relationships developed during that time. Tickled (yes, a Black man from Scarborough used that term) to have talked about Tupac and Notorious B.I.G. with Layne. Hope I led him to understand the greatness of Biggie—I feel like he was undercover a Tupac guy though.

Through *Born Ready*, *Pusha-Man*, *Hip Hop (Who Stole the Soul?)*, and *Shakespeare's Nigga* I have been too loud, too bright, and broken some limbs as I truly poured my soul onto the TPM stage.

Bless.

From the Backspace to the Mainspace and all things in between, JOSEPH JOMO PIERRE has been fortunate to not only perform but also develop as a creator and performer through his many relationships through TPM. The place where *Shakespeare's Nigga* was *Born Ready* to be his culture's *Pusha-Man*.

I LOVE THEATRE PASSE MURAILLE

BY D'BI.YOUNG ANITAFRIKA

Theatre Passe Muraille is for me the most magical theatre space in the city. I am completely biased of course because it is in this space that I first began my professional theatre work as a monodramatist in this country. But before that Theatre Passe Muraille took under its wing a bunch of idealist twentysomethings in the form of *'da Kink in my hair*.

I was nominated for a Dora Mavor Moore Award in Theatre Passe Muraille's version of *'da Kink*. What a ride this was, one that took us all the way to the Princess of Wales Theatre! Then a couple years later it was Layne Coleman who took a chance on two young practitioners, Weyni Mengesha and myself, when we said we wanted to do my first solo play, *blood.claat*. Layne actually took his own personal funds to help produce the show, which went on to be nominated for five Dora Awards, winning two of them. It was also at Theatre Passe Muraille, ten years later in 2016, that I produced another monodrama, *She Mami Wata & The Pussy WitchHunt*, which also went on to win a Dora. Is that magick or is that magick!

I love Theatre Passe Muraille because it nurtured me as a developing artist and it continues to do the same for many practitioners. It taught me the responsibility of not only creating but also sustaining spaces that are committed to the growth and development of our future storytellers. This city and country need Theatre Passe Muraille!

Finalist for the 2017 Ontario Premier's Awards for Excellence in the Arts, D'BI.YOUNG ANITAFRIKA is a triple Dora Mavor Moore Award–winning playwright-performer, director-dramaturge, and emerging scholar. She is an internationally celebrated arts educator and the founding artistic director of the Watah Theatre. anitafrika is also the instigator of Spolrusie Publishing, a unique micro press that publishes original works by Black and QTIPOC creators.

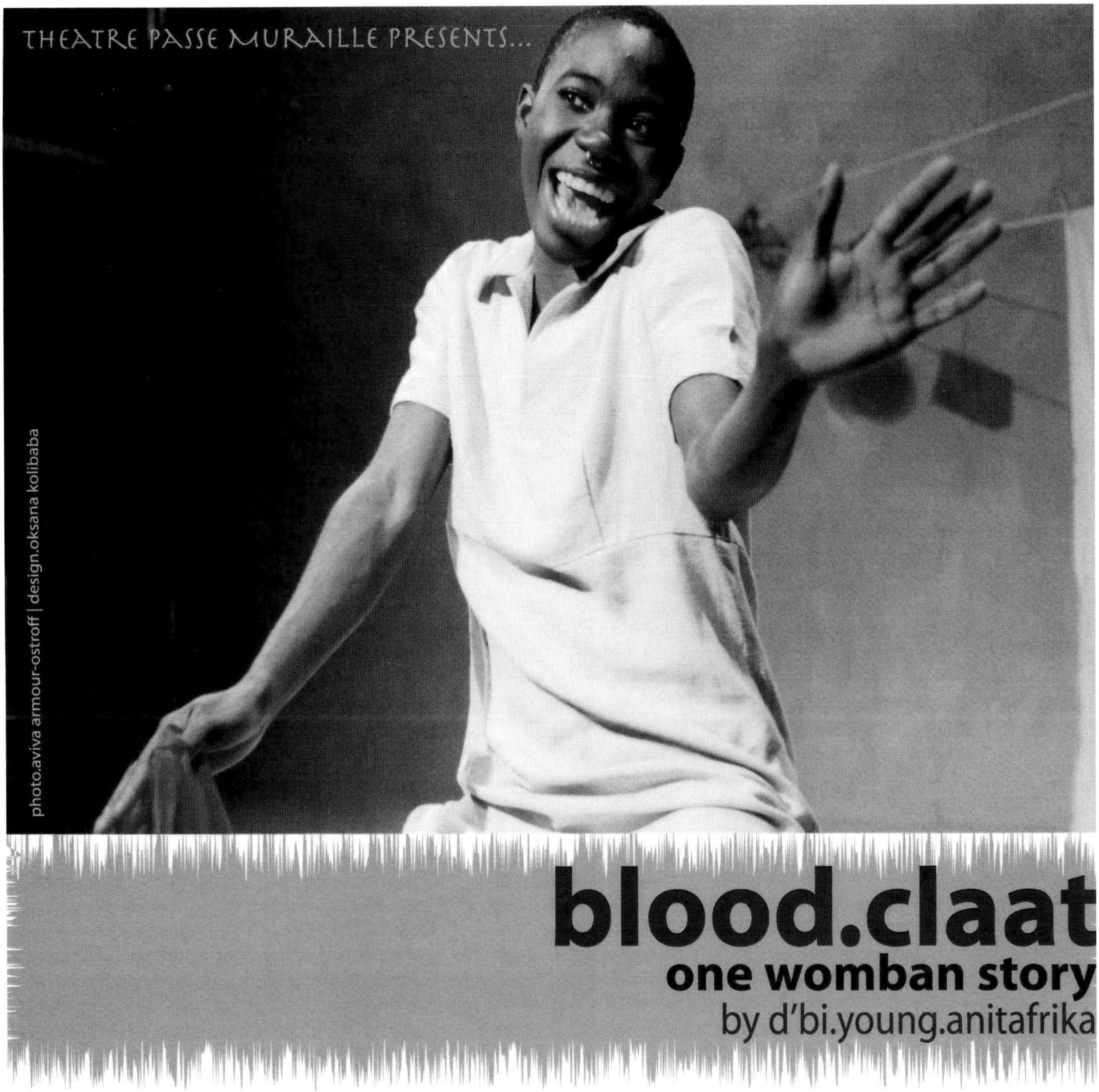

***BLOOD.CLAAT* HOUSE POSTER**
D'BI.YOUNG ANITAFRIKA. PHOTO BY AVIVA ARMOUR-OSTROFF.

GETTING MARRIED AT TPM!

BY JULIE TEPPERMAN AND AARON WILLIS

Our fondest memories of doing *YICHUD (Seclusion)* at Theatre Passe Muraille are most definitely the pre-show wedding celebration. We invited the audience to arrive half an hour early, and the moment they entered the lobby they were made to feel like they were guests at Rachel and Chaim's wedding. Thanks to the vision of our amazing designer Beth Kates, TPM was completely transformed to look and feel like a synagogue—from the playing space itself, to the lobby, and even the bathrooms! This design was so detailed and transformative that several times people who were new to TPM came up to Julie (who played the bride) and said, "How ever did you get permission to do a play in an old synagogue?!"

When people arrived they were plunged into full-on wedding hoopla—there was a klezmer band, the men could go up to the balcony and dance and drink and make toasts (l'chaims) with the groom and his groomsmen, and the women could receive a special blessing from the bride, as is the tradition at an Orthodox Jewish wedding. People's level of "buy in" was the most moving part of all. Some people would improvise: "You don't know me, I'm on the groom's side of the family!" And often people would ask for special blessings for very real things, such as for sick relatives or blessings for fertility. Though the play itself was text-based and quite traditional in terms of the audience sitting in seats, this pre-show celebration invited them, based on their own comfort level, to participate, to improvise, to role-play, to celebrate with our characters as if they were part of our family. Even if someone chose to simply sit in their seat and watch it all unfold, they felt *immersed in a world*. The result being that people were all the more connected to and invested in the characters and the story once the "play proper" began. So much so that several times, at the end of the "wedding montage" after the groom broke the glass, people would shout out, "mazel tov!"

Theatre Passe Muraille proved to be the perfect home for our little synagogue. It's in huge part due to Andy and the staff's belief in the value of "immersion" as an entry point into the world of the play that made the experience incredibly enriching and memorable for us and the audience alike.

We founded Convergence Theatre in 2006, and it has thrice been voted the Best Site Specific Theatre in Toronto by *NOW Magazine*. With each new project we challenge ourselves to find innovative ways to push the boundaries of intimacy between

performer and audience. We believe the audience is integral to the theatregoing experience; by creating shows in site-specific and non-traditional venues, as well as completely reimagining traditional theatre spaces such as TPM, we aim to more fully immerse the audience in the world of our plays.

In 2009 Artistic Director Andy McKim attended an early incarnation of *YICHUD (Seclusion)* at the Next Stage Theatre Festival. This began AARON WILLIS and JULIE TEPPERMAN's long and immensely fulfilling relationship with Theatre Passe Muraille in partnership with Convergence Theatre to develop *YICHUD* and bring it to a full production. This production received two sold-out runs in TPM's Mainspace in 2010 and 2011, as well as an invitation to headline the 2011 Magnetic North Theatre Festival in Ottawa, where it was nominated for a Capital Critics Circle Award for Outstanding Production. *NOW Magazine* listed it as one of Toronto's Top Ten Productions of 2010. *YICHUD* is published by Playwrights Canada Press.

YICHUD (SECLUSION)
AARON WILLIS AND JULIE TEPPERMAN. PRODUCTION DESIGN BY BETH KATES. PHOTO BY KEITH BARKER.

THE LIGHT OF AUDIO DESCRIPTION AT THEATRE PASSE MURAILLE: INCLUSIVE ACCESSIBLE THEATRE FOR BLIND AND LOW VISION THEATREGOERS

BY MALA D. NARAINE

I feel blessed to have been a friend of the Theatre Passe Muraille community since 1991. I was introduced to TPM by Layne Coleman, who was the artistic director. We met at the Blyth Festival in the summer of 1991. I happened to be sitting beside him during an afternoon matinee. Having low vision, I was using a telescope magnifier, which is similar to binoculars and allows me to see from a distance what is happening on stage. I was really enjoying the performance. During intermission Layne asked me to explain to him how much I am able to see using the telescope magnifier. He was very pleased that I was enjoying the play and indicated that he was interested in encouraging blind and low-vision people to come to the theatre.

Layne invited me to come to TPM and gave me a complimentary season pass. I offered to volunteer at TPM, but at that time we could not think of anything that I could help with as a low-vision person. He encouraged me to try writing a play. However, with no experience or formal training, I soon abandoned that idea. Layne and I often met for coffee at the Epicure Cafe to explore ideas to get more blind and low-vision people to come to the theatre. Given that audio description was not available in 1991, we were not successful in achieving this goal.

Layne continued to provide me with complimentary season passes throughout his tenure as artistic director. I attended every play for several seasons. In 1993 I got a short-term contract position at Trent University as Human Rights Advisor and had to move to Peterborough, Ontario. I looked forward to Sunday afternoons when I would get the bus into Toronto to see a play at TPM. I moved back to Toronto in 1995 upon the completion of my contract at Trent. Layne was no longer the artistic director of TPM, but we continued to keep in touch with long chats over coffee.

I was a doctor of education candidate at the Ontario Institute for Studies of Education, and TPM sold me a student season pass for the duration of my postgraduate studies. After completing my doctorate, I continued to purchase season passes for TPM and would often go with friends. I set up a special arrangement with TPM where they would reserve seats for me at the front. When I call to reserve tickets, the box office is alerted to my special needs. Even though audio description was not

—

ANDY AND THE STAFF AT TPM HAVE SET A SHINING EXAMPLE WITH THEIR WILLINGNESS TO PROVIDE INCLUSIVE AND ACCESSIBLE THEATRE.

available, having a seat at the front enhanced my enjoyment of the theatre.

As Bob Dylan says, "The times, they are a changin'." Progressive disability legislation was established in Ontario. The Accessibility for Ontarians with Disabilities Act has motivated organizations to comply with accessibility requirements for the provision of customer service. Small experimental theatres such as TPM realized that they need to be inclusive and accessible through the provision of American Sign Language (ASL) and audio description.

My post-doctoral fellowship at Ryerson University entailed conducting research on audio description for theatre, film, and television. At Ryerson we are promoting an integrative model for audio description, where the directors of the plays are encouraged to be the audio describers. In light of this legislation and the focus of my academic research, in 2010 I approached the current artistic director, Andy McKim, to find out if TPM would be willing to have one of their plays audio described.

Andy was enthusiastic about trying this new model of audio description and agreed to have our Ryerson research team assist with the audio description for two performances of *Highway 63: The Fort Mac Show* in 2011. It was indeed ironic that the director/describer of *Highway 63: The Fort Mac Show* was Charlotte Corbeil-Coleman, the daughter of Layne Coleman. As the playwright and director, she had a unique perspective as an audio describer, and her description of *Highway 63* was superb. It was a wonderful experience, not only for the blind and low-vision audience, but also for Charlotte.

Andy was persistent in his pursuit of funding for a pilot project on audio description. In 2016 he was successful in obtaining funding for an audio description pilot project for the 2016/17 season. I was delighted when he recruited me to be a consultant for this project and welcomed this opportunity to contribute to TPM as a volunteer.

Each of the four plays selected for the pilot project, *Alien Creature*, *John & Waleed*, *Stupidhead!*, and *Sound of the Beast*, required unique strategies for integrative audio description. It was decided that *Alien Creature* and *Stupidhead!* would be described with "closed" audio description, heard only by the blind audience on wireless headsets, and *John & Waleed* and *Sound of the Beast* would be described with "open" audio description, heard by the entire audience as the description is integrated as part of the play.

Andy and I collaborated with the audio description research team from the Inclusive Media and Design Centre at Ryerson University, namely Dr. Deborah Fels and Margot Whitfield, to train the directors/describers: Chelsea Dab Hilke, Marjorie Chan, Aaron Willis, and Jivesh Parasram. They were extremely committed to this pilot project and worked tirelessly to produce an audio description script in a very short time frame. Because the four plays represented different styles and genres, the directors/describers had to respond to various challenges that were specific to each play when developing the integrative audio description script.

TPM did extensive marketing to promote all of the audio description performances to the blind and low-vision communities in Toronto. All of the blind and low-vision theatregoers who attended the audio description performances indicated that their entertainment experience was enhanced by the audio description.

Andy and the staff at TPM have set a shining example with their willingness to provide inclusive and accessible theatre through American Sign Language and audio description. It is indeed poignant that a peer-reviewed research article on Charlotte's experience as director/describer co-authored by me, Margot Whitfield, and Dr. Deborah Fels was published in *Visual Communication* in February 2018—the year of TPM's fiftieth anniversary.

Layne saw the light of inclusion emerging from the cracks; Andy expanded the cracks and brought forth the light of inclusive accessible theatre to shine brightly on TPM.

Happy fiftieth anniversary, TPM!

MALA D. NARAINE is a passionate human-rights and accessibility-issues expert. She completed a three-year post-doctoral fellowship in the Inclusive Media and Design Centre at Ryerson University. For over fifteen years she has helped educational institutions, other organizations, and human resources professionals find the right solutions for accommodation of disabilities in the workplace and in post-secondary environments.

THEATRE WITHOUT WALLS
THEATRE WITHOUT WALLS
THEATRE WITHOUT WALLS

the rochdale drama project

THÉÂTRE PASSE MURAILLE
THÉÂTRE PASSE MURAILLE
THÉÂTRE PASSE MURAILLE

Theatre Passe Muraille

CHALLENGE AND OPPORTUNITY

—

COVER PAGE FROM THE ROCHDALE DRAMA PROJECT, TPM'S FOUNDING PROPOSAL

THE BEST OF TIMES, THE WORST OF TIMES

BY HRANT ALIANAK

When I was asked to write something in commemoration of Theatre Passe Muraille's fiftieth anniversary, I thought I had better go through my resumé and try and remember some of the shows I had done there. I was a little stunned to see that I was actually involved as writer, director, producer, or actor in twenty-seven various productions since 1972—more than with any other theatre company. Sixteen of these shows were productions in the seventies when Paul Thompson was the artistic director, and those are the ones that had the most impact on my career.

It was the best of times; it was the worst of times. The best because I would often go to Paul with a half-baked idea without even having written a word and he would green-light me for a production two months down the road. He had faith enough that any new play that I would write and direct would at the very least be different from the norm, which it always was. And that was predominantly what Passe Muraille was about in those days, experimenting and discovering new forms of storytelling, truly going beyond walls. It didn't matter if it succeeded, as long as it was genuinely trying to explore new territory, however raw it may have been. This is a luxury that has long been lost in Canadian theatre in the last few decades, when everything has to be subjected to the long, laborious process of workshops and rewrites. I will always be indebted to Paul for repeatedly showing me this trust and allowing me unrestricted playtime on the stage.

The worst because Passe Muraille at that time was the most chaotic, technically inept place to work at and my work was inevitably always technically demanding. Opening nights were often fraught with disaster. On the opening night of *Noah's Kiosk*, a large portion of the set fell on the audience, including the critics, all of whom of course panned the play. At the opening night of my spaghetti western version of *Titus Andronicus*, unfinished pieces of lumber and other stage detritus inadvertently became part of the set, because there were only two crew people who designed, hung, and operated the lights as well as designed and constructed the set, and hung and operated the sound, all in three weeks. Paul and I would have screaming matches out in the streets, as I would curse him for never budgeting enough for tech support and he would yell back that if he

NIGHT HOUSE POSTER

had to budget for extra crew, that would mean doing one less play a year, and that would certainly be my play.

Of course a lot of magic happened as well. When Passe Muraille was between theatres in 1975 and only had a dinky office space in a back alley on Breadalbane Street with a long, narrow upper room for storage, I approached Paul with the idea of doing a play up on the second floor, assuring him that I would just move the stored set pieces around and make use of them as part of the set. He was dubious but game. I told him I was planning the play for a cast of five. He said he could only afford four. I quickly agreed, and my play *Night* became a reality in accordance with the financial restrictions imposed on it. I learned with that show that sometimes good art happens because of those very restrictions. The play was very successful and was the beginning of my cycle of cinematic plays that informed all my later works.

In 1976 my play *The Blues* became, I believe, the first play to be staged at the Ryerson Backspace. The entire cast of four quit after four days of rehearsal and Paul once again challenged me. Was he going to lose money or was I going to do something about it? I quickly recast the show and used up the remaining ten days of rehearsal and opened it, with both the space and the play in its usual state of chaotic half readiness, but somehow it worked and it became a hit show.

I could go on, but one gets the idea. In retrospect there is a lot to be said for getting a show done properly and yet . . . a lot more to be said for just getting a show done, period. And that in a nutshell was Passe Muraille. And without it I would probably not have had my plays done. So what can I say, but thanks and long live Passe Muraille!

HRANT ALIANAK made his debut as a writer in 1972 at Theatre Passe Muraille with his play *Tantrums*. Other plays he has written and directed include his gangster trilogy, *Night*, *Passion and Sin*, and *Lucky Strike*, as well as *The Blues*, *The Big Hit*, and *The Walls of Africa*. His play *Lucky Strike* has been performed to rave reviews in such cities as New York, Washington, Liverpool, London, and Tel Aviv.

NIGHT
ANNE ANGLIN AND BOOTH SAVAGE.
PHOTO BY DAVID GROSKIND.

O.D. ON PARADISE
SHARON DYER, JOHN WINSTON CARROLL, LAYNE COLEMAN, BRUCE WILSON, JANET-LAINE GREEN, AND NANCY BEATTY. PHOTO BY KENNETH DAVISON.

THE THREE-HEADED ARTISTIC DIRECTOR?

BY JIM PLAXTON

In the beginning I had never worked with founder Jim Garrard, nor Paul Thompson and his now famous collective-creation process, but then Hrant Alianak asked me to design a production of *I Love You, Baby Blue 2* he was to direct. The play was to open the 1976/77 TPM season in a freshly renovated building on Ryerson Avenue. However, the day before our first preview, the theatre was locked up by the city as "unsafe" for the public. Surprised but undaunted, we tore down the two-thousand square feet of airbrushed canvas art flats and moved to the larger Bayview Playhouse while others at the theatre dealt with the city and building code.

I returned happily to TPM for *Coming Through Slaughter* and *Maggie and Pierre*. I was hooked. When Clarke Rogers took the reins as artistic director and invited myself and Layne Coleman as his co-artistic directors, I gave up my freelance work and took the job. *O.D. on Paradise* and *Alligator Pie* were early successes that lived on and toured.

Another personal favourite in our first season was *D & C*, a two-hander credited to "Claude Roberts."* The script suggested

* The author of the play *D & C* was actually Clarke Rogers. We/he used a pen name to avoid the expected criticism that we were being self-indulgent in presenting our own work rather than the work of others—which was true. I suppose too it was a way of avoiding the expense of an outside writer's fee. A forensic audit might reveal a payment to one Claude Roberts. It was the end of our first season when the inevitable cash crunch hit and accounting practices had to be "creative."

ALLIGATOR PIE
MICHEL LEFEBVRE, NORMA DELL'AGNESE, MATT HORNER, JAN KUDELKA.

there would be violence on set as the couple dealt with "personal issues." We suspended a 20' x 20' platform from the grid and supported its centre with rubber tires—not unlike a wrestling ring. Sturdy wire mesh protected the audience on three sides, stage to grid, in case of flying props. On the fourth side we constructed an unseen backstage area using steel studs and drywall with a stage door entrance, a bedroom, kitchen, and a fully functional bathroom! The first real actor's dressing room/green room in TPM history! The mesh cage shook audibly and the drywall was damaged during every performance. Bob Nasmith was summoned in for coffee and plaster repairs each morning.

One night over beers, Clarke and I decided to take out the second floor, making one space out of two. Layne must have agreed. And while we were at it, why not provide permanent dressing rooms for actors? There was government money available for restoring "heritage buildings" and our plate-glass and plywood window openings cried out for historically accurate mullions and paint to bring the Nasmith Bakery back to its original look. Safety first and up to code was the rule. Upgraded fire-sprinkler systems, lobby washrooms for patrons, an actual box office, actor dressing rooms with showers, a new grid for lights, and a repurposed two-foot wood floor dropped to the new Mainspace, to say nothing about the heavy steel work to stabilize the whole structure.

This work was done by professionals aided by theatre folks over the summer in time for the opening of *The Passe Muraille Hamlet*. We techies even broke through the bakery's cobbled concrete floor and bricked in a pit for the grave of "poor Yorick." Alas, it may have been filled in years ago, but the trap in the floor remains. The set was built out of the 12" x 4" wood beams from the second floor, splayed like fingers at two angles in one corner, forming a staircase to connect the new balcony to the main deck. An old velvet drape from the Victory Theatre dressed the set.

We opened on time with no technical or building code issues with the city. But we had created other problems. Before this second renovation we had three performance spaces in the Ryerson building, so losing one produced new economic realities.

In our second season together, we brought back the alligator and *O.D. on Paradise*. *Alligator Pie* was sent off on tour and *O.D.* was scheduled after *Hamlet*. But our production budgets had not changed from the previous year. The original *O.D.* design budget was $1,200. In a meeting with Alana, my co-designer, it became clear that $1,200 was just not enough to make it happen in the larger space. There were two young companies on the road with her wonderful quilted design for *Alligator Pie*, but we had a big job to do with the remount and some finishing work in our new space. I walked into Clarke's office and explained the matter. His response was short and sweet: "You wrote the budget—so change it!" and went back to his newspaper. So it was done. I returned to the meeting with ten thousand dollars to spend on finishing the renovations and remounting *O.D.*

In those good old days, for better or worse, decisions were still made by the artists, not theatre boards. That came later as the dreaded term "deficit financing" entered our vocabulary.

There was a break-in during pre-production and a Dora Award had gone missing. It was quickly recovered by the Toronto police, who willingly posed for photos on our Jamaican beach with bikini-clad body builders as I was presented for a second time with my award for the first *O.D.* Was it a shameless promotion? Absolutely—anything for a free newspaper spot. And a writer—who was coerced by a certain unnamed, unfriendly, and vengeful reviewer—published a story in the *Toronto Star* accusing the actors of smoking ganja on stage. Clarke joined with the actors, sued, and won in what I like to remember as the Strawberry Tea Party, after the actual substance smoked by the cast. More square inches of free promotion helped to fill the house.

I am a little bit saddened by what I perceive as a loss of control of our theatre spaces by our younger artists. How many names and productions over fifty years can we celebrate? How many have we lost? Theatre Passe Muraille is just one theatre among many in Toronto, but surely it stands proudly among the best Canadian theatres for its dedication to new work and its support of artists.

As a freelance designer JIM PLAXTON's tenure at TPM was a wonderful opportunity to stretch his wings and host a few young designers during a time of transition in the theatre's history. When Paul passed the baton to Clarke Rogers, Layne Coleman and Jim were brought in as co-artistic directors to support a new vision based more on the playwright rather than the collective.

A DIFFICULT BIRTH (AT THE BARNYARD AND FRACTIONS THEREOF)

BY PAUL J. STOESSER

The tumult of the 1975/76 Toronto theatre season witnessed two singular events: Theatre Passe Muraille closed its four-month run of *I Love You, Baby Blue* at the Bathurst Street Theatre and Gina Mallet arrived at the *Toronto Star* as theatre critic.

Almost immediately Ms. Mallet's opening salvo across the bow of the alternative theatres was a review that brutalized Tom Hendry's *Byron* at Toronto Free Theatre. Within a couple of months she spurned the Canadian Mime Theatre. For her the preferred model, or perhaps more precisely the only model, was Broadway. There is no record that Mallet saw the immensely popular *Baby Blue*, which was anything but Broadway, yet by alternative-theatre standards it was boffo at the box office. So much so that its profits guaranteed the viability of Paul Thompson's negotiations for Sol Friendly's iron and sheet metal works at 16 Ryerson Avenue, housed in what was originally Nasmith Bakery with its attached stables, which, in spite of several years of neglect, was a superb example of late-nineteenth-century industrial architecture.

By midsummer, following another TPM residency in Petrolia (*Oil* and *1837: The Farmers' Revolt* had been previously presented in conjunction with the official reopening of the historic Victoria Playhouse, and *Them Donnellys* had premiered there as well), the numerous details of real-estate matters had been settled and the deal for 16 Ryerson Avenue all but signed. However, instead of jumping into his beloved MG and heading to Toronto, Thompson and Anne Anglin bundled into their pickup and set out for the Red River Valley to develop *The West Show*. Theatre Passe Muraille was on the move again. The Toronto paperwork of closing the building deal was delegated to Janet Amos. A unique event in the Canadian alternative theatre that passed unremarked and without egotism.

With the building finally in TPM's possession but with scant progress on its refurbishment, the early months of 1976 were spent emptying and cleaning the building by a patchwork of effort and individuals. During the summer I was hired as production director with ranging responsibility for both the building and the production schedule, as well as designing

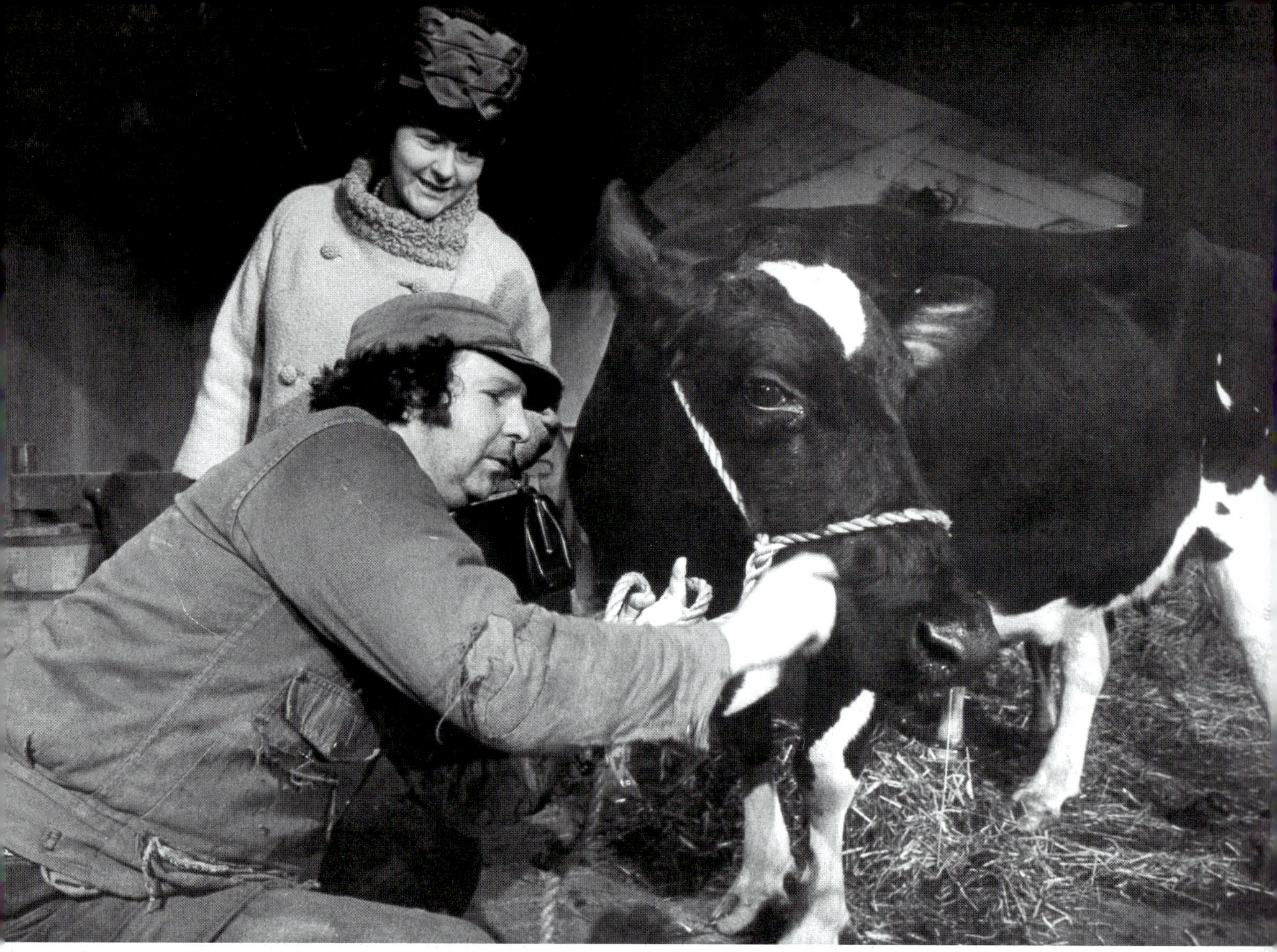

HE WON'T COME IN FROM THE BARN
CLARE COULTER AND TED JOHNS. PHOTO BY DAVID GROSKIND.

OUR CAST MORE THAN DOUBLED IN SIZE TO INCLUDE TWO COWS, THREE PIGLETS, AND A ROOSTER.

lighting and settings for several of the productions. By that first autumn season a concerted and coordinated effort of an unusually large work force for a small theatre was underway to develop three performance venues, one on each floor of the main building and a smaller studio in the stables, which has since become known as the Backspace. These efforts also included the installation of related production-support facilities while at the same time attending to all of the system requirements for heating, plumbing, air conditioning, and electrical services as well as fire separations, particularly in the rated stairways.

Throughout this time not only were we struggling to get the building on its feet, but we were also working under dire physical as well as critical circumstances.

Simultaneous production schedules intertwined with building concerns, which were unnecessarily complicated by an intransigent building inspector and a black hole of near-dysfunctional municipal offices under the aegis of the deputy chief building official comprising the department of works, the building department, the legal department, and the engineering department, among others. This hurdles-and-pitfalls scenario has been well documented as standard fare for the general public. However, in Theatre Passe Muraille's case, while it had enjoyed great public expressions of support during the morality fiasco surrounding *Baby Blue*, it would be naive to think that there wasn't equally staunch opposition and lingering distaste for Thompson personally and Passe Muraille generally at city hall, where egos bruise easily and memories are long.

In October, in spite of increasing frustrations with civic red tape and related obstructions, we prepared and produced three shows for various venues: CODCO's *Laugh Your Guts Out with Total Strangers*, hosted at Factory Theatre Lab's Adelaide Street East premises; *John Hornby* at the Central Library Theatre (among the last, if not the last, professional production there before the building was sold to the University of Toronto); and a touring production of *1837: The Farmers' Revolt* that was pre-staged at Ryerson Theatre in Toronto before opening its Southwestern Ontario tour in the Thistle Theatre at Brock University in St. Catharines three days later. From the "new" old premises on Ryerson Avenue in unseasonable temperatures, averaging only slightly above eight degrees Celsius, all of this local activity was coordinated while concurrently building and rehearsing a four-show repertoire travelling in early November to Ottawa's National Arts Centre. These productions comprised of another *1837*, featuring most of the original cast; Hrant Alianak's *The Blues*; and *John Hornby*, fresh from its Toronto run; and all were staged in the 350-seat studio. Ted Johns's *Naked on the North Shore* was presented as a lunchtime offering.

Rehearsing and producing our shows in the unheated building was the insult; the injury was in the continuous and unrelenting onslaught by Gina Mallet, whose critical stance invariably dismissed any—nay, virtually every—attempt in the city at producing native theatre. A bile invective that was not exclusively but especially expressed against TPM. Her *nostalgie de la boue* was a mystery to us all and completely at loggerheads with her current position, especially considering the empathy of her immediate predecessor.

In late November/early December Thompson and Mallet had a "lengthy" conversation about what was uppermost in the minds of the city's artistic directors: venue affordability. The subsequent article bore "almost no resemblance whatsoever" to their discussion according to Thompson, who was now equally disappointed by her misrepresentation and distrustful of her motives. Rather than focusing primarily on George Luscombe's "plight" in making rent at Toronto Workshop Productions, her article instead suggested that Thompson had "run out of energy," supposedly under the burden of the building. Thompson's response to Mallet was typed on a series of lush postcards printed by Coach House Press featuring John Boyle's illustrations for TPM's *Canadian Heroes Series Number 1*, mounted in the previous season. (A couple of years later Boyle would be commissioned by the TTC to decorate the Queen Street subway station in the same style with his mural *Our Nell* on both platforms.) Thompson's unsent response was later retrieved by me from the wastebasket.

His comments, which ostensibly regarded Luscombe's financial difficulties, was the surface concern. The sub-theme was the changing practice of various governmental granting agencies, which had begun relating box-office receipts to funding disbursements. In large part a bums-in-seats consumption equation was adopted by these agencies as a result of conservative and reactionary political pressures that questioned the nature of art supplied by public monies. Like Passe Muraille, several Toronto theatre companies, among them Tarragon, Factory Theatre Lab, and Toronto Free Theatre, were just coming into home ownership of larger spaces with commensurately larger operating costs. Canadian Actors' Equity Association exacerbated these financial pressures by reassessing individual theatre classifications based on weekly potential gross box office, which was then used to determine minimum payments to performers, further driving production costs up without any compensatory balancing of income from the funding bodies.

In the meantime a single letter from our lawyer, John Longmire, leveraged from the city a permit for the emergency installation of our heating plant, lest the fabric of the building be jeopardized and the city held liable. A powerful instrument, a lawyer's letter. When we finally opened our warmer but still not officially authorized barn at 16 Ryerson Avenue, the first production mounted was *He Won't Come in from the Barn* by the promising new playwright and recent Passe Muraille discovery, Andrew

McKeever. Staged in January at the south end of the main floor, the who's who of the production included Paul Thompson at the helm, Ted Johns as the He, Billy Dunlop as his son, Paul Kelman as a veterinarian, Ken Parnell as a neighbouring farmer, and Clare Coulter as He's wife. Appearing without Equity or ACTRA sanction, but nevertheless under the watchful eye of the Toronto Humane Society, Thompson cast some farm critters, temporarily on leave from auction. Our cast more than doubled in size to include two cows (perhaps inspiring an eponymous software company some several years and one digital communications revolution later), three piglets, and a rooster.

Bob Pearson, quite likely the single best craftsperson to have worked at Passe Muraille, provided the set design, which featured a barn interior that included a pigpen and a stall for the cattle whose south ends faced north, all located within a framing post-and-beam structure, a rural proscenium portal, which was remarkably sympathetic to the heavily wooden-beamed ceiling of the room. The rooster had free range of the set, indeed the entire room, but was rehearsed by Bob with some judiciously placed treats to make appearances along the beam.

These structural roof beams were among several of the original architectural features that had attracted Paul Thompson immediately to the building, and for them we fought long and hard with the city to prove that they met fire-code conditions for heavy-timber construction so as to prevent these massive beams from being hidden beneath acres of insipid Sheetrock and drywall. For the enduring beauty of those nineteenth century factory features, generations of patrons and artists owe a huge debt to structural engineer Roger Empensando, who obsessed tirelessly and ultimately prevailed on our behalf. Roger's work figured significantly in the 1977 designation of Passe Muraille's new home as a "historical building" by the Toronto Historical Board.

And so, back to the barn . . .

It's opening night. Gina was "on the aisle" per usual as we dimmed to black for the beginning of the show. Unbeknownst to all, and especially her, during that initial blackout as we settled the house to the gentle lowing of the cattle, our cock of the walk perched itself on the back of the empty seat immediately behind her. As my first "light of dawn" cue gently faded up, Cocky responded as only he could, crowing a mighty welcome to this new-come day and sent poor Ms. Mallet halfway to the roof and likely to the laundry as well. Among the many apocryphal moments and scenarios over the years of the varied responses to her vitriol—such as a group collection among the theatres for a one-way ticket back to New York City—this particular incident of the rooster sounding off, as in one voice for all those of us performers and producers and publicists who had chafed under Mallet's merciless and even at times mean critiques, was especially gratifying in the moment. But alas, it added nothing positive ultimately to the subsequent review. Gina "the Hammer" Mallet (a much-used sobriquet amongst the theatre community) was not amused. McKeever, our playwright, might have been, had he been real, but rather he served as a pseudonym for yet another TPM collective creation—his name borrowed from Thompson's uncle and RCAF pilot. Perhaps even, one might think, as a ruse to throw off a certain critic's predispositions.

Concurrently, in the north end of the second floor—long before the big dig of '83 punched a hole through the floor and the economics of 16 Ryerson Avenue—we rehearsed and ran Sharon Pollock's *No! No! No!*. Troubled Howie Cooper opened the show by breaking into the living-room setting of a house and then coming downstage to the very edge of my lighting, within a few feet of the audience, sniffing at the air, and ad libbing, "Smells like a barn in here." Which it did. With the benefit of hindsight, our production of *He Won't Come in from the Barn* perhaps prefigured what would become TPM's future artistic predicament: it can't get out of the barn and it has had considerable difficulty staying in touch with that founding ethos of *passe muraille* that invigorated and informed the earliest TPM productions.

And about the parenthetical title of this essay? Let's just say, much to Bob Pearson's delight, I stepped right into one of those cow patties. One day in the theatre we had just finished cueing my lighting design; I thought I would show off my rural chops and remarked to Bob, who hailed from a Southwestern Ontario pig farm in Ethel, that I knew the larger black-and-white cow to be a Holstein, but didn't know what to call the smaller brown one. Without missing a beat he turned to me and proclaimed, "Well that's a Half-stein of course!"

A short-lived member of the Rochdale community, PAUL J. STOESSER was, as a graduate theatre student, aware of TPM in the early '70s, but made his first real contact with the company following *Oil*. Paul Thompson and Stoesser later met in the heat and summer dust of 16 Ryerson Avenue and decided they liked the sniff of each other well enough to give it a go. For several years and scores of shows as production director, designer, and sometime theatre technician, their achievements in the building, and most importantly in the productions, were immensely satisfying. Thompson provided Stoesser all the rope needed to hang himself and with it built a glorious home for the marvellous talent that graced their lives with art and beauty. Stoesser thinks maybe Thompson missed him, because he retired from TPM the year after Stoesser did. Of course, they've both worked there again since.

OFF TO DUBLIN, EH?

BY NEIL FOSTER

The Immigrant is a play written by Jim Sheridan (*My Left Foot*, *The Boxer*, *The Field*, *In the Name of the Father*), and was workshopped at Theatre Passe Muraille in 1981 with Jim Sheridan playing the immigrant and David Fox playing a dozen (give or take a few) characters that the immigrant comes across, all the while trying to obtain refugee status in order to eventually rescue his family from his war-torn (mythical) country of Badswanavilla and have them join him in Canada.

As I said, the play was workshopped in Toronto at Theatre Passe Muraille, but was to be given its premiere at Theatre Calgary in the Late Night Series, a series that ran concurrently with its main-stage productions, which in this case was the premiere of John Murrell's *Farther West*. Fox was in *Farther West*, so *The Immigrant* came to Calgary to premiere. As it turned out, Equity wouldn't let Sheridan perform in the play as he wasn't Canadian, and so the part went to me, Neil Foster—who was on hand as I too was in *Farther West*. Sheridan directed and it all went very well.

It went so well that Sheridan, a Dubliner, sold the production to the Project Arts Centre in Dublin to include it in the 1982 Dublin Theatre Festival.

I was living in Edmonton at the time and made the trek to Toronto to hook up with Fox and travel to Dublin a few weeks before the festival was to begin. My first phone call to David Fox:

FOSTER: Hey, David. I'm here.

FOX: Where?

FOSTER: Toronto.

FOX: Oh shit.

Turns out we were $1,500 short in airfare, because Sheridan was in New York City and not in Dublin, where he was supposed to be. I was to call Susan Serran at TPM and talk to her.

Susan informed me they had tried all the funding sources except Alberta Culture because TPM wasn't Albertan. But I was. She speed-dialled Alberta Culture and handed the phone to me. Gordon Gordie at Alberta Culture couldn't help me—their budget was spent—try the Canada Council for the Arts. The Canada Council told me they didn't fund actors, only directors and playwrights, and I should try the Minister of External Affairs. She gave me a name: Mr. Claude Du Lang. By this time my story of an actor trying to get to the festival had been refined/polished/adapted to become a production that was so successful in a local market it was to be tested in an international venue with the long-term goal of me directing subsequent national and international tours.

DU LANG: Call me back in one hour and a half.

An hour and a half later.

Fifteen hundred dollars, that's okay. You'll get the money at the end of April.

This was a Tuesday in September.

FOSTER: I need the money by Friday.

And we got it.

Friday, I met up with Fox at the airport. He was off to get some duty-free rye whisky—in case there was no rye in Dublin, I guess, and I was going for a beer with my aunt who drove me to the airport.

The bar I was in turned out to be at the opposite end of the terminal from our departure gate and I had misjudged the length of the terminal.

I missed the flight.

BUT! Because we had just bought the ticket a few days before, it was full fare and I could get on the next flight in forty-five minutes. PHEW!

BUT! There was only a thirty-minute window to make the connecting flight from Heathrow to Dublin, and I was already forty-five minutes delayed.

I got to Heathrow, a lovely flight, and got in line to get behind six hundred or so other travellers, only to see Fox at the front of the line just getting through customs. Desperate, I squeezed, ducked, dodged, elbowed, and somehow—without being beaten up—got to the front of the line in time to make the connection.

The connecting flight was boarding and there was no sign of Fox until I boarded and clocked him in the back of the craft reading a newspaper. I pulled out a newspaper, hid my face, and sat beside him for a few moments before speaking.

FOSTER: Wow, these transatlantic flights really take the wind out of you, eh?

You can only imagine FOX's face.

FOX: Where the fuck were you, man??

FOX could tell this part better than me.

I had you paged on the plane!! We checked the washrooms! I was freaking out!

Turns out the flight I missed was delayed on the tarmac for about thirty minutes so—even for Foxy—it was a tight squeeze to make the connecting flight.

We landed, we rehearsed, we performed, and a grand time was had by all. And I wouldn't have missed it. And I will never forget it.

Regards, eh?

NEIL FOSTER first worked at TPM performing at the 1982 Dublin Theatre Festival in *The Immigrant*. In the late '80s, with his good friend Greg Spottiswood and their company Exploded Satellite Projects, he produced an Amnesty International benefit called the Open Door, an actor-as-writer evening of monologues, and a workshop of Colleen Murphy's *Down in Adoration Falling*. In the '90s, as an associate director at Factory Theatre, he had the privilege to work with TPM and all the other mid-size theatres in several advocacy committees to help seek out and establish sustainable long-term funding commitments for theatre, dance, and other arts groups.

Passe Murai

CREDIBILITY AND CLASS

BY SUSAN FELDMAN

I'm not really sure why Clarke Rogers wanted me to come and work at Passe Muraille. He had a more than able admin and production team led by Jerry Doiron and Stephan Droege, and I'd never managed a theatre before. But I had founded a few key organizations, the Guild of Canadian Playwrights and the Performing Arts Development Fund of Toronto, which set up the half-price ticket booth that's now part of the Toronto Alliance for the Performing Arts, plus I was a past president of the Toronto Theatre Alliance. So, as Clarke saw it, I would bring "some credibility and class to the place." I think I was supposed to be the kinder, gentler face of the two-headed beast. But "managing director" was an odd job description, and after a few years and our best efforts we both realized the shoe didn't quite fit.

These were difficult years for Passe Muraille. Audiences were fickle, money was incredibly tight, and the bank continually threatened to call in the line of credit. Clarke was doing his best to reinforce the cliché of the tortured, self-destructive artist, and the theatre lurched from crisis to crisis. But he always managed to come up with some gems each season. Like a divining rod, Clarke had the ability to zero in on artists connected to the zeitgeist in a palpable way.

Under his watch, Cathy Jones came to town with her hilarious, feminist, one-woman show, *Wedding in Texas and Other Stories*. Brad Fraser explored the angst of teenage boys and sexuality in *Wolfboy*, starring a young Keanu Reeves. Linda Griffiths's powerful and dark piece *Jessica: A Transformation* was developed in collaboration with Métis writer Maria Campbell. It was based on her novel *Halfbreed* and featured Tantoo Cardinal, Graham Greene, Tom Jackson, and Makka Kleist. Then there were the ongoing partnerships with Buddies in Bad Times Theatre (*Murder in High Park: Steele Kiss*), Nightwood Theatre (*This is for you, Anna*), and VideoCabaret (*The History of the Village of the Small Huts*)—all companies that were politically fuelled with stories of the present and from the past. Throughout these years Passe Muraille's stages were filled with a parade of heroes, outliers, rebels, and iconoclasts. Sometimes raw, sometimes funny, these were the characters that Clarke was drawn to, and he wanted to confront audiences with their worlds.

The last show I was around for was a huge, operatic, mess of brilliance, *Tragedy of Manners*, by writer and critic Donna Lypchuk. It chronicled the Queen West scene that emerged in the 1980s from the creative hub of the Cameron House. The play featured forty-two mostly non-actors on stage. Visual and video artists, musicians, bartenders, and hangers-on came together to tell the story of bohemian life on the strip. It gave us characters who made art, who fell in and out of love, who died of drug overdoses, and who were ill with the disease that became known as AIDS. This was the culmination of Clarke's drive to make edgy, honest theatre within a vibrant community, and it was his pride and joy.

Art imitating life and life imitating art.

SUSAN FELDMAN was the managing director at Passe Muraille from 1986 to 1988.

FENDING OFF THE BANKERS

BY LASCELLE WINGATE

My time as general manager of Theatre Passe Muraille was relatively brief but represented one of the most memorable times in my theatre career.

The board that hired me, mostly made up of artists, was unfailingly supportive of all my efforts. It was a unique and wonderful experience for me—other boards I worked for were more traditional and business-oriented, and the artists of TPM's board were dedicated, hard-working, and a pleasure to work with, even if they didn't have deep pockets and rich contacts.

The staff was equally wonderful. I came in after Producing Director Jane Buss to work with Artistic Director Brian Richmond, and our team included Artistic Associate Peter Hinton; marketing and fundraising whiz Roxanne Moffitt, who worked wonders with a minuscule budget; and intern Randy Miller, who went on to great things with Jest in Time and the Department of Canadian Heritage.

My time was short but intense. It was a whirlwind time at TPM, including the groundbreaking co-production with VideoCabaret of *Rigoletto* and a breathtaking production of *Abingdon Square* directed by Peter Hinton.

Most memorably, our co-production with Native Earth Performing Arts of the world premiere of Tomson Highway's *Dry Lips Oughta Move to Kapuskasing* ended the season with an artistic and organizational bang, directed by Larry Lewis. I worked closely with Native Earth's general manager, Elaine Bomberry, and, as always, financing a huge new original Canadian work wasn't easy.

Cash flow was minimal, to say the least. Toward the end of the rehearsal period I realized we were just about to exceed our credit line. There weren't any obvious solutions. My dilemma was whether or not I should alert the bank to our situation or hope that opening and box-office revenues would arrive before I had to confess.

Two weeks before opening I received a call from our bank manager asking to see me.

My only card was that our theatre neighbour down Bathurst Street, Factory Theatre, had recently gone through some tough times and our common local bank had cut off Factory's credit line, leading to some very bad press for the bank.

I marshalled all my composure and negotiating style. While the bank manager wanted to talk about when we would be able to cover the line of credit, I told him about *Dry Lips*, about how it was by Canada's most important and well-known Indigenous playwright, how it featured an all-Indigenous cast. I asked him how it would look if the bank was seen to be silencing that voice and depriving audiences of that experience.

That veiled threat must have resonated—he granted us a grace period until the show opened, and from day one it was almost completely sold out. It was, of course, a huge success then and, in the future, winner of the 1989 Dora Award for Outstanding New Play, shortlisted for the 1989 Governor General's Literary Award, winner of the 1990 Chalmers playwriting award, and was the first piece of Indigenous theatre to be seen in a major Canadian commercial production—the Mirvish Productions and National Arts Centre co-production in 1991.

My ties with Tomson continued throughout my theatre career—at the Grand Theatre, Artistic Director Martha Henry and I produced a barnburning production of *The Rez Sisters*, which was Larry Lewis's last production. I feel blessed to have been part of such a dynamic group of theatre folks and my fondness and respect for Theatre Passe Muraille has continued to this day.

LASCELLE WINGATE has general managed three Ontario theatre companies: Theatre Passe Muraille in 1989/90, preceded by Theatre Plus, and followed by London's Grand Theatre. She has also led the Writers' Trust of Canada, but began her career as a professor of German literature.

DRY LIPS OUGHTA MOVE TO KAPUSKASING
BEN CARDINAL, ERROLL KINISTINO, AND GRAHAM GREENE. PHOTO BY MICHAEL COOPER.

YEARS SPENT IN THE VORTEX

BY JACOBA KNAAPEN

Theatre Passe Muraille has always been a grand seductress. Over the expansive time that I worked at TPM, I watched artists of all ages and stages of their careers compelled to hone their craft inside her walls. She is a powerful "beast" of a building that inspires exploration, and a little madness. The words risk and grit are customs, forever bonded to her dirty walls. Many of the artists who thrived there helped to shape my artistic bones, and some became lifelong friends. There were also many, mostly forgotten, TPM administrators who toiled tirelessly and invisibly to amplify her voices.

In the early '90s, the then artistic producer, Susan Serran, offered me my first job as "audience relations manager." The title encompassed an extensive list of responsibilities ranging from box-office manager to group sales to fundraising to organizing the theatre's infamous art auctions. Led by celebrity auctioneer Jack Layton, the then city councillor called for bids on pieces of art from an accomplished group of Canadian artists that included Carl Beam, Lorne Wagman, Rae Johnson, and Screamin' Sam Ferrera. Inside and outside of Passe Muraille's literal walls, stitched together with the programming of live theatre productions and playwriting workshops and readings, we also delivered an exhaustive schedule of events: talk shows, debates, concerts, book launches, street festivals, parades, cabarets, birthdays, memorials, and anniversaries. All combined this was a profoundly formative sink-or-swim period of growth that challenged all my skills and propelled my learning curve off the charts.

Stunningly it is now TPM's fiftieth anniversary. I remember the *other* benchmark anniversary, the quarter of a century grand celebration—the twenty-fifth! The Mainspace was packed with a phantasmagoria of artists, wound together in circles intensely chattering, drinking, smoking, more chattering, and more drinking! Many of them wore pink cardboard party hats, cut out in the image of the TPM building that had been designed and donated by Coach House Books for the celebration. They watched glorious performances by Andy Jones from CODCO and Linda Griffiths, and listened to Paul Thompson wax philosophically about the legacy. They drunkenly placed bids during the silent auction to win free tickets to TPM shows. They danced sexily to the raucous music of a live band—though I can't remember who was playing. They eyeballed an exhibit highlighting a twenty-five-year TPM history, featuring show posters that I had spent months carefully selecting. These were the productions that had dazzled and broken new ground—and forever revered by TPM's old guard. The memories made them howl. Sadly, to my eye, other less-successful show posters representing unrealized dreams remained unlaminated and ignored. The smaller Backspace was set up as an intimate poker room, hosted by Jim Garrard. It felt exclusive, and the mood was enveloped in cigar smoke. Drinks of Scotch flowed and were served by a "punky" waitress. If I remember correctly, with all of the proceeds going to TPM, we exceeded our financial target on *that* night.

Over the years I worked with two artistic directors, five general managers, and had three different office locations in two adjoining buildings. I started off in the basement offices at 54 Wolseley Street next to the costume shop, and as I typically arrived before everyone else, my first responsibility was to disarm the alarm system every morning. Other "top of the day" duties included venting the carpentry shop of marijuana smoke and cleaning the cat-litter box for Byron and Shelley—TPM's resident felines. I didn't mind these curious chores because there was an advantage of being the first to arrive. TPM had just one computer that we all had to share, and the computer sign-up sheet was always full, so being early guaranteed me at least *some* computer access. My second office was next door at 16 Ryerson Avenue, where I now had to share a doorway with the theatre's men's washrooms. In the winter that office was like a brick-lined fridge, so my compatriot Nick Tracey and I frequently worked at our desks wearing coats. Space heaters did nothing to cut through the icy breeze that blew through the porous windows, and our hands would get numb, as it was impossible to wear gloves and get the computer work done. Years later with the reconstruction of the TPM lobby, this space would become infinitely more hospitable and warmer—and is now the women's washroom. My office moved back over to 54 Wolseley Street, but upstairs this time, as TPM had given up both the old basement offices and the costume shop, retaining only the carpentry shop. But at the end of these days, no matter the office location, the workload was always vast; there was always a mountainous climb for another TPM opening night.

I will never forget the previously mentioned feline souls Byron and Shelley. After finding a dead mouse squeezed in the mechanism of TPM's photocopier, actor Michael Copeman brought them as kittens to TPM to "help us get rid of the fucking mice!" For a while the strategy worked, but Shelley began to disappear for days at a time. Eventually she resurfaced at the Writers' Trust office next door, where she had happily been adopted as *their* cat and responded to her new name, Peaches, abandoning her brother Byron. Byron was social and craved attention while hanging out at the TPM bar's post-show parties. I vividly remember a drunken actor eating his kibble one night from a small dish on top of the bar, mistaking it for a kind of bits-and-bites mix. The actor satisfyingly declared that it tasted great. A unique part of the front of house job description was to do a complete "cat check" and make sure that the Mainspace was cat free before the house opened. In advance of a performance of Timothy Findley's adaptation of *The Stillborn Lover*, Byron had remained hidden in the house and surprised actors Marion Gilsenan and David Fox with an onstage appearance! This unscripted stage debut both delighted the audience and was reported in a newspaper review of the show. Ticket sales boomed. Several seasons later Byron suffered a nervous breakdown from being exposed to one too many noisy machine-shop sessions. I brought him home to live with my family on Bathurst Street where he recovered and flourished; living to be nearly twenty years old and outlasting my tenure at the theatre.

These are but a few of my marked moments in the swirling span of an eleven-year-long ride. Ultimately, it was a family affair. My partner Stephan Droege had worked there as technical director and resident designer in the previous five years. Both of our toddler-aged sons, Max and Nico, grew up scrambling adventurously under the seating risers acting as floor-sweepers, emerging as dust magnets covered in grime. Juggling my role as a mother with the unrelenting demands of my TPM job was a constant test for me. The sacrifice of innumerable days and evenings spent working at the theatre instead of time spent with my young boys still haunts me. So now, when I walk back into Theatre Passe Muraille, wrapped in the "blanket" of so many diverse memories, seeing all of her grand ghosts, I smile—choosing to remember her magnificence.

As a champion for the performing arts, JACOBA KNAAPEN has passionately worked in Toronto's cultural sector for over three decades. Deeply committed to the ongoing development of theatre, dance, and opera, she is the past recipient of a Harold Award for her contribution and mentorship to the independent theatre community and a recipient of a Vital People Award from the Toronto Community Foundation. She is the executive director of the Toronto Alliance for the Performing Arts.

—

TPM WAS THE FIRST PLACE THAT WELCOMED ME IN TORONTO, AND I STILL FEEL A TRUE SENSE OF BELONGING HERE.

WORKING BEYOND WALLS

BY RÉGINE CADET

In 2013 I had just moved to Toronto from Montreal and was searching for a job in arts management when I saw the posting for the general manager position at Theatre Passe Muraille. I knew virtually nothing about the theatre at the time.

I was drawn to the mandate and the socio-political stance of the theatre, as it was in some ways very similar to the work that I had been doing for the last twelve years at the MAI (Montréal, arts interculturels)—advocating for diversity, inclusion, and representation on stage. "Giving voice to under-represented groups" was what excited me the most, as well as the concept of working "beyond walls."

TPM was the first place that welcomed me in Toronto, and I still feel a true sense of belonging here. Hiring a Black Francophone woman to lead such an institution meant a lot to me, and it had more significance than any value statement they might have had.

My first day of work was also the first day I had ever set foot in the theatre. I remember it quite vividly: Andy gave me the grand tour of his cherished theatre building and I thought, "Oh my God, this place is falling apart!" The office washroom flooded that same morning when I flushed the toilet . . . not really my idea of a great beginning. To make things worse, in my first week, as I was transitioning with the previous general manager, I uncovered a big deficit and fully comprehended the difficult financial situation the organization was facing . . . I almost ran away right then and there!

After some thought I decided to stay to take on the challenge. I have not regretted it so far. It's been three and a half years since that day and I'm still leading this institution alongside Andy McKim, who has become a good friend and a mentor.

I can say that it has not been an easy ride. Running this institution remains a big struggle. It's not a secret to anyone that TPM has very limited resources, but it is also very generous in nature. To be inclusive you have to be generous; you have to be ready to share your limited resources with many, ready to share your experiences, ready to collaborate, ready to give more. It's a constant three-way battle between the art, the finances, and our big-heartedness. I'm not sure who the big winner will be in the end, but so far the finances (or should I say the lack of finances) seem to have the upper hand. But still the combat continues—fifty years and still alive and striving.

This theatre has such strong values and has created such a rich and inspiring legacy that it's hard not to want to fight to keep it alive. I have high hopes for TPM for the next decades and will continue dedicating myself to the achievement of the many goals and projects we have set collectively with the staff and board.

I'm so proud to be leading this institution at this pivotal moment in its existence and to be actively fabricating its history. *TPM, pour longtemps encore!*

RÉGINE CADET spent twelve years with MAI (Montréal, arts interculturels), where she held the position of artistic and executive director for seven years, before becoming the general manager at TPM in January 2014. She trained at the Haitian American Academy of Ballet and Arts and later joined the Ballet Folklorique d'Haiti. On her arrival in Canada she founded the dance company, EKSPRESYON.

FUTURE FOLK
AURA CARVUEVA, CATHERINE HERNANDEZ, AND KAREN ANCHETA. PHOTO BY ALEX FELIPE.

OH MY IRMA
HALEY MCGEE. PHOTO BY AVIVA ARMOUR-OSTROFF.

MY FIRST MEETING

BY ADAM VAUGHAN

The first meeting I ever had as a politician involved Theatre Passe Muraille. Deanne Taylor from VideoCabaret and Ron Struys from Factory Theatre's board set up the meeting on my first official day in office. They came with staff from the theatre with an urgent plea: you must save Passe Muraille. We need a million dollars. Fast.

While I knew where the theatre was and had attended plays there for years, I had no idea where the stapler was in my office, let alone where a million dollars might be hiding at city hall. The cast and crew for this meeting had a business plan, a political argument, and a new staffing strategy. What they were looking for was funding from city hall in order to save a critical part of the city's cultural ecosystem.

I didn't need convincing. The impact of small theatres and arts venues and the critical role they play in local neighbourhoods cannot be understated. Whether it's the Bloor Cinema in the Annex, Harbourfront Centre and the Power Plant on the waterfront, or the historic role musical venues like the Bamboo, the Rivoli, and the Cameron House have played in creating Queen Street West, healthy arts organizations are synonymous with great neighbourhoods and wonderful streets.

The mayor of the day was David Miller. His staff and the city's arts wing all helped us raise the money and draft the motions needed to save the theatre. It also turned out that the *Toronto Sun*, and other city councillors, not to mention talk radio, were also paying attention.

A play about the plight of Palestinians, queer musicals, nudity, and shocking political drama, not to mention the strange concept of the city buying into a non-profit building and then using the purchase price to fix the theatre, not only confused the anti-arts crowd, it enraged them!

The city ignored the heckling; we saved the theatre, and even though months later critics thought city ownership of the building bestowed censorship rights on the city (it didn't), Theatre Passe Muraille not only survived, it thrived. And it wasn't censored!

—

THE IMPACT OF SMALL THEATRES AND ARTS VENUES AND THE CRITICAL ROLE THEY PLAY IN LOCAL NEIGHBOURHOODS CANNOT BE UNDERSTATED.

New plays, new audiences, and new vitality flowed from the city's investment. Strong leadership from an artist-led board and brilliant leadership from Andy McKim saw Theatre Passe Muraille take centre stage in Toronto's theatre community. From the Fringe Festival to showcasing new voices, the theatre remains a unique and valued icon in the city's arts community. It remains a mainstay in the local community and continues to provide a platform for understanding our city and society.

In the years afterward the theatre thanked the community and the city by engaging in even more community-based theatrical productions. Local stories, local youth, and the culture embedded in the surrounding neighbourhood all found their way on stage.

The theatre provided space for community meetings ranging from forums on new development to the revitalization of Alexandra Park, a public-housing community next door. The theatre also hosted victims of Queen Street's epic fire and helped neighbours rebuild their lives.

The life of Torontonians is found on stage, and the lives of Torontonians are made better by being an audience to their own stories. The neighbourhood is lucky to have Theatre Passe Muraille as a neighbour!

It was a million dollars well spent, and that meeting remains one the best I've ever had as a politician!

ADAM VAUGHAN was first elected to the House of Commons as Member of Parliament for Trinity-Spadina in 2014 and was elected twice to Toronto City Council in 2006 and 2010. Before entering politics Adam was a broadcast journalist for more than twenty years, specializing in municipal affairs for both the CBC and Citytv. He covered all three levels of government and has written about urban issues too.

MAKING IT THROUGH HUMOUR

BY HUGH NEILSON

I remember thinking to myself how strange it was to be walking into the offices of the "theatre beyond walls" on my first day as general manager only to be faced with walls everywhere, literally and figuratively. In fact, there were so many walls I wasn't even sure that anyone was working there. It was deafeningly quiet, though I could vaguely hear someone using a keyboard. One had to navigate through some weird maze to find anyone's desk, and when you did find someone they were reluctant to look you in the eye. It was very emblematic of the state of the organization at that time.

"You know, most of us have given up on TPM. Many think it should just die," someone said to me when I told them I had just accepted the job as general manager at TPM in 2007. In a way I already knew that nobody expected much from us at all, and I think Andy knew that as well, though we never talked about it. We never talked of failure because we didn't have that luxury, except for one brief moment about a month after I started. The conversation was short. It went like this:

ME: This could be the shortest gig we've ever had.

ANDY: I know.

Pause.

ME AND ANDY: Hahahahaha!

And that is how we made it through: humour. And since nobody was expecting anything from TPM at the time, when we did do something, people were appreciative, maybe even surprised.

A lot of good people worked at TPM before us. And I was so chuffed (as Colin Rose, the general manager before me would say) to have been chosen to work at this historic company. One that I had read about and studied at university many years before. But now it was in crisis. The season we inherited had been bankrolled by the sale of our theatre building. In fact, my second week into the gig, two managers from our bank visited the theatre to meet the new general manager. I expect they were hoping to find an experienced, confident miracle worker who had a history of running, managing, and turning theatres in crisis around. They asked what other theatres I had managed before, and when I told them this was the first one—well, I can only imagine how disappointed they were after that meeting. We had very little to work with—our marketing budget for the year was thirty-five thousand. Once you accepted the reality that there really were no financial resources then, in a strange way, it actually became kind of easy to run the place.

I like to believe that we channelled the creativity from the past—the creativity that had helped TPM survive forty years of hard luck. But we were new to the job, so we improvised everything, and there is a catharsis in working from a blank slate—there is nothing to screw up.

For example, there was no real subscription audience, so letting people know that we were open for business was our

TPM OFFICES BEFORE THE REMOVAL OF THE TEMPORARY WALL

first priority. Andy came up with the idea to sell subscriptions at Word on the Street, an annual book festival. People could buy them at the ridiculously low price of $35. That day we sold 375 subscriptions, and we could not have been happier.

We had precious little money for advertising, so we could not afford to create and distribute a poster for each show. The solution was that we advertised three of our productions on one poster. That saved printing costs, but where could we afford to put them up that would have any impact? Well, we knew we wanted our audience to look like the people who rode the subway every day. Talking about the subway prompted one staff member to say that they had noticed that there were certain locations on the subway line where advertising was always out of date. In other words, in those select locations, posters were left up for months until new advertising finally replaced them. So we decided to place our ads in those locations, pay for one month and hope that the posters were not replaced until after the final production on the poster closed, three months later. Our gamble paid off and the posters remained in place for over two months. I actually remember one poster staying up in the subway system for a year.

Before I left TPM in 2010, we had managed to post three surpluses in a row, which was a blessed relief. But more importantly, we were also creating great art.

HUGH NEILSON graduated from the University of Ottawa with a degree in theatre direction and animation. Hugh spent seven years with the Professional Association of Canadian Theatres (PACT), where he had a broad role ranging from advising on membership development to labour negotiations. While remaining a volunteer with PACT, he moved to his first general manager position at Theatre Passe Muraille before moving to Young People's Theatre, Persephone Theatre in Saskatoon, and then to the Great Canadian Theatre Company in Ottawa.

PASSE
Carl Marotte and Keanu Reeves in Brad Fraser's
WOLFBOY
With Bob Collins, Beverly Cooper, Joanne Vannicola & Shirley
Directed by John Palmer Set Concept: Tom Dean Lighting Design:
Opening March 30, 1984 8:30 p.m.
THEATRE PASSE MURAILLE 16 RYERSON AVE. TORONTO

Theatre Passe Muraille

CONNECTIONS

—

***WOLFBOY* HOUSE POSTER**
CARL MAROTTE AND KEANU REEVES. PHOTO BY DAVID HLYNSKY. DESIGN BY R.A. GLEDHILL.

Muraille

SLAPSTICK STAGE MANAGEMENT

BY KENDRA FRY

While out with two TPM alumni the other night, I was reminded of two things.

Thing One: People who worked at Passe Muraille together share a unique and unbreakable bond that defines all their interactions thereafter.

Thing Two: That bond often involves horrifically embarrassing moments that we wish would go away.

Over the years I grew from a young assistant stage manager, wide-eyed at working with the iconic Layne Coleman, to the general manager of TPM, equally wide-eyed at having the opportunity to work with the incomparable Andy McKim. However, it's not the great moments of budgeting genius or the awesome collaborative team problem-solving that people remember. Nope. It's the night that I pushed a desk off stage wearing a schoolgirl skirt.

I was working on *The School Show*, Ted Johns's one-man show about the destruction of the Canadian education system. Layne Coleman was directing and, given that the show was two hours long, all delivered by Ted, Layne decided that we needed the scene changes to be a bit longer to give Ted a moment to breathe. In the rehearsal hall at the Blyth Festival where the show initiated, all eyes turned to me as the young assistant stage manager, charged with changing the scenery. Could I maybe take a little longer moving that big desk around? Could I twirl the chair a little bit as I repositioned it? Could I act like it was all very tiring and I was bored of it? Oh, and could you do it in a private schoolgirl outfit complete with the short skirt?

It all kind of snuck up on me really. Like many an assistant stage manager over the years, one minute I was organizing props and tidying costumes and the next I was on stage with a relatively developed (albeit non-speaking) character. But I loved working with Layne and Ted and the whole team, so, fine.

A year later the show was staged at Passe Muraille and I revamped my role as Schoolgirl/Assistant Stage Manager. On opening night many, many people who I knew were in the audience, including people I had worked for or wanted to work with and, of course, my fiancé.

About halfway through the show I flounced on stage, grabbed the very heavy desk (which was on slides), gave it a twirl around, kicked my heels up as I leaned over it (for real, I did say that this was embarrassing), and pushed it off stage. ALL THE WAY OFF STAGE. The stage right side at that point ended in a flight of steps and had no kick rail around it. I pushed that damned oak desk with all its desk accessories on it, right off the stage.

There was a thump as the first two legs went over, a scattering noise as the file folders and pens went flying, a gasp from the audience, and an "oof!" from me. I madly grabbed hold of the end of the desk and stopped it going completely off, precariously balancing it on the edge.

Ted seemed not to have heard anything and came on stage to do the next scene. And all through the scene I desperately and quietly laboured to push an oak desk back on stage from below and reset it with all of its bits, which had scattered bloody everywhere in the dark. Occasionally I could hear the audience laughing at the obvious noises coming from off stage. At one point I let myself dream that my fiancé would leap from his seat, push through the curtain, and come to my rescue. Or perhaps that was a nightmare, hard to say in this situation.

Anyhow, I got it back on stage on time and at the end of the scene danced my ridiculous and red-faced way back out to push the desk on once more, to a scattering of applause from my colleagues.

The longest night of my life at Passe Muraille.

KENDRA FRY was the general manager at TPM from 2009 to 2013, but her first job at Passe Muraille was as an assistant stage manager in 1999. While at Passe Muraille, Kendra's commitment to new work included nineteen productions, fourteen collaborative productions, and five BUZZ Festivals. She also spearheaded upgrades to the building and its theatres, including the replacing the roof, installing a building-wide HVAC, and a new state-of-the-art lighting system in both theatre spaces. She is currently the general manager for Trinity-St. Paul's Centre for Faith, Justice and the Arts.

SUSPENSION OF DISBELIEF, *THE DRAWER BOY*
BY BROOKE JOHNSON.

FOUND A HOME

BY RYAN MCDOUGALL

I worked at TPM in some capacity for nine years. First catching crew calls, then filling in for the Backspace technician, whom I later took over for. I then moved to the Mainspace in a tech/technical director role. When the current production manager left I took over and occupied that role for about five years.

I am from a very small town. My first introduction to professional theatre was the Blyth Festival, so not a major culture shock. My next jump, however, was to Toronto as a production manager apprentice. As much as I would grow to love this city for all its intricacies and foibles, at the time this transition was terrifying.

Luckily for me one of the first places I worked at was TPM. It was a warm, welcoming group of weirdos dedicated not only to art but to the community. A community I was fortunate enough to become a part of. Layne Coleman had a way of referring to TPM as a ship. This always seemed appropriate to me, as it was the place that allowed me to stay afloat during my transition years and then became my home away from home for years to come.

A special place in my heart will always be held by that old building full of imagination and love.

RYAN MCDOUGALL started taking crew calls that led into house teching in TPM's Backspace and Mainspace, then took over as production facilities manager after Jonathan Rooke left, for a total of seven years with the company.

AN EVER-CHANGING ARTWORK

MICHAEL COOPER

The first theatre to hire me professionally was Theatre Passe Muraille. It was just after I completed a season as an assistant at the Shaw Festival. I called and the person on the phone said, "We can't hire you; we don't have that kind of money." I think they wanted to hang up on me. But alas, I did manage to work there in the late '70s and early '80s.

Every time I went to the theatre, the stage moved around. An ever-changing piece of artwork in itself. I do remember Graham Greene in a VideoCabaret production wearing a gaffer-tape moustache. The newspapers all went crazy trying to find the infamous photo of Keanu Reeves and Carl Marotte from *Wolfboy* I shot where Keanu looked like he was . . . shall I say, enjoying himself. Timing is everything. Such a vibrant creative theatre, I'm honoured to have a small place in its history.

MICHAEL COOPER has been a commercial photographer for almost forty years. Michael's dramatic flair and ability to capture mood and moment comes from his involvement with the performing-arts community. The first theatre in Toronto Michael worked for was Theatre Passe Muraille. He has photographed for many performing-arts companies in Toronto, including thirty-five years capturing the Canadian Opera Company's performances.

MY COMMUNITY

LINDSAY ANNE BLACK

This is my least incriminating story about my years with Passe Muraille.

I can't recall which show was opening that night, but TPM had become a homey place for me by then. I had been painting their scenery since 2003, and my designs were starting to hit both of their stages as part of their own season programming, and no longer with rental companies alone. My camera bag was with me, as it almost always was in those days—a gift from my partner at the time, Michelle, plus a group of delightful friends who had all contributed. For several years I had been taking photos around the various theatres where I worked whenever I was triggered by interesting light and texture, or an item that struck me as unique. Where other people might (probably, at the time) light a cigarette to occupy themselves while they waited for something, I would wander around with my camera. I would often walk the hour and a half home instead of taking transit, just so I could follow the alleys or waterfront paths in search of fodder. I had also begun to do PR shots for a few theatre companies, TPM included.

On that particular night, the camera kit was carefully hidden underneath my long leather coat on the back of my bar stool during the performance. After the show came down, I stayed by its side and allowed people to come to me. As the crowd began to thin out, however, I walked the six steps toward Trevor Schwellnus and the bar, turning back toward my things during our conversation. I never strayed from the area. When it was time to leave, I returned to the chair and put on my coat, but after a desperate assessment of what had happened I let the staff know that my camera kit was no longer there. A Nikon D80 and three lenses, plus batteries and chargers, were all now missing. Whoever had taken them had clearly been waiting specifically for their moment.

Since my Michelle had raised money for the first camera, she felt it would be inappropriate to do so again, and let it slide. A couple of weeks later, however, she got a call from Ryan McDougall, who was the TPM production manager at the time. He let her know that the staff had felt so badly about the theft that they had taken up a collection themselves, and he wanted to know the best way to turn over their contribution toward a replacement. Not only had the staff chipped in, artists from the shows currently in the building had donated as well—even some who did not know me personally. From there it spread to other theatres where I worked regularly. By the time I learned of all of this, the community had gathered more than a third of the cost of a completely new kit, which is what made the purchase possible at all. I couldn't believe the generosity of that place and our community—that so many people would support me in this way when my spirit—and livelihood—had taken a beating.

The replacement camera kit, which I still use and love, is to this day a reminder of how unified the theatre community can be when it's at its best. That was neither the first nor the last time I have had that overwhelming feeling of gratitude toward my friends and colleagues. Now that I have had to leave theatre to work in the digital realm, the camera is a regular reminder of a community I miss and respect tremendously. When trying to choose the right anecdote for this project, I first thought of all the late-night silliness or the diverse pieces of art we made together, but to me, the core quality of Passe Muraille is that spirit of support and generosity, of which I am grateful to have been a part. My great thanks.

LINDSAY ANNE BLACK is a social media manager based out of her home in Stratford, Ontario. She once built a successful career as a set and costume designer, scenic artist, and props builder for the performing arts, but left the industry in 2014.

I COULDN'T BELIEVE THE GENEROSITY OF THAT PLACE AND OUR COMMUNITY.

THE MAIN SPACE DURING REHEARSALS FOR *LIFE, DEATH AND THE BLUES*, 2014
PHOTO BY PETER MACCALLUM.

Passe Muraille

MEMORIES OF THE THEATRE BRATS COLLECTIVE'S *FOREVER YOUNG*, 1986

BY RACHEL THOMPSON

For many theatre brats, Theatre Passe Muraille was our playground when we were kids. It was a magical place to play dress-up, and the best for playing hide-and-go-seek. So many dark corners and heavy curtains to disappear into.

So one evening in 1986, when some kind of celebration was happening in the upstairs bar area, a twelve-year-old girl (that was me) decided to set the story straight. Clarke Rogers was the artistic director and we always loved his smile and wild hair. He was like an uncle to my sister Severn and me—he always wanted to know what we were doing and was our greatest fan. That's one thing about growing up in the theatre family—you end up with a huge, loving fan support of theatre aunties and uncles.

So on this evening of conversation, music, and ideas, Clarke and I sat on these tall stools discussing the fate of theatre in Canada. Sipping on my Shirley Temple, I plumped up my naive chick feathers and challenged Clarke that we kids could make a better play than any boring adult. We knew what it was all about. And instead of laughing this challenge away, Clarke said, "Okay let's see it."

So a few months later a group of theatre brats worked on a collectively written piece about being young, and the title was *Forever Young*. We went together on the streetcar across town for rehearsals and felt like our ideas were being taken seriously. We thought we were pretty fantastic and very funny as we portrayed our "real" version of the movie *The Breakfast Club*. We were an eclectic group of individuals who had the biggest theatre support you can imagine and Clarke Rogers was our supportive director who never once doubted us.

I can't remember how many performances we did in the Backspace, but it was magical. I can still hear Bob Dylan's song "Forever Young" playing when the lights went out to cue us to get into our first positions. We were taking to the stage to tell our story and people were listening. Theatre is indeed a live place of discourse and seeing the world through different lenses.

I'm not saying that this show solidified our future endeavours, but it sure played a role to strengthen our confidence to follow our passions. We became actors, directors, stage managers, writers, filmmakers, teachers, hair stylists, makeup artists, architects, and businesspeople.

Thank you, Clarke Rogers. Thank you, Theatre Passe Muraille.

RACHEL THOMPSON is a teacher and documentarian.

Sipping on my Shirley Temple, I plumped up my naive chick feathers and challenged Clarke that we kids could make a better play than any boring adult.

***FOREVER YOUNG* CAST PHOTO AND HOUSE PROGRAM**
STARRING SEVERN, JESSIE, RACHEL, DAVID, JENNIE, ADRIAN, PAUL, ARWEN, GABRIEL, AND HAIDA
STAGE MANAGED BY A SEVENTEEN-YEAR-OLD GAL NAMED KISS. PHOTO BY MATTHEW LEVEN.

JESSIE AND DAVID FYFE (ACTOR NANCY BEATTY'S CHILDREN)
RACHEL AND SEVERN THOMPSON (DIRECTOR PAUL THOMPSON AND ACTOR ANNE ANGLIN'S CHILDREN)
GABRIEL AND JENNIE HOGAN (ACTORS SUSAN AND MICHAEL HOGAN'S CHILDREN)
ARWEN MACDONELL (ACTOR/PROP MASTER FINA MACDONELL'S CHILD)
PAUL BRAUNSTEIN (ACTOR JEFF BRAUNSTEIN AND ACTOR/DIRECTOR MAJA ARDAL'S CHILD)
ADRIAN BURNETT (PAINTER RAE JOHNSON'S CHILD)
HAIDA HARPER (ACTOR KYRA HARPER'S CHILD)

Passe Muraille

ON THEATRE PASSE MURAILLE

BY JACOB RICHMOND

In the way that any human life can have chapters like a novel, Theatre Passe Muraille, the building, the company, has been significant in my life as a teenager, a young man, and a father.

As a teenager, when my father worked there, it was my summer job. I got paid to clean up, paint things, grunt work mostly. I got paid by Dad from his own pocket, twenty bucks a week, if I can recall. Through the periphery of my own pubescent self-obsession I remember clear moments.

The electric Toronto premiere of Tomson Highway's *Dry Lips Oughta Move to Kapuskasing*.

On my first ever grown-up date watching *Echo* by an obscure theatre artist by the name of Robert Lepage. The date went remarkably well, considering the play featured a scene where God had sex with a nun in a revolving bed. No kissing. We never made a love connection. But she really liked the play and went back again and took her mother.

Going to *Rigoletto* every night. As a young teen who listened to bands like Megadeath, Slayer, and Iron Maiden, I was rigid in my musical tastes, and certainly would go out of my way to voice my utter contempt for any and all forms of musical theatre. But there I was, every night, at *Rigoletto*, singing along . . . I remember Dad would ask if I liked it. "It's okay I guess . . . " said with a non-committal teenage shrug . . . "But you've seen it like thirty times," Dad would say. I would avert my eyes and stare at my shoes, not liking being called out for liking things. "There's nothing else to do in Toronto."

As a young neurotic playwright who had hidden his interest in theatre like a drug addiction from his parents. Having my second play produced in, of all places, Theatre Passe Muraille, passing like a wild animal in the alley, climbing the Theatre Beyond Walls. Near opening, having my first ever anxiety attack, then receiving an opening night card from Dad's friend that read, "One billion people in China couldn't possibly give a fuck. Love David Ferry." Oddly enough this actually worked, and I have used this sage joke several times over my professional career whenever I feel I am taking myself too seriously.

Parties in the shop! They never told me about those as a teen! It's a whole entire world down there!

Theatre Passe Muraille Backspace . . . falling in love in the green room with my future wife.

The first play my son Ira would ever see.

Approaching the anniversary of my mom's death (actress Janet Wight, March 8, 1945–November 14, 2016) I am struck by the ephemeral nature of her life's work. Yes, she did a lot of film and TV, and that is probably where she is best known—but I am sure she would agree her proudest moments as an artist happened on stage.

And for this there is no record of her Hedda Gabler, her Martha, her King Lear: all of it lives only in memory of those still

RIDE THE CYCLONE
ELLIOTT LORAN, RIELLE BRAID, SARAH PELZER, MATTHEW COULSON, KELLY HUDSON, AND KHOLBY WARDELL. PHOTO BY FAIREN BERCHARD, COURTESY OF ATOMIC VAUDEVILLE.

alive who were in the audience. And once time trudges on, even that memory will gradually fade. This idea used to terrify me, but as I get older I find the idea rather beautiful and in keeping with why the theatre will always draw us together. The strange practice of a large group of people sitting in chairs, staring at a smaller group of people pretending to be other people—usually damaged people (people you wouldn't want to have over for dinner). We watch them go through their paces, their hopes, dreams, anxieties, neurosis, prejudices in front of us. Just the act itself is ritualistic, and one of the oldest rituals the human species has. Good or bad I always find something intrinsically noble about the practice—no one does it for money, fame, or influence, and after a lifetime of hard work as a performer on stage, your best work will have no permanent record—mostly it will disappear.

My mom raised three kids on a theatre actress salary. It was a hard life, and she was always in a panic about the next gig. It's a job, a hard one. One where your performance review is in a newspaper and will greatly decide how much work you will get in the next year. You find yourself doing gigs you know aren't right for you; you deal with fragile egos, blowhards, dilettantes.

Why would anyone choose such a life? I don't think you can help yourself. I certainly didn't choose to be a playwright . . . I just couldn't stop myself from writing plays. As I remember my mom, I feel she couldn't help herself either. Because for all of her funny bluster and late-night "fuck fucking-theatre," there were moments she would refer to it as "secular church," and would speak of those few times where the alchemy was just right. Those rare moments where you walk off stage and feel an endorphin rush better than any stimulant, and think to yourself, "This day I've truly lived."

I feel a lot of those days for myself, both professionally and personally, have happened at that converted warehouse on Ryerson and Wolseley. Three separate chapters of my life, three separate mindsets, goals, priorities under one roof. The name of the theatre, "a theatre beyond walls" has gathered more significance with each passing year, and how much that company has meant to me as a human.

I look forward to the next!

JACOB RICHMOND's plays include *The Qualities of Zero*, *Small Returns*, and *Legoland*. He has also written pieces for CBC Radio as well as for film and television. Having worked as a writer and performer at numerous cabarets in Montreal, he was inspired to collaborate with director Britt Small to create Atomic Vaudeville, a monthly award-winning cabaret in Victoria, British Columbia, where he now resides.

PASSE MURAILLE SAVED MY LIFE

BY ANDREW MOODIE

My first memory of Theatre Passe Muraille is that it saved my life.

I was working as a sous-chef in a failing restaurant on Granville Island in Vancouver. An old high-school friend of mine was the head chef and, as he saw the owners turn all the profits of the place into a little white powder, he told me I should be prepared to get the hell out of there.

I had moved to Vancouver from my hometown of Ottawa, brought out by David Bloom to act in a wild and creative version of *Macbeth* set in a prison camp. I loved doing the show, and I loved Vancouver. Really loved it. I was hoping after the production to stay and just go from one theatre to another. But back in those days there were few opportunities for an actor in theatre, and even fewer for an actor of colour in BC. And it became very clear, very quickly, that I was going nowhere fast.

Before moving to Vancouver I attended a rally at city hall in Toronto to protest cuts to arts funding. A man by the name of Layne Coleman saw me at that protest, and he, for some strange reason, thought I could act. So he called a friend of mine, George Seremba, to get my contact info. And he asked me to come out and act in a play by John Allen called *Cafe Negril*. He asked if I could do a Jamaican accent. "Absolutely!" I lied.

So when I finally made it to the Backspace of Theatre Passe Muraille, the first thing that struck me was the smell. It was the smell of paint, cigarettes, alcohol, and youth. I was working with the stunningly beautiful Jane Spidell. Her talent and beauty were really too much. It was like staring into the sun. I had the good sense to never tell her what I thought of her because I don't think I'd be able to do so without sounding a tad obsessed and a little creepy. Hopefully she never reads this.

John Allen was the playwright, and he had written a really touching, complex personal play about his experiences in Jamaica, and I was so happy and eager to be a part of it. When I discovered he was also acting in the show I remember thinking to myself, why the hell would a playwright want to act in his own show? Wow, that's a mistake. Someone should tell him. I mean, who would do that? Really! But he was really great. Generous. Funny. And tortured. Just like me.

And Layne . . . Layne was every ounce the theatre royalty he appeared to be. Gracious, kind to a fault, encouraging, and I could tell, just from looking in his eyes, that he was an old soul and a brilliant actor. During rehearsal I would coax Layne and John to tell me stories about "The Old Days." The early days of Passe Muraille. And I very quickly realized that I had stumbled onto something like Camelot. It wasn't Camelot, but that's the way I liked to think of it. In my imagination Paul Thompson was the bearded wizard Merlin. Clarke Rogers was King Arthur. Linda Griffiths was Lady Guinevere. And it soon became very clear that before me, in the rehearsal hall, sitting behind a table, dolling out pithy words of wisdom, was Lancelot.

From what I could gather the play *O.D. on Paradise* was a seminal moment in their lives, and a truly bacchanalian production both on and off the stage. I imagined all those young, drunk, drugged-up, horny bodies getting on stage every night. Lots of drama, lots of laughs, and tears.

But Passe Muraille wasn't Camelot. It was something new. Breaking boundaries. It was sexual. It was political. It was raw. It was profane. It was something that went . . . beyond.

By the time I worked at Passe Muraille in John's play, times had changed. The pot smoke in the play was just oregano—a prop that had to be replaced when someone who saw the show thought I was smoking real weed and broke into the dressing room to steal the whole bag. There was no drama behind the scenes, just respectful professionalism. But the energy was still there. The ghosts. The imprint of the spirit of all those artists who created this theatre; you can feel it when you get close to the walls. Still to this day I am overcome every now and then by the fact that so many lives, so many people have had such an impact on this theatre. And I'm so happy to have taken a small part in its life. After all, it saved mine.

ANDREW MOODIE is an award-winning film, television, and theatre actor, director, and playwright. He has received a Chalmers Award for his play *Riot*, a Dora Mavor Moore Award for his performance in *Health Class*, and a Writers Guild of Canada Screenwriting Award for his work on *Afghanada*.

THREE FATHERS

BY ALAN DILWORTH

In 2004 I wrote and directed a piece called *The Unforgetting*. It was developed and produced by Belltower Theatre (myself, Maev Beaty, and Patrick Robinson) at the SummerWorks Festival. Maev, Patrick, and Andrew Penner starred in it—Andrew was also the music director. It was a haunting piece about a young woman and her husband after the recent death of her father. The question at hand was who her father really was and a mystery around who owned the mill they called their own. It was inspired by the story of my mother's father, who had been a street kid in London, England, and sent via the Home Children program to work on a farm in Southern Ontario at eight years of age. After about a year he ran away to Toronto with his eleven-year-old brother, who was a Home Child on another farm. They learned to survive on the streets of Toronto. My grandfather ended up making a beautiful life for himself and his family in Toronto, but he had many secrets. *The Unforgetting* was a very personal and poetic work. I fell madly in love with the Mainspace working on it. *The Unforgetting* won the SummerWorks Jury Prize and marked the beginning of my relationship with Andy McKim and, ultimately, Theatre Passe Muraille. I returned to the Mainspace four more times, three were for SummerWorks productions: *Eustache Wake* (which I co-wrote and co-directed with Jorge Gidi), *If We Were Birds* by Erin Shields, *The Middle Place* by Andrew Kushnir (which was later offered as a co-production between TPM, Project: Humanity, and Canadian Stage in their 2011/12 seasons), and I will discuss the fourth Mainspace project below.

In 2012 I had the privilege of directing Pamela Mala Sinha's *Crash* in the Backspace at Passe Muraille as part of their 2012 season. *Crash* is a stunningly poetic piece about love and loss. It is one of the most poignant pieces I have ever worked on, with the most dedicated and extraordinary creative team. In *Crash*, the loss of a girl's father sends her on a "trauma logic odyssey" through a labyrinth of love, loss, and memory. During *Crash*, Pamela, Debashis, Ruby, and the rest of Pamela's family taught me many things about love, loss, and grief. I never met Pamela's father but felt close to him as we worked, through the love of his family and friends. I am grateful to them for all they shared, and to Andy McKim and TPM for their support for this important project.

In the fall of 2014 I returned to the Mainspace to direct *The De Chardin Project* by Adam Seybold as part of TPM's 2014/15 season. This production had particular significance to me. It starred my friend Cyrus Lane and my wife Maev Beaty and was designed by two of my favourite collaborators and friends, Lorenzo Savoini (production design) and Thomas Ryder Payne (sound). But what was most significant for me about working on *De Chardin* was that my father was dying while we were working on it. *The De Chardin Project* is the story of the scientist and Jesuit priest Teilhard de Chardin. The structure of the play revolves around De Chardin's reckoning with his life as he is dying. My father was a devout Catholic and had been educated by the Basilian Fathers. Toward the end of his life, my father became increasingly inspired by the Jesuit fathers, in particular some of their spiritual practices and orientation to social justice and service. For his and my mother's social engagement, the Jesuit Regis College at U of T bestowed a joint honorary doctorate upon my mother and father the spring before we began rehearsal. Life and art were closely linked for me on *De Chardin*. Never before had I experienced such a confluence between meaning and aesthetics in the work, been so in love with the Mainspace, or felt it so transformed as it was in this project. Just before we began rehearsal, my father, then very ill, asked me when we were opening. We opened November 25. On November 27 my father died.

Theatre Passe Muraille is and always will be held very close to my heart. The history, the space, Andy and his team, and the work my collaborators and I have created there all run right through me. I am one of many that have been shaped by TPM, and I am very grateful.

ALAN DILWORTH is a theatre director, playwright, and teacher. He is the acting artistic director and a Drummond-Dorrance Fellow at Soulpepper Theatre Company in Toronto. He is also co-artistic director of Sheep No Wool. His work explores personal, social, and political transformation and is rooted in questions of "self," inspired by the tension between Zen Buddhism and modernity.

CRASH

BY PAMELA MALA SINHA

I'm an actress. Before 2012 I had never thought of myself as a playwright. The only thing I had written up to that time was a short story about PTSD that had been published in an anthology called *Dropped Threads*. It was not until a few years later, after experiencing a different kind of grief—the loss of a parent—that I felt the need to express myself in the medium I loved. I started writing a play, not knowing if I would ever finish it, or if it would one day be produced. Looking back I think there are three main reasons why both occurred.

The main precondition for a production, you might think, is the play itself; without its existence, there would be no "premiere." In the case of *Crash*—without the possibility of a premiere, there would have been no play.

In 2010 I wrote an OAC Recommender Grant for Theatre Creators to Factory Theatre to start a draft of the play. When I received notification of that award by letter, scrawled across the bottom of it were the words "call me." A week or so later, by the stone bench in the Factory courtyard, I met the brilliant and formidable Iris Turcott for the first time. When I told her the only thing I had written was a short story a few years back, she took a long drag of her cigarette and said, "Well, now you're going to write a fucking play." That's the first reason the play exists.

The following year, when I had completed two-thirds of the play, Chris Abraham asked me what I was looking for in a director. I said, "Unsentimental, but sensitive." He said, "Alan Dilworth." He gave me his email and I sent what I had to Alan—whom I had never met. He called back almost immediately. I didn't know at the time that this phone call would be the beginning of one of the most important creative partnerships of my life. Before we hung up, I told Alan that I had no idea how or where we would do the play—he said, "We'll do it on a doorstep if we have to, but we will do it." That's the second reason.

With a director on board, I applied to TPM's BUZZ Festival in September 2011. After a brief rehearsal with Alan I found myself sitting on a very high stool, alone in a pool of light on the stage of the Mainspace, reading an excerpt from my first solo play. Not long after, as I was getting on the Bathurst streetcar, I heard a voice I recognized. When Alan saw me he said—into his phone—"She's right here! I'll ask her." Andy had called to say that the April slot had just come open in the season—could I finish the play in time? There was no time to think about it—we would have to answer now, on the streetcar! I don't know if I ever would have finished my play if Andy hadn't offered to produce it in that phone call. The risk he took is the third reason.

Less than five months later, under Alan's brilliant direction and with Kimberly Purtell's poetic lighting and set, Cameron Davis's stunning projections, and Debashis Sinha's haunting soundscape, *Crash* came to life in a way that I couldn't have imagined as I was writing it. Though I have performed the play on many stages since then, that first production is still the most special to me, perhaps because of the love that compelled me to start the play, and the space that inspired me to finish it—for our premiere in the magical Backspace, at our beloved Theatre Passe Muraille.

PAMELA MALA SINHA is an award-winning actress and playwright working in theatre, film, and television. Her first solo play, *Crash*, which she also performed, garnered six 2012 Dora Mavor Moore Award nominations and four wins, including Outstanding Performance by a Lead Actress and Outstanding New Play. Her second play, *Happy Place*, premiered at Soulpepper Theatre, Toronto, in September 2015. Pamela is currently adapting *Happy Place* into a film for Sienna Films.

—
CRASH
PAMELA MALA SINHA. PHOTO BY MICHAEL COOPER.

LATE NIGHT SHENANIGANS

BY BEVERLEY COOPER

I think of TPM as my first theatrical home, complete with deep love, nurturing, slamming doors, and "fuck yous." Shortly after I moved to Toronto, I acted in a show called *Rude Noises (For a Blank Generation)*, written (with the company) and directed by a young, über-talented Brad Fraser. I played a store-window mannequin and spent most of the show holding various poses for as long as I could. Rehearsals involved some improv sessions and one day an actor came in with a story about how the previous night he had dropped acid, gone dumpster diving, and ate a live rat. My young, naive mind was quickly opened to new possibilities.

I was in awe of the master legend, Paul Thompson, who was hovering around the periphery of the show. After a run-through, his note to me was "she's every woman." I wasn't quite sure how to translate that into something actable, but that was only the beginning of my journey to understand Paul's enigmatic, metaphoric take on theatre. I performed in several more shows at TPM (including the infamous John Palmer–directed *Wolfboy* starring Keanu Reeves), all made with controversy, anxiety, and a deep devotion to creativity.

In 1984 Ann-Marie MacDonald and I created a short play for Rhubarb satirizing the Nancy Drew mystery books for girls. Clarke Rogers was, by then, the artistic director at TPM. He saw our piece and invited us to do a late-night serial show. So for six weeks every Sunday morning, Ann-Marie and I would meet and decide on what the next week's story would be; we'd divvy up scenes and then head off to our respective corners to write. On Tuesdays we'd meet up, share, and rewrite each other's work. On Wednesdays we'd meet with our director, the marvellous Maureen White. She gave us writing notes; we'd figure out the casting and decide what props, costumes, or sound we'd need. Friday afternoons we rehearsed and Friday nights at eleven p.m. we'd put on these wild, fly-by-the-seat-of-your-pants shows.

Nancy Drew: Clue in the Fast Lane was based in political satire, centring on Nancy Drew, teen detective, who was yanked out of her books to help solve a modern-day mystery: a right-wing zealot had taken over the presidency and was trying to take America back to the "good old days" of white picket fences and apple pie (sound familiar?). The shows began in the Backspace, but by the end of the run we were packing out the Mainspace, standing room only. That all led to a longer, rehearsed run, consolidating the writing into three "action packed" episodes. We had a wildly talented group of people acting with us along the way, folks like Layne Coleman (Carson Drew), Kate Lynch (Hannah Gruen), Ken Girotti, and Saul Rubinek (villains). Derek Boyes, Stuart Clow, Henry Czerny, Tony DeSantis, Paul Gross, and Colin Mochrie all played Hardy Boys at some point.

I remember arriving at the theatre at about ten p.m. to set up for the late-night show. I was carrying a large box of props, various bits of costumes, and a cassette tape of weird sound effects. The dressing room was dark. I was fumbling around for a light and tripped over one of the tech guys who was sleeping on an old grubby mattress on the floor: someone always seemed to be crashing in the theatre then. The tech guy lurched out, in a daze, to set up for the show, and I bent down to pick up the mattress and drag it out of the dressing room. My hand touched something warm, wet, and sticky. The tech guy had also been jacking off. It was the way of the TPM world then. Kind of crazy, but a whole lot of fun.

Both BEVERLEY COOPER's acting and writing work have deep roots in TPM. Highlights include workshopping/improvising a new Linda Griffiths play; acting on a eleven-foot high dangerously raked stage with Shirley Douglas in *Wolfboy*; being mentored by the great and wild Clarke Rogers; and having her dear friend Ann-Marie MacDonald be both acting, writing, and tap-dancing partner for their serial high-jinx projects, *Nancy Drew: Clue in the Fast Lane* and *The Road Shows*.

Clues to women's modern ways

By JON KAPLAN

"A girl's gotta do what a girl's gotta do."

That's the motto for a show that looks like three weeks of fun theatre — Nancy Drew: Clue in the Fast Lane. The work, by Prewd Productions in association with Theatre Passe Muraille, is now running in the Backspace of Passe Muraille.

The show began a few years ago as a short skit in a Rhubarb series. Then, last fall, it ran as late-night

NOW THEATRE

theatre at Passe Muraille. After a workshop session at Factory Theatre's Brave New Works, the show is finally getting a "prime-time" release.

The work has been written (and rewritten) by Beverley Cooper and Ann-Marie MacDonald, who sit in the interview with magnifying glasses close at hand. Looking for clues, of course.

"The first Nancy Drew books were written in the late 30s," says Cooper. "By the 50s, they were being doctored and giving a different view of Nancy. Now they're being updated, with the teen detective looking for clues in rock videos."

"The books were a formula for conditioning girls," notes MacDonald. "For us, while we were writing the script, Nancy became mixed up with all the TV shows we watched as kids, with a perfect family and house, better-than-real-life situations, and all the ideals we should aim for. Nancy became an impossible role model for all these things; she was as squeaky-clean as sliced white bread."

The show obviously spoofs all of this. Nancy is teamed with a flawed and outrageous modern girl, Janice the Babysitter, who has been blitzed by "sugar overload, Halloween 25, and Porky's 87. She is a victim of mass-hysteria pop culture, but she still knows what it'll be like when they push the button," says MacDonald.

Powder-blue roadster

The first episode opens in 1955, just as Nancy is proposed to by Ned Nickerson, a childhood beau. In a quandary because she doesn't want to hang up her magnifying glass, she goes out for a drive in her powder-blue roadster. Somehow she time travels and ends up in 1985, at the house where Janice is baby-sitting. The two are terrorized by everything from recent schlock films, including *him* on the extension phone upstairs and a blood-thirsty chain saw. They escape from the house, right into a series of adventures and dastardly plots.

More than that Cooper and MacDonald won't say, except that over the three weeks that the episodes will be running (one per week, Wednesday-Sunday through June 2), there will be travel back and forth through time and across several other pieces of teen fiction. The Hardy Boys, for instance, in the persons of Derek Boyes and Henry Czerny, will be part of the action; the actors also double as villains in the piece.

Also in the company are Kate Lynch as Hannah, Nancy's motherly housekeeper ("June Cleaver if she had never married"), and Layne Coleman as Carson Drew, "the best of dads." We're also warned to expect visits from such diverse personalities as Barbie Doll and Flipper.

"Our idea," says MacDonald, "was to take the ideal girl from the past and have her collide with modern society. Both she and Janice are amazed at each other's views of the world. Yet both want a free world, and the two seeming ends of the spectrum finally come together. At base they're not so different."

Since both writers wanted to play Nancy and Janice, they're sharing the parts. Neither sees the show as a heavy piece of agitprop theatre, despite the satire on right-wing politics and values that is part of the work. Director Maureen White has spoken of it as theatre of the obvious. "But," adds MacDonald, "we hit you with a funny-bone hammer, not something out of the Gong Show."

This is a "new and improved" show, with recaps and previews of the next episode each week. It's worth coming to even if you've seen it in some other version.

"We want people to think that anything can happen here," says Cooper. "It will."

Beverley Cooper (left) and Ann-Marie MacDonald use teenage sleuths to make grownup statements about women.

SUSIE KING

—

NANCY DREW: CLUE IN THE FAST LANE* HOUSE AD AND REVIEW IN *NOW MAGAZINE

REMEMBERING

BY PAULETTE PHILLIPS

Paulette Phillips remembers . . .

"You've got to be careful with what you choose to write about. The conflict at the core of your writing commonly infects your real world and becomes the conflict in your life." That was the piece of wisdom I received from Jacob Wren when I confided to him that I was at my wits end during the rehearsal phase of my play *Controlling Interest*.

Staged in the Backspace at Theatre Passe Muraille in 1995, *Controlling Interest* was conceived as a feminist play that took a cold look at jealousy and competition within women's working relationships, how women struggle to make art, and struggle to collaborate. I wonder now how I could have been so naive or inexperienced to think I would not have trouble directing a play about a woman directing a film, in which a beautiful young woman is cast in a sexually charged role in a feminist erotic film.

So in this play about the making of a film, Linda, a forty-year-old filmmaker, is recognized, to comic effect, to be her own worst enemy. She is ornery, combative, and desperate to make her film. The audience connected with the self-effacing humour of it all.

The brilliant Tracy Wright played Linda the filmmaker; Les, the cameraman boyfriend, was played by the wonderful Brian Tree; and the talented Brian Sweetapple and Sigrid Johnson played Frank and Zoe, the actors cast in Linda's art film. The play revolved around sexual tension, jealousy, the toxic relationship between Zoe and Linda, the fraying relationship between Les and Linda, and the frisson between Linda and Frank. Linda was the centre of it all.

The play was about women and power, their working relationships, sexuality and aging. What I didn't expect was that the conflict would really be between me and Tracy as we struggled to mount the play and define a shared vision. It was one of the most challenging and difficult working relationships in my life. The rehearsals were tense and painful. For me, the full extent of what I wanted to explore, the rich difficulties of that particular cultural moment for a certain kind of sexualized feminist artist, became the *coup de grâce* of the development period for that play. I don't think my friendship with Tracy ever recovered from

—

***CONTROLLING INTEREST* HOUSE POSTER**

that difficult time of working together, but I will always carry with me huge respect and love for her and her brilliance.

At this moment, as I conjure these memories, I find myself again struggling with the inevitability of how an art subject casts a spectre on real life. This time the subject is life and death—or is there such a thing as death . . . as I develop the strategies and visual language to explore wilding and the succession of a house succumbing to nature. The nature of that struggle is not for discussion here.

In reality, thinking back on that period, I remember a lot of laughter and fun and intense conversations about theatre, art . . . I think that TPM most definitely had a family, was a series of families, and, given that was the nature of the place, I was a foster child, taken in for a short time and made to feel at home. I will always be grateful to the team that supported my work . . . Susan Serran, David Baile, and Robin Fulford, with whom I worked with closely as a producer. Tracy, Sigrid, Nadia Ross, Daniel Brooks, Daniel MacIvor, Val Buhagiar, Caroline Gillis—these were my pals and for that time, there, I felt very connected to a large network of theatre artists.

PAULETTE PHILLIPS is a visual artist whose practice combines film and video installation, sculpture, photography, and performance. Phillips is a professor at OCAD University. In the 1990s Phillips worked in theatre, writing and directing the experimental performance installations *Under the Influence* at Factory Theatre (1992) and *Controlling Interest* (1995) at Theatre Passe Muraille. Phillips shared a Dora Mavor Moore Award for Best Female Performance with Tracy Wright, Nadia Ross, Ali Riley, Valerie Buhagiar, Caroline Gillis, and Maria Vacratsis for their work in the *Lorca Play*, directed by Daniel MacIvor and Daniel Brooks.

POSSIBLE WORLDS
LISA RYDER AND RANDY HUGHSON.
PHOTO BY GREG TJEPKEMA.

POSSIBLE WORLDS

BY JOHN MIGHTON

One of the most rewarding experiences of my career as a playwright was working with Daniel Brooks on a remount of my play *Possible Worlds* in the Backspace in 1998 (with producers Robin Fulford and Susan Serran).

A few years before the remount I had been fortunate enough to see, in the Mainspace, the extraordinarily funny and thought-provoking *The Noam Chomsky Lectures* by Daniel Brooks and Guillermo Verdecchia. I had never seen a play that made me feel, so viscerally, the importance of political ideas. I eventually approached Daniel to see if he would consider directing *Possible Worlds*.

In his production Daniel employed many of the groundbreaking directorial techniques that he had developed working on his own plays and on the plays of writers like Daniel MacIvor.

Because *Possible Worlds* is about the power and the limitations of the imagination, Daniel and his designers, Richard Feren and Andrea Lundy, set out to create a series of new worlds and shifting atmospheres, using the most minimal elements of light and sound. In the first scene the curtain rose to the sound of a skipping record and revealed two detectives standing over the body of a man whose brain has been removed. A single bulb in a grey casing swung back and forth—almost imperceptibly—over the heads of the detectives. This movement produced a disorienting effect, which mirrored the confusion and discomfort of the detectives, as the entire stage seemed to be swinging slowly with the pool of light cast by the bulb.

Daniel and his actors and designers approached every scene and every set change with the same sense of rigour and inventiveness. Until this production I had never really understood the possibilities of light and sound, or the power of great direction. I am grateful to have had such a magical production and will always remember the little black box theatre that somehow—through the boundless imaginations of these artists—seemed to contain the universe.

JOHN MIGHTON is a mathematician, author, playwright, and the founder of JUMP Math, a successful school program designed to tutor children who are having difficulties in math. Mighton's plays *Scientific Americans*, *Possible Worlds*, *A Short History of Night*, *Body and Soul*, *The Little Years*, and *Half Life* have been performed across Canada, as well as in Europe, Japan, and the United States, and have won several national awards, including the Governor General's Literary Award for Drama.

Passe Muraille

PASSE MURAILLE AND THE PUPPETMONGERS

BY DAVID AND ANN POWELL

Puppetmongers Theatre has a long and fruitful history with Theatre Passe Muraille. We first performed in the Backspace in the mid-1980s, with a double bill of our *Walidad the Grass Cutter* (an old tale told as a travelogue of our 1976 tour in Iran) paired with *The Brick Bros. Circus* (a circus of performing building bricks). We also seem to remember that when we approached to repeat the next year, the theatre had programmed in Dennis Lee's *Alligator Pie*.

Having built a strong professional friendship with Andy McKim when he was at the Tarragon Theatre, in 2010 we came to Passe Muraille with our production of Charles Dickens's *Hard Times*. The play was directed by Chris Earle and featured us and Anand Rajaram, and it was designed and built to fit perfectly in the Backspace: it was our biggest and longest show to date, and we ran for a wonderful two weeks. It was during this run that we got a telephone call just after a school matinee to tell us that our ailing mother was dying—and the final news came at the end of the show that she'd died just as the show had started. There was nothing we could have done, as she was living up north of Kingston, but that awareness and sadness put an extra twist into the performance that night.

In 2012, when our usual venue was not available for our annual winter holiday production, we ran *Cinderella in Muddy York* in the Mainspace, for this so-far twenty-seven-year-old tradition for family audiences. The run was fun, but the venue switch was not great for Puppetmongers's box-office revenue.

In 2014 we remounted our oldest show, *The Miller & His Wife*, in the Backspace for a week of performances for school groups, and then through March break for families. This show is a retelling of two classic folk tales of greed and dastardly doings.

We are currently developing a Puppetry Hive to nurture puppetry and theatre artists and collaborations. This program is in partnership with Theatre Passe Muraille and supported with funds from the Ontario Hive Councils. We anticipate Hive members presenting their works in progress at Passe Muraille events in the near future.

The brother and sister team of ANN POWELL and DAVID POWELL have been creating award-winning puppet theatre for school, family, and adult audiences since 1974, earning a reputation as leaders and innovators in puppetry arts. Ann and David have toured their productions around the world, while here at home they have had a long and fruitful history with Theatre Passe Muraille, since first performing in the Backspace in the 1980s.

PASSE MURAILLE IN A NUTSHELL

BY DIANA BELSHAW

. . . or perhaps it would be better to say "impressions and experiences of Passe Muraille," as there have been so many different manifestations of my relationship to the theatre.

It seems appropriate that my first recollection of Passe Muraille was from a confusing and utterly fruitless visit to the building on Trinity Square. Fresh out of theatre school with a thin veneer of New York sophistication, I was in Toronto to meet artistic directors and restart my Canadian career after four years away. All I remember of that visit was darkness, a mystifying chaos, and a deep relief at heading back out the door. Not actually a metaphor for how I feel about TPM, but certainly representative of many moments along the way!

Years later I returned to Toronto after time back in Vancouver. I had seen a number of Passe Muraille productions on tour, *Doukhobors*, *Naked on the North Shore*, and a hilarious CODCO parody of Passe Muraille's collective-creation process. Even before encountering the TPM world, I had a sense of what it was and the gulf between it and what most theatres were doing in the late '70s. It was mythical and groundbreaking theatre made by giants about stories we didn't know but needed to . . . and funny.

Clarke Rogers engineered my first job in Toronto (I suspect simply to prove to Paul Thompson that he actually knew more people in Toronto than Paul did) by telling Paul that he should hire me for the about-to-happen *Les Maudits Anglais* (1978). The expected audition turned into something else. It became more of a conversation, an argument—nothing to do with acting—and suddenly I was part of a collective, based in Montreal, working in fractured French and preparing to perform in front of an audience of highly political Montrealers at Théâtre d'aujourd'hui. Eric Peterson quit within a week; David Fox and Paul Kelman soldiered on, dragging Linda Griffiths, John Jarvis, and myself into the ring. Anyone who has ever been part of a Paul Thompson collective knows that the process can be life-threatening—I have never been as confused, out on the edge, terrified, and enraged (engaged?) as I was through that long, hot Montreal summer. We went on tour to campgrounds in the Gaspé, banging drums to summon an audience (to my complete horror), performing fragments of confused material in bad French to bewildered campers, and mostly despairing that there would ever be anything performable. In Paul's inimitable miracle-building fashion, there eventually was a show; it played

IT WAS MYTHICAL AND GROUNDBREAKING THEATRE MADE BY GIANTS ABOUT STORIES WE DIDN'T KNOW BUT NEEDED TO . . . AND FUNNY.

to sold-out houses, created an uproar in the French theatre community, and gave birth to Linda's iconic *Maggie and Pierre* a year later. We even played the show with surtitles (take that, COC!) in Toronto.

The Passe Muraille link led to another company that was part of the TPM diaspora, the Blyth Festival, where I worked for many years with Janet Amos, Ted Johns, Miles Potter, and many artists who came through the TPM crucible. Even there, there are indelible images of the cast working on another collective with Thompson, trekking into the Rubber Boot after a hard day of boiling animal carcasses for the show. TPM has always had an experiential element in its makeup. Over the years I did workshops at TPM on plays that often remained in the development phase (including Paul Quarrington's *Pumpkin* with David Fox's delivery of, "You take a pumpkin, you put it on the window sill . . . and then you drink it" seared into my brain). I watched the extraordinary first workshop of *The Crackwalker*. I saw a magical production directed by Miles Potter of Dennis Lee's *Alligator Pie* with a two-year-old daughter whose eyes widened and whose love of theatre ignited.

Then back in the later '80s to do Hector Bunyan's *Three Beats to the Bar*. Hector's play was notable for a number of things—no one else was writing about the deep agony of displacement the way Hector was; the cast included Veronica Moreno, a South American actor who should, by rights, have been working more than she ever did; and the rehearsals coincided with one of the many financial crises to which TPM was subject over the years. A Canada Council grant was in the works, but cash flow had dried up. So Sarah Wakely, our amazing stage manager, cashed in her RRSPs to cover payroll and we journeyed on to opening. It was not a great production (although I often think that the play might have done better twenty years later, weaving as it did poetic language and imagery with the political and social wounds of a generation of refugees).

TPM and I went our separate ways for almost twenty years after this. I remember productions that still sit deeply in my memory (*The Yoko Ono Project*, *A Midsummer Night's Dream*, *The Drawer Boy*), but I moved outside the circle of artists whose artistic lives were bound up in the company. And then, in 2009, I was asked to sit on the board of directors. Andy McKim and Hugh Neilson had hauled the company out of yet another financial morass and were looking for allies on the board to support their vision of the company. I was privileged to be able to work along with them, and then Kendra Fry and Régine Cadet, on what have become the herculean struggles and challenges that beset theatre companies today.

Around the same time, I came to Andy in despair, as the theatre building at Humber (where I was then director of the Theatre Performance Program) was being demolished and we were to become homeless for a year. Bless TPM. The theatre not only took us in and rented us space, but the staff devised a mentorship program for the graduating students so that they would be integrated into the company. This was a brilliant and generous initiative to bridge young artists from the conservatory into the professional world, and it remained in place for a number of years. Humber's Backspace Project was a testing ground for our young creators to devise and produce their own work, as they would be required to do once they graduated, and, not surprisingly, many have remained part of the TPM community ever since. Only at TPM!

And now I am back to being an audience member. As I said at the beginning, I have experienced TPM from so many directions that my sense of the company is a collage of images, of passionate moments of discovery and risk, disaster always imminent, but a wild will to survive and breed new artists. It's a huge legacy that is living and ready to subvert the community anew.

DIANA BELSHAW has been part of the TPM community since the late 1970s as an actor, supporter, and chair of the board of directors. Through her early association with TPM she also formed long-lasting relationships with the Blyth Festival and many other companies across Canada. She is an actor, director, dramaturge, educator, and arts administrator.

THEATRE PASSE MURAILLE

Artistic Producer
Susan Serran

General Manager
Colin Rose

February 14, 1993

Dear Jubilee Participant (and Equity Member)

Two weeks ago, Theatre Passe Muraille received a letter from Ron Haney over at Equity demanding that all actors involved in this evening's fund raiser be payed 175.00 for donating our services. Now, none of us had ever raised the issue of being payed, and no one can think of an instance in the past of actors ever having been payed for fund raisers, so we're not sure why Theatre Passe Muraille was singled out for this privilege. Phone calls and letters were sent to Equity, but Mr. Haney stood firm. The office of Passe Muraille has therefore been going nuts the last few days printing up over thirty contracts and paycheques, with the necessary duplicates sent to Equity, the end result being that over $6000.00 of the money earned from tonight's fund raiser is earmarked to go to us actors.

Attached you will find your contract. Please sign it. You will also find a cheque for your fee. I would like to suggest you sign it back to Theatre Passe Muraille. Yes, its a kickback. But since its the nineties, Passe Muraille will send you a charitable receipt for the same amount.

Sorry to put you through all this. Perhaps you'd like to call or write Ron Haney at Equity and tell him how you feel about all this. I did.

Thanks for your participation in tonight's show.

Kate Lynch

Theatre Passe Muraille

DEFINING MOMENTS

—
THE DRAWER BOY
TOM BARNETT, DAVID FOX, AND JERRY FRANKEN. PHOTO BY NIR BAREKET.

OPENING NIGHT, *THE DRAWER BOY*, FEBRUARY 1999

BY MICHAEL HEALEY

Alcohol is absolutely useless as a manager of stress. You can't get enough of it down to do the job properly, and then, when the stress is suddenly removed, you're just awash in alcohol: useless, defenseless, vowels your long enemies and consonants AWOL.

We had had two previews, sparsely attended. I believe we were told, on the afternoon of the first preview, that zero was the number of reservations for that evening. The previews taught us little, except they were great for giving the actors no premature inkling they were in a comedy.

I was on those steps, at the back of the house—how many of us have watched from those steps to see if the thing worked, Linda and Hrant and dozens more, watching from back there, watching the audience, not the play, to see if it was working. First act goes okay. Audience is with the thing. Stress unmitigated, Scotch tasting like nothing at all. Miles Potter a five-foot, eight-inch tight smile.

In Act Two, the audience changes, and the actors can feel it, and so they change too. The audience and actors are doing something now, together, and I'm just a witness. And then it's over, and the looks on Tom's face, David's face, Jerry's face, called back and back: they're stunned. We all were.

MICHAEL HEALEY worked as an usher at Theatre Passe Muraille while at theatre school in 1983. He watched Layne Coleman's *Hamlet* a half dozen times. He's now a playwright and actor and owes everything to TPM.

Passe Muraille

MY FIRST TIME

BY LYNN SLOTKIN

How Theatre Passe Muraille broke down my square walls and my blinkered view of the world.

Up until 1971 my theatregoing was spent watching respectable, conservative fare at the Royal Alexandra Theatre and the O'Keefe Centre (now the Sony Centre). But in 1971 I discovered Theatre Passe Muraille when I went to see *Vampyr*. It was playing at Trinity Square—the juxtaposition of *Vampyr* playing next to a church speaks to the irreverent fearlessness of the man running the theatre at the time, Paul Thompson. He was the managing director at the time. Why he wasn't called the artistic director is a mystery, but never mind.

I walked into that creaky building that evening, a bit timorous, trying to figure out where the "theatre" was in what I thought was a cavernous place. In a small office to the side, sitting at his desk, was Paul Thompson. He had that distinctive white beard and a full head of white hair, and he was as boyish as ever. Does that man ever age? On the floor was a small wood cradle in which was one of his daughters (I don't know which). He gently rocked the cradle with his foot. And he was smoking a joint. My staid attitude was taken aback when I smelled that distinctive oddly sweet fragrance coming from that office. I got over that prissy attitude quickly.

The play and the production was a revelation and an awakening of the kind of in-your-face, challenging theatre that company did and is known for. I recall that when I went into the sanctuary to a seat close to the front, the theatre was full of an atmospheric smoky mist. The production started. I was gripped. At one point a character was possessed by some spirit or other. She was played by a young Clare Coulter, who was compelling, mesmerizing, and topless. Except for myself and perhaps a few close relatives I'd never seen a woman topless before in public. I might have thought, "You're not in Kansas, Slotkin." I would have looked away in embarrassment, but it was all so arresting I just watched, mouth agape. A few years later Paul Thompson produced *I Love You, Baby Blue* at Theatre Passe Muraille, which celebrated blue movies and sexuality in which the whole cast was naked. And so my education in public nudity was complete. Thank you, Paul Thompson and Theatre Passe Muraille, for beginning my education in wall-busting theatre.

LYNN SLOTKIN's first show at Theatre Passe Muraille was *Vampyr* in 1971, at Trinity Square. She loved that wild, rocking show. Paul Thompson was not the first artistic director of the company, but he was for Lynn. She has been going to see Passe Muraille shows regularly since then, to be shaken up, challenged, and turned upside down with its stories. She's supported it vocally and financially, and has been reviewing its productions for years. It's been wonderful in every single way.

VAMPYR
BOOTH SAVAGE AND BRENDA DONAHUE. PHOTO BY BOB NASMITH.

I found myself very close to the sun, exposed to TPM's financial woes and triumphs, its campaigns and causes, its history of patronage, wading through the paper pools to learn the ambitions of Coleman, Serran, Thompson, and Garrard—to name a few.

IN ORBIT

BY DAN DALEY

It was in the middle of May that I took a turn down a rainy Ryerson Avenue to discover something surprising—something that I, as a young east-ender, never expected to find in what was, to me, the far reaches of the city's "west end." I was leaving teenhood for adulthood that summer. I couldn't shake the words of my twelfth-grade drama teacher: "Your mind will open to the mess of possibilities." This was her way of telling me to ditch my sensible pursuit of auto mechanics and spend the next four years in theatre school. How nuts was that? . . . A responsible adult telling me to do such a thing. Stepping out of the rain and through those red doors, the lights faded, the set illuminated, Rick Roberts and Jenny Young walked on stage, *The Anger in Ernest and Ernestine* erupted, and like that my world view fell to pieces; the possibilities became endless and it was there in that old bakery that I knew theatre was the messiness I, as a "sensible" young person, so desperately needed.

In the ten years that followed this moment I came to orbit that theatre like a planet drawn by the sun's gravity. As many may know, Theatre Passe Muraille—in its acrobatic way—contorted through great loss and great challenge between 2005 and 2015. This was really no surprise, considering that this theatre was founded to reflect social change and the realities of Canadian life. It was the people behind this Canadian drama that stirred the imagination of this young theatre student.

Early on, in a less dramatic turn of events, I found myself not on its stage but in its administrative offices. SummerWorks had a single desk in the far corner where I eagerly set up shop as their artistic associate. This was short-lived, before the venerable Jennifer Brewin of Theatre Columbus quickly found work for me with her. I inched my chair to her desk and, to my awe, found myself rubbing shoulders with the likes of Martha Ross and Leah Cherniak. That was kind of how it went there; TPM was the sun and these great stars formed the constellations on its galactic mission to bring indie theatre beyond walls.

It felt like a final chapter in 2012 when I was set to go abroad, not sure when I'd return. Andy McKim said to me, "I suspect we'll have you back in the office. Somehow we'll find a way." He was right. Upon my return the following year I landed right back there heading up the Paprika Festival, whose new home was to be that stage. Now, like my twelfth-grade drama teacher, I was telling tales of possibility to a new tide of young theatre makers. I was between those walls again not as a young thing, but as a young thing with a lot of responsibility. So the next logical step was to head up TPM's fundraising. Perfectly sensible, right? Andy and Régine thought so. Now I found myself very close to the sun, exposed to TPM's financial woes and triumphs, its campaigns and causes, its history of patronage, wading through the paper pools to learn the ambitions of Coleman, Serran, Thompson, and Garrard—to name a few.

I've gone away again. Now I'm not sure how I'll return to that space. But I know that, if I do, it will be to support what so many there work tirelessly to do—to continue the work of genuinely connecting with people of Toronto, of Canada—telling their stories, fostering understanding and inspiration within our diverse communities. It is the most difficult, messy, and sensible thing anyone can do.

DAN DALEY worked out of Theatre Passe Muraille's offices in various capacities from 2010 to 2015, including the role as the associate producer of growth and development for TPM. He was artistic producer of the Paprika Festival when the festival returned to TPM's Mainspace in 2014. That same year, then a Paprika artist, Bilal Baig conceived of *Acha Bacha*, which premiered in TPM's 2017/18 season.

—
TORONTONIANS
KATE LYNCH, JIM GARRARD, AND JOHN JARVIS..

IMPRINTS

BY RICHARD GREENBLATT

Where to begin? So much history for me; mostly good, some bad, all indelible. A fair amount of my professional and personal life is interwoven in and around—and yes, through—its walls.

So, in no particular order or chronology:

Watching the first production of *The Crackwalker* by Judith Thompson in the Backspace and knowing that this play changes everything. I'll never forget Graham Greene crashing through the side exit door on the house left side—now bricked up—and being scared out of my head.

The first time I worked there, writing a song for *The School Show* by Ted Johns in 1979.

Performing in the Strawberry Tea Awards—a fundraiser for a legal defense fund to take Gina Mallet to court when she impugned the theatre by writing in the *Toronto Star* that real weed was used in *O.D. on Paradise*. The fundraiser was everyone reading their worst reviews. I never laughed so hard in my life—and I wasn't even stoned—as I'd wince in pain and wicked enjoyment at the most cutting ones (usually written by Urjo Kareda).

Mini-putt fundraisers. Directing Adam Pettle's *Misha* and falling in love with the Backspace. Then falling in love with it again when I directed Sara Farb's *R-E-B-E-C-C-A*.

Watching the Jays win the '92 World Series on a TV brought into the Mainspace after a performance of *Resistance 500*, then going out onto Queen Street to party. Arguing with Clarke Rogers—many times—and still liking him in spite of myself. And himself. Thursday nights in the shop. New Year's Eve '03 in the upstairs bar, dancing and falling in love with Tanya Greve.

Directing Julie Tepperman's *YICHUD (Seclusion)* and watching Beth Kates transform the Mainspace, the lobby, the upstairs bar area, and the exterior of the building into a synagogue, to the point where audience members were heard to say, "I never knew there was a synagogue here," and, "How nice that this synagogue let them do a play here."

Competing in the Ultimate Theatre Championship with Dykstra. Then co-hosting the next year with Northan.

Watching shows that thrilled: *Fire*; *This is for you, Anna*; *The Noam Chomsky Lectures*; *Maggie and Pierre*; *The Drawer Boy*;

and more. The ever-filthy dressing rooms and green room that no amount of cleaning can ever seem to get even moderately livable.

Way too many memorials.

Watching a reading in the BUZZ Festival of my daughter Natasha's play *The Peacemaker* and watching my son Will act in *Better Than This* in the Backspace, and *shepn nakhes* for both of them (it's a Yiddish expression—google it if you don't know what it means).

And lastly . . .

I heard about my son Luke's death just outside the theatre. It was after a late-night performance of *Essay* by Hannah Moscovitch in which I was performing during SummerWorks '05. The police found me there, chatting with audience members post show, and after checking I was who I was, told me the worst news one can ever hear. I vaguely remember slumping against the wall next to the main entrance, just saying the word "no" over and over. For months afterward I was afraid to go anywhere near the building, until I had to, for some work reason or other. I went up to the spot where I had been that night and forced myself to look at it for a long time. I realized that it was not the building's fault that Luke had died, or that I happened to be there when I was told. But it is where I was.

And so this theatre, this building, and that wall will always have a part of my grief imprinted on it. But these other things, too.

RICHARD GREENBLATT has been making theatre for over forty-two years as an actor, director, playwright, and musician. He has worked at Theatre Passe Muraille numerous times in all four capacities and has a great love for both the building and for the artists whose imprints are on its walls.

RESISTANCE 500
JANE LUK, RICHARD GREENBLATT, AND ALISA PALMER.

BURN (OR ADVICE TO THE YOUNG)

BY RAOUL BHANEJA

How fitting that my submission for a book on the fiftieth anniversary of TPM is late! It's fitting because at Theatre Passe Muraille we don't adhere to the norms. We break rules; we push "beyond the walls"; we do it how it has to be done to get it done.

There is a kind of quiet chaos at TPM that has roared at different decibel levels during various eras, but it is always present. This is not a theatre that runs on autopilot. It can't! Not because of a lack of skill on the part of those working in the building, but because at TPM we are trying to do more. More than we should with the money we have, the time we have, the resources we have—and that's what makes it a special place to make theatre.

In 1994, when my wife Birgitte Solem first moved to Toronto, she lived around the corner from TPM, and a few years later it became my home as well. Passe Muraille was always in the neighbourhood, just a part of the landscape, as much as the Cameron House (where I was a busboy and a terrible bartender for a spell) or the convenience store we'd purchase from almost every day. My very first theatre audition in Toronto was in the Mainspace of TPM for *Baņuta Rubess*!

Passe Muraille became even more a part of our lives when Birgitte joined the collective that created *The Rochdale Project* there, or when I workshopped and debuted *Hamlet (solo)* in the Backspace, or, even more recently, my show *Life, Death and The Blues*. There were concerts and tributes and gigs and jams and parties in the shop and fights in the alley and tears on the corner of Wolseley; it is all left on the floor at Theatre Passe Muraille.

The greatest lesson I ever learned about the place came one day when I was having a conversation with Passe Muraille legend and mentor Paul Thompson, who presided over some of the most successful productions the theatre had ever seen; a man who with his own sweat, genius, and tenacity had pushed beyond the walls, helping thrust Theatre Passe Muraille onto the local and national stage.

As was customary I was the young theatre artist complaining to Paul about TPM. I can't even exactly recall what I was so indignant about, but I suspect it was that they hadn't given me enough help (or more precisely enough money) for my Hamlet show, and if only they had my life would be so much easier!

Wasn't the point of a place like TPM to support someone like ME and MY work? Wasn't the iconic Nasmith Bakery building, which housed our beloved TPM, the kind of building that should foster the creation of work like mine from people like me? If it wasn't then why did it even exist?!!!

"Burn it down then," Paul said with no hint of irony.

"What?!" I said.

"If you don't like it, burn it down. Build a new one."

"But how can you say that? You helped build this place?!"

"It's just a building. If you don't like it, change it," Paul said.

And that was it. End of conversation.

In that moment I realized not only what Paul was about, but also the soul of Theatre Passe Muraille. In a time when so many of our conversations in the theatre are about everything but the ART, I was reminded that the ART is the only part of the conversation that matters. On top of that, if a man who helped build the theatre was suggesting I burn it down if I wanted to make change . . . well, you can't get much more TPM than that.

It is the pushing of ideas and concepts "beyond the walls" that quickens my heart whenever I walk in the building. Here is to fifty more years of Theatre Passe Muraille, wherever and whatever form it takes, may it never lose that spirit!

RAOUL BHANEJA began his career out of the National Theatre School at the Blyth Festival in a collective creation directed by Paul Thompson, and he's never been the same since. He debuted his world-touring one-man show *Hamlet (solo)* in the Backspace in 2006 and after a number of years of development with TPM premiered his Dora-nominated musical *Life, Death and The Blues* in the Mainspace in 2014, which went on to tour nationally.

AT THEATRE PASSE MURAILLE WE DON'T ADHERE TO THE NORMS. WE BREAK RULES; WE PUSH "BEYOND THE WALLS"; WE DO IT HOW IT HAS TO BE DONE TO GET IT DONE.

LIFE, DEATH AND THE BLUES
JAKE CHISHOLM, TOM BONA, RAOUL BHANEJA, DIVINE BROWN, AND CHRIS BANKS. PHOTO BY MICHAEL COOPER.

MY THEATRE DAD

BY ANUSREE ROY

My relationship with Theatre Passe Muraille is intertwined with my relationship with my "theatre dad," Andy McKim.

I can't remember if it was spring or summer, but the sky was clear blue as director Thomas Morgan Jones and I sat on the rock in front of TPM's big red door, drinking coffee and discussing our upcoming meeting with Andy. Although this was ten years ago, every detail of that day is still so clear to me. We were early for our meeting. We knew Andy wanted to discuss programming our show, *Pyaasa*, in his season the following year, but we didn't know what would be discussed at the meeting.

At the appointed time, we ascended the narrow TPM stairs and met with Andy in his office. It was a large shared space, with lots of personal items on the walls and on his desk.

We settled in. We were nervous.

After the obligatory greetings, Andy said he wanted to discuss the details of programming *Pyaasa* and specifically wanted to speak with me, the playwright. I was anxious. I was a young writer, and this was going to be my first professional production. I genuinely didn't know what to anticipate.

What followed has shaped the business side of my writing career. With a clear, authoritative, and kind tone, Andy explained that he wanted to program the play without any changes. He wanted to showcase the work exactly as it was conceived, written, and performed. He wanted my voice, my authentic writing voice, out there. He didn't want to change it to *suit* his audience's needs, even though he was aware that a significant amount of the text was written in Bengali, my native language. He wanted the audience to experience the play how he experienced it. I was taken aback. The young, inexperienced writer in me was anticipating demands for rewrites to cater to the audience, which I knew I would vehemently decline. But Andy was not interested in that. His need was to tell an authentic story with integrity.

The meeting continued and we went on to discuss various other aspects of the production. In the end, as we were about to leave, Andy called me back into his office. He spoke with great calm and clarity. He told me that as a young writer who was about to enter the business, I had to keep remembering to fight to retain my authenticity. To keep demanding it. To keep insisting on that being a priority and never to cater to demands that wouldn't serve the writing. I said thank you. We shook hands, and Thomas and I left.

Back on the sidewalk, in front of the bright red door, I let the last part of our meeting sink in. I spoke the words over and over to myself to make sure my mind absorbed their meaning. *I have to keep being authentic.* Ten years later TPM's red door and Andy's words warm my heart. Over the years his words have shaped each contract I have negotiated, and I am ever so grateful for that.

ANUSREE ROY is a Governor General's Literary Award–nominated writer and actor whose work has premiered internationally. Her plays include *Trident Moon*, *Sultans of the Street*, *Brothel #9*, *Roshni*, *Letters to my Grandma*, and *Pyaasa*. She is the recipient of the KM Hunter Artist Award, the RBC Emerging Artist Award, and the Carol Bolt Award, was named as a protégé of the Siminovitch Prize, and was a finalist for the Susan Smith Blackburn Prize.

WITH A CLEAR, AUTHORITATIVE, AND KIND TONE, ANDY EXPLAINED THAT HE WANTED TO PROGRAM THE PLAY WITHOUT ANY CHANGES.

ANDY AND ANUSREE

PYAASA
ANUSREE ROY. PHOTO BY AVIVA ARMOUR-OSTROFF.

Passe Muraille

FRIGGIN' TREMENDOUS NEWS

BY FABIAN JENNINGS

Early 1971: TPM considers my play *Charles Manson a.k.a Jesus Christ* for production and agrees to do it in December.

Friggin' tremendous news. I return home from the meeting with Paul Thompson on a crowded subway, obliged to stand, swaying and holding onto a strap. In my excitement (young playwright, first play), my left arm goes numb and I can't release the strap. This is no shit. Am I having a stroke? I'm panicking as my stop approaches. Just in time I pry my hand loose with my free hand. Good thing I had two. Make my exit. Find a bench. Sit and talk myself down.

Paul Thompson, I was told, took me for the leader of a motorcycle gang when he first saw me. That was a lumberjack kind of jacket/shirt I was wearing, Paul, not colors! Long hair, beard . . . a lumberjack, Paul, a lumberjack . . . Alas, only on the outside. Inside I was prone to anxiety attacks. (Read above.)

The play was a success, but weird. After one performance I meet the leader of the Canadian chapter of the Sharon Tate fan club. (Tate was a starlet, Roman Polanski's wife and one of the Family's victims.) He congratulates me effusively on honouring Tate's memory and I am beginning to be concerned he might fall in love with me, too. (Don't forget, at the time I considered myself a lumberjack.)

Even stranger, in the months following the play I see a performance of *The Farm Show* and am so impressed I abandon playwriting and become a dairy herdsman. That's right, milking cows. Earned a certificate from Kemptville Ontario Agricultural College and got to stroking those teats. A step down from lumberjacking, but still plenty masculine.

(Little did I know that decades later I would recognize myself as a non-practising bisexual. I've now been fifty years faithfully married to a gorgeous woman, but let me put it this way: if I were prone to philandering, I know two or three guys that would definitely be of interest.)

But back to cows. While I'm on a dairy farm north of Toronto (belonged to an ol' guy named McDonald—Scout's honor), I get a phone call from a reporter—*Toronto Star*. How'd he find me? Anyhow, he's pretty sure with my connections I'd know a Hell's Angel named Danny something-or-other, who had hung out with the Manson Family. He'd supposedly crossed the border and was somewhere in Canada. He actually thought this biker might drop by to visit me! I told the reporter that was ludicrous and, should he find him, please don't tell him where *I* was.

Now, to be clear: I have nothing against the Hell's Angels. In fact, so far, I haven't met any save for once at Grossman's on Spadina. The reason I didn't want this guy to know where I was wasn't out of disrespect for the Angels. It was . . . well . . . something else.

And now on to Sal Mineo, who became aware of the Manson play when he was in TO in some play by Arthur Marx that dealt peripherally with the Manson phenomenon. Urjo Kareda panned Marx's play and praised mine, saying if Mineo wanted to do Manson he should look me up. Mineo phones me wanting to see the play and asks me if he sends a taxi around will I send him the play. I say, "Sure, if you'll pay for the taxi."

Mineo gets the play, is interested, and tells me to get an agent and we'll deal. Negotiations are slow going anywhere and some months go by; then I hear Mineo has been shot dead in the underground garage of his high-rise apartment in LA. I still think of a copy of that play lying around upstairs among his last effects.

A final oddity about the play: it was cast for maybe ten actors and a rock band. I wanted Mick Jagger and the Rolling Stones, but we settled for some pick-up musicians from the Horseshoe Tavern on Queen. Anyhow, where was Theatre Passe Muraille going to get the money to mount a production of that size? Well, I wound up loaning three or four thousand from some *Globe and Mail* reporter friends I knew (long story) and contributed it to the budget. TPM put in the rest and away we went. The play did well enough that I was able to pay the three or four thousand back and have a couple of hundred left over for myself and my composer friend, Allan Rae, who created the music.

TPM. Fiftieth anniversary! Well, I wish us both fifty more. As an institution, you may make it. As a person, I know I won't, but I'm okay with that. Thanks for the memories.

Though unconnected to theatre, FABIAN JENNINGS continues to write humongous third-rate plays with casting and technical demands that even Bill Gates hasn't the means to mount.

CHARLES MANSON A.K.A. JESUS CHRIST
PETER JOBIN.

REMEMBERING *CHARLES MANSON A.K.A. JESUS CHRIST*

BY VINETTA STROMBERGS

There are some theatre experiences that leave a mark on you. Whether or not you remember all the details clearly is not important. What you remember is the impact. After the show ends, you're not sure if you can even applaud. Sometimes you do, and sometimes you are just glued to your seat and do not want to move. You need time to process what you've just experienced. And then you want to go out with your friends and talk about it, voraciously and passionately.

In the early '70s one such experience was Theatre Passe Muraille's production of *Charles Manson a.k.a. Jesus Christ*. It happened in a church-hall space in a hidden square behind Eaton's. You entered into a large, high-ceilinged open space surrounded by natural brick walls with scaffolding braced against all four walls. I can't remember if anyone sat on the ground floor. I sat with my friends up above the action and looking down at the playing area. In retrospect, it was very Thunderdome.

I remember a suspended platform, about twelve feet in the air, and someone lying on it. I remember blood dripping from the platform to the ground. I remember a bathtub on the ground floor and someone taking a bath. People came and went and interacted. Was there someone on roller skates? I don't remember the dialogue or the musical numbers, but everything painted a picture of the lifestyle of the Manson acolytes, the "hippies" who committed the terrible crime. It was appropriately icky and shocking and set us up for judging the final outcome.

Then the scene became the courtroom where Manson was on trial. Peter Jobin (as Manson) delivered a huge final monologue at the end of the trial. He spoke directly to the surrounding audience and was charismatic. I was totally drawn to the actor and repulsed by the character he was portraying. We, the audience, were being challenged for our beliefs and our complicity in what happened.

VINETTA STROMBERGS was part of the "alternative theatre" movement in Toronto in the early '70s. Vinetta was associated with Global Village, but people often flowed between theatres and regularly supported each other's work. She got to actually work at TPM in 1988 when she had the great pleasure of directing Daniel MacIvor in his first personal one-man show, *Wild Abandon*. The show was a huge success in the TPM Backspace and was remounted the following year.

THEATRE PASSE MURAILLE

BY SKY GILBERT

Things I remember . . .

The rumour that everyone who was involved with *The Passe Muraille Hamlet* was high on pot. ("You've heard of the Passe Muraille warm-up, haven't you?"—then the person telling the joke mimes taking a big huff of a spliff.)

I remember thinking that one day I might graduate to the *big dressing room*. I remember the door that used to be on the stage right side of the Backspace stage that led to the alley outside; I remember Graham Greene coming in that door as a vagrant Indigenous person in the first production of *The Crackwalker*. I remember asking the powers that be at Passe Muraille—the same year—if Micah Barnes could climb up on top of that doorway and sing a song in my play *Torch Song*.

I remember the offices that went on and on, and then there was storage and sets—I never realized it was so big. What did you guys get up to back there!

I remember the first reading for Linda Griffiths's *The Duchess*. Paul Thompson told us not to read our parts but, instead, to read "any lines we felt like reading!" I didn't know what to do.

I remember wondering what might be living in the couch in the green room.

I remember Clarke Rogers telling me that my work had nothing to do with Canada.

I remember thinking how politically incorrect it was for Moo to get pushed down the stairs by her rotten boyfriend—and have it be funny—in Sally Clark's play of the same name.

I remember looking at Ken McDougall in the dressing room after he had a blood transfusion during rehearsals of Hillar Liitoja's *Sick* and thinking, "*How thin he is!*"

I remember Paul Bettis telling beautiful boys to kiss each other in *Provincetown 1919*.

I remember watching Cynthia Grant face off with somebody in the Passe Muraille office.

I remember hiding up in the balcony in the main theatre when a play was on and being really, really glad, because if I was very quiet I could walk around and have a drink and no one would ever know.

I remember getting the first cheque for one of my first plays, *Lana Turner Has Collapsed*, from Theatre Passe Muraille's Seed Program and thinking maybe I was worth something.

There are other things, but I can't think of any more right now.

SKY GILBERT is a writer, director, and drag queen extraordinaire. He was the co-founder and artistic director of Buddies in Bad Times Theatre (North America's largest gay and lesbian theatre) for eighteen years. He was recently the recipient of the Margo Bindhardt Award (from the Toronto Arts Foundation), the Silver Ticket Award (from the Toronto Alliance for the Performing Arts), and the ReLit Award (for his fourth novel, *An English Gentleman*), and also recently received a Ph.D. from the University of Toronto. By day Sky holds a University Research Chair in Drama and Creative Writing at the University of Guelph.

WEST MEMPHIS MOJO
TYRONE BENSKIN AND NICKY GUADAGNI.

I REMEMBER—

BY NICKY GUADAGNI

I remember sitting in my backyard one evening with Jacoba Knaapen in March 2017 after seeing an opening at TPM, lamenting that we didn't know what to contribute to their collective history.

My husband Robin suggested we use the "I remember" method. So we started jamming and up shot a flood of memories from all three of us—each eruption beginning with "I remember."

So, I remember:

John Winston Carroll as Fred in *O.D. on Paradise* fiercely pounding his chest each performance, raging at his son Vic (Layne Coleman) that he was the one who was head of the family. So one night, around the half-hour, John's complaining about chest pains and was getting very anxious thinking he was having a heart attack (he was in his sixties). John was sweating and bug-eyed and freaked. So we called an ambulance.

Turned out the heart attack was the bruising on his chest from pounding it every night in performance.

I remember certain performances and productions that will never leave me:

Géza Kovács sitting up high on the Backspace upper level, his legs dangling down talkin' about going to Horny Tim's in *The Crackwalker*.

Clare Coulter in *He Won't Come in from the Barn*. Clare told me that one night they only had two people in the audience at the five-minute call, and she decided she would make this the best show she'd ever done. She would be completely focused and playing her best game for those two theatregoers. Then just as the lights went down another two people walked in and Clare couldn't handle it. It was too many people.

Gary Reineke as Al Cornell.

Jan Kudelka's *American Demon*.

O.D. ON PARADISE
BRUCE WILSON, JANET-LAINE GREEN, NICKY GUADAGNI, AND ANDY MCCURBIN. PHOTO BY KENNETH DAVISON.

Layne Coleman's *Blue City Slammers*.

John Blackwood turning into a Jamaican.

Linda Griffiths's breasts in *The Duchess*.

My breasts in *O.D.*

Jim Plaxton's *O.D.* sets—sand in my socks all winter. And tan makeup marks on all my clothes.

Brooke Johnson doing "to be or not to be" from the upper level as Alice Riverton in *In the Wings*.

Best Indigenous actors on the continent: the cast of *Jessica: A Transformation*.

Layne Coleman about to dive from the upper level as Vic in *O.D.*

Maggie Huculak, who transformed herself into the hulking gifted mathematician in *The Little Years*.

Alligator Pie.

I don't remember:

Sharing the green room with Keanu Reeves (who was acting in the Backspace) for two weeks around 1983, but apparently I did. Never even noticed him.

I remember:

My husband knocking on doors around TPM asking neighbours to sign a petition to get the alley beside the theatre named after Linda Griffiths. Many neighbours couldn't speak English, but Robin assured them she was a "nice lady" and they signed.

I remember:

The packed opening night of *In the Wings*, when I'd never felt so fantastic, and coming out the next afternoon to a matinee audience of four. TPM was trying out mid-week matinees on us. Four wasn't enough, Clare.

Originally from Montreal, NICKY GUADAGNI majored in drama at Dawson College and went on to train at the Royal Academy of Dramatic Art in London. Her theatre work for Passe Muraille includes *O.D. on Paradise* and *In the Wings*, which she adapted for the stage from the Carole Corbeil novel.

SNATCHES FROM A SPACE I HAVE INHABITED

BY DONNA-MICHELLE ST. BERNARD

Quickly cocking up one leg on the big white rock out front, looking super cool but also nonchalant because she's coming, not that I care.

Squeezing into the backmost corner of the Backspace, where proximity of bodies, walls, and darkness enable community, privacy, tears, and observation.

Pre-show, scanning the grid, counting lenses (instruments) as if they will give some clue of what's to come.

Tiptoeing across the catwalk above the Mainspace, stepping over an unseen actor in repose, crossing through her energy, sanctified.

In the lobby, arguing in taut, low tones about what a jerk he's being, unaware of lobby mics and program sound in the booth, but about to find out.

On the Cabaret stage, being a bear, rising on haunches, snuffling wetly, pawing air and snout, settling back.

Spilling my wounded guts out in public acts of grief that never find a private counterpart.

Praying he makes it through the run. Praying he will live. Joking with him about the prospect he might not.

Wishing he'd made it to opening. Trying to remember everything he said he wanted.

Playing to the seat they have saved in his name, wishing the lights were lower so I couldn't see it empty, imagining I see him applauding gently and smiling with every tooth in his head at the end. He had such a good smile.

Smudging, stomping, singing the space from sacredness to secular. Pretending to eat an orange that I forgot to bring.

WATCHING HER TAKE NO SHIT AND DECIDING THAT IS THE PRECISE AMOUNT OF SHIT I INTEND TO TAKE FROM HERE ON OUT.

On a liminal level sitting silently with the idea of Linda.

Sitting within spitting distance of a reliving that cracked my heart, smacked my face, bruised my spirit, took my tongue.

Exploding into laughter at what was not at all a joke, my coping callous. My date: "Never sit beside me again."

How did he do that? HOW DID HE DOOOOOO THAT?!?!?!??!

Please don't make me go out there. Please, please just let me lie down and cry. What do you people want from me?— Oh! That's my song!

Wondering what she meant by that.

Crouching in the alley to get my mind right. Nobody talks to me like that, but she already said there's no punching allowed. So, now what?

That time she threatened to slap me for stepping on her lines and I thought for sure the director would do something . . .

Saying, "I'm gonna cry now, and I don't know why," and they let me.

Look at this. We did this. OMG, we're magic.

"To my surprise, your show didn't give me a migraine."

"You make me feel seen."

Up in the office, sitting cross-legged under the table with my crayons and cue cards, just being left to be.

Up the creepy staircase, through some good, heritage grime, out onto the roof . . .

In the shadowed mezzanine, serving the work but apart from it, world shrunk to spots on stage, pages turning in sync under little pools of just enough light. Shrinking myself to non-existence, so surprised when he finds me and . . . apologizes, then swelling with love.

The man who will always be my mayor being a norm, laughing at a joke exactly like a guy who actually gets it, who wants to be here.

Good Lord, what is he doing to that pig?!

Watching her take no shit and deciding that is the precise amount of shit I intend to take from here on out.

DONNA-MICHELLE ST. BERNARD is an emcee, playwright, and arts administrator. Her work has been recognized with a SATAward nomination, the Herman Voaden Playwriting Award, the Enbridge playRites Award, a Dora Mavor Moore Award for Outstanding New Play, and two nominations for the Governor General's Literary Award for Drama.

RIGOLETTO
MARTIN JULIEN. PHOTO BY MICHAEL COOPER.

MY TPM

BY MARTIN JULIEN

1980. Flop sweat in the unrenovated second floor at 16 Ryerson Avenue. Flubbing my card tricks, at the age of nineteen, playing Norman Bethune—the supposed sleight-of-hand manoeuvre a theatrical metaphor—in a producer's showcase performance of Theatre North's canoe-touring production of *The Spirit of Muskoka* by Jerry Prager. I'd just recovered from hepatitis A. The performance, however, was impossible to recover. My young professionalism? Exposed!

1987. Playing "The Trotskyite" in the Clarke Rogers–helmed production of Donna Lypchuk's *Tragedy of Manners*, about the Cameron House. Me, along with forty other sweating, striving denizens of the Queen West art scene. This is Paradise. Shotgunning cans of Molson Ex throughout rehearsals while different liquids got cooked up in the Backspace. An incendiary and stunningly committed performance by Bob Nasmith as invented beat-generation painter Jack Frost. But hey, I simply tucked my parents' red paperback copy of Saul Alinsky's *Rules for Radicals* into the pocket of a pilfered red-wool jacket and then expressed an intense affect of post-adolescent myopia on stage, punctuated by occasional outbursts of disdainful rhetoric. When my dad saw the show, the year before his death, he simply said, "You were just playing me and your mother from before you were born." My nurture/nature? Exposed!

1988. Green room. (Green from mould, that is.) Listening to Christopher Newton and Brian Richmond chat through the crack in the doorway leading to the Backspace about the shitty second callback audition I'd just massacred to play the part of Herchel Blackwell in Ledoux and Young's Toronto premiere of *Fire*. This is never a good idea, kids. Needless to say, Michael Riley got the part. My self-discipline? Exposed!

1989. *Rigoletto*—the rock-opera adaptation! Entering as the evil Charles Manson/Lou Reed/Iggy Pop–inspired Sparafucile on a Yamaha XJ550 motorcycle! Which, of course, I couldn't ride for shit without freaking out and falling over; I was actually pushed on, in "neutral"—VROOM! VROOM!—by Glenn Davidson. My cool factor? Exposed!

1989. My eight-month-old son Lucas playing "Charles the baby" to Ann-Marie MacDonald's mama in Peter Hinton's translucent production of *Abingdon Square* by María Irene Fornés. We needed the two hundred dollars a week. Only missed one performance, due to a cold. Only cried once on stage—during opening-night curtain call. That poor baby was traumatized. My fitness as a father? Exposed!

2001. Playing many, many scenes with the strong and beautiful Philippa Domville, both of us in our underwear, during the run of *Time After Time: The Chet Baker Project* by James O'Reilly. My diet and exercise regime? Exposed!

2012. The Songbook Series. Singing "Surfer Girl" by the Beach Boys in a slurred, guttural a cappella half-moan/half-whisper—alone at the microphone in a business suit—while my wife does a silent go-go dance in ski wear under a spotlight far stage right. My erotic obsessions? Exposed!

It really was, at times, it so seemed . . . Beyond Walls.

MARTIN JULIEN is an actor, singer, writer, and educator with over three decades of experience in Canadian theatre. He made his stage debut at the age of ten for the Factory Theatre Lab in Toronto, and has been nominated for three Dora Mavor Moore Awards as best performer.

UBU RAW
GORDON MAY, LEN SEDUN, FRANÇOIS-RÉGIS KLANFER, DINI BAKER, ASHELEIGH MOORHOUSE, DANNY FREEDMAN, AND BOB DERMER.

PRODUCTION HISTORY

Every best effort has been made to compile a detailed and accurate production history of Theatre Passe Muraille. However, due to the vagaries of memory, time, and record-keeping, we acknowledge that there will be gaps and mistakes in this listing. Much of this history is due to the diligent work of TPM staff and volunteers, including Petra Chevrier, Barbara Fingerote, Jasmine Wang, Sophie Lewycky, Kate Maguire, and Andrea Renaud (the original 1996 TPM production history author); the staff and volunteers of the L.W. Conolly Theatre Archives at the University of Guelph Library; and Judith Rudakoff, from her book *Dangerous Traditions: A Passe Muraille Anthology* (1992), with work from her assistants Sally Szuster and Beverly Taft, who compiled a very accurate Play Calendar for the period from 1969 to 1974.

JIM GARRARD

1968

October–November: The Relationship by Al Morgan, directed by Al Morgan

December: Tom Paine by Paul Foster, directed by Jim Garrard

1969

Santa Claus by e e cummings, directed by unknown

The Babies by Anna Lippman, directed by unknown

Project X by Phillip J. Hopcraft, directed by Phillip J. Hopcraft

The Laundromat Special by Collective, directed by Mary Gardner

March 05–March 22: Futz by Rochelle Owens, directed by Jim Garrard, produced by Trio Productions and TPM

May 27–June: New Step by Leonard Cohen, directed by Mary Gardner

May 27–June: Balls by Paul Foster, directed by Jim Garrard

May 27–June: The Marriage Proposal by Anton Chekhov, directed by Jim Garrard

June 27–June 29: Portrait / Itch by Jeffrey Levy, directed by Paul Holtfretter and Jeffrey Levy, produced by The Company and TPM

July 03–July 12: Escurial by Michel de Ghelderode, directed by Asheleigh Moorhouse

July 17–July 26: Home Free by Lanford Wilson, directed by Jim Garrard

August 04–August 09: Forensic and the Navigators by Sam Shepard, directed by The Company, produced by The Company and TPM

August 04–August 09: Nightmare with Hat by Jeffrey Levy, directed by The Company, produced by The Company and TPM

August 04–August 08: The Maids by Jean Genet, directed by Jim Garrard

August 20–August 24: Endgame by Samuel Beckett, directed by Chris Brookes, produced by The Company and TPM

November 04–November 16: Memories for my Brother, Part One: Before the Guns by John Palmer, directed by John Palmer

November 20–December 20: Tom Paine by Paul Foster, directed by Jim Garrard

MARTIN KINCH

1970

January 13–January 20: Richard III by William Shakespeare, directed by Martin Kinch

January 29–March 14: Sweet Eros by Terrence McNally, directed by Martin Kinch

January 29–March 14: In His Own Write by John Lennon, adapted by Adrienne Kennedy and Victor Spinetti, directed by Martin Kinch

March 12: Charlie—In So Many Ways by Collective, directed by Paul Thompson

March 27–April 10: A Bond Honoured by John Osborne, directed by Asheleigh Moorhouse

May 07–May 19: Notes from Quebec, adapted by Penny Williams, based on Diguidi, Diguidi, Ha! Ha! Ha! by Jean-Claude Germain, directed by Paul Thompson

PAUL THOMPSON

May 27–June 15: The Hanging of William O'Donnell by David Helwig, directed by Jim Garrard

September: Oedipus Rex by Sophocles, directed by Asheleigh Moorhouse

October 08–October 25: Spring Awakening by Frank Wedekind, directed by Martin Kinch

October 09–October 10: 6 of a Kind by Louis Del Grande, directed by Louis Del Grande

November 09–December 06: I Had It But It's All Gone Now by Richard De Canio, directed by Louis Del Grande

November 27–November 28: Niobe by Phillip J. Hopcraft, directed by Phillip J. Hopcraft

December 12–December 19: Noah by Anne Anglin and Clare Coulter, directed by Anne Anglin and Clare Coulter

December 21–December 31: The Little Prince by Antoine de Saint-Exupéry, adapted by Paul Thompson, directed by Paul Thompson

1971

January 07–January 24: Out to Breakfast by Collective, directed by John Palmer

February 11–March 21: Vampyr by Shain Jaffe, directed by Martin Kinch

April 02–April 25: Doukhobors by Collective, directed by Paul Thompson

May 13–May 30: Wrestler's Son by Louis Del Grande, directed by Mel Tuck, produced by LM&N Productions in association with TPM

11 TRINITY SQUARE NOON HOUR THEATRE SERIES INVITATION, SUMMER 1969

August 03–September 15: Buzzer by Dean Taylor, directed by Conrad Ishpemming (John Davies), produced by Echelon Productions and Proto Theatre, with the support of TPM

August 19–September 21: Ubu Raw, based on Ubu Roi by Alfred Jarry, directed by Paul Thompson

September 30–October 17: Free Ride by Collective, directed by Paul Thompson

October 21–November 07: Me, You, Us and the Raincoat by Louis Del Grande, directed by Louis Del Grande

October 21–November 07: Renegade in Retrospect by Frank Parman, directed by Eileen Thalenberg

November 19–January 02: Charles Manson a.k.a. Jesus Christ by Fabian Jennings, directed by John Palmer

1972

January 13–January 30: The Black Queen Is Going To Eat You All Up by Frank Powley, directed by Jim Garrard

January 15: The Steadfast Tin Soldier by Miles Potter, directed by Miles Potter

February 11–March 05: Bethune! by Collective, directed by Peter Boretski

March 23–April 16: Tantrums by Hrant Alianak, directed by Louis Del Grande

May 18–June 08: Buffalo Jump by Carol Bolt, directed by Paul Thompson

June 01–June 30: Jack and the Beanstalk by Collective, directed by Collective, presented by Children's Pantomime Theatre

August 13: The Farm Show by Collective, directed by Paul Thompson

October 25–November 19: Dog in the Manger by Lope de Vega, directed by Louis Del Grande

November 03–November 11: The Violinist and the Flower Girl by Hrant Alianak, directed by Hrant Alianak

November 29–December 17: Pilk's Madhouse by Ken Campbell, directed by Ken Campbell

December 27–January 10: The Separate Condition by Barbara Nye, directed by John Juliani

1973

January 18–February 18: 1837 by Collective, with Rick Salutin as writer, directed by Paul Thompson

March 02–March 18: The Master by Will Seymour (Phillip J. Hopcraft), directed by Jim Garrard

March 22–April 07: Pauline by E. Pauline Johnson (Tekahionwake), adapted by the Collective, with Carol Bolt as writer, directed by Paul Thompson

April 11–April 22: The Farm Show (tour) by Collective, directed by Paul Thompson

May 09–May 27: Show of Shows by Collective, directed by Collective, produced by Homade Theatre, a TPM guest production

May 13–May 19: Brandy by Hrant Alianak, directed by Hrant Alianak

September 19–October 14: Under the Graywacke by Collective, directed by Paul Thompson

October 10–October 27: Noah's Kiosk by Hrant Alianak, directed by Hrant Alianak

October 16–November 20: Them Donnellys by Collective, with Frank McEnaney, directed by Paul Thompson

October 17–October 27: Cod on a Stick / Crime and Punishment by Dudley Cox, directed by CODCO, produced by CODCO, presented by TPM

October 25–November 23: So Who's Goldberg? by Louis Del Grande, directed by Louis Del Grande

December 05–December 26: All the Ghosts by Larry Fineberg, directed by Louis Del Grande

December 12–December 23: Christmas by Hrant Alianak, directed by Hrant Alianak

1974

Remember the Truth Dentist by Heathcote Williams, directed by unknown, a TPM Seed Show

THE WEST SHOW
JANET AMOS, DAVID FOX, MILES POTTER, CONNIE KALDOR, ANNE ANGLIN, TED JOHNS, PAUL THOMPSON, ERIC PETERSON, PAULA JARDINE, AND BOB PEARSON. PHOTO BY PAUL THOMPSON.

January 09–January 30: Toronto Pixie Caper by Collective, directed by Ken Campbell

February 14–March 03: The Adventures of an Immigrant by Rick Salutin, directed by Paul Thompson

March 06–April 28: Naked on the North Shore by Ted Johns, directed by Paul Thompson

March 13–April 07: The Farm Show (tour) by Collective, directed by Paul Thompson

April 22–May 05: The Tempest by William Shakespeare, directed by Cheryl Cashman

May 10–May 26: Rail Tales by Hrant Alianak, Raymond Canale, and Rod Langley, directed by Hrant Alianak

June 24–July 15: Oil by Collective, directed by Paul Thompson

September 12–October 12: 1837: The Farmers' Revolt by Collective, with Rick Salutin as writer, directed by Paul Thompson

October 09–November 03: Them Donnellys by Frank McEnaney, directed by Paul Thompson

October 21–October 26: Almighty Voice by Collective, directed by Clarke Rogers

October 24–November 30: Sickness, Death & Beyond the Grave by Collective, directed by Greg Malone, produced by CODCO, presented by TPM

November 20–December 03: The Joke Show by Phil Schreibman, directed by Phil Schreibman, a TPM Seed Show

December 04–December 15: Brutal Paradise by Peter Melnick, directed by Peter Melnick

December 21–January 05: Alligator Pie by Dennis Lee, adapted by Janet Amos, Clare Coulter, and Géza Kovács, directed by Janet Amos

1975

Simone by Megan Terry, directed by Frank Canino, a TPM Seed Show

January 09–January 23: Tony's Woman by Michael Sestito, directed by Hrant Alianak

January 18–April 24: I Love You, Baby Blue by Collective, directed by Paul Thompson

February 26–March 08: Follies of Conviction by James Roy, directed by James Roy, a TPM Seed Show

March 10–March 30: The False Messiah by Rick Salutin, directed by John Palmer

March 12–March 26: Family/ Entertainment by Collective, directed by Paul Kelman, a TPM Seed Show

April 07–April 08: Canadian Heroes Series Number 1: Gabriel Dumont by Collective, directed by John Gray and Paul Thompson

April 23–May 14: Alive by Collective, directed by Janet Amos

May 07–May 28: Night by Hrant Alianak, directed by Hrant Alianak

May 14–May 25: Monomania by Peter Melnick, directed by Peter Melnick, a TPM Seed Show

June 19–June 21: Field of On and Off by David Type, directed by David Type, a TPM Seed Show

June 24–July 17: The Farm Show (tour) by Collective, directed by Paul Thompson

September 05–September 18: The Spell of the Yukon by Robert Service, adapted by Collective, directed by Hrant Alianak

September 17–October 04: City: The Toronto Show by Collective, directed by Cheryl Cashman

October 08–October 19: Breathing Space by Collective, directed by Jordan Deitcher, a TPM Seed Show, created by Raven Production Company

October 24–November 02: The Alberta Cowboy Show by Collective, directed by Paul Kelman

October 29–November 12: Titus Andronicus by William Shakespeare, directed by Hrant Alianak

November 27–December 17: The Empress of China by Peter Melnick, directed by Peter Melnick

December 03–December 09: The West Show by Collective, directed by Paul Thompson

1976

January: The Peep Show by Collective, directed by Paul Thompson, CBC TV series

January 02–January 05: 30 Minutes from Downtown by Collective, directed by Howie Cooper, a TPM Seed Show

January 21–February 15: Would You Like to Smell My Pocket Crumbs by Collective, directed by Collective, produced by CODCO, presented by TPM

February 18–March 14: Operation Finger Pinkie by Collective, directed by Janet Amos

February 26–February 26: The Follies of Conviction by James Roy, directed by James Roy

March 03–March 10: Letters to the Editor by James Roy, directed by James Roy

March 10–April 04: The Horsburgh Scandal by Betty Jane Wylie, directed by Paul Thompson

March 18–March 21: The Writing of the Painting of Martha by Dennis Tourbin, directed by Dennis Tourbin, a TPM Seed Show

March 31–April 11: Faustus by Christopher Marlowe, directed by Des McAnuff

April 17–April 26: Brébeuf by Collective, directed by Eldon Garnet, a TPM Seed Show

April 21–May 02: Landscapes by Collective, directed by Cheryl Cashman

April 21–May 08: The Collected World of David McFadden by David McFadden, directed by Doug Rodger

May 18–June 06: The Blues by Hrant Alianak, directed by Hrant Alianak

May 25–June 06: The Wringing of Hearts by Peter Melnick, directed by Peter Melnick

May 25–June 06: 1837: The Farmers' Revolt / The Farm Show (tour) by Rick Salutin and TPM, directed by Paul Thompson

May 25–June 06: Star by Robert Louis Stevenson, adapted by Collective, directed by Paul Kelman, a TPM Seed Show

May 25–May 29: Gilgamesh by Janis Rapoport, directed by David McIlwraith, a TPM Seed Show in association with Theatre Balagan

July 07–July 28: The Athletes' Show by Collective, with Bruce Kidd, directed by Paul Thompson

October 05–October 16: Laugh Your Guts Out with Total Strangers by Collective, directed by Collective, produced by CODCO, presented by TPM

October 20–October 31: John Hornby (Canadian Heroes Series Number 2) by Collective, directed by David Fox

November 10–November 21: Two Miles Off by Collective, directed by Mark Manson

November 13–November 21: So Inside, No Closer by Chris Hallgren, directed by Chris Hallgren, a TPM Seed Show in association with Another Theatre Company

November 15–November 25: Naked on the North Shore by Ted Johns, directed by Paul Thompson

November 24–December 11: The Patty Rehearst Story by Anthony Lorraine, directed by Marion Lewis and Deanne Taylor, produced by Hummer Talent Cartel and TPM

December 18–January 02: Gullband by Susan Musgrave, adapted by Paula Jardine, directed by Paula Jardine, a TPM Seed Show

December 29–January 06: The Road to Charlottetown by Milton Acorn and Cedric Smith, directed by Cedric Smith and Paul Thompson, a TPM Seed Show

1977

January 25–February 06: He Won't Come in from the Barn by Andrew McKeever, directed by Paul Thompson

February 10–February 19: The Empire Builders by Boris Vian, directed by Kevin Ward

February 10–February 27: No! No! No! by Sharon Pollock, directed by Hrant Alianak

March 02–March 20: 18 Wheels by John Gray, directed by John Gray

March 30–April 24: I Love You, Baby Blue 2 by Hrant Alianak, Collective, and Paul Kelman, directed by Hrant Alianak

April 13–April 17: Con/Notes by Richard Shoichet, directed by Richard Shoichet and Wyndham Wise, a TPM Seed Show

April 23–April 30: Convicted But Not Convinced by Anthony Lorraine, directed by Anthony Lorraine, a TPM Seed Show

May 20–May 29: Cheap Thrills by Michael Hollingsworth, directed by Michael Hollingsworth, a TPM Seed Show

May 28–June 12: The Empress of China by Peter Melnick, directed by Peter Melnick, a TPM Seed Show

May 28–June 12: Loose Connections by Collective, directed by Steven Bush, a TPM Seed Show

September 05–September 18: The Spell of the Yukon by Robert Service, adapted by the Collective, directed by Hrant Alianak

September 16–October 01: Punc Rok by Michael Hollingsworth, directed by Michael Hollingsworth, a TPM Seed Show

September 21–October 01: Shakespeare for Fun and Profit: A Canadian Dream by Collective, directed by Paul Thompson

October 11–October 15: Paper Wheat by Collective, directed by Guy Sprung, produced by 25th Street Theatre, a TPM guest production

November 09–December 03: Kaspar by Peter Handke, directed by Alexander Hausvater, produced by Montreal Theatre Lab and TPM

November 28–December 18: Far as the Eye Can See by Rudy Wiebe, directed by Paul Thompson, produced by Tarragon Theatre and TPM

December 10–February 25: The Bible as Told to Karen Ann Quinlan by the Hummer Sisters, directed by the Hummer Sisters, a TPM Seed Show

1978

February 08–February 19: Eros Rising by Penn Kemp, directed by Anne Anglin, a TPM Seed Show

March 11–March 17: Beatrice Cenci by Steve Ballantine and Kevin Ward, directed by Kevin Ward, a TPM Seed Show

March 15–April 15: Nite of De Lite by Dale Cameron and Lynda Davy, directed by Dale Cameron, produced by The De Lite Company in association with TPM (a TPM Seed Show)

April 19–April 30: Everything Must Go by Peter Melnick, directed by Peter Melnick, a TPM Seed Show

April 26–May 07: Queen Street Show by Simon Malbogat, directed by Simon Malbogat, a TPM Seed Show

May 26–June 12: The Empress of China by Peter Melnick, directed by Peter Melnick

June 01–June 11: Headspace by Judith Merril, adapted by Collective, directed by Paul Kelman

BILLY BISHOP GOES TO WAR HOUSE PROGRAM

August 25–September 03: He Won't Come in from the Barn by Andrew McKeever, directed by Paul Thompson

September 26–September 30: Sunset Strippers Show by Collective, directed by Enrico Campana, a TPM Seed Show

October 03–October 22: Commedia Dell'Arte by Collective, directed by Claude Jutra, produced by Theatre Pepperoni, presented by TPM

October 18–October 31: The True Story of Ida Johnson by Sharon Riis, adapted by Paula Jardine, directed by Paula Jardine, a TPM Seed Show

October 25–November 01: The Indictment by Dick Dale, directed by Tony Bogue, produced by Mixed Company Theatre and TPM (a TPM Seed Show)

October 25–November 01: Tillie's Punctured Romance by Charlie Ledds, directed by Tony Bogue, produced by Mixed Company Theatre and TPM (a TPM Seed Show)

November 03–December 16: Les Maudits Anglais by Gary Geddes, directed by Paul Thompson

November 07–December 10: The Road to Charlottetown by Milton Acorn and Cedric Smith, directed by Cedric Smith and Paul Thompson

November 14–December 23: Brush-Off by Joann McIntyre, directed by John Palmer

November 28–December 16: Pan Meets a Flower by David Type, directed by David Type, a TPM Seed Show

December 26–December 31: Wizard of TV Land by Collective, directed by Collective, a TPM Seed Show

1979

1837: Nationalist Rebellion in Frontier Canada (tour) by Rick Salutin and TPM, directed by Pam Brighton

January 06–February 03: Dream Girls by Collective, directed by Janet Amos and Clarke Rogers

February 06–February 25: Without a Parachute by David Fennario, directed by Simon Malbogat

February 13–March 25: Billy Bishop Goes to War by John Gray, directed by John Gray, produced by Vancouver East Cultural Centre in association with TPM

March 01–March 10: Circus Gothic by Jan Kudelka, directed by Cheryl Cashman, a TPM Seed Show

March 15–March 25: Ballads of Canada by Wiz Bryant, directed by Wiz Bryant

March 20–April 04: Les Canadiens by Ken Dryden and Rick Salutin, directed by Miles Potter

April–June: 1837: The Farmers' Revolt by Rick Salutin and TPM, directed by Paul Thompson

April 01–May 30: The Farm Show (tour) by Collective, directed by Paul Thompson

April 05–April 21: After the Opera by Jack Blum and Lenny Blum, directed by Jack Blum

June–July: Modern Living, based on 1984 by George Orwell, adapted by the Hummer Sisters and Collective, directed by Michael Hollingsworth and Deanne Taylor, produced by VideoCabaret, a TPM guest production

June 07–July 01: Watchtower by Thom Sokoloski, directed by unknown, produced by Theatre of the Autumn Leaf, a TPM guest production

July 24–August 05: The Last Tango Monster by Victor Solitario, directed by Victor Solitario, produced by Theatre Solitude, a TPM guest production

September 20–October 20: The Waning Moon Café by Collective, directed by CODCO, produced by CODCO, with Figgy Duff in concert, presented by TPM

October 06–October 21: Night by Hrant Alianak, directed by Hrant Alianak

October 10–November 10: October's Soldiers by Alun Hibbert, directed by Clarke Rogers

October 19–December 04: Electra by Sophocles, directed by Richard Rose, produced by Necessary Angel Theatre Company in collaboration with TPM

November 13–November 25: Sarah and Gabrial by Tanya Ryga and Sharon Stearns, directed by Svetlana Zylin

November 27–December 15: Burnt Toast Revue by Sheila Gostick and Jim Tuck, directed by unknown, a TPM Seed Show

LES CANADIENS
JAMES RANKIN AND JEAN RICARD.

November 30–December 23: Maggie and Pierre by Linda Griffiths and Paul Thompson, directed by Paul Thompson

1980

1980–1981: Maggie and Pierre (tour) by Linda Griffiths and Paul Thompson, directed by Paul Thompson

January 05–February 03: Coming Through Slaughter by Michael Ondaatje, directed by Paul Thompson

March 18–April 05: The School Show by Ted Johns, directed by Clarke Rogers

March 27–April 20: Stallers' Fam by Franz Xaver Kroetz, directed by Peter Froehlich

April 08–May 18: Circus Gothic by Jan Kudelka, directed by Jan Kudelka

May 03–May 20: When You Comin' Back Red Ryder? by Mark Medoff, directed by Marc Diamond, produced by Phantom Theatre and TPM

May 20–May 24: Half Human, Half Heartache by The Clichettes, with Marni Jackson, directed by Michael Glassbourg, a TPM Seed Show

May 20–May 30: From Saigon to Sudbury by Collective, directed by Gord McCall, produced by Theatre Lifeline, with support from TPM

June: Hotch Potch Suite by Fabian Boutilier, directed by Fabian Boutilier

June 18–June 28: Glazed Tempera by Cynthia Grant, Kim Renders, and Maureen White, directed by Cynthia Grant, produced by Nightwood Theatre, with the support of the TPM Seed Fund

August: West by Maria Campbell, directed by Paul Thompson

August 24–September 08: The Death of the Donnellys by Ted Johns, directed by Paul Thompson, produced by the Blyth Festival and TPM

September 25–October 12: Lana Turner Has Collapsed by Frank O'Hara, adapted by Sky Gilbert, directed by Sky Gilbert, produced by Buddies in Bad Times and TPM

October 04–November 04: Boom by Georg Büchner, adapted by Collective, directed by Richard Rose, produced by Necessary Angel and TPM

October 16–October 26: Phantom of the Opera by Victor Solitario, directed by Victor Solitario, a TPM Seed Show

November: Comedie by Hrant Alianak, directed by Hrant Alianak

November 12–December 14: Torontonians by Collective, directed by Paul Thompson

November 26–December 21: The Crackwalker by Judith Thompson, directed by Clarke Rogers

December 31–April 18: Half Human, Half Heartache (tour) by Marni Jackson and The Clichettes, directed by Hrant Alianak

1981

100 Years by G. Marquery, directed by Cynthia Grant

January 22–January 25: Torch/Song by Sky Gilbert, directed by Sky Gilbert, presented as part of Brief New Works

January 22–January 25: Measures by Andri Haller, directed by Candace O'Connor, presented as part of Brief New Works

January 22–January 25: Willy, Sinton and Jill by John Coulter, directed by David Cox, presented as part of Brief New Works

January 22–January 25: The Nature of the Beast by Mary Vingoe, directed by Cynthia Grant, presented as part of Brief New Works

January 28–February 15: Nathan Cohen: A Review by Rick Salutin, directed by Paul Thompson

March 17–April 19: Prodigals in a Promised Land by Hector Bunyan, directed by Clarke Rogers

May: Dead Heat by Jim Garrard, directed by Jim Garrard, a TPM Seed Show

May 07–May 31: Studhorse Man by Robert Kroetsch, adapted by Collective, directed by Paul Thompson

May 20–May 21: Where's Fluffy? The Rise and Fall of Babyland by Janet Burke, Jennifer Puidokos, and Deanne Taylor, directed by Janet Burke, Jennifer Puidokos, and Deanne Taylor, a TPM Seed Show

May 28–May 31: FLQ/CBC by Dennis Tourbin, directed by Clarke Rogers

August 20–September 13: Kaddish by Allen Ginsberg, directed by Mordecai Greenberg, produced by Nephesh Theatre Company, presented by TPM

August 20–September 13: The Irish Hebrew Lesson by Wolf Mankowitz, directed by Howard Rypp, produced by Nephesh Theatre Company, presented by TPM

September 03–September 05: Emily by Tony Di Franco, directed by Tony Di Franco, a TPM Seed Show

September 04–September 05: The Party by Victor Coleman, directed by William Lane

October 27–November 01: Running by Ann Skinner, directed by Cindy Cowan and Richard Pochinko, a TPM Seed Show

November 03–November 22: Picnic in the Drift by Rina Fraticelli and Tanya (Mars) Rosenberg, directed by David McIlwraith, produced by Mutan Productions, with the support of TPM

November 26–December 20: The Gods of Money by Bembo Davies, directed by Jeff Braunstein

1982

January 12–January 31: Cold Comfort by Jim Garrard, directed by Jim Garrard

February 02–March 21: The Crackwalker by Judith Thompson, directed by Clarke Rogers, produced by 25th Street Theatre and TPM

February 02–February 07: The Second by Paul Quarrington, directed by David Fox, a TPM Seed Show

February 18–March 06: O.D. on Paradise by Patrick Brymer and Linda Griffiths, directed by Clarke Rogers, produced by 25th Street Theatre and TPM

March 18–March 28: Rude Noises by Brad Fraser, directed by Brad Fraser

March 25–April 17: Hank Williams, The Show He Never Gave by Maynard Collins, directed by Paul Thompson

April 06–April 25: The Crackwalker by Judith Thompson, directed by Clarke Rogers

April 13–May 01: The Al Cornell Story by Bill Ballantyne, directed by Hrant Alianak, a TPM Seed Show

April 28–May 16: Bridal Polonaise/Polonez Weselny by Steven Rumbelow, directed by Steven Rumbelow, produced by TPM, with Triple Action Theatre Group (UK)

June 08–June 27: Pantomime by Derek Walcott, directed by Calvin Butler, produced by Theatre Fountainhead, a TPM guest production

CLARKE ROGERS

October 13–November 07: Satin Thigh by Liberty Jane Carter, directed by Hrant Alianak

October 22–November 07: The Decameron by Alexander Hausvater, directed by Alexander Hausvater

November 05–November 20: Jessica by Maria Campbell, adapted by Maria Campbell, Linda Griffiths, and Paul Thompson, directed by Paul Thompson, produced by 25th Street Theatre and TPM

November 10–November 20: Hank Williams: The Show He Never Gave by Maynard Collins, directed by Paul Thompson

November 11–November 28: Green Dolphin by M. T. Kelly, directed by Layne Coleman

November 24–December 05: Bad Taste by Robyn Butt, directed by Clarke Rogers

December 26–February 13: Alligator Pie by Dennis Lee, adapted by Janet Amos, Clare Coulter, and Géza Kovács, directed by Janet Amos, produced by TPM in association with Blyth Summer Festival

1983

January 12–March 06: O.D. on Paradise by Patrick Brymer and Linda Griffiths, directed by Clarke Rogers, produced by TPM in association with 25th Street Theatre

January 21–February 06: Just Us Indians by David Type, directed by Michel Lefebvre

February 24–March 06: Generals Die in Bed by Charles Yale Harrison, adapted by Miles Potter, directed by Miles Potter

March 30–April 17: D & C by Claude Roberts [Clarke Rogers], directed by Clarke Rogers

May 04–June 11: Two Can Play by Trevor Rhone, directed by W. Lloyd Jackson and Trevor Rhone

November 17–December 11: The Passe Muraille Hamlet by William Shakespeare, directed by Clarke Rogers

December 01–December 07: The Cockroach Trilogy by Alan Williams, directed by Mike Bradwell

December 19–December 31: Alligator Pie by Dennis Lee, adapted by Janet Amos, Clare Coulter, and Géza Kovács, directed by Miles Potter

1984

January 20–February 12: The Warlord of Willowdale by Alan Williams, directed by Alan Williams

February 10–March 11: O.D. on Paradise by Patrick Brymer and Linda Griffiths, directed by Clarke Rogers, produced by TPM in association with 25th Street Theatre

March 01–March 18: Until We Part by Collective, directed by David McIlwraith, produced by Theatre Columbus, a TPM guest production

March 30–April 22: Wolfboy by Brad Fraser, directed by John Palmer

April 10–May 06: School for Emigrants by Collective, directed by Paul Thompson

April 24–May 06: Tighten the Traces / Haul the Reins by Robbie O'Neill, directed by Peter Froehlich, produced by Mulgrave Road Co-op Theatre and TPM

April 24–May 06: The Boat by Alistair MacLeod, directed by Peter Froehlich, produced by Mulgrave Road Co-op Theatre and TPM

May 01–May 15: Lost Souls and Missing Persons by Sally Clark, directed by Clarke Rogers

May 15–May 27: This is for you, Anna by Collective, directed by Shauna Janssen, produced by The Anna Project, a TPM guest production

May 30–June 02: Fight by Christopher Gerrard-Pinker, directed by Christopher Gerrard-Pinker, produced by Sword Theatre, VideoCabaret, and TPM

June: La Musica by Marguerite Duras, directed by Cynthia Grant

June 29–July 04: Three Beats to the Bar by Hector Bunyan, directed by Arif Hasnain

September 01–April 01: Alligator Pie (tour) by Dennis Lee, adapted by Janet Amos, Clare Coulter, Géza Kovács, and Eric Peterson, directed by Michel Lefebvre

November 01–November 28: O Canayen by Collective, with Michelle Smith, directed by Dean Gilmour, produced by Theatre Smith-Gilmour and TPM

November 15–December 02: Dance Hall Boys by David Sereda and Henry van Rijk, directed by John Palmer, produced by Buddies in Bad Times and TPM

November 21–November 24: Tango for Two Continents by Collective, directed by Paul Thompson

FRONT AND BACK COVER OF *ALLIGATOR PIE* HOUSE PROGRAM

November 21–December 16: American Demon by Jan Kudelka, directed by Clarke Rogers

November 24–December 16: Heat Lightning by Jan Kudelka, directed by Kate Lushington

1985

January 04–February 17: The Go-Go Boys by Howard Lester and Andrew Alty, directed by Howard Lester and Andrew Alty

March 05–March 18: Of Ice and Men by Collective, with Leon Rooke and Paul Thompson, directed by Paul Thompson

April 07–June 23: Nancy Drew: Clue in the Fast Lane by Beverley Cooper and Ann-Marie MacDonald, directed by Maureen White, produced by Prewd Productions in association with TPM

April 25–May 16: Master Harold and the Boys by Athol Fugard, directed by Maurice Podbrey

April 25–May 16: Fifth Molimo Street by Ben Halm, directed by Clarke Rogers

May: The History of the Village of the Small Huts, Part One: New France by Michael Hollingsworth, directed by Michael Hollingsworth, produced by VideoCabaret and TPM

September 10–October 03: Balls and Chains by Howard Lester and Andrew Alty, directed by Howard Lester and Andrew Alty

September 11–October 03: The Go-Go Boys by Howard Lester and Andrew Alty, directed by Howard Lester and Andrew Alty

October 13–November 03: Blue City Slammers by Layne Coleman, directed by Layne Coleman

October 31–November 21: Supermale by Alfred Jarry, adapted by Joann McIntyre, directed by Richard Pochinko, produced by Theatre Resource Centre and TPM

December 17–December 21: Trickster's Cabaret by Collective, directed by Richard Pochinko, produced by Native Earth Performing Arts and TPM

1986

January 01–February 01: The History of the Village of the Small Huts, Part Two: The British by Michael Hollingsworth, directed by Michael Hollingsworth, produced by VideoCabaret and TPM

January 14–January 26: This is for you, Anna by Suzanne Odette Khuri, Ann-Marie MacDonald, Baņuta Rubess, and Maureen White, directed by Suzanne Odette Khuri, Ann-Marie MacDonald, Baņuta Rubess, and Maureen White, produced by Nightwood Theatre and TPM

March: Spirit of '85 by Collective, directed by Collective, with Paul Thompson

March 27–April 01: Jessica: A Transformation by Maria Campbell, adapted by Linda Griffiths, with Maria Campbell, directed by Clarke Rogers

June 04–June 22: Discords by Christopher Gerrard-Pinker and Daniel Brooks, directed by Christopher Gerrard-Pinker, produced by Sword Theatre Productions, VideoCabaret, and TPM

June 17–June 28: La danse des poules by Dominique Abel and Fiona Gordon, directed by unknown, produced by Theatre Columbus and TPM

August: The Farm Show (tour) by Collective, directed by Paul Thompson

August 21–August 21: The Bespoke Overcoat by Wolf Mankowitz, directed by unknown, produced by Nephesh Theatre Company and TPM

August 21–August 21: P.S. The Cheque is in the Mail by Gabrielle Emanuel, directed by unknown, produced by Nephesh Theatre Company and TPM

TRICKSTER'S CABARET
MAKKA KLEIST, MONIQUE MOJICA, GARY FARMER, AND BILLY MERASTY.

September 22–November 07: The Beavers by Ronald Weihs, directed by Richard Pochinko, produced by Theatre Resource Centre in association with TPM

October 03–October 05: Pythagoras: The Mystery by Ian Wallace, Joann McIntyre, and Neil Gordon, directed by Joann McIntyre, produced by Theatre Resource Centre and TPM

October 07–October 26: By Grand Central Station I Sat Down and Wept by Elizabeth Smart, adapted by Anne Anglin and Nancy Beatty, directed by Anne Anglin

October 07–December 07: Jessica: A Transformation (tour) by Maria Campbell, adapted by Linda Griffiths, with Maria Campbell, directed by Clarke Rogers

October 17–October 31: The Road Shows by Beverley Cooper and Ann-Marie MacDonald, directed by Maureen White

November 05–November 23: White Dreams & Bad Money by Jim Bartley, directed by Sky Gilbert

December 28–January 04: Forever Young by Theatre Brats Collective, directed by Clarke Rogers

1987

January 09–February 01: Young Art by Brad Fraser, directed by Paul Thompson

February 17–March 29: Wedding in Texas and Other Stories by Cathy Jones, directed by Cathy Jones, Andy Jones, and Mary Walsh, produced by CODCO, presented by TPM

March 09–March 09: The 5 Minute Feminist Cabaret by Collective, directed by unknown, produced by Nightwood Theatre, Women's Cultural Building, and TPM

April 09–April 26: Pericles, Prince of Tyre by William Shakespeare by René-Daniel Dubois, directed by Alexander Hausvater

April 14–May 03: The History of the Village of the Small Huts, Part Three: The MacKenzie/Papineau Rebellion by Michael Hollingsworth, directed by Michael Hollingsworth, produced by VideoCabaret and TPM

May 28–June 21: The Last Will and Testament of Lolita by Collective, directed by unknown, produced by Nightwood Theatre and the Humbert Humbert Project in association with TPM

June 09–June 23: Other Voices: The Women Speak by Collective, directed by Susan Hogg, produced by The English Shakespeare Company (UK) and TPM

July 15–August 22: Pythagoras: The Mystery by Joann McIntyre and Ian Wallace, directed by Joann McIntyre and Richard Pochinko, produced by Theatre Resource Centre and TPM

August 10–August 24: Great Canadian Women by David Demchuk, directed by Robert Scott, produced by Gemini Productions and TPM

August 14–September 06: Ma Rainey's Black Bottom by August Wilson, directed by Jon Michaelson, produced by Mercury Theatre, a TPM guest production

October 01–October 25: Tragedy of Manners by Donna Lypchuk, directed by Clarke Rogers, produced by Paradise Productions, the Cameron House, and TPM

November 12–December 06: Bachelor-Man by Winston Kam, directed by Peter Hinton

1988

January 06: Lana Lust: The Bitch Stops Here! by Kent Staines, directed by unknown, produced by Sword Theatre Productions and TPM

February 04–March 20: Peggy's Song by Jim Garrard, directed by Clarke Rogers

March 08–April 03: Private Members by Andrew Alty and Howard Lester, directed by Andrew Alty and Howard Lester

JANE BUSS AND BRIAN RICHMOND

October 28–November 27: Fire by Paul Ledoux and David S. Young, directed by Brian Richmond, produced by TPM in association with the Shaw Festival

November 08–November 27: Scientific Americans by John Mighton, directed by Kathleen Flaherty, produced by Particle Zoo, Stonz Theatre, and TPM

1989

January 13–February 12: Under the Skin by Betty Lambert, directed by Susan Wright

March 03–April 02: West Memphis Mojo by Martin Jones, directed by Peter Hinton and Brian Richmond

March 21–April 02: Wild Abandon by Daniel MacIvor, directed by Vinetta Strombergs, produced by Sword Theatre Productions and TPM

April 18–May 21: Dry Lips Oughta Move to Kapuskasing by Tomson Highway, directed by Larry Lewis, produced by Native Earth Performing Arts and TPM

BRIAN RICHMOND

September 19–October 21: Rigoletto by Giuseppe Verdi, adapted by Michael Hollingsworth and Deanne Taylor, directed by Brian Richmond, produced by VideoCabaret International, TPM, and the National Arts Centre

November 10–December 10: Abingdon Square by María Irene Fornés, directed by Peter Hinton

1990

February 02–March 04: Echo by Ann Diamond, directed by Robert Lepage

February 09–March 04: Princess Pocahontas and the Blue Spots by Monique Mojica, directed by Muriel Miguel, produced by Nightwood Theatre and TPM

March 16–April 15: The Butcher's Apron by Charles Tidler, directed by Brian Richmond

October 12–November 04: Clutching the Heat by Maristella Roca, directed by Peter Froehlich

October 12–December 04: Hush by Allen Cole and Naomi Riches, directed by Peter Hinton and Alisa Palmer

November 16–December 16: Bag Babies by Allan Stratton, directed by John Bourgeois

1991

January 15–February 10: The Darling Family by Linda Griffiths, directed by Sandra Balcovske

February 01–February 24: Lilies by Michel Marc Bouchard, translated by Linda Gaboriau, directed by Brian Richmond

March 14–March 31: A Game of Inches by Linda Griffiths, directed by Sandra Balcovske

—
LILIES
DAMON D'OLIVEIRA, RICHARD PARTINGTON, AND CHRISTOPHER SHORE.

LAYNE COLEMAN

July 01–July 21: The History of the Village of the Small Huts, Part Five: Laurier by Michael Hollingsworth, directed by Michael Hollingsworth, produced by VideoCabaret and TPM

September 12–October 06: The Stone Angel by Margaret Laurence, adapted by James W. Nichol, directed by Brian Richmond and Maureen White, produced by the Blyth Festival and TPM

September 13–September 29: Hunter's Moon by Booth Savage, directed by Booth Savage

October 08–October 27: Cafe Negril by John L. Allen, directed by Layne Coleman

November 08–December 08: Second Nature by Deanne Taylor, directed by Deanne Taylor, produced by VideoCabaret and TPM

November 22–December 15: A Live Bird in its Jaws by Jeanne-Marc Delisle, directed by Deborah Porter, produced by Particle Zoo Productions and TPM

December 26–January 05: Old King Cole by Ken Campbell, directed by Booth Savage

1992

January 10–January 26: The Tyrant of Pontus by Thomas Coyle, directed by Sally Han, produced by Compleat Theatre and TPM

January 14–February 09: A Fertile Imagination by Susan G. Cole, directed by Layne Coleman

February 05–February 23: Jump! by Daniel MacIvor, directed by Daniel MacIvor, produced by da da kamera in association with TPM

March 11–April 05: The Seaford Tapes by Clare Coulter, Andrew Scorer, and Tracy Wright, directed by Clare Coulter

April 08–April 26: House by Daniel MacIvor, directed by Daniel Brooks

April 21–May 10: The League of Nathans by Jason Sherman, directed by Ian Prinsloo

MAY: THE GATHERING FESTIVAL

Universal Highway by Bruce Bell, directed by Laura J. Forth

Anything You Want Baby by John Dolin, directed by Wendy Hopkins

Baglady by Frank McGuinness, directed by Maureen White

"X" by Andrea Freeman and Caitriona Murphy, directed by Kirsten Johnson

Suzi Got Her Lips Tattooed by Collective, directed by Brenda McFarlane

The Love Talker by Deborah Pryor, directed by Erika Varga

Margaret and Ureason by Dona Paul Massel, directed by Heather Dick

Underwater, Overseas by Emil Sher, directed by Louise Nolan

Precipitous by Kathleen McDonnell, directed by Rebecca Cann

Apart by Colleen Craig, directed by Kerri MacDonald

Making Ends Meet by Janice Israeloff and Michael Smith, directed by Michael Smith

The Duel by Natasa Tanska, directed by Bathsheba Garnett

Speculum by Betty Jane Wylie, directed by Ines Buchli

Caveman Rainbow by Caroline Gillis, directed by Daniel MacIvor

SUSAN SERRAN, KEN MCDOUGALL, AND BAȚUTA RUBESS

September 29–October 25: How an Intellectual Can Aspire to Savagery by Death Waits, directed by Death Waits, produced by Candid Stammer Theatre in association with TPM

September 29–October 25: The Enthusiasm of the Species by Michael McMurty, directed by Phillip Nessel and Death Waits, produced by Candid Stammer Theatre in association with TPM

October 02–October 25: Resistance 500 by The Hour Company Collective, directed by unknown, produced by The Hour Company in association with TPM

November 03–December 06: Head in a Bag by Bańuta Rubess, directed by Bańuta Rubess

November 06–December 06: Ghetto by James O'Reilly, directed by Ken McDougall

November 23–November 23: Sacrifice by Jan Komárek, directed by unknown

1993

January 06–January 24: Sleeproom by Sally Clark, Robin Fulford, Daniel MacIvor, and John Mighton, directed by Ken McDougall, produced by Platform 9 and TPM

February 02–February 21: Dance of the Blue Harlequins by Rainer Maria Rilke, adapted by Jan Komárek, directed by Jan Komárek, produced by Sound Image Theatre and TPM

February 05: The Stone Angel by Margaret Laurence, adapted by James W. Nichol, directed by Maureen White

March 17–April 04: Say Zebra by Sherry Coman, directed by Stewart Arnott, produced by Compleat Theatre and TPM

April 13–April 25: A Play About the Mothers of Plaza de Mayo by Alisa Palmer, directed by Alisa Palmer, produced by Froth Productions in association with TPM

October 07–October 31: Urban Donnellys by Collective, directed by Colin Taylor and Paul Thompson, produced by TPM in association with Theatre WUM

October 12–November 07: The Last Supper by Hillar Liitoja, directed by Hillar Liitoja, produced by DNA Theatre in association with Platform 9 and TPM

November 17–November 22: Canadian Monsoon by Sheila James, directed by Lynda Hill, produced by Cahoots Theatre Projects in association with TPM

November 24–November 28: The Moon and Dead Indians by Daniel David Moses, directed by Colin Taylor, produced by Cahoots Theatre Projects in association with TPM

December 01–December 05: Noran Bang: The Yellow Room by M. J. Kang, directed by Marion de Vries, produced by Cahoots Theatre Projects in association with TPM

1994

The Chocolate Bath by Mark Christmann, directed by Paulette Phillips, produced by The Believer Project, a TPM guest production

January 11–February 06: The Alistair Trilogy by Diane Cave and Nadia Ross, directed by Diane Cave and Nadia Ross, produced by STO Union in association with TPM

January 18–February 13: Never Swim Alone by Daniel MacIvor, directed by Ken McDougall

February 15–March 06: Requiem for an Angel by Jan Komárek, directed by Jan Komárek, produced by Sound Image Theatre in association with TPM

March 08–March 27: Body and Soul by John Mighton, directed by Diane Cave, produced by Crow's Theatre and TPM

March 15–April 03: Still by Leah Cherniak and Martha Ross, directed by Baņuta Rubess, produced by Theatre Columbus, a TPM guest presentation

April 12–May 01: Pretty Blue by Ron Chambers, directed by Lindsey Robinson, produced by LR Productions in association with TPM

SUSAN SERRAN, BAŅUTA RUBESS, AND COLIN TAYLOR

September 27–October 30: INTO by Dave Carley, directed by Bill Lane, produced by Theatre Cognito and TPM

November 08–December 04: The Earth is a Witch, The Witch is a Saint, The Saint is Applause by Death Waits, directed by Daniel Brooks

1995

January 03–January 15: The America Play by Suzan-Lori Parks, directed by Colin Taylor, produced by Theatre WUM, a TPM guest production

January 12–February 19: The Stillborn Lover by Timothy Findley, directed by Baņuta Rubess

February 07–February 26: Excerpts from the Emo Journals by Collective, directed by Daniel MacIvor and Nadia Ross, produced by STO Union and TPM in association with da da kamera

March 14–April 09: Mom, Dad, I'm Living With a White Girl by Marty Chan, directed by Sally Han, produced by Cahoots Theatre Projects and TPM

April 18–May 07: Metamorphosis of a Shadow by Jan Komárek, directed by Jan Komárek, produced by Sound Image Theatre and TPM

April 25–May 14: Motherhood, Madness and the Shape of the Universe by Kim Renders, directed by Trisha Lamie

June 06–June 18: Joy/Joie by Pol Pelletier, directed by Pol Pelletier and Gisèle Sallin, produced by La Compagnie Pol Pelletier, with the support of TPM

October 17–November 05: Controlling Interest by Paulette Philips, directed by Paulette Philips, produced by Paulette Philips, Platform 9, and TPM

October 31–November 19: The Little Years by John Mighton, directed by Herbert Olschok, produced by TPM in association with the Why Theatre Festival

November 22–December 03: I Hate You On Mondays by Kate Miles, directed by Jennifer Brewin, produced by Head on a Stick, a TPM guest production

December 01–December 03: The Tommy Prince Story by Alanis Odjig, directed by Paul Thompson, produced by De-ba-jeh-mu-jig Theatre Group and TPM

1996

January 02–January 28: The Indian Medicine Shows, i. The Moon and Dead Indian by Daniel David Moses, directed by Colin Taylor

January 02–January 28: The Indian Medicine Shows, ii. Angel of the Medicine Show by Daniel David Moses, directed by Colin Taylor

January 16–February 11: Not Spain by Richard Sanger, directed by Naomi Campbell and Deborah Lambie, produced by Grand Theatre Collective and TPM

February 27–March 17: The Freud Project: Civilization and its Discontents by Paul Bettis, directed by Paul Bettis, produced by Civilized Theatre and TPM

March 01–March 31: Lucky Strike by Hrant Alianak, directed by Hrant Alianak, produced by Canadian Rep Theatre and TPM

April 23–May 12: The Threepenny Epic Cabaret by Bald Ego Theatre and Stan Rogal, directed by Adam Nashman, produced by Bald Ego Theatre and TPM

May 07–June 02: Wedding Day at the Cro-Magnons' by Wajdi Mouawad, translated by Shelley Tepperman, directed by Baņuta Rubess, produced by TPM and the National Arts Centre

June 15–June 23: Canadian Monsoon by Sheila James, directed by Lynda Hill, produced by Cahoots Theatre Projects and TPM

THE INDIAN MEDICINE SHOWS
PHILIPPA DOMVILLE AND BILLY MERASTY. PHOTO BY MICHAEL COOPER.

SEPTEMBER: THE GATHERING FESTIVAL

Christiane: Stations in a Painter's Life by Marguerite Anderson and Elizabeth Schwaiger, directed by Vikki Anderson

Daughters of Lot, Or, The Lot of Daughters by Aron Tager, directed by Aron Tager

Bananafish's Dog Poetry by Kelly Thornton, directed by Chad Dembski

Mid Life Crisis by Tracey Hoyt, Alison Field, and Alex Dallas, directed by Tanja Jacobs

Sheboobie by Lisa Brooke, Kate Huband, and Shoshana Sperling, directed by Moynan King

A Tidy Package by Amy House and Berni Stapleton, directed by Lois Brown

Bert and Staff by Shoshana Raven Guy, directed by ahdri zhina mandiela

Biff by Alison Lawrence, directed by Alison Lawrence

The Persephone Project by La Compagnie Petit Jeu, directed by Philippa Domville

The Slow Eviction of Ruby Rosenholtz by Toby Rodin, directed by Dean Gilmour

September 24–October 20: Gulag by Robin Fulford, directed by Sarah Stanley, produced by Platform 9 and TPM

October 31–November 24: Still the Night by Theresa Tova, directed by Anne Anglin, produced by Tapestry Music Theatre, Tova Entertainment, and TPM

1997

January 11–February 02: Marisol by José Rivera, directed by Colin Taylor

February 04–February 16: Possible Worlds by John Mighton, directed by Daniel Brooks, produced by Platform 9, Possible Worlds Company, and TPM

March 04–April 06: Maggie and Pierre by Linda Griffiths and Paul Thompson, directed by Paul Thompson

April 15–May 04: Stuck by David Rubinoff, directed by Chad Dembski, produced by Topological Theatre, Playing For Keeps, and TPM

April 26–May 18: Beast on the Moon by Richard Kalinoski, directed by Hrant Alianak, produced by Alianak Productions and TPM

LAYNE COLEMAN

July 17–August 10: The Convict Lover by Merilyn Simonds, adapted by Collective, directed by Layne Coleman, produced by The Kingston Summer Festival and TPM

September 20–October 19: 1837: The Farmers' Revolt by Rick Salutin and TPM, directed by Colin Taylor

October 22–December 14: Possible Worlds by John Mighton, directed by Daniel Brooks

1998

January 27–February 26: The Duchess a.k.a. Wallis Simpson by Linda Griffiths, directed by Paul Thompson

February 15–March 15: Quartet by Eugene Stickland, directed by Alisa Palmer, produced by Froth Productions and TPM

May 01–June 07: Aurash by Bahrām Beyzāie, translated and adapted by Soheil Parsa and Brian Quirt, directed by Soheil Parsa, produced by Modern Times Stage Company and TPM

October 20–November 29: Sir John, Eh? by Jim Garrard and Grant Heckman, directed by Layne Coleman, produced by The Kingston Summer Festival and TPM

November 05–November 29: Hunger Striking by Kit Brennan, directed by Janet Amos

1999

January 08–January 24: Miss Chatelaine by Damien Atkins, directed by Stephen Heatley

January 21–February 14: The Death of General Wolfe by Brian Quirt, directed by Brian Quirt

February 23–March 21: The Drawer Boy by Michael Healey, directed by Miles Potter

April 02–April 25: Health Class by David S. Craig and Robert Morgan, directed by Leah Cherniak

April 08–May 02: Babes on Bay Street by Lila Csorgo, directed by Michael Waller

May 18–June 06: Stay by David Demchuk, directed by Anne Driscoll, produced by White Queen and TPM

September 21–September 23: The Drawer Boy by Michael Healey, directed by Miles Potter

October 05–October 24: Act of God by James O'Reilly, directed by Susan Potvin

November 11–December 12: Alien Creature: A Visitation from Gwendolyn MacEwen by Linda Griffiths, directed by Simon Heath, produced by TPM in association with Duchess Productions

2000

January 13–February 06: The Yoko Ono Project by Jean Yoon, directed by Jean Yoon and Marion de Vries, produced by Loud Mouth Asian Babes and TPM

February 17–March 12: The Mother's Saint by Edward Roy, directed by Edward Roy, produced by Topological Theatre and TPM

March 23–April 16: The Lady Smith by Andrew Moodie, directed by Layne Coleman

May 09–May 28: The Rediscovery of Sex by Collective, directed by Paul Thompson, produced by Alianak Theatre Productions in association with Mainstage Productions and TPM

June 01–June 18: Circles of Love by Al-Noor Peera, directed by Layne Coleman, produced by Ego Productions and TPM

ALIEN CREATURE: A VISITATION FROM GWENDOLYN MACEWEN
LINDA GRIFFITHS. PHOTO BY HEATHER MORTON.

September 26–October 15: White Mice by Darren O'Donnell, directed by Darren O'Donnell, produced by Mammalian Diving Reflex, presented by TPM

October 10–October 29: Sheroes by Sarah Martyn, directed by Layne Coleman

November 07–November 26: The Kabbalistic Psychoanalysis Of Adam R. Tzaddik by Anton Piatigorsky, directed by Chris Abraham, produced by Moriah Productions in association with TPM

November 14–December 03: The Vic by Leanna Brodie, directed by David Oiye, produced by Cahoots Theatre Projects and TPM

2001

January 18–March 21: The Drawer Boy (tour) by Michael Healey, directed by Layne Coleman

February 06–February 25: Alien Creature: A Visitation from Gwendolyn MacEwen by Linda Griffiths, directed by Simon Heath

February 08–February 21: The Drawer Boy (tour) by Michael Healey, directed by Layne Coleman

March 20–April 15: Time After Time: The Chet Baker Project by James O'Reilly, directed by Jim Millan, produced by Crow's Theatre in association with TPM

May 08–May 27: This Hotel by Alex Poch-Goldin, directed by Kelly Thornton, produced by Planet 88 Productions in association with TPM

September 18–October 07: You Are Here by Daniel MacIvor, directed by Daniel MacIvor, produced by da da kamera in association with TPM

October 30–November 25: Passe Muraille's A Midsummer Night's Dream by William Shakespeare, directed by Kate Lynch

December 05–December 16: Body Geometry: The Seventh Angel by Collective, directed by David Duclos, produced by The Theatre Centre, with the support of TPM

2002

January 22–February 10: Dreams of Blonde and Blue by M. J. Kang, directed by Guillermo Verdecchia, produced by Cahoots Theatre Projects and TPM

March 12–March 31: The School Show by Ted Johns, directed by Layne Coleman

April 16–May 05: Thunderstick by Ken Williams, directed by Paul Thompson

May 25–June 16: [boxhead] by Darren O'Donnell, directed by Chris Abraham, produced by Go Chicken Go, presented by TPM

September 24–October 13: To The Wall by Andy Jones, directed by Charlie Tomlinson

October 15: The Drawer Boy (tour) by Michael Healey, directed by Layne Coleman

November 05–December 08: In the Wings by Carole Corbeil, adapted by Nicky Guadagni, directed by Layne Coleman

2003

January 07–January 26: William & James by Robert Tsonos, directed by George Pothitos, produced by Sometimes Y Theatre in association with TPM

February 18–March 09: Finding Regina by Shoshana Sperling, directed by Kelly Thornton, produced by Nightwood Theatre and TPM in association with the Globe Theatre

March 25–April 13: The Blues by Hrant Alianak, directed by Hrant Alianak

May 07–June 01: Me, Dad and the Hundred Boyfriends by Cathy Jones, directed by Charlie Rhindress, produced by Half Apple Productions in association with TPM

June 10–June 29: 'da Kink in my hair by Trey Anthony, directed by Weyni Mengesha, produced by Plaitform Entertainment in association with TPM

November 13–December 07: Tequila Vampire Matinee by Kevin Quain, directed by Ted Dykstra

2004

January 20–February 15: Blood by Tom Walmsley, directed by Kate Lynch

January 20–February 15: One Good Marriage by Sean Reycraft, directed by Shari Hollett

February–March 07: The Adventures of Ali & Ali and the Axes of Evil by Marcus Youssef, with Guillermo Verdecchia and Camyar Chai, directed by Guillermo Verdecchia, produced by Cahoots Theatre Projects, with NeWorld Theatre, presented by TPM

April 23–May 16: Unity (1918) by Kevin Kerr, directed by Chris Abraham

June 03–June 20: Platinum Travel Club by Franca Miraglia, directed by Layne Coleman, produced by By The Word Productions in association with TPM

September 21–October 10: PppEeeAaaCccEee by Darren O'Donnell and Rebecca Picherack, directed by Darren O'Donnell and Rebecca Picherack, produced by Mammalian Diving Reflex and TPM

October 19–November 07: One Good Marriage by Sean Reycraft, directed by Shari Hollett

November 16–December 05: Small Returns by Jacob Richmond, directed by Michael Kesser, produced by Jack in the Black Theatre in association with TPM

2005

January 04–January 30: Little Dragon by Keira Loughran, directed by Marion de Vries, produced by k'Now Theatre and TPM

February 05–February 27: Poochwater by Mike McPhaden, directed by Patrick Connor, produced by The Poochwater Collective in association with TPM

March 29–April 17: St. Christopher by A. Shay Hahn, directed by Vikki Anderson, produced by DVxT Theatre Company in association with TPM

March 04–March 20: Dream Machine by Blake Brooker and David Rhymer, directed by Blake Brooker, produced by One Yellow Rabbit and TPM

October 04–November 05: Fish Eyes by Anita Majumdar, directed by Gregory Prest, presented as part of Stage 3

—
***PPPEEEAAACCCEEE* HOUSE PROGRAM**

October 04–October 29: Better Parts by Nicole Stamp, directed by Nicole Stamp, presented as part of Stage 3

October 04–October 19: Born Ready / Pusha Man by Joseph Jomo Pierre, directed by Philip Akin, produced by Obsidian Theatre Company and TPM, presented as part of Stage 3

November 01–November 20: Jamaica Man by John Blackwood, directed by Rudi Quammie Williams, produced by Obsidian Theatre Company and TPM, presented as part of Stage 3

November 09–November 27: Territories by Niki Landau, directed by Paul Lampert, produced by Theatre PANIK and TPM

November 15–November 27: blood.claat—one womban story by d'bi.young anitafrika, directed by Weyni Mengesha, produced by Obsidian Theatre Company and TPM, presented as part of Stage 3

2006

February 16–March 12: 3 Squares a Day by Tom Walmsley, directed by Kate Lynch

March 02–March 19: The Rochdale Project by Collective, directed by Simon Heath

April 20–May 08: Sparta by Sarah Martyn, directed by Layne Coleman

May 19–June 11: Cringeworthy by Alex Poch-Goldin, directed by Chris Abraham, produced by Planet 88 Productions in association with TPM

October 21–November 19: Descent by Tom Walmsley, directed by Kate Lynch

2007

February 13–March 11: The Sheep and the Whale by Ahmed Ghazali, translated by Bobby Theodore, directed by Soheil Parsa, produced by Cahoots Theatre Projects, Modern Times Stage Company, and TPM

April 05–April 29: Noble Parasites by Mike McPhaden, directed by Rebecca Brown

ANDY MCKIM

October 23–December 02: The Drawer Boy by Michael Healey, directed by Ruth Madoc-Jones

2008

February 09–March 09: Smokescreen / Born Ready by David S. Craig and Joseph Jomo Pierre, directed by Ed Roy and Philip Akin, produced by Roseneath Theatre, Obsidian Theatre Company, and TPM

March 14–April 06: Last Days of Graceland by Franca Miraglia, directed by Patricia Vanstone, produced by By The Word Productions and TPM

April 11–May 11: People Power, based on poems by Len Cervantes, adapted by CBT Collective, directed by Nina Lee Aquino, produced by Carlos Bulosan Theatre in association with TPM

September 30–October 18: An Evening with Uncle Val by Andy Jones and Michael Jones Sr., directed by Lois Brown, produced by Andy Jones Productions in association with TPM

October 22–November 15: Pyaasa by Anusree Roy, directed by Thomas Morgan Jones

October 23–November 15: The Misfit by Anita Majumdar, directed by Mark Cassidy

November 14–December 06: Legoland by Jacob Richmond, directed by Jacob Richmond and Britt Small, produced by Atomic Vaudeville in association with TPM

November 14–December 06: Trudeau Stories by Brooke Johnson, directed by Allyson McMackon

2009

January 06–January 31: Them & Us by Tracy Dawson, directed by Ruth Madoc-Jones

January 26–February 14: You Fancy Yourself by Maja Ardal, directed by Mary Francis Moore, produced by Contrary Company in association with TPM

March 09–March 28: Tijuana Cure by Layne Coleman, directed by Ashlie Corcoran, produced by Theatre Smash in association with TPM

April 13–April 26: Appetite by Collective, directed by Sarah Sanford, produced by the Exchange Rate Collective in association with Volcano Theatre and TPM

September 16–October 04: The Refugee Hotel by Carmen Aguirre, directed by Carmen Aguirre, produced by Alameda Theatre Company in association with TPM

October 14–October 31: BASH'd! by Chris Craddock and Nathan Cuckow, directed by Ron Jenkins

November 20–December 12: Letters to my Grandma by Anusree Roy, directed by Thomas Morgan Jones

2010

January 04–January 23: You Fancy Yourself by Maja Ardal, directed by Mary Francis Moore, produced by Contrary Company in association with TPM

January 14–February 06: Such Creatures by Judith Thompson, directed by Brian Quirt

February 05–March 07: YICHUD (Seclusion) by Julie Tepperman, directed by Richard Greenblatt and Aaron Willis, produced by TPM in association with Convergence Theatre

February 18–March 13: Future Folk by Sulong Theatre Collective, directed by Sulong Theatre Collective, produced by Carlos Bulosan Theatre, Sulong Theatre Company, and TPM

March 18–March 27: Birnam Wood by Allyson McMackon, directed by Allyson McMackon, produced by Theatre Rusticle in association with TPM

THE CURE FOR EVERYTHING
MAJA ARDAL. PHOTO BY AVIVA ARMOUR-OSTROFF.

April 13–April 24: Crocosmia by Collective, directed by Alexander Scott, produced by Little Bulb Theatre in association with TPM

September 30–October 16: Hard Times by Chris Earle, directed by Chris Earle, produced by Puppetmongers in association with In The Night Kitchen and TPM

October 21–November 20: The Middle Place by Andrew Kushnir, directed by Alan Dilworth, produced by TPM and Canadian Stage

November 10–December 04: The Cure for Everything by Maja Ardal, directed by Mary Francis Moore, produced by Contrary Company and TPM

November 18–December 11: Roshni by Anusree Roy, directed by Thomas Morgan Jones, produced by Theatre Jones Roy and TPM

2011

January 05–January 29: Oh My Irma by Haley McGee, directed by Alisa Palmer

February 03–February 26: Highway 63: The Fort Mac Show by Collective, with Layne Coleman, directed by Charlotte Corbeil-Coleman, produced by Architect Theatre and TPM

March 17–April 02: Montparnasse by Maev Beaty and Erin Shields, directed by Andrea Donaldson, produced by Groundwater Productions in association with TPM

April 06–April 16: The Last 15 Seconds by Collective, directed by Majdi Bou-Matar, produced by MT Space in association with TPM

May 21–May 26: YICHUD (Seclusion) by Julie Tepperman, directed by Richard Greenblatt and Aaron Willis, produced by Convergence Theatre and TPM

September 14–October 09: The Tale of a Town by Lisa Marie DiLiberto, directed by Varrick Grimes, produced by FIXT POINT and TPM

October 06–October 29: Those Who Can't Do . . . by Erin Fleck, directed by Shari Hollett

November 10–December 03: Ride the Cyclone by Brooke Maxwell and Jacob Richmond, directed by Britt Small and Jacob Richmond, produced by Atomic Vaudeville, presented by The Musical Stage Company and TPM

November 29–December 11: Jesus Chrysler by Tara Beagan, directed by Michael Wheeler, produced by Praxis Theatre in association with TPM

2012

February 09–February 26: Dancing With Rage by Mary Walsh, directed by Karen Carpenter, produced by RCA Theatre Company and TPM

April 10–April 28: Prisoner of Tehran by Marina Nemat, adapted by Maja Ardal, directed by Maja Ardal, produced by Contrary Company in association with TPM

May 01–May 13: Crash by Pamela Mala Sinha, directed by Alan Dilworth

September 12–September 23: Queen West Project by Deborah Pearson, directed by Deborah Pearson

September 12–September 15: The Toybox by Ben Chaisson and Beth Kates, audience-directed, produced by Playground Studios and TPM

September 20–September 29: Mister Baxter by Kate Fenton, directed by Adam Seybold, produced by The Quickening Theatre, presented by TPM

September 29–September 29: The Four Corners by Lisa Marie DiLiberto and Charles Ketchabaw, directed by Lisa Marie DiLiberto, produced by FIXT POINT and TPM

October 04–October 27: This Must Be The Place: The CN Tower Show by Architect Theatre Collective, with Layne Coleman, directed by Jonathan Seinen

November 16–December 08: Fare Game: Life in Toronto's Taxis by Collective, directed by Collective

November 29–December 08: The 501: Toronto In Transit by Collective, directed by Collective

December 11–December 15: It's a Wonderful Toronto: The Rob Ford Holiday Spectacular! by Matt Baram, directed by Chris Earle, produced by The National Theatre of the World in association with TPM

2013

January 16–January 26: Body 13 by Collective, directed by Majdi Bou-Matar, produced by MT Space in association with TPM

February 01–February 23: Shakespeare's Nigga by Joseph Jomo Pierre, directed by Philip Akin, produced by Obsidian Theatre in association with 3D Atomic and TPM

April 02–April 13: Legoland by Jacob Richmond, directed by Jacob Richmond and Britt Small, produced by Atomic Vaudeville, presented by TPM

September 25–September 28: On The Rocks by Louise Pitre, directed by Jen Shuber

September 26–October 19: Crash by Pamela Mala Sinha, directed by Alan Dilworth

October 31–November 16: Moss Park by George F. Walker, directed by Patrick McDonald, produced by Green Thumb Theatre and TPM

November 14–November 23: Crash (tour) by Pamela Mala Sinha, directed by Alan Dilworth

November 14–December 07: Heaven Above, Heaven Below by Linda Griffiths, directed by Karen Hines, produced by TPM in association with Duchess Productions

2014

January 16–February 08: The Way Back to Thursday by Rob Kempson, directed by Briana Brown

February 14–March 08: Same Same But Different by Anita Majumdar, directed by Brian Quirt, produced by TPM and Alberta Theatre Projects in association with Nightswimming

March 18–April 16: Same Same But Different (tour) by Anita Majumdar, directed by Brian Quirt, produced by TPM and Alberta Theatre Projects in association with Nightswimming

April 29–May 17: Vitals by Rosamund Small and Jean Webb, directed by Mitchell Cushman, produced by Outside the March Theatre Company in association with TPM

September 25–October 19: Life, Death and The Blues by Raoul Bhaneja, directed by Eda Holmes, produced by TPM in association with Hope and Hell Theatre Company

October 24–November 16: My Treasure Island!!! by Sara Levine, adapted by Karen Woolridge, directed by Kate Lynch, produced by The Johnson Girls in association with TPM

November 20–December 14: The De Chardin Project by Adam Seybold, directed by Alan Dilworth

2015

January 21–2016: Life, Death and The Blues (tour) by Raoul Bhaneja, directed by Eda Holmes

February 05–March 01: R-E-B-E-C-C-A by Sara Farb, directed by Richard Greenblatt

February 14–March 07: The Sound of Cracking Bones/Le bruit des os qui craquent by Suzanne Lebeau, translated by Julia Duchesne and John Van Burek, directed by John Van Burek, produced by Pleiades Theatre in association with TPM

April 16–May 10: Hooked by Carolyn Smart, adapted by Nicky Guadagni, directed by Layne Coleman

June 18–June 21: The Way Back to Thursday (tour) by Rob Kempson, directed by Briana Brown

October 21–November 01: Baram & Snieckus: You and Me Both A Sketch Comedy Revue by Naomi Snieckus and Matt Baram, directed by Kurt Smeaton, produced by The National Theatre of the World, with the support of TPM

2016

January 14–January 31: Elle by Robert Glover, adapted by Severn Thompson, directed by Christine Brubaker

February 03–February 27: Chelsea Hotel, The Songs of Leonard Cohen by Leonard Cohen, adapted by Tracey Power, directed by Tracey Power, produced by Firehall Arts Centre and Theatre 20, with the support of TPM

March 03–March 27: Pyaasa by Anusree Roy, directed by Thomas Morgan Jones

March 1–April 24: Caught by Jordi Mand, directed by Sarah Garton Stanley

April 28–May 15: Ultrasound by Adam Pottle, directed by Marjorie Chan, produced by Cahoots Theatre and TPM

September 27–October 16: Brave New World by Aldous Huxley, adapted by Matthew Thomas Walker, directed by Matthew Thomas Walker, produced by Litmus Theatre and Kabin, with the support of TPM

November 10–November 20: Secrets of a Black Boy by Darren Anthony, directed by Kimahli Powell, produced by Playing With Crayons, with the support of TPM

2017

January 12–February 05: Alien Creature: A Visitation from Gwendolyn MacEwen by Linda Griffiths, directed by Jani Lauzon

January 26–March 12: Elle (tour) by Robert Glover, adapted by Severn Thompson, directed by Christine Brubaker

February 16–March 05: John & Waleed by Waleed Abdulhamid and John Millard, directed by Marjorie Chan, produced by TPM in association with Cahoots Theatre

March 16–April 02: Stupidhead! A Musical Comedy by Katherine Cullen and Britta Johnson, directed by Aaron Willis

April 13–May 07: Sound of the Beast by Donna-Michelle St. Bernard, directed by Andy McKim and Jivesh Parasram

October 24–November 05: Kiinalik: These Sharp Tools by Elysha Poirier, Erin Brubacher, Evalyn Parry, and Laakkuluk Williamson Bathory, directed by Erin Brubacher, produced by Buddies in Bad Times Theatre and TPM

November 17–December 03: Cake by Donna-Michelle St. Bernard, directed by Clare Preuss, produced by New Harlem Productions, with the support of TPM

December 13–December 17: The Tale of a Town—Canada by Lisa Marie DiLiberto, directed by Lisa Marie DiLiberto, produced by FIXT POINT, with the support of TPM

2018

January 28–February 25: Krapp's Last Tape by Samuel Beckett, directed by Mac Fyfe, produced by Singing Swan Productions, with the support of Wily Pig, VideoCabaret, and TPM

February 01–February 18: Acha Bacha by Bilal Baig, directed by Brendan Healy, produced by Buddies in Bad Times Theatre and TPM

February 28–March 25: The Drawer Boy by Michael Healey, directed by Nina Lee Aquino

April 10–April 22: Take d Milk, Nah? by Jivesh Parasram, directed by Tom Arthur Davis, produced by Pandemic Theatre and b current, with the support of TPM

KRAPP'S LAST TAPE
BOB NASMITH. PHOTO BY GRAHAM ISADOR.

September 28–September 29: Sound of the Beast by Donna-Michelle St. Bernard, directed by Andy McKim and Jiv Parasram

October 3–October 14: Sound of the Beast (tour) by Donna-Michelle St. Bernard, directed by Andy McKim and Jiv Parasram

October 11–October 27: Pearle Harbour's Chautauqua by Justin Miller, directed by Byron Laviolette, produced by Pearle Harbour, with the support of TPM

October 25–November 11: Will You Be My Friend by Janice Jo Lee, directed by Matt White, produced by Green Light Arts, with the support of TPM

November 25–December 9: The Runner by Christopher Morris, directed by Daniel Brooks, produced by Human Cargo, with the support of TPM

2019

January 29–February 9: Hook Up by composer Chris Thornborrow and librettist Julie Tepperman, directed by Richard Greenblatt, produced by Tapestry Opera in partnership with TPM

February 16–March 3: Paolozzapedia by Adam Paolozza, directed by Adam Paolozza, produced by Bad New Days, with the support of TPM

March 7–March 24: CHICHO by Augusto Bitter, directed by Claren Grosz, presented by Pencil Kit Productions and TPM, with the support of Aluna Theatre

March 12–March 16: Sound of the Beast (tour) by Donna-Michelle St. Bernard, directed by Andy McKim and Jiv Parasram

March 20–March 24: Crying Hands: Deaf People in Hitler's Germany by Bentein Baardson, directed by Bentein Baardson, produced by Theatre Manu, presented by TPM

April 4–April 21: The Chemical Valley Project by Kevin Matthew Wong and Julia Howman, directed by Kevin Matthew Wong and Julia Howman, produced by Broadleaf Theatre and TPM

April 23–April 28: The Things I Carry by Lee Su-Feh, with excerpts from On a Plane by Chris Bose, directed by Lee Su-Feh, produced by battery opera, presented by Dancemakers and TPM

ABOUT THE EDITORS

Martin Julien is an actor, singer, writer, and educator with over three decades of experience in Canadian theatre. He made his stage debut at the age of ten for the Factory Theatre Lab in Toronto, and has been nominated for three Dora Mavor Moore Awards as best performer. He recently defended his Ph.D. dissertation on acting methodologies at the Centre for Drama, Theatre and Performance Studies at the University of Toronto, where he held a SSHRC Doctoral Fellowship. His work has been published by Routledge, *TDR*, *Stanislavski Studies*, *Intermission*, Cambridge Scholars Publishing, and *Canadian Theatre Review*.

Samantha Serles is a writer and editor based in Toronto. She worked at Theatre Passe Muraille from 2010 to 2014 as a dramaturge and holds an M.F.A. in theatre from York University and a graduate certificate in professional writing and communications from Humber College.

Rae Johnson is an artist who began teaching drawing and painting at OCAD in 1988. She has lectured about her work across Canada in universities and art centres. In the early 1980s Rae formed the collective ChromaZone with fellow artists Oliver Girling, Andy Fabo, Brian Burnett, Sybil Goldstein, Tony Wilson, HP Marti, and, later, Tim Jocelyn.

ACKNOWLEDGEMENTS

A debt of gratitude is owed to Petra Chevrier for her help with this book. Petra poured over photos and archival material to create credits and captions, she coralled TPM staff and board members to identify others, and painstakingly reviewed everything to ensure accuracy and consistency. The book wouldn't be nearly as complete without Petra's work and we are forever grateful for her involvement.

We further owe thanks to Barbara Fingerote for her help in assembling the definitive Theatre Passe Muraille performance history. It's a thing of beauty.

And finally, we would like to thank all the contributors to this book, both written and visual. We greatly appreciate your willingness to celebrate the theatre and give so freely of your time and energy.

BY GRAND CENTRAL STATION I SAT DOWN AND WEPT
NANCY BEATTY.

INDEX

B

C

D

E

U

V

W

Y